PHARMACEUTICAL AND MEDICAL DEVICE SAFETY

This book examines how regulatory and liability mechanisms have impacted upon product safety decisions in the pharmaceutical and medical devices sectors in Europe, the USA and beyond since the 1950s. Thirty-five case studies illustrate the interplay between the regulatory regimes and litigation. Observations from medical practice have been the overwhelming means of identifying post-marketing safety issues. Drug and device safety decisions have increasingly been taken by public regulators and companies within the framework of the comprehensive regulatory structure that has developed since the 1960s. In general, product liability cases have not identified or defined safety issues, and function merely as compensation mechanisms. This is unsurprising as the thresholds for these two systems differ considerably; regulatory action can be triggered by the possibility that a product might be harmful, whereas establishing liability in litigation requires proving that the product was actually harmful.

As litigation normally post-dates regulatory implementation, the 'private enforcement' of public law has generally not occurred in these sectors. This has profound implications for the design of sectoral regulatory and liability regimes, including associated features such as extended liability law, class actions and contingency fees. This book forms a major contribution to the academic debate on the comparative utility of regulatory and liability systems, on public versus private enforcement, and on mechanisms of behaviour control.

Volume 8 in the series Civil Justice Systems

Civil Justice Systems

Series General Editor: Christopher Hodges, Director, Swiss Re/CMS Research Programme, Centre for Socio-Legal Studies, University of Oxford

This series covers new theoretical and empirical research on the mechanisms for resolution of civil disputes, including courts, tribunals, arbitration, compensation schemes, ombudsmen, codes of practice, complaint mechanisms, mediation and various forms of Alternative Dispute Resolution. It examines frameworks for dispute resolution that comprise combinations of the above mechanisms, and the parameters and conditions for selecting certain types of techniques and procedures rather than others. It also evaluates individual techniques, against parameters such as cost, duration, accessibility, and delivery of desired outcomes, and illuminates how legal rights and obligations are operated in practice.

Volume 1: *The Costs and Funding of Civil Litigation: A Comparative Perspective*
edited by Christopher Hodges, Stefan Vogenauer and Magdalena Tulibacka

Volume 2: *Consumer ADR in Europe*
Christopher Hodges, Iris Benöhr and Naomi Creutzfeldt-Banda

Volume 3: *Law and Corporate Behaviour: Integrating Theories of Regulation, Enforcement, Compliance and Ethics*
Christopher Hodges

Volume 4: *A Comparative Examination of Multi-Party Actions*
Joanne Blennerhassett

Volume 5: *Redress Schemes for Personal Injuries*
Sonia Macleod and Christopher Hodges

Volume 6: *Ethical Business Practice and Regulation: A Behavioural and Values-Based Approach to Compliance and Enforcement*
Christopher Hodges and Ruth Steinholtz

Volume 7: *Delivering Collective Redress: New Technologies*
Christopher Hodges and Stefaan Voet

Pharmaceutical and Medical Device Safety

A Study in Public and Private Regulation

Sonia Macleod
and
Sweta Chakraborty

HART PUBLISHING

Bloomsbury Publishing Plc

Kemp House, Chawley Park, Cumnor Hill, Oxford, OX2 9PH, UK

HART PUBLISHING, the Hart/Stag logo, BLOOMSBURY and the Diana logo are trademarks of Bloomsbury Publishing Plc

First published in Great Britain 2019

A catalogue record for this book is available from the British Library.

Library of Congress Cataloging-in-Publication data

Names: Macleod, Sonia, author. | Chakraborty, Sweta, author.

Title: Pharmaceutical and medical device safety : a study in public and private regulation / Sonia Macleod, Sweta Chakraborty.

Description: Oxford, UK ; Chicago, Illinois : Hart Publishing, 2019. | Series: Civil justice systems | Includes bibliographical references and index.

Identifiers: LCCN 2018057164 (print) | LCCN 2018057920 (ebook) | ISBN 9781509916733 (EPub) | ISBN 9781509916696 (hardback)

Subjects: LCSH: Medical laws and legislation. | Drugs—Law and legislation. | Medical instruments and apparatus—Safety regulations. | Products liability—Drugs | Products liability—Medical instruments and apparatus. | Medical laws and legislation—Great Britain. | Medical laws and legislation—European Union countries. | Medical laws and legislation—United States. | BISAC: LAW / Arbitration, Negotiation, Mediation.

Classification: LCC K3601 (ebook) | LCC K3601 .M327 2019 (print) | DDC 344.04/233—dc23

LC record available at https://lccn.loc.gov/2018057164

ISBN: HB: 978-1-50991-669-6 (Hart Publishing)
HB: 978-3-8487-5463-2 (Nomos)
HB: 978-3-406-73714-5 (CH Beck)
ePDF: 978-1-50991-672-6
ePub: 978-1-50991-673-3

Typeset by Compuscript Ltd, Shannon
Printed and bound in Great Britain by CPI Group (UK) Ltd, Croydon CR0 4YY

MIX
Paper from responsible sources
FSC® C013604

To find out more about our authors and books visit www.hartpublishing.co.uk. Here you will find extracts, author information, details of forthcoming events and the option to sign up for our newsletters.

FOREWORD

This book is a study of two overlapping fields: regulation and litigation in cases where the safety of medical products overlaps them both. The primary purpose is to identify how safety issues with medical products came to light after they were in use, and what steps were then taken. The term 'medical products' is a generic one, since we are in fact looking at several distinct product types, which act differently and are regulated under different regimes: medicinal products (drugs), vaccines, biologicals, medical devices and combination products.

The primary theoretical purpose of this study is to provide empirical evidence to answer the question: how did the safety issues come to light? Was it through litigation, or through a post-marketing safety vigilance system that is part of the regulatory system? The reason for answering that question is that it has been maintained, especially by some American scholars and lawyers, that litigation is a mechanism that identifies safety issues. The data set of case studies in this book provides minimal support for that assertion. In the cases here, involving litigation in the UK and sometimes from other EU states and the US, safety issues with these products were all, apart from one case, identified by the medical community and established through identification of data and subsequent more detailed research, and not through litigation.

A further theoretical point follows. It is sometimes asserted that a purpose of private enforcement by private actors of private law rights in civil courts (litigation based on theories of product liability) is to provide deterrence so as to increase product safety. The primary targets of this litigation are manufacturers of the product, hospitals where procedures were carried out and the medical staff who treated the patient. The theoretical idea is that internalising the cost of harm caused to patients will deter future harm. Whilst this study does not address that point directly, it does have some relevance to system design.

The principal finding of this study, as noted, is that it is the regulatory system, rather than the litigation system, that affects product safety for these types of products and for medical practice in relation to them. Accordingly, it is those regulatory and medical research systems that should be relied on and strengthened rather than the litigation system.

It is important to recognise the context in the late twentieth and early twenty-first centuries. Regulation of medicinal products and medical devices has been transformed in Europe since the 1960s, after the spur of the Thalidomide tragedy. The regulatory system in the US was centralised much earlier, in the 1930s, but has still undergone considerable evolution since its inception. Regulation of quality of products goes back centuries, but things were completely transformed from the 1960s for medicines and from the 1990s for medical devices.

In contrast, private enforcement of law goes back many centuries. One is reminded of the saying, 'If you only have a hammer, everything looks like a nail.' If private enforcement of law is the principal tool and firm focus of lawyers, judges, the legal system and scholars, it would not be surprising if theories were to arise that use of that tool is effective in various ways (beyond its obvious effect of transferring money to people who have suffered harm), and that the system is therefore considered effective and justified by theories such as that it has an effect on future behaviour.

However, we have now developed regulatory systems (classified as public or administrative law, and therefore perhaps less familiar to private lawyers) aimed specifically at establishing the safety of products both before they are placed on the market and throughout their lifetime of use through constant monitoring (vigilance). The evidence of this study is that it is the more focused and sophisticated systems of product regulation, coupled with opportunities for detailed medical studies, that are currently able to deliver effective and timely safety information, which can then be acted upon, rather than the somewhat blunt instrument of litigation. That conclusion is hardly surprising: the regulatory approach involves data produced by *ex ante* and *constant* monitoring of experience with products and practice, rather than the theory that identification of harm *ex post* will be able to drive future decisions by the economic actors (in which regulators and their actions are rarely considered).

The policy conclusions are clear. Safety is achieved by systems that produce data and have direct effect on ongoing actions and decisions. We should strengthen those regulatory, research and data systems to improve safety. If we are seeking to deliver compensation then the fact that a compensation system does not need to have a behavioural effect to support safety opens the door to adoption of contemplating mechanisms that may be more efficient and deliver better outcomes.

This is not to say that the regulatory and research systems could not be improved. Indeed, if we look at the case studies here in a chronological sequence, we can see the development of regulatory monitoring techniques and mechanisms over time. The teratogens series demonstrates the obvious progress from no effective regulation to a more comprehensive regulatory system. Within the individual case studies on valproate and Accutane/RoAccutante there is evidence of evolving regulatory requirements on labelling and prescribing practices based on ongoing monitoring of adverse events.

These systems depend essentially on having reliable data from monitoring – either real-time usage in mass patient populations, or smaller specific studies. Obtaining accurate adverse event reporting is notorious difficult, as is described in the conclusions. Additional complications arise when claimants' lawyers report adverse events and then seek to utilise such reports during subsequent litigation, as can be seen from the Accutane MCL.

It is important to note that mechanisms other than litigation are now increasingly used to deliver compensation. Macleod and Hodges recently studied around 40 such administrative compensation schemes from around the world.[1] The administration and eligibility criteria of those schemes provide an interesting contrast to the liability thresholds applied in litigation. Cost is another important differential: litigation is relatively expensive. Given that litigation appears to be of little importance in detecting safety signals, a question is raised as to whether it would be better to compensate using administrative schemes. This would

[1] S Macleod and C Hodges, *Redress Schemes for Personal Injuries* (Hart Publishing, 2017).

avoid the adversarial nature of litigation and could help to resolve conflict and emotional distress. Recent evidence from the evolving interdisciplinary field of Compensation Health Research suggests that the legal arrangements and procedures may have an anti-therapeutic effect on those who have suffered an injury. Further empirical evidence is needed in order to enable informed changes in policy and practice.[2]

Christopher Hodges
Professor of Justice Systems and Director,
Swiss Re/CMS Research Programme,
Centre for Socio-Legal Studies, University of Oxford

[2] For examples of such projects, see the Australian Institute for Safety, Compensation and Recovery Research portal at www.iscrr.com.au/home.

ACKNOWLEDGEMENTS

Particular thanks are due to Christopher Hodges for his unstinting help and support.

We owe enormous thanks to a number of people, including those listed below, who have given us considerable help with case studies:

Paul Balen, Consultant, Freeths LLP
Mary E Bartkus, Special Counsel, Hughes Hubbard & Reed LLP
Ina Brock, Partner, Hogan Lovells International LLP
Ian Dodds-Smith, Partner, Arnold & Porter Kaye Scholer LLP
Deborah Jack, Executive Director, The Thalidomide Trust
Martin Johnson, former Executive Director, The Thalidomide Trust
Arundel McDougall, former partner Ashursts LLP
Dr June Rayne CBE, Director of Vigilance and Risk Management of Medicines, MHRA
Benjamin Schulte, Senior Associate, Hogan Lovells International LLP
Paul Sim, S&P Medical Devices Knowledge Manager, BSI
Tom Spencer, Lawyer, GlaxoSmithKline
John Wilkinson OBE, Director of Vigilance and Risk Management of Medicines, MHRA

CONTENTS

Foreword by Christopher Hodges ... v
Acknowledgements ... ix
Abbreviations ... xix

1. Introduction ... 1
   I. The Legal Context ... 1
      A. Basis of Liability ... 10
      B. Litigation Systems ... 11
      C. Funding and Costs ... 11
      D. US: The Class Action and MDL ... 12
      E. Europe ... 14
      F. Settlement Schemes ... 16

2. The Regulation of Medicines and Medical Devices ... 17
   I. Medicinal Products ... 18
      A. Historical Drug/Pharmaceutical Regulation in the UK ... 18
         i. 1948–59: The Birth of the National Health Service ... 21
         ii. 1959–62: Thalidomide ... 22
         iii. 1963–71: Voluntary Self-regulation ... 23
         iv. 1971 Onwards: Statutory Regulation ... 24
      B. European Regulation of Medicinal Products ... 25
         i. A Brief History of European Medicinal Products Regulation ... 26
         ii. Current EU Structures and Procedures for Regulating Medicinal Products ... 30
      C. European Regulation of Medical Devices ... 42
         i. Classification and Standards ... 46
      D. General Product Safety Regulation in Europe ... 50
      E. Medicinal Product Regulation in the US ... 50
         i. Historic Regulation of Medicinal Products in the US ... 51
         ii. Current Regulation of Medicinal Products in the US ... 56
         iii. Marketing Authorisations within the US ... 58
         iv. Requirements for Developing and Marketing Medicinal Products in the US ... 60
      F. US Regulation of Medical Devices ... 73
         i. US Classification and Standards ... 73

3. Detailed Case Descriptions and Regulatory Histories ... 82
   I. Teratogens and Foetal Damage ... 82
      A. Thalidomide (alpha-phthalimido-glutarimide) ... 82
         i. Description ... 82

ii. Safety Issue ... 82
iii. Marketing and Regulatory History ... 83
iv. Litigation ... 85
v. Conclusion ... 87
B. Hormonal Pregnancy Tests – Including Primodos ... 88
i. Description ... 88
ii. Safety Issue ... 88
iii. Marketing and Regulatory History ... 89
iv. Litigation ... 91
v. Conclusion ... 91
C. Diethylstilboestrol (DES) ... 92
i. Description ... 92
ii. Safety Issue ... 92
iii. Marketing and Regulatory History ... 92
iv. Litigation ... 97
v. Conclusion ... 99
D. Epilim/Depakote/Depakene (sodium valproate, valproic acid, magnesium valproate, valproate semisodium or valpromide) ... 100
i. Description ... 100
ii. Safety Issue ... 100
iii. Marketing and Regulatory History ... 101
iv. Litigation ... 105
v. Conclusion ... 107
E. Accutane/Roaccutane (isotretinoin) ... 108
i. Description ... 108
ii. Safety Issue ... 108
iii. Marketing and Regulatory History ... 108
iv. Litigation ... 116
v. Conclusion ... 118
II. Contraceptives and Hormone Replacement Therapy ... 119
A. Gravigard or Copper 7 Intrauterine Device ... 119
i. Description ... 119
ii. Safety Issue ... 119
iii. Marketing and Regulatory History ... 120
iv. Litigation ... 121
v. Conclusion ... 124
B. Third-Generation Oral Contraceptives ... 125
i. Description ... 125
ii. Safety Issue ... 125
iii. Marketing and Regulatory History ... 125
iv. Litigation ... 128
v. Conclusion ... 128
C. Norplant (levonorgestrel) ... 129
i. Description ... 129
ii. Safety Issue ... 129
iii. Marketing and Regulatory History ... 129

iv. Litigation 130
v. Conclusion 131
D. Hormone Replacement Therapy 132
i. Description 132
ii. Safety Issue 132
iii. Marketing and Regulatory History 132
iv. Litigation 136
v. Conclusion 137
III. Vaccines 138
A. DTP Vaccine 138
i. Description 138
ii. Safety Issue 138
iii. Marketing and Regulatory History 139
iv. Litigation 142
v. Conclusion 144
B. MMR Vaccine 145
i. Description 145
ii. Safety Issue 147
iii. Marketing and Regulatory History 147
iv. Litigation 148
v. Conclusion 149
IV. Neuromodulators 150
A. Benzodiazepines 150
i. Description 150
ii. Safety Issue 150
iii. Marketing and Regulatory History 150
iv. Litigation 151
v. Conclusion 153
B. Merital (nomifensine) 154
i. Description 154
ii. Safety Issue 154
iii. Marketing and Regulatory History 154
iv. Litigation 156
v. Conclusion 156
C. Selective Serotonin Reuptake Inhibitors 157
i. Description 157
ii. Safety Issues 157
iii. Marketing and Regulatory History 159
iv. Litigation 161
v. Conclusion 163
D. Sabril (vigabatrin) 164
i. Description 164
ii. Safety Issue 164
iii. Marketing and Regulatory History 164
iv. Litigation 165
v. Conclusion 165

E. Mirapexin/Sifrol/Daquiran (pramipexole) 166
i. Description 166
ii. Safety Issue 166
iii. Marketing and Regulatory History 167
iv. Litigation 168
v. Conclusion 169
V. Non-Steroidal Anti-Inflammatories 170
A. Opren (benoxaprofen) 170
i. Description 170
ii. Safety Issue 170
iii. Marketing and Regulatory History 170
iv. Litigation 171
v. Conclusion 172
B. Vioxx (rofecoxib) 173
i. Description 173
ii. Safety Issue 173
iii. Marketing and Regulatory History 174
iv. Litigation 175
v. Conclusion 176
VI. Pancreatic Function (Endocrine and Exocrine) and Obesity Treatments 177
A. Adifax/Isomeride/Redux (dexfenfluramine) and Ponderax (fenfluramine) 177
i. Description 177
ii. Safety Issue 177
iii. Marketing and Regulatory History 178
iv. Litigation 179
v. Conclusion 180
B. Mediator (benfluorex) 181
i. Description 181
ii. Safety Issue 181
iii. Marketing and Regulatory History 181
iv. Litigation 184
v. Conclusion 184
C. Human Insulin 185
i. Description 185
ii. Alleged Safety Issue 185
iii. Marketing and Regulatory History 187
iv. Litigation 188
v. Conclusion 189
D. Pancreatic Enzymes 190
i. Description 190
ii. Safety Issue 190
iii. Marketing and Regulatory History 190
iv. Litigation 192
v. Conclusion 192

VII. Contaminated Human-Tissue-Derived Products 193
A. Blood Products 193
i. Description 193
ii. Safety Issue 193
iii. Marketing and Regulatory History 194
iv. Litigation 194
v. Conclusion 196
B. Human Growth Hormone 197
i. Description 197
ii. Safety Issue 197
iii. Marketing and Regulatory History 197
iv. Litigation 197
v. Conclusion 197
VIII. Cardiovascular Pharmaceuticals 198
A. Eraldin (practolol) 198
i. Description 198
ii. Safety Issue 198
iii. Marketing and Regulatory History 198
iv. Litigation 199
v. Conclusion 200
B. Manoplax (flosequinan) 201
i. Description 201
ii. Safety Issue 201
iii. Marketing and Regulatory History 201
iv. Litigation 203
v. Conclusion 203
C. Lipobay (cerivastatin) 204
i. Description 204
ii. Safety Issue 204
iii. Marketing and Regulatory History 205
iv. Litigation 207
v. Conclusion 207
IX. Anti-Protozoan Medications 208
A. Emaform, Entero-Form or Chinoform (clioquinol) 208
i. Description 208
ii. Safety Issue 208
iii. Marketing and Regulatory History 209
iv. Litigation 210
v. Conclusion 211
B. Lariam (mefloquine) 212
i. Description 212
ii. Safety Issue 212
iii. Marketing and Regulatory History 212
iv. Litigation 215
v. Conclusion 216

X. Breast and Other Cosmetic Implants ... 217
A. Dow-Corning Silicone Implants ... 217
i. Description ... 217
ii. Safety Issue ... 217
iii. Marketing and Regulatory History ... 218
iv. Litigation ... 219
v. Conclusion ... 220
B. Trilucent Breast Implants ... 221
i. Description ... 221
ii. Safety Issue ... 221
iii. Marketing and Regulatory History ... 221
iv. Litigation ... 222
v. Conclusion ... 223
C. Poly Implant Prothese (PIP) Hydrogel Breast Implants ... 224
i. Description ... 224
ii. Safety Issue ... 224
iii. Marketing and Regulatory History ... 225
iv. Litigation ... 225
v. Conclusion ... 227
D. Poly Implant Prothese (PIP) IMGHC Silicone Breast Implants ... 228
i. Description ... 228
ii. Safety Issue ... 228
iii. Marketing and Regulatory History ... 230
iv. Litigation ... 232
v. Conclusion ... 234
XI. Urinary Incontinence and Pelvic Prolapse Treatments ... 235
A. Micturin (terodiline) ... 235
i. Description ... 235
ii. Safety Issue ... 235
iii. Marketing and Regulatory History ... 235
iv. Litigation ... 236
v. Conclusion ... 236
B. Urogynaecological Mesh ... 237
i. Description ... 237
ii. Safety Issue ... 238
iii. Marketing and Regulatory History ... 239
iv. Litigation ... 259
v. Conclusion ... 264

4. Conclusions ... 265
I. Prevention is Better than a Cure ... 266
II. Adverse Event Reporting ... 266
III. Correlation or Causation? ... 269
IV. Thresholds ... 269
V. Product Withdrawals ... 272

VI. Compensation or Redress? 274
VII. Public Regulation v Private Regulation....278
A. Compensation – Redress....278
B. Deterrence....280
VIII. Conclusions....280

Index....*283*

ABBREVIATIONS

ADR	adverse drug reaction
AFFSAPS	Agence Française de Sécurité Sanitaire des Produits de Santé (the French Regulator for the safety of health products from 1 July 1998 to 30 April 2012)
AIMDD	Active Implantable Medical Devices Directive
AIMDs	active implantable medical devices
ANSM	Agence nationale de sécurité du medicament et des produits de santé, the French regulator for the safety of health products from 1 May 2012 to date
ATMPs	advanced therapy medicinal products
BfArM	Bundesinstitut für Arzneimittel und Medizinprodukte, the German Federal Institute for Drugs and Medical Devices from 1994
BGA	Bundesgesundheitsamt, the German Federal Health Agency from 1952 to 1994
BLA	Biologics License Application
CDC	Centers for Disease Control and Preventions, US national public health institute 1 July 1946 onwards
CDER	Center for Drug Evaluation and Research
CHMP	Committee for Medicinal Products for Human Use
COCs	combined oral contraceptives
CPMP	Committee for Proprietary Medicinal Products of the EU
CSD	Committee for the Safety of Drugs
CRM	Committee on Review of Medicines
CSM	Committee for the Safety of Medicines
doi	digital object identifier, a unique identifier assigned by the journal publisher to individual articles
DVT	deep vein thrombosis
DTP	diphtheria, tetanus and pertussis
EMA	European Agency for the Evaluation of Medicinal Products/European Medicines Agency

FACD	Fellow of the Australasian College of Dermatologists
FAERS	Food and Drug Administration Adverse Event Reporting System
FDA	Food and Drug Administration, the regulatory authority in the USA
GLP	Good Laboratory Practice
GLO	group litigation order
GMC	General Medical Council
GPS	General Product Safety
HDE	humanitarian device exemption
HRT	hormone replacement therapy
HUD	humanitarian device
IGAS	Inspection générale des affaires sociales, the French Government audit, evaluation and inspection office for health, social security, social cohesion, employment and labour policies and organisations
IUD	intrauterine device
IVDD	In Vitro Diagnostics Directive
IVDs	in vitro diagnostics
LSC	Legal Services Commission
Licensing Authority	The UK statutory authority under the Medicines Act 1968, originally comprising the Health and Agriculture Ministers of England, Scotland, Wales and Northern Ireland
MAUDE	Manufacturer and User Facility Device Experience Database
MCA	Medicines Control Agency, the UK regulatory authority for medicines from 1999 to 2003
MCL	Multi-County Litigation
MDA	Medical Devices Agency
MDD	Medical Devices Directive
MDs	medical devices
MDL	Multi-District Litigation
MHRA	Medicines and Healthcare products Regulatory Authority, the UK regulatory authority for medicines and medical devices, created in 2003
MSIFI	Monitoring System for Illness Following Immunization of the CDC
NCES	National Childhood Encephalopathy Study

NIH	National Institutes of Health
NHS	National Health Service of the UK
NLF	New Legislative Framework
OCs	oral contraceptives
ONIAM	Office national d'indemnisation des accidents médicaux, the French compensation scheme for injuries from medical treatment
OTC	over-the-counter
PID	pelvic inflammatory disease
PIP	Poly Implant Prothèse
PMA	pre-market approval
POP	pelvic organ prolapse
PRAC	Pharmacovigilance Risk Assessment Committee
SmPC	summary of the product characteristics
SSRIs	Selective Serotonin Re-uptake Inhibitors
SUI	stress urinary incontinence
TüV	*Technischer Überwachungsverein*, German businesses that provide inspection and product certification services
UK	United Kingdom of Great Britain and Northern Ireland
US	United States
USA	United States of America
VAVFL	Vigabatrin Associated Visual Field Loss
VTE	venous-thromboembolism
WRAIR	Walter Reed Army Institute of Research

1

Introduction

People do not engage in medicinal product litigation unless they feel they have been harmed in some way. It is by definition a personal, visceral experience, and while this book focuses on the collective process, it does not in any way seek to diminish or detract from the individual experience.

This book is structured as an introduction, which briefly outlines the legal context in which litigation takes place and provides a summary of the regulation of medicines and medicinal products, including a brief history of the development of the relevant legislation, a series of 35 case studies and a chapter detailing the research conclusions.

The 35 case studies illustrate the interplay between the regulatory regimes and litigation. These case studies include medicines, biologics and devices marketed from the 1940s to the present day. The case studies were selected on two bases: first, they were all the major medical product safety cases that had resulted in extensive litigation in the UK since the 1960s; and, second, they were other large cases of interest from around the world (SMON from Japan, Mediator in France, Dow Corning in the US. We do not set out to cover the very much larger corpus of medical product litigation that has occurred in the US.

The case studies are divided into broad categories, the majority of which are based on the active ingredients in the drug or the indication being treated. There is one category that is the exception to this – the first grouping, drugs known to be teratogens or thought to cause foetal damage. These drugs impact beyond their immediate recipient, so despite being different drugs for varied indications, they have been classed together. This enables an overview of how the regulation on teratogens has evolved over time, from a position where the there was no effective regulation to today's position.

A brief summary of each of the products is set out in Table 1.1: inevitably this summary is highly selective and a fuller picture can be obtained in the case studies.

I. The Legal Context

This chapter is a short summary of the legal context within which the case studies are set, presented consciously more for non-medical or other non-legal readers in fairly simple terms. Two aspects need to be explained: the legal basis of liability, and the legal system's procedures for processing

First, a word about legal systems. Countries have their own jurisdictions, rules and approaches. England and Wales is a unified jurisdiction, whilst Scotland and Northern Ireland have some rules that are common throughout the UK but some aspects that are distinct (such as court and civil procedure systems). The USA has some aspects that are federal and unified across the country, but also strong maintenance of individual State laws and courts.

Table 1.1 Summary of the case studies

	Product	Indications and Date of First Use	Date of First Safety Signal and Description	Litigation Start Date	Conclusion
1	Thalidomide	Sold in West Germany as an over-the-counter sedative from 1957. On prescription there May 1961 to November 1961. Prescription only in the UK from April 1958 to December 1961.	1961: Two Independent reports by Dr Lenz and Dr McBride in Germany and Australia respectively, in November 1961.	Germany: May 1968–December 1970. UK group action 1962 writs are issued.	December 1970 the German Trial was closed down, and a law passed preventing further litigation. The Contergan Foundation was created. UK voluntary settlements in 1968 and 1973: the Thalidomide Trust was created from the latter.
2	Primodos and other hormonal pregnancy tests	Pregnancy test from 1950s.	1967: Medical paper in England re teratogenicity followed by several years of medical research in order to establish its truth. Regulatory responses 1970, 1975; withdrawn 1978.	UK group action in 1975 followed regulatory warning.	Regulatory change prompted litigation, and no further regulatory changes resulted from litigation.
3	DES (diethylstilbestrol)	Sedative and to prevent miscarriage; 1941 in US. Post-coital contraceptive in the US 1970–75. Various other indications including cancer treatment and curtailing 'excess height' in girls.	1971: Medical journal article in USA that made the association to vaginal cancer.	USA 1970s; 1987 Netherlands.	Supply in 1950s–1960s pre-dated the introduction of regulatory controls in the EU. US litigation developed 'market share liability'. Litigation in the Netherlands developed 'alternative liability'.
4	Epilim (sodium valproate)	Anticonvulsant for epilepsy, 1970s.	1968: Epidemiological surveys from around the world reporting increase in birth defects; CSM warnings 1983 and 2003. Progressively more detailed labelling. EMA Reassessment in 2014	UK litigation 2003 followed regulatory warning. French litigation started in 2011 and is ongoing. US litigation commenced in 2010 and is ongoing.	UK: Marketed before regulatory system. Concluded as a risk–benefit issue, on which doctors should advise patients about known risks. France and USA: Pending litigation outcomes.

	Product	Indications and Date of First Use	Date of First Safety Signal and Description	Litigation Start Date	Conclusion
5	Accutane/ Roaccutane (isotretinoin)	Skin conditions (severe acne), 1982.	1982: Launched as a teratogen 1982: ADR reports from indicated risk of depression, psychotic symptoms and in rare cases suicidal ideation. 1983: Bowel conditions reported; regulation response was stricter warnings and access.	USA: MCL 2003, MDL 2004 UK: 1999 following amendments to warnings.	Product information was determined to be accurate; risk–benefit issue but strict guidelines for access. MDL ended in summary judgment for defence in 2012, MCL cases dismissed 2018. UK litigation ceased in 1999.
6	Gravigard/ Copper7	Intrauterine device for contraception, 1971.	Case reports in early 1970s. 1977: label change in USA warning of association with PID.	USA: 1985/86. UK: 1988. Australia: issued 1987, served 1991, settled 2001.	USA: Kociemba case in 1986 prompted settlement. UK: Legal aid funding withdrawn in 1996 Australia: Long running case that finally settled in 2001 in an out of court settlement
7	Third-generation oral contraceptives	Combined oral contraceptives, 1982 onwards.	1995: UK CSM letter describes studies that third-generation combined oral contraceptives might carry increased risk of thrombo-embolism as compared to second-generation products. 1988: First regulatory action following ADR reports, more regulatory actions followed.	UK group action 1995 after regulatory warning.	Continuous scrutiny in medical studies and coordinated ADR reporting; a risk–benefit issue, on which doctors should advise patients about known risks. Litigation followed; in 2003 judgment for defendant based on absence of causation

(continued)

Table 1.1 *(Continued)*

	Product	Indications and Date of First Use	Date of First Safety Signal and Description	Litigation Start Date	Conclusion
8	Norplant (levonorgestrel)	Subdermal device releasing contraceptive drug, 1983.	1991: ADR reports re irregular bleeding, headaches, depression, implantation and removal issues; withdrawn 1999.	US: 1995 MDL, class action in Louisiana. UK: Threatened from 1995 but legal aid withdrawn in 1999 and no litigation arose.	ADR reports, followed by litigation. MDL and class action settled, UK litigation ceased in 1999 as legal aid was withdrawn.
9	HRT	Menopausal symptoms and some products for osteoporosis, 1942.	1996: Three new epidemiological studies published in *The Lancet* result in 5 studies total that suggest a small increase of risk in cardiovascular events and cancer; regulator begins investigation.	UK claims 1997, not pursued.	Constant regulatory review; advice remains that benefits outweigh risks.
10	DTP vaccine	Diphtheria, pertussis (whooping cough), and tetanus, 1940s.	1974: Retrospective UK study re neurological conditions; withdrawn 1998.	Single claim in Scotland 1980s; UK group action 1980s.	Medical study signal; litigation followed.
11	MMR vaccine	Measels, mumps and rubella, 1971.	1998: Medical paper re autism and bowel disease; no regulatory action save for individual 'yellow card' reports made by defendants when claims were notified.	1998: UK Group action followed medical paper.	Medical paper signal caused media frenzy; public response of a supposed risk led to significant fall in child vaccination, and increase in incidence of measles and some deaths.
12	Benzodiazepines	Tranquillisers, 1960.	1980: Beginning of medical literature re dependence and withdrawal effects.	1988: UK group action following regulatory change.	Signal from medical literature prompted major litigation.
13	Merital (nomifensine)	Norepinephrine-dopamine reuptake inhibitor, antidepressant, 1976.	1975: ADR reports of kidney and liver toxicity and haemolytic anaemia, possible death; withdrawn voluntarily.	No litigation.	Following ADR reports, the company voluntarily withdrew the product worldwide.

	Product	Indications and Date of First Use	Date of First Safety Signal and Description	Litigation Start Date	Conclusion
14	SSRIs	Anti-depressants, late 1980s	Mid-2000s: Medical studies re dependence and withdrawal effects and suicidal ideation; stricter warnings resulted in decrease of prescriptions.	2001: US litigation; following success in Tobin case (Paxil), 2002: group action in the UK for Seroxat.	Risk–benefit issue; claims ongoing.
15	Sabril (vigabatrin)	Anti-epileptic, 1989.	1997: Medical paper re visual field constriction effects; warnings introduced.	UK litigation 2000, group action 2003.	Medical report preceded litigation.
16	Mirapexin (pramipexole)	Non-ergoline dopamine agonist for Parkinson's disease and restless legs syndrome, 1997.	1997: ADR reports and medical studies from 1990s re compulsive gambling, hyper-sexuality and overeating.	USA: 2002, class action certified in 2008, settlement achieved. 2005: Canada (certified as class action in 2012). 2006: UK class action, fizzled out.	Alleged safety signal known from ADR reports for 8 years before being added to product label in 2005, which triggered litigation. Product remains marketed with strong warnings.
17	Opren (benoxaprofen).	Non-steroidal anti-inflammatory for arthritis, 1980.	1982: Medical article re deaths from hepato-renal complication; withdrawn worldwide 1982.	UK group litigation followed withdrawal.	Safety signal followed by swift regulatory action and a voluntary withdrawal, with litigation then ensuing.
18	Vioxx (rofecoxib)	Non-steroidal anti-inflammatory, 1999.	2004: Placebo controlled post-marketing study re increased cardiovascular disease; voluntarily withdrawn.	US claims brought in 2004; England group failed to get funding; Claims brought in Canada and many other countries beginning in 2004.	Post-marketing study triggered US litigation. Accusations of regulatory failure resulted in studies of regulatory oversight and legislative investigations; most noticeably focused on increased transparency.

(continued)

Table 1.1 *(Continued)*

	Product	Indications and Date of First Use	Date of First Safety Signal and Description	Litigation Start Date	Conclusion
19	Adifax/isomeride/Redux (dexfenfluramine) and Ponderax (fenfluramines)	Adifax: Appetite suppressant for anti-obesity, 1976. Ponderax: Combination Fen-Phen appetite suppressant, early 1970s.	1982: ADR reports listing a possible association; study undertaken and reported in a 1996 NEJM report linking the drug to heart valve disease. Worldwide withdrawal 1997.	US claims from 1997; few cases in France, none in UK.	Medical reports preceded claims. ADR and medical reports; the small number of EU cases likely to be because regulatory warnings were stricter in the EU; and medical practice favoured use of the product on its own for obesity, not (as in USA) in combination with phentermine (as Fen-Phen).
20	Mediator (benfluorex)	Overweight diabetes, 1976; off-label use as appetite suppressant.	1998: Early concerns including a letter to French regulator re heart valve damage and death. 2003: Spanish report of association between the drug and heart valve disorder reported in 2003; voluntary withdrawal in Spain 2003; regulator removed from the market in EU in 2010.	France claims 2010, ongoing pending the outcome of an associated criminal trial.	Same class as isomeride and fenfluramine so not licensed in many countries; withdrawn in most countries from 2003, but left on the market in France until 2009.
21	Human insulin	Diabetes, 1982.	1991: medical articles suggested loss of hypoglycaemic awareness; regulations changes reflected evidence from scientific community.	UK group action 1991 after medical debate.	Signal from medical studies; no regulatory changes resulted from litigation.
22	Pancreatic enzymes	Cystic Fibrosis, 1992.	1993: ADR reports re fibrosing colonopathy, and medical paper in *The Lancet* 1995 re stenosis; withdrawn voluntarily in the US in 1995.	UK change in warnings threatened group action.	Drug withdrawn in the US but stayed in the market in the UK with stricter warnings.

	Product	Indications and Date of First Use	Date of First Safety Signal and Description	Litigation Start Date	Conclusion
23	Blood products: Factor VIII and IX	Transfusion and haemophiliacs, 1970s.	1982: Contamination with HIV; testing then heat treatment introduced 1984/85.	UK and Ireland group litigation 1997 followed regulatory action over heat treatment.	Medical and regulatory developments, followed by litigation. No regulatory action arose out of the litigation.
24	Human growth hormone	Growth stimulant, extracted from pituitary of cadavers, 1959.	1985: US post-mortems identified CJD.	UK group action in 1994.	Signal from US post-mortems.
25	Eraldin (practolol)	Cardi-specific beta-blocker, 1970.	1970s: ADR reports of fibrosing and sclerosing of the mucus membranes, severe psoriasis-like skin rashes; sclerosing of the serous membrane; sclerosing peritonitis. Withdrawn voluntarily in 1975	No claims, a voluntary compensation scheme was set up in 1975.	Signals from case reports and yellow card system, voluntary withdrawal followed, and the compensation scheme prevented litigation.
26	Manoplax (flosequinan)	Chronic congestive heart failure, 1992.	1993: Company sponsored post-marketing study; UK Licensing Authority set to revoke licence 1993; withdrawn from market 1993.	Claims threatened but not pursued after regulatory action.	Company-sponsored study resulted in voluntary withdrawal and notifications sent to the authorities and doctors.
27	Lipobay (cerivastatin)	Statin to lower cholesterol, 1998.	1999: Spontaneous reports from outside the UK raised concern of increased cases of rhabdomyolysis of the drug, particularly in combination with gemfribrozil; 2001 worldwide withdrawal.	US litigation 2002; Germany 20 cases all won by company; UK isolated attempt to get funding rejected.	Litigation followed after increased regulatory warnings and withdrawal from worldwide market. Issue more acute in US where co-prescriptions with gemfribrozil more frequent; relatively limited practical impact in the UK.

(continued)

Table 1.1 *(Continued)*

	Product	Indications and Date of First Use	Date of First Safety Signal and Description	Litigation Start Date	Conclusion
28	Emaform, Entero-Form or Chinoform (Clioquinol)	Anti-microbial agent, 1920s.	1950s: patients with SMON, cause only identified in 1970; regulatory change followed; formulation banned in Japan.	Japan: 1971, settlements achieved in various districts between 1978 and 1987.	Large-scale search for the causative agent, which lasted 20 years. Regulatory change followed, including in the administration of settlements for victims.
29	Lariam (mefloquine)	Malaria, 1989.	1993: Observational studies re association with neuropsychiatric adverse effects.	UK group action 1996 after a TV programme.	Studies noted risks: UK regulator determined that the risk–benefit balance remained acceptable; strict dosing guidelines.
30	Dow Corning Silicone implants	Breast and other silicone implants, 1964.	Mid-1970s: the safety of implants began to be questioned. 1991: The FDA required a PMA, which effectively removed the product from the market in 1992.	US individual cases from the late 1970s, litigation increased, peaking with an MDL in 1992. Settlement agreed in 1994, as a result Dow Corning filed for bankruptcy in 1995.	No definitive link between silicone implants and systemic diseases has been demonstrated. Despite this the cost of litigation was sufficient to bankrupt Dow Corning.
31	Trilucent Breast implants	Breast implants filled with TrilipidZ, 1993.	1999: ADR reports of high capsular contraction rates; upon examination the filler was found to be oxidised; voluntary withdrawal 1999.	Cases were commenced, but a settlement was reached.	ADR reports preceded regulatory response: no litigation as voluntary settlement.
32	PIP Hydrogel breast implants	Breast implants filled with hydrogel, 1994.	Minimal ADRs reported prior to voluntary withdrawal in 2000; however, a review by the UK MDA in 2000 concluded that the manufacturer's biological safety assessment of the filler was inadequate.	Litigation followed in the UK, which was then transferred to France for enforcement of the debt; before it could be enforced the company went into administration.	No actual evidence of lack of safety existed before the product was withdrawn, but was subsequently found. Litigation followed, but was unsuccessful due to PIP's becoming bankrupt.

	Product	Indications and Date of First Use	Date of First Safety Signal and Description	Litigation Start Date	Conclusion
33	PIP IMGHC silicone breast implants	IMGHC silicone filled breast implants, 1997.	2010: after suspicion about ADR reports the French regulator discovered that PIP was substituting the filler with a non-compliant filler.	PIP entered voluntary bankruptcy. Substantial criminal and civil litigation followed.	Fraud had been committed, but, testing of the non-compliant filler concluded it was not a risk to health. Litigation followed, but was not satisfactory for many claimants.
34	Micturin (terodiline)	Incontinence, 1986.	1991: UK ADR reports result in warning to doctors of link between drug and cardiac arrhythmias; withdrawn voluntarily 1991.	Claims threatened 1992 after withdrawal.	ADR reports preceded regulatory response: no litigation.
35	Urogynaecological mesh	Synthetic mesh to provide support during urogynaecological surgery; 1970s onwards mesh used, first specific kit in 1996.	Adverse events including mesh exposure, pain, impaired mobility, recurrent infections, incontinence/urinary frequency, prolapse, fistula formation, sexual and relationship difficulties, depression, social withdrawal or exclusion/loneliness and lethargy. Regulatory action followed in many countries, including 522 studies in 2012 in the USA and reclassification in many countries. Use of mesh in urogynaecological surgery has been heavily restricted in many countries.	Huge-scale litigation in the USA, many MDLs starting from 2011 onwards. UK: no GLO listed at present, but ongoing litigation.	Adverse event reports contributed to a changing knowledge base, and consequent regulatory restrictions on mesh use in urogynaecological surgery. US litigation has been extensive, and has resulted in billions of dollars being paid in settlements. UK litigation is much smaller-scale and is ongoing.

A. Basis of Liability

Legal liability almost throughout the world is based on two main theories. The universal one is where the person who is legally considered to have caused the claimant's harm acted negligently, that is was at fault. Under English and US law, the actions, or failure to act, of the defendant fell below a standard of reasonableness that breached a legal duty of care. These concepts of individual actors, evaluation of reasonable acting and causation can be applied to any defendant – an individual doctor or nurse, a hospital or a manufacturer. It is well known that it can be extremely complicated to investigate and examine the actions that led to harm in a medical context, and to establish whether a healthcare professional's actions were or were not below a legal standard of reasonable care, and that a patient's injury was caused by such a failure.

Since establishing negligence can be complicated, and hence slow and costly, a different criterion was developed in the USA and England in order to make it simpler for people to sue the manufacturers of products. This is known as 'strict liability', which merely refers to a liability system that is not based on either negligence or 'absolute' liability (since strict liability sets out some criteria and affords certain defences).

Debate in the UK on introducing strict product liability was stirred up as a result of the Thalidomide tragedy, since it was likely that the children affected would be unlikely to have been able to succeed in establishing negligence, and the same result might occur in similar cases on medicines. The Law Commission and the Scottish Law Commission led the debate on draft laws, but the new regime was not introduced until the Consumer Protection Act 1987 was passed, with rules that are harmonised throughout the EU under Directive 85/374/EC.

The EU strict liability regime requires a producer (usually a manufacturer but also an entity whose brand is on the product, and possibly a supplier) to have placed into circulation a product that is legally 'defective', since it does not provide the level of safety that persons generally are entitled to expect. There are various defences, and an important one for medical product manufacturers is where the state of scientific and technical knowledge at the time the product was put into circulation was not such that the defect could have been discovered (known as the 'state of the art' defence).[1]

Although the introduction of strict liability was intended to make it easier, and hence quicker and cheaper, for consumers to be able to claim compensation from manufacturers for injuries caused by products, this is rarely the outcome with medical products. This study shows problems arising in cases on causation (Vioxx, Hormonal Pregnancy Tests), market share liability (DES) and defect (MMR, valproate).

Since at least the 1960s, there has been debate over whether to shift the compensation system further, into a 'no fault' regime. A better description of such schemes would be 'administrative compensation schemes', since the structure and context are what constitute the primary changes. The inquiry moves from the adversarial context of litigation, with lawyers fighting lawyers to 'win', to a system in which a patient claims from an administrative body, providing basic details which are then investigated by the body with the assistance of expert medical and legal experts, to see if the criteria for payment are met.

[1] Directive 85/374/EC, Art 7(e).

The description 'no fault' is not specific, since it describes a feature of a scheme that is absent rather than present. Every system has specific criteria for triggering payment of money. The legal system uses criteria of negligence and strict product liability. Administrative schemes tend to use a list of factual medical criteria. For example, the Florida Birth-Related Neurological Injury Compensation Association[2] will compensate a living child who was born weighing at least 2,000 grams either in a participating hospital or delivered by a participating physician, and who suffered injuries to the brain or spine caused by oxygen deprivation or mechanical injury during labour, delivery or during resuscitation in the immediate post-delivery period, which rendered the child permanently and substantially mentally and physically impaired. Disabilities caused by genetic or congenital abnormalities are excluded from compensation.

B. Litigation Systems

We have referred to the fact that litigation systems are adversarial. Civil procedure systems have the same basic format around the world. A claimant files a claim form and details of the claim with a court, naming the defendant(s). The defendants respond in writing. Both sides produce documentary evidence and the evidence of independent experts that support their respective positions. If the case is not settled, a public trial will be held in which the allegations and evidence, usually involving oral testimony by witnesses of fact and experts, will be set out, and a decision will be made on liability. Continental systems generally have 'trials' that extend over multiple successive hearings in court, whereas in the American and British common law legal systems trials will be concentrated single events, even if lasting some days or weeks.

There are major differences in procedure between the USA and UK. One is that decisions on liability and damages are made by juries in the former jurisdiction and by judges in the latter. A related difference is that levels of damages are typically far higher in USA, and it is also possible for juries to award punitive damages against defendants.[3]

C. Funding and Costs

Another major difference exists in how litigation is funded and how costs are charged and allocated at the end. All litigation requires intermediaries: lawyers, courts and experts. In the US, access to justice is often virtually free to claimants, as lawyers will act on a contingency fee basis, under which they are paid out of the proceeds of success. A no-win result means no fee. But a win may mean a very large fee. In a class action (see section I.D) the court, rather than one or more class members, usually awards the claimant lawyers their fee. There is no general rule that a claimant who loses will be liable to pay the defendant's legal costs.

[2] See at www.nica.com.

[3] Recent examples: *Ingham v Johnson & Johnson*, no 1522-CC10417, Circuit Court, City of St Louis, Missouri awarded \$550m in compensation and \$4.1bn in punitive damages to 22 women in July 2018, upholding an allegation that talcum powder was contaminated with asbestos; *Dewayne Johnson v Monsanto Co*, CGC-16-550128, California Superior Court (San Francisco) awarded \$289m, including \$250m punitive damages, in August 2018, upholding an allegation that glyphosate in weedkiller caused non-Hodgkin's lymphoma.

In England and Wales, claimants must pay their lawyers, and are subject to a 'loser pays costs' (cost-shifting) rule. From the 1950s until around the later 1990s, large personal injury cases could only be brought if the claimants were funded by the state, through the legal aid scheme.[4] Individuals applied to the Legal Aid Board, later the Legal Services Commission, and were awarded a certificate of funding if their personal assets were below certain limits and their cases satisfied a 'reasonable merits' test. The system was inherently one-sided and many cases were funded that failed.[5] This legal aid mechanism was orchestrated by leading claimant lawyers to fund multiparty cases, especially multiparty medicines cases. The tactical battle became one over the grant and subsequent continuation of legal aid funding.[6] Over time, legal aid became unaffordable for the state,[7] and was subject to successive cuts and restrictions until it was significantly reduced in 1999 (to be replaced by the unsuccessful experiment of conditional fee agreements[8]), virtually disappearing in 2013 for most civil cases.[9]

Experiments have been made with methods of payment of one's lawyers by means of insurance policies, either 'before the event' (BTE) or 'after the event' (ATE), where the premium for latter type of policy might be very high. Such BTE legal expenses insurance policies are widely available for small individual cases in many European states, and are widely used in Germany, but appear not have been popular in UK for personal injury cases. After legal aid became unavailable, some large or multiple-claimant cases in England and Wales were funded by ATE policies.

Since 1974, experiments have been made in England and Wales with 'qualified one way cost shifting' rules to try to assist personal injury claimants, on the assumption that most personal injury claims were valid and defendant insurers should be encouraged to settle more quickly.[10]

D. US: The Class Action and MDL

Cases involving medicinal products and medical devices can typically involve large cohorts of patients. Legal systems have developed mechanisms for processing multiple claims, the classic model being the class action procedure. The courts and the class action regime are highly politicised in the US,[11] and involve very large sums of money going to successful attorneys.[12]

[4] Introduced by the Legal Aid Act 1949.

[5] J Peysner, *Access to Justice: A Critical Analysis of Recoverable Conditional Fees and No-Win No-Fee Funding* (Palgrave Macmillan, 2014) 26–27.

[6] C Hodges (ed), *Multi-Party Actions* (Oxford University Press, 2001).

[7] S Hynes and J Robins, *The Justice Gap* (LSAG, 2009) 71; J Sorabji, 'Austerity's Effect on English Civil Justice' (2015) 8(4) *Erasmus Law Review* 159, 163.

[8] J Peysner, 'Tail Wags Dog: Contingency fees (and Part 36 and third party funding)' (2013) 231 *Civil Justice Quarterly* 1.

[9] Access to Justice Act 1999; Legal Aid, Sentencing and Punishment of Offenders Act 2012.

[10] Lord Justice Jackson, *Review of Civil Litigation Costs: Final Report* (Judiciary, 2010) chs 9 and 10; *Written Ministerial Statement: Implementation of Part 2 of the Legal Aid, Sentencing and Punishment of Offenders Act 2012: Civil Litigation Funding and Costs* (Ministry of Justice, 2012).

[11] BG Garth, 'Power and Legal Artifice: The Federal Class Action' 26 *Law & Society Review* (1992) 237 ('The class action is a politically empowering legal artifice'); RA Kagan, *Adversarial Legalism: The American Way of Law* (Harvard University Press, 2001); W Haltom and M McCann, *Distorting the Law: Politics, Media, and The Litigation Crisis* (University of Chicago Press, 2004); WV McIntosh and CL Cates, *Multi-Party Litigation: The Strategic Context* (UBC Press, 2009).

[12] DR Hensler, B Dombey-Moore, B Giddens, J Gross, EK Moller and NM Pace, *Class Action Dilemmas. Pursuing Public Goals for Private Gain* (RAND Institute for Civil Justice, 2000).

The class action procedure had existed for some decades in the US, but became a powerful tool of civil enforcement after Rule 23 of the Federal Rules of Procedure was reformed in 1966. A huge volume of class litigation occurred over the following three decades.[13] Strenuous debates ensued on the extent of the benefits and the harm produced. Reforms were introduced to shift cases from State courts to federal courts under the Class Action Fairness Act of 2005.[14]

United States federal and State courts generally do not certify classes of personal injury claimants in product litigation, as it is felt that individual differences among personal injury claimants would make class treatment inappropriate. A different means of coordinating large numbers of individual personal injury claims has evolved, the Multi-District Litigation (MDL). In federal courts a Multidistrict Litigation Panel of federal judges may designate a single federal judge (the MDL judge) to oversee the MDL. Under the MDL procedure, all individual claims in federal courts are transferred for centralised case management before being returned to their original courts (unless settled meanwhile) for trial locally. Examples of an MDL are the Dow Corning silicone implants, Vioxx and vaginal mesh cases. A similar model, the Multi-County Litigation (MCL), uses State procedure rules to coordinate individual cases pending in different courts within a State. That has been used in Accutane, Vioxx and vaginal mesh cases.

The essential reason why the US adopts some of the above features is the theory that private enforcement is equivalent to public enforcement (the latter being itself politically unpopular in some quarters, as it is felt that certain American regulators are captured by political and business forces[15]) since they both provide regulation through deterrence, and fines and damages have the same disciplining effect. The sheer size of the sums of money involved in litigation in the US (damages and costs) means that sizeable battles occur over preliminary motion practice in federal multidistrict personal injury product litigation, and over whether class litigation in related securities and statutory consumer litigation will be certified or not. It has typically been the case that if a class action is certified, the defendant manufacturer will then settle the case rather than fight it.[16] A mechanism that has been used in recent years in personal injury multidistrict litigations is for a series of individual trials to act as 'bellwether' trials, to gauge the strengths and weaknesses of opinion on different aspects of liability and damages from multiple juries, rather than one 'bet the company' case. The bellwether mechanism was used in the Vioxx and Depakote/valproate cases.

A major shift in disputes away from courts and into largely invisible arbitration has also occurred for consumer and employment cases. This followed US Supreme Court decisions that upheld the validity of arbitration clauses in standard consumer or labour contracts in the *Conception*[17] and *American Express*[18] cases in 2011 and 2013 respectively. (That result

[13] S Farhang, *The Litigation State. Public Regulation and Private Lawsuits in the US* (Princeton University Press, 2010).

[14] JC Coffee Jr, *Entrepreneurial Litigation: Its Rise, Fall, and Future* (Harvard University Press, 2015); C Hodges, *US Class Actions: Promise and Reality*, EUI Florence Working Paper 2015/36 (ERC ERPL 14) hdl.handle.net/1814/36536; in German at hdl.handle.net/1814/46464.

[15] S Farhang 'Public Regulation and Private Lawsuits in the American Separation of Powers System' (2008) 52 *American Journal of Political Science* 821.

[16] See eg B Garth, IH Nagel and SJ Plager, 'The Institution of the Private Attorney General: Perspectives from an Empirical Study of Class Action Litigation' (1987–88) 61 *Southern California Law Review* 353.

[17] *AT&T Mobility v Conception*, 131 S Ct 1740 (2011).

[18] *American Express Co v Italian Colors Restaurant*, 133 S Ct 2304 (2013).

would not be lawful in European states.) The result has been a general disappearance of such disputes from view.

E. Europe

Europe has expressed great reluctance to adopt US-style class action mechanisms, referring to the US system as a 'toxic cocktail' of ingredients that produce abuse (especially by lawyers).[19] The European Commission stated in 2017 that the collective action mechanism is 'too complex, costly and lengthy to fully reach its objectives'.[20] Debates on how to deliver collective redress to consumers have continued for at least 20 years. Individual European states have introduced local collective mechanisms, which all differ, as the decisions on which individual elements or safeguards against abuse are to be introduced is a political one, and different outcomes have been reached in different national contexts. It is interesting that little collective litigation exists in those states where alternative mechanisms exist. The Nordic states are examples of this: almost all consumer–trader disputes are handled by the Consumer Disputes Board and similar sectoral boards, and personal injury cases are handled by the relevant Compensation Board for workplace, or road traffic, or patient, or medicines injuries.

The Netherlands has a strong culture of settling disputes. In order to conclude the DES case, it invented a Class Action Settlement procedure (the 2005 Collective Settlements Act, known as WCAM) in order to give legal finality to a settlement reached between the claimant group and the manufacturers under which a compensation scheme had been agreed.[21] That procedure has since been adopted successfully in other (non-injury) mass claim cases.[22]

[19] Recommendation 2013/396 of the European Commission of 11 June 2013 on Common Principles for Injunctive and Compensatory Collective Redress Mechanisms in the Member States Concerning Violations of Rights granted under Union Law [2013] OJ L206/60. See also Joint Information Note, Towards a coherent European approach to collective redress: Next Steps, SEC(2010) 1192, 5 October 2010; Commission Staff Working Document, Public Consultation: Towards a coherent European approach to collective redress, SEC(2011)173 final, 4 February 2011; European Parliament Resolution of 2 February 2012 on 'Towards a coherent European approach to collective redress', 2011/2089 (INI), 2 February 2012; Inception Impact Assessment, *A New deal for Consumers – revision of the Injunctions Directive* (European Commission, 31/10/2017) Ares(2017)5324969, citing Study supporting the assessment of the implementation of 2013 EC Recommendation on Collective Redress.

[20] Inception Impact Assessment, *A New deal for Consumers – revision of the Injunctions Directive* (European Commission, 31/10/2017) Ares(2017)5324969, citing Study supporting the assessment of the implementation of 2013 EC Recommendation on Collective Redress.

[21] Dutch Civil Code, arts 7:900–7:910 and Dutch Judicial Code, arts 1013–1018. See WDH Asser, 'New Trends in Standing and Res Iudicata in Collective Suits (the Netherlands)' in AW Jongbloed (ed), *The XIIIth World Congress of Procedural Law: The Belgian and Dutch Reports* (Intersentia, 2008) 17; J Fleming and JJ Kuster, 'The Netherlands' in PG Karlsgodt (ed), *World Class Actions: A Guide to Group and Representative Actions around the Globe* (Oxford University Press, 2012) 286; I Tzankova and D Lunsingh Scheurleer, 'The Netherlands' (2009) 622 *Annals of the American Academy of Political and Social Science* 149; and MJ van der Heijden, 'Class Actions' in JHM van Erp and PW Van Vliet (eds), *Netherlands Reports to the Eighteenth International Congress of Comparative Law* (Intersentia, 2010) 197.

[22] In addition to the commentaries in the previous footnote, see case studies in S Voet, 'Public enforcement and A(O)DR as mechanisms for resolving mass problems: a Belgian perspective' in Hodges and Stadler (eds), *Resolving Mass Disputes: ADR and Settlement of Mass Claims* (Edward Elgar, 2013); DR Hensler, C Hodges and I Tzankova (eds), *Class Actions in Context: How Culture, Economics and Politics Shape Collective Litigation* (Edward Elgar, 2016); and C Hodges and S Voet, *Delivering Collective Redress: New Technologies* (Hart Publishing, 2018) 125–28.

A mechanism that is attractive to claimants is where the state investigates a case, at its cost, and private parties can 'piggy-back' with their compensation claims. Most European states have this piggy-back option in relation to prosecutions of individuals or companies, where a private party may join as a *partie civile*.[23] If relevant defendants are convicted (and assuming they have deep pockets), the criminal court may then, as a second stage, process the damages actions and determine the issues of compensation, restitution and legal costs. If French *parties civiles* are found to be victims of a criminal act they are entitled to compensation from the statutory fund SARVI. In many European countries, criminal courts can decline to process the damages actions, but there is no opt out in Belgium and France.[24] However, an *action civile* gives the claimant full access to the proceedings of the criminal court, including disclosure of supporting documents, access to court files, witness interviews conducted by the judge, and rights to participation in the trial, including representation by a lawyer. This procedure has been used in France in the valproate, Mediator and PIP silicone implants cases.

In England and Wales, criminal courts that convict those found guilty can (and since 2012 must[25]) consider making a compensation order[26] to benefit people who have suffered harm or loss. However, it is rare that manufacturers, doctors or hospitals are prosecuted in England and Wales. The related technique of 'regulatory redress', in which a regulatory authority orders or agrees with a defendant that the latter will pay compensation, is now becoming widespread in many consumer sectors in UK and elsewhere, not least because it is highly efficient and swift.[27] However, it has yet to find an equivalent in the personal injury context.

A sequence of multiparty personal injury cases was brought in England and Wales from the 1970s onwards, funded by legal aid. That demand caused the courts to innovate in procedure, since no 'class action' mechanism was available. Coordinated arrangements were developed based on judicial case management techniques,[28] which were subsequently codified in the group litigation order (GLO) when the Civil Procedure Rules were reformed by Lord Woolf in 1999.[29] The GLO procedure requires an application to be made to the Lord Chief Justice, and now to the Senior Master, and it has operated well in case management terms.

Examples of multi-party cases that were discontinued by claimants in this study are: Primodos (1982), insulin (1993), Benzodiazepines (1994, £30–35 million spent on legal aid), Gravigard (1996), HRT (1997), Lariam (1998), Norplant (1999), MMR vaccine (2003, £15 million spent on legal aid), Valproate (2010, after £4 million spent on legal aid), Seroxat (2010) and Vioxx (Scotland).

[23] Hodges and Voet, n 22, ch 4.

[24] S Voet, 'Cultural Dimensions of Group Litigation: The Belgian Case' (2012–2013) 41 *Georgia Journal of International & Comparative Law* 433; Voet, n 22, 27; Hodges and Voet, n 22, 145–48.

[25] The Legal Aid, Sentencing and Punishment of Offenders Act 2012, s 63.

[26] Powers of Criminal Courts (Sentencing) Act 2000, s 130.

[27] Hodges and Voet, n 22, ch 5.

[28] See case studies in Hodges, n 6.

[29] Lord Woolf, *Access to Justice: Interim Report to the Lord Chancellor on the Civil Justice System in England and Wales* (HMSO, 1995); Lord Woolf, *Access to Justice: Final Report to the Lord Chancellor on the Civil Justice System in England and Wales* (HMSO, 1996).

Cases in which judgment was given for the defendants included: DTP vaccine (1988, £2 million spent on legal aid), DTP vaccine in Scotland (single claim, 1991) and oral contraceptives (2003).

Cases that was successful at trial (outside the USA) included SMON (1978, Japan), human growth hormone (1999, after which a compensation scheme was established) and PIP hydrogel implants (2010, but the company went into bankruptcy).

F. Settlement Schemes

Lastly, it should not be forgotten that some cases are concluded when the parties agree to refer cases to a voluntary compensation scheme, or when the manufacturer makes such a scheme available for people to use, whether it is a pre-existing mechanism or created on an ad hoc basis. Examples in this study are the Thalidomide Trust (UK 1973), Opren (1987), fenfluramine etc (USA, 1999, fund of around $20 million), blood products (UK 1988), Trilucent breast implants (2000), human growth hormone (2001) and Sabril (2008). In France a compensation fund was created by the Government for valproate in 2016.

2

The Regulation of Medicines and Medical Devices

> These are dangers that might follow the use of any drug, and therefore it is important to stress that no drug is without some hazard; that the safety of a drug is a relative and not an absolute quality of the drug, and that whether a drug is safe for human use depends on many factors.
>
> Lord Cohen of Birkenhead[1]

This chapter summarises the regulation of medicines and medical devices, outlining how the systems have evolved over time and identifying major differences between the US and UK (EU) regimes. The description of the modern regimes draws on previous work by Hodges, who defines regulation as follows:[2]

> Product regulation is the system of administrative control over the marketing of products. It may potentially cover all the activities of producers and distributors, including design, research, manufacture, labelling, distribution, advertising, post-marketing vigilance, and recall. It does not currently generally impose regulatory duties on users of products (except for some human tissue products), but imposes regulatory duties on producers or others responsible for placing products on the market, and sometimes distributors. Breach of such duties is enforceable by regulatory authorities, through sanctions applied by administrative authorities or ultimately by the criminal courts.[3]

Three points should be noted at the start. First, the history of regulation of medicines (in particular) stretches back many centuries in the context of guarding against adulterated or quack products, but was revolutionised in the twentieth century, especially after the Thalidomide tragedy in the 1960s.

Second, the modern regimes for both medicines and medical devices (and other consumer products) have gradually been extended since the 1960s, in relation to safety aspects, from initial focus on pre-marketing assessment to cover continuous post-marketing scrutiny of safety information (known as vigilance).

Third, the regimes for medicines and medical devices differ, and should not be confused (as they often are). For example, in Europe marketing approval for a medicine, and its

[1] Testing of New Drugs, HL Deb 3 March 1964, vol 256, col 67.

[2] C Hodges, 'The Regulation of Medicinal Products and Medical Devices' in J Laing and J McHale (eds), *Principles of Medical Law*, 4th edn (Oxford University Press, 2017). See also C Hodges, *European Regulation of Consumer Product Safety* (Oxford University Press, 2005).

[3] Hodges, 'The Regulation of Medicinal Products and Medical Devices', n 2, para 17.01.

manufacture and wholesale distribution, requires an authorisation from a national regulatory authority. In contrast, marketing approval for placing a medical device on the European market requires a manufacturer to sign a declaration of conformity of a product with the legal requirements. For devices in higher risk classes, such a declaration may only be signed after specified aspects of design and manufacture have been positively assessed by a notified body, but a national authority is not involved and does not license a product.

This important difference between the European regulatory regimes for medicines and devices is apparent in the basic criteria that are applied to them. For medicines, the criteria are 'safety, efficacy and quality', whereas for devices they are 'safety and performance'. In contrast the US system requires that the studies within the medicines licence applications show that the drug is safe and effective for its proposed use.[4] Devices must also demonstrate that they are safe and efficacious, but this can be inferred by conformity with consensus standards[5] or by studies included in the particular application.

Regulation of activities, rather than of products, was introduced for human blood and blood components from 2005,[6] and for human tissues and cells from 2006.[7] Regulation of gene therapy medicinal products and somatic cell therapy medicinal products became mandatory from 2012, and of tissue engineered products from 2013.[8]

I. Medicinal Products

In contrast to the USA, the regulation and marketing of medicines in the UK was not centralised and was governed piecemeal by a variety of Acts.

The following summary of the history of medicinal products in the UK and the EU is intended to provide a brief synopsis, rather than a detailed outline. The following sections on historical regulation are intended to provide context and background for the earlier drugs and biologics, for example DES and the DTP vaccine, which were both used during the 1940s.

A. Historical Drug/Pharmaceutical Regulation in the UK

Concerns about impure or adulterated drugs and cures have a long history,[9] dating right back to medieval times. The guilds (essentially early trade bodies) played a key role, with the

[4] It is recognised that no drug is absolutely safe and that all drugs have side effects. 'Safe' in this sense means that the benefits of the drug or device appear to outweigh the known risks.

[5] Section 514(c) of the Food, Drug and Cosmetics Act 1938 Pub L No 75-717, 52 Stat 1040, as amended by the 21st Century Cures Act 2016 Pub L No 114-255.

[6] Directive (EC) 2002/98 and Commission Directives (EC) 2004/33, (EC) 2005/61 and 2005/62/EC.

[7] Directive (EC) 2004/23 and Commission Directives (EC) 2006/17 and (EC) 2006/86.

[8] Regulation (EC) 1394/2007 and Commission Directive (EC) 2009/120.

[9] For a detailed description, see IH Harrison, *The Law on Medicines*, vol 1: *A Comprehensive Guide* (MTP Press Ltd, 1986); and J Wingfield and K Pitchford (eds), *Dale and Appelbe's Pharmacy and Medicines Law*, 11th edn (Pharmaceutical Press, 2017).

Grocer's Company being granted powers to inspect and destroy adulterated wares, which included both foods and medicines. The earliest known specific 'pharmaceutical' (in the loosest possible sense) regulation[10] dates to the middle of the sixteenth century, when Henry VIII enacted regulations to permit a committee of physicians to visit and inspect London apothecaries' shops, and to destroy any products they considered to be defective or unfit for human consumption.

Despite its long history, the regulation of pharmaceuticals progressed in a piecemeal, disorganised fashion right up until the latter half of the twentieth century, with the Medicines Act 1968 providing the first comprehensive reorganisation. There had been recommendations for centralised effective regulation of medicines far earlier than this.[11] In 1914 the Report from the Select Committee on Patent Medicines,[12] chaired by Sir Henry Norman, produced far-sighted plans for a comprehensive system for regulating the advertising, sale and distribution of medicines. The recommendations included a register of manufacturers/sellers/distributors and each medicine having a specific product registration number, with an annual fee to be charged for registration. All medicines would have to list their ingredients and any claims made about the product, with the Department of Health having powers to test product composition and to require that the active ingredient of a medicine be detailed on the product label. The new regime would be overseen by the Department of Health Minister, who would be the ultimate regulatory compliance enforcer. To aid the Minister, it was recommended that a Medicines Division be set up within the Department of Health, which had the power to permit or prohibit the sale or advertising of a medicine. These prescient suggestions were never taken up; the Select Committee Report was published on 4 August 1914, the same day Great Britain declared war on Germany. It took another 54 years before such a comprehensive plan for medicine regulation was enacted by the British Government.

Social context has clearly impacted upon pharmaceutical regulation, from the large-scale geopolitical upheavals of the First World War to more mundane national politics. As such, the drivers of pharmaceutical regulation ought to be considered within their wider socio-legal context. A substantial shift in emphasis on the rationale for drug regulation has occurred during the twentieth century. In his comprehensive 1986 book, Ivor Harrison made a very interesting point about the changing priorities within pharmaceutical regulation:[13]

> Currently, an *emphasis on consumer protection has also contributed to the demand for stricter controls over medicines.* In the past, laws have been made for the following purposes:
>
> (a) to ensure the purity of drugs,
> (b) to use them as a source of revenue,
> (c) to prevent their misuse,
> (d) to protect the public from charlatans and 'quacks'.

[10] 1540 Henry VIII ch 40.

[11] See SR Walker and JP Griffin (eds), *International Medicines Regulations: A look forward to 1992* (Springer, 2011), first published 1989.

[12] Available at archive.org/details/b28269901.

[13] Harrison, n 9, at 1(emphasis added).

Table 2.1 outlines the main legislative provisions detailed in *The Law on Medicines*, according to the classification detailed by Ivor Harrison.

Table 2.1 The main legislative provisions according to Harrison, *The Law on Medicines*

Act	Outcome	Purpose
Adulteration of Food and Drugs Act 1872	Obliged local authorities to ensure the quality of drugs on public sale.	(a)
Therapeutic Substances Act 1925	To ensure appropriate manufacturing and testing of biological agents, such as vaccines, sera, toxins, etc.	(a)
The Medicines Stamp Act 1802, The Stamp Act 1804, and The Medicines Stamp Act 1812	Medicine sellers had to be licensed, and a stamp affixed to the medicine container at the point of sale. This was aimed at taxing 'quack' medicines, as affixing a stamp provided immunity from the requirements of disclosure of contents.	(b)
Arsenic Act 1851	To restrict and record sales of small amounts (under 10lb, larger amounts were needed in agriculture) of arsenic and to prevent it from being added to food.	(c)
Pharmacy Act 1868	Listed substances that should be controlled as poisons and restricted the retail sale of these.	(c)
Poisons and Pharmacy Act 1908	Created a system of licensing sellers for arsenic and nicotine for use in agriculture and horticulture.	(c)
Regulation 40B under the Defence of the Realm Act 1916	Prohibited the sale or supply of opiates and cocaine to servicemen during the war except on prescription. This was the first time that a prescription was legally required for a medicine.	(c)
Dangerous Drugs Act 1920	To control and regulate the possession and use of addictive drugs, opiates and cocaine (the sale of these substances was already regulated as they were classed as poisons). Improved record keeping and licensed the manufacture and import of these drugs.	(c)
The Pharmacy and Poisons Act 1933	Created the Poisons Board to advise the Home Secretary on which substances should be on the poisons list and what controls should be placed on the individual substance. (Poisons included painkillers, tranquilisers and other medicines, including some that were not very toxic but which needed a control mechanism.)	(c)
The Penicillin Act 1947	To restrict the sale of penicillin to reduce the risk of antibiotic resistance (replaced in 1956 by the Therapeutic Substances Act).	(c)
Therapeutic Substances Act 1956	Replaced the 1925 and 1947 Acts. Controlled the manufacture of antibiotics and biologicals. Repealed by the Medicines Act 1968.	(c)
Venereal Diseases Act 1917	Prevented the advertising and sale of medicines for venereal diseases and the giving of advice or treatment except by medical practitioners.	(d)

(continued)

Table 2.1 *(Continued)*

Act	Outcome	Purpose
Cancer Act 1939	Prevented the advertising and sale of medicines for cancers and the giving of advice or treatment except by medical practitioners.	(d)
The Pharmacy and Medicines Act 1941	Prohibited advertising remedies for Bright's disease (nephritis), cataract, diabetes, epilepsy, glaucoma, paralysis and tuberculosis. It also prevented the advertising of products worded in terms that were likely to cause the product to be used to procure an abortion or miscarriage. Repealed the Medicine Stamp Acts and required that all proprietary medicines listed their contents on their labels.	(d)

Harrison demonstrates that by the 1950s there was a patchwork of legislation in place that, in the main, achieved these four purposes: ensuring the purity of drugs; generating revenue; preventing the misuse of drugs; and protecting the public from snake oil salesmen. However, the problems outlined in the 1914 Select Committee Report – a lack of cohesion (some of these Acts were enacted under the auspices of the Home Office, some under the Ministry of Health) and of consistent enforcement of the provisions – remained as they had been prior to the First World War. Additionally, consumer protection was limited to ensuring that the medicines contained the ingredients they were supposed to, and that the public were protected from 'quacks'. There was no statutory requirement to demonstrate that a drug on the market was safe and efficacious. This was hardly satisfactory.

Curiously, the provisions for the licensing, sale and manufacture and quality control of biologicals were more advanced than those for medicines. This was in part due to the inherent qualities of biologicals, such as antibodies and vaccines, which could not be heat sterilised without destroying the integrity of the biological.[14] This had led to several cases of contaminated or live vaccines inadvertently being given.[15] The Therapeutic Substances Act 1956[16] provided a far more coherent and comprehensive system for biologicals, but did not extend to pharmaceuticals.

i. 1948–59: The Birth of the National Health Service

An additional driver for pharmaceutical regulation was tied to the creation of the National Health Service (NHS) in 1948. If an NHS prescriber listed a proprietary or brand name then the agreement was that that branded product would be supplied; if the prescriber

[14] Ministry of Health, *Report of the Departmental Committee appointed to consider and advise upon the Legislative Measures to be Taken for the Effective Control of the Quality and Authenticity of such Therapeutic Substances offered for Sale to the Public as cannot be tested adequately by Direct Chemical Means* (Cmd 1156, 1921).

[15] The most well-known accidental use of live vaccine was the Cutter incident in 1955, when over 200,000 children in the western USA were given a live polio vaccine produced by Cutter Laboratories, California. 40,000 children developed polio and around 200 were left with some paralysis; 10 died. See P Offit, *The Cutter Incident: How America's First Polio Vaccine Led to a Growing Vaccine Crisis* (Yale University Press, 2005).

[16] This replaced the 1925 Act of the same name and the Penicillin Act 1947.

listed a generic drug name on the prescription then the cheapest version of that drug would be supplied. Since its foundation the NHS has always been the major purchaser and prescriber of pharmaceuticals in the UK. When it was founded, the majority of the drugs the NHS purchased and prescribed were non-proprietary (generic) medicines. Proprietary (branded) medicines were considerably more expensive, but in the decade following the formation of the NHS there was a tenfold increase in the proportion of proprietary medicines prescribed.[17] The need to manage costs was recognised almost from the start of the NHS. In 1949 the Joint Standing Committee on the Classification of Proprietary Preparations was set up to classify pharmaceutical products and to recommend that some products (those advertised directly to the public and those that had not demonstrated therapeutic value) ought not to be prescribed. The Committee was chaired by Lord Cohen of Birkenhead until May 1965, and was often known as the Cohen Committee. It acted as a restraint on prescribers, but more influential was the Report of the Committee on the Classification of Proprietary Preparations, a 1959 technical report on the equivalence between unbranded and proprietary pharmaceuticals. This function was later undertaken by the Ministry of Health.[18] The success of trying to persuade prescribers preferentially to prescribe generics was limited. The primary focus of the Joint Standing Committee on the Classification of Proprietary Preparations was economic; it had no powers to prevent a drug from being put on the market. Within its remit there was a nod towards consumer protection in the Committee's assessment of the efficacy of a product as part of its classification of it, but its primary aim was protecting the public purse rather than protecting the public.

ii. 1959–62: Thalidomide

The need for more effective control of pharmaceutical safety was recognised by the UK Government in the late 1950s. Various bodies and organisations were providing advice and recommendations on regulatory reform, including the Pharmaceutical Society of Great Britain, an Inter-Departmental Working Group (jointly held by the Ministry of Health and the Home Office), the Guillebaud Committee, the Hinchcliffe Committee and the Inter-Departmental Committee on Drug Addiction, and later the Sainsbury Committee. However, the major impetus for regulatory reform came when the shortcomings of the pharmaceutical regulatory system were painfully highlighted by the Thalidomide tragedy. Thalidomide was available in the UK in various forms between 1959 and 1962, with devastating consequences for those exposed in utero. Thalidomide has had the largest impact of any drug in shaping the UK's pharmaceutical regulatory system.

It is important to remember that drug companies were, generally, carrying out pre-market testing prior to the Thalidomide disaster, which often included teratogenicity testing. Although there were no mandatory testing requirements, the majority of pharmaceutical manufacturers behaved in a responsible fashion. There will always be exceptions,

[17] S Anderson, 'Drug Regulation and the Welfare State: government, the pharmaceutical industry and the health professions in Great Britain, 1940–80' in V Berridge and K Loughlin (eds), *Medicine, the Market and the Mass Media. Producing Health in the Twentieth Century* (Routledge, 2005).

[18] Initially as the *Handbook on Prescribing* in 1960, then as *Prescribers' Notes*, which morphed into the *Prescribers' Journal* in 1961.

and public protection demands a mandatory system, rather than a voluntary assumption of responsibility. It should also be remembered that even with the best pre-market testing, the adverse effects of some pharmaceuticals will slip through the net; it has been proposed that the teratogenic effects of thalidomide might have been difficult to detect even with a far more sophisticated pre-marketing testing regime than was standard at the time.[19]

The regulatory response triggered by the Thalidomide scandal had two stages: initially the response was voluntary, with later mandatory provisions under the Medicines Act 1968.

iii. 1963–71: Voluntary Self-regulation

The immediate response to the Thalidomide tragedy came in the form of the Committee for the Safety of Drugs (CSD), set up on the advice of Lord Cohen of Birkenhead, established in June 1963, with new drug submissions being accepted from 1 January 1964. The Committee was chaired by Sir Derrick Dunlop, and became commonly known as the Dunlop Committee. The Dunlop Committee was tasked with advising upon whether new drugs should be submitted for clinical trials and/or released onto the market, and to study adverse drug reactions (ADRs) of pharmaceuticals that were already on the market. The Dunlop Committee terms of reference were as follows:

1. To invite from the manufacturer or other person developing or proposing to market a drug in the UK, any reports they may think fit on the toxicity tests carried out on it; to consider whether any further tests should be made and whether the drug should be submitted to clinical trials; and to convey their advice to those who submitted the reports.
2. To obtain reports of clinical trials of drugs submitted thereto.
3. Taking into account the safety and efficacy of each drug, and the purposes for which it is to be used, to consider whether it may be released for marketing, with or without precautions or restrictions on its use; and to convey their advice to those who submitted reports.
4. To give manufacturers and others concerned any general advice they may think fit.
5. To assemble and assess reports about adverse effects of drugs in use and prepare information thereon that may be brought to the notice of doctors and others concerned.
6. To advise the appointing ministers on any of the above matters.

For the first time the specific issue of safety was the foremost concern of the Committee, which was focused on whether a medicine provided 'reasonable safety for its intended purpose'. The Dunlop Committee comprised independent experts, including statisticians, pharmacologists, toxicologists, pharmacists and doctors. It had no powers to prevent a drug from being placed on the market – it was an entirely voluntary arrangement. However, pharmaceutical firms and members of the Association of British Pharmaceutical Industries (ABPI) and the Proprietary Association of Great Britain (PAGB) voluntarily undertook not to place drugs on the market unless the drug had CSD approval. The Dunlop Committee met monthly from the start of 1964 to 1 September 1971 to consider 'new' drug applications. The term 'new' was applied loosely to include 'new formulations of existing drugs, drugs to be present for a new purpose, and existing substances not previously used as drugs'. All applications had their own identifying number. Each manufacturer was allocated

[19] R Greek, N Shanks and MJ Rice, 'The History and Implications of Testing Thalidomide on Animals' (2011) 11 *Journal of Philosophy, Science & Law* at jpsl.org/archives/history-and-implications-testing-thalidomide-animals/.

a four-number code, starting at 0001 for Geigy (UK) Ltd, which was the first manufacturer to apply. Each product was then given a four-digit number code, based on the order in which the applications were made to CSD, which followed the manufacturer code. For example, applications made by Geigy would be numbered 0001/XXXX.

Various subcommittees, which also met monthly, were set up to serve the Dunlop Committee. The three most prominent subcommittees were:

- the Toxicity Subcommittee, chaired by Professor Frazer, which dealt with aspects relating to animal testing;
- the Clinical Trials Subcommittee, chaired by Professor Robert Hunter, which advised on all aspects of clinical trials; and
- the Adverse Reactions Subcommittee, chaired by Professor Leslie Witts.

The actions taken by the Adverse Reactions Subcommittee have long outlived the Subcommittee itself. The origins of the 'yellow card system' of reporting ADRs were devised by the Adverse Reactions Subcommittee in 1964. In May 1964, letters were sent out to doctors with pre-paid reply cards and a request to report cases of suspected ADRs to the Committee for the Safety of Medicines (CSM) using the yellow-card system. Doctors and manufacturers were later mandated to use the yellow-card system to report adverse events. An updated version of the yellow-card system, including an app for digital reporting, is still in operation today.[20]

The Dunlop Committee took on some of the functions that had previously been undertaken by the Joint Standing Committee on the Classification of Proprietary Preparations (the Cohen Committee). As a result, the Joint Standing Committee on the Classification of Proprietary Preparations issued new terms of reference:[21]

> (1) To advise on the classification of proprietary pharmaceutical preparations with the object of helping doctors to decide which should be used in the treatment of their patients, and to identify those preparations the prescribing of which appears to call for special justification.
> (2) To keep under review the principles for determining whether preparations should properly be regarded as drugs, foods, toilet preparations or disinfectants and to give advice on the classification of particular preparations submitted to the Committee.

At this time the chairmanship of the Joint Standing Committee on the Classification of Proprietary Preparations passed to Professor Alistair MacGregor, and while under his chairmanship the Committee was often known as the MacGregor Committee. The McGregor Committee sent out a regular booklet to prescribers called the Proplist. As in its previous incarnation, the focus of this Committee was cost-saving, but there was a nod to efficacy and safety.

iv. 1971 Onwards: Statutory Regulation

The Medicines Act 1968 formalised and centralised drug regulation in the UK. The 1968 Act introduced licensing, with requirements that licence holders demonstrate the safety and

[20] At yellowcard.mhra.gov.uk/.

[21] New Drug Classification: Statement of Principles by New Committee' (1965) 1 (5445) *British Medical Journal* 1306.

efficacy of their products before they were placed on the market. Although it had received Royal Assent in October 1968, the Medicines Act came into effect on 1 September 1971.[22] From this point onwards new powers were obtained by the Licensing Authority, which was responsible for the regulation of drug safety, efficacy and quality. The Licensing Authority had the legal powers necessary to approve drugs and to remove drugs from the market. All new medicines required a licence, and in section 19(1) of the Act (as originally enacted) the factors relevant to the determination of an application for a licence were set out:

> (1) Subject to the following provisions of this Part of this Act, in dealing with an application for a product licence the licensing authority shall in particular take into consideration—
>
> (a) the safety of medicinal products of each description to which the application relates;
> (b) the efficacy of medicinal products of each such description for the purposes for which the products are proposed to be administered; and
> (c) the quality of medicinal products of each such description, according to the specification and the method or proposed method of manufacture of the products, and the provisions proposed for securing that the products as sold or supplied will be of that quality.

For the first time, safety headlined the requirements, showing how far consumer protection had come.

In order to assist the Licensing Authority the CSM took over the function of assessing pre-marketing applications, previously undertaken by the Dunlop Committee. New pharmaceuticals were considered by the CSM, using the criteria set out above. Products that had been on the market before 1 September 1971 were automatically granted a licence as of right[23] during the transitional period.[24] The Committee for the Review of Medicines was created and tasked with reviewing all Product Licences of Right before 20 May 1990.

In 1971 some of the functions of the MacGregor Committee were taken over by the Medicines Commission, and the MacGregor Committee was disbanded. The residual functions of advising on whether a product was truly a 'drug or medicine' (so eligible to be prescribed) fell to the non-statutory, aptly named Advisory Committee on Borderline Substances.

B. European Regulation of Medicinal Products

The Treaty of Rome, signed on 25 March 1957,[25] created the European Economic Community (EEC), the founding members being Belgium, France, Holland, Italy, Luxembourg and West Germany. As the name suggests, this was primarily an economic arrangement at the outset.[26] On 1 January 1973, the United Kingdom (UK) (along with Ireland and Denmark) joined the EEC. Under the architecture of the (now) European Union (EU), legislation

[22] The transitional period was to allow for consultation with the pharmaceutical industry and to allow time to adjust to the new regime.

[23] Medicines Act 1968, ss 25–27.

[24] Medicines Act 1968, ss 16–17 and 25–27.

[25] The Treaty establishing the European Economic Community ('EEC Treaty' or 'Treaty of Rome'), effective date 1 January 1958, at eur-lex.europa.eu/legal-content/EN/TXT/?uri=legissum:xy0023.

[26] The Treaty on European Union ('Maastricht Treaty'), signed on 7 February 1992, removed the word 'Economic'; available at eur-lex.europa.eu/legal-content/EN/TXT/?uri=LEGISSUM%3Axy0026.

passed at EU level (Directives or Regulations) have to be applied at national level by Member States (save that Regulations have direct effect), and (usually) have to be enforced at national level by national competent authorities. Domestic legislation has therefore been aligned with EU requirements since 1973. Since then the EU has grown to include (at present) 28 Member States.[27]

In addition to the Member States, two European Free Trade Area (EFTA) states, Iceland and Norway, agreed to adopt a complete *acquis* on medical products, effective from 1 January 2000.[28] These states are in effect choosing to operate under community rules, the difference being that any legally binding acts from the EU do not automatically confer rights or obligations in these two states but have to be transposed into national legally binding Acts. Lichtenstein is also eligible to join on the same basis as Iceland and Norway, but it usually adopts the Swiss decisions made by the Swiss regulatory agency Swiss Medic, rather than adhering to community decisions. As Switzerland is not part of the EU, Swiss Medic authorisations are not deemed to be community authorisations and have no legally binding status in the EU.

At the time of writing (autumn 2018) the UK is still a full member of the EU. The impact on pharmaceutical and medical device regulation of the UK's proposed departure from the Union (so-called 'Brexit') has yet to be fully ascertained.

The essential basis of all product regulation in the EU relates to regulating the *market* in products, rather than social considerations such as safety, which may be included as elements within the market structure. Thus, the fundamental basis of the new extensive EU legislation regulating medicines and medical devices is to create a level playing field in relation to the *marketing* of those products. However, the regulatory requirements also inevitably govern the *safety* aspects of these products. Indeed, the scope of the EU legislation has been extended regularly since its inception, from controlling some aspects of placing a medicinal product on the market, not only to specifying more extensive pre-marketing controls but also to encompassing an extensive post-marketing safety surveillance system.

i. A Brief History of European Medicinal Products Regulation

The following brief summary of the EU's regulation of medicinal products is intended to provide an outline rather than a detailed description.[29]

a. 1965–95: The First 30 Years

The first EU legislation on control of medicinal products[30] was passed on 26 January 1965, as a direct consequence of the Thalidomide tragedy. The preamble to the Directive explicitly

[27] Belgium, France, Germany, Italy, Luxembourg, Netherlands (1 January 1958); Denmark, Ireland, UK (1 January 1973); Greece (1 January 1981); Portugal, Spain (1 January 1986); Austria, Finland, Sweden (1 January 1995); Cyprus, Czech Republic, Estonia, Hungary, Latvia, Lithuania, Malta, Poland, Slovakia, Slovenia (1 May 2004); Bulgaria, Romania (1 January 2007); Croatia (1 July 2013).

[28] This was effected through the European Economic Area (EEA) Agreement of 28 May 1999.

[29] Further detail can be found in JP Giffin, J Posner and JR Barker (eds), *The Textbook of Pharmaceutical Medicine*, 7th edn (Wiley-Blackwell/BMJ Books, 2013).

[30] Council Directive 65/65/EEC.

mentions consumer safety, providing that 'the primary purpose of any rules concerning the production and distribution of medicinal products must be to safeguard public health'.

Both the breadth of activities covered and the detailed requirements were expanded in successive decades. Table 2.2 details the major legislation and key EU communications between 1965 and 1995. Five key enabling acts are highlighted in bold font: these Directives created the underpinnings of the European medicines regulatory structures, and their impact is explored in further detail later in this chapter.

Table 2.2 Major EU medicinal product legislation and communications 1965–95

Year enacted	Enabler	Effect
1965	**Directive 65/65/EEC**	**Established EEC-wide regulation of medicinal products.**
1975	**Directive 75/318/EEC**	**Introduced standardised requirements for testing proprietary medicines for safety, quality and efficacy.**
1975	**Directive 75/319/EEC**	**Established the Committee for Proprietary Medicinal Products (now known as 'old' CPMP) and established the multi-state procedure (now known as the mutual recognition procedure).**
1975	**Directive 75/320/EEC**	**Established the Pharmaceutical Committee.**
1978	Directive 78/25/EEC	Regulated the use of colourings in medicinal products.
1982	Communication C/115/82	Guidance on parallel imports for which marketing authorisations have already been granted.
1983	Directive 83/570/EEC	Defined purpose and scope of Summary Product Characteristics.
1986	Directive 86/609/EEC	Introduced standards for protecting animals used in research.
1987	Directive 87/18/EEC	Standards for Good Laboratory Practice.
1987	Directive 87/19/EEC	Amending and updating Directive 75/318/EEC.
1987	Directive 87/21/EEC	Amending and updating Directive 65/65/EEC.
1987	**Directive 87/22/EEC**	**Established the concertation procedure (now known as the centralised procedure)**
1988	Directive 88/320/EEC	Further Standards for Good Laboratory Practice.
1989	Directive 89/105/EEC	Medicinal pricing and reimbursement within national health systems.
1989	Communication C/310/86	Communication on the Article 30 compatibility of measures taken by Member States relating to price controls and reimbursement of medicinal products.
1989	Directive 89/342/EEC	Directive on immunologicals.
1989	Directive 89/343/EEC	Directive on radiopharmaceuticals.
1989	Directive 89/341/EEC	Amending Directives 65/65/EEC, 75/318/EEC and 75/319/EEC.
1989	Directive 89/381/EEC	Regulation of human blood- or human plasma-derived products.

(continued)

Table 2.2 *(Continued)*

Year enacted	Enabler	Effect
1991	Directive 91/356/EEC	Standards for Good Manufacturing Practice.
1992	Directive 92/25/EEC	Regulating wholesale distribution.
1992	Directive 92/26/EEC	Classification for supply.
1992	Directive 92/17/EEC	Regulating labelling and package inserts.
1992	Directive 92/28/EEC	Regulating advertising of medicinal products
1992	Regulation 1798/92	Extended patent protection for medicinal products
1992	Directive 92/73/EEC	Regulating homeopathic medicinal products.
1993	Directive 93/39/EEC	Pharmacovigilance and a resolution mechanism for disputes between Member States on the efficacy, safety or quality of a medicinal product, by binding decision.

As can be seen from Table 2.2, a number of Directives were modified and amended after their initial adoption. To provide clarity, a number of these key pieces of legislation were consolidated in 2001 in Directive 2001/83/EC.

b. January 1995–April 2004

During the 1990s, a considerable effort was made to further harmonise pharmaceutical regulation within the EU, in what was known as the 'future systems' movement. The majority of these changes became effective on 1 January 1995 and introduced substantial alterations, including the creation of new bodies, such as the European Agency for the Evaluation of Medicinal Products (EMA),[31] and the creation of the 'new' CPMP. As in the preceding 30 years, this decade involved considerable change to the medical regulatory system in the EU. The key legislative provisions and communications are detailed in Table 2.3.

Table 2.3 Major EU medicinal product legislation and communications 1995 and April 2004

Year enacted	Enabler	Effect
1993	**Regulation 3209/93**	**Established the European Agency for the Evaluation of Medicinal Products (EMEA); replaced the old CPMP with the 'new' CPMP.**
1995	Regulation 297/95	Mandated the payment of fees to support the EMEA.
1995	Regulation 540/95	Mandatory reporting of non-serious ADRs that are associated with the use of an EU authorised medication, whether the use occurred within the EU or not.

(continued)

[31] The European Agency for the Evaluation of Medicinal Products (commonly abbreviated to 'EMEA') changed its name to become the European Medicines Agency (EMA). For ease of use the abbreviation 'EMA' will be used throughout this book for all incarnations of the organisation.

Table 2.3 *(Continued)*

Year enacted	Enabler	Effect
1995	Regulations 541/95 and 542/95	Harmonised the examination of any variations between Member States in marketing authorisation terms.
1995	Regulation 1662/95	Detailed some Community decision-making protocols and established the Standing Committees on Medicinal Products for Human and Veterinary use.
2000	Regulation 141/2000	Orphan drug procedures (drugs for rare diseases).
2000	Regulation 847/2000	Specification of 'similar medicinal product' and 'clinical superiority'.
2000	Directive 2001/20/EC	Clinical trials directive, regulating the conduct of trials.
2002	Directive 2002/98/EC	Amended 2001/83/EC, setting new standards for human blood- or human plasma-derived products.
2003	Regulations 1084/2003 and 1085/2003	Regulated variations between Member States in marketing authorisation terms.
2003	Directive 2003/63/EC	Replaced Annex 1 of 2001/83/EC and required that all marketing application dossiers be standardised to the Common Technical Document (CTD) format.
2003	Directive 2003/94/EC	Replaced 91/356/EEC and expanded the Good Manufacturing Practice framework.
2004	Directive 2004/24/EC	Regulated traditional herbal medicinal products.
2004	**Regulation 726/2004**	**Overhauled the authorisation and supervision procedures for medicines, replacing EEC/2309/93.** **Created the Committee for Medicinal Products for Human Use (CHMP) (replacing the 'new' CPMP).** **Morphed the European Agency for the Evaluation of Medicinal Products into the European Medicines Agency (EMA).**

Possibly the most notable of these developments was the creation of the EMA. Article 71 of Regulation EEC/2309/93, which established the EMA, stated that the Commission should publish a report on the experience of the procedures outlined in the Regulation, which was to be conducted within six years of the Regulation's coming into force. The EMA had a six-year health check booked in from the date of its establishment. In 2000 the review was carried out by Cameron McKenna and Arthur Anderson. In response the EU produced a consultation document that led to a raft of reforms commonly known as Review 2001.

c. May 2004 Onwards

The Review 2001 reforms were contained within Regulation 726/2004, and generally went live on 1 May 2004. The Review 2001 reforms had three key outcomes:

- an overhaul of the authorisation and supervision procedures for medicines, replacing EEC/2309/93;

- substantial changes to the European Agency for the Evaluation of Medicinal Products, which morphed into the European Medicines Agency; and
- the creation of the CHMP (replacing the 'new' CPMP).

Although substantial, the 2001 Review reforms were not the only legislative changes at this time. Table 2.4 details the key EU legislation and communications from May 2004 to date.

Table 2.4 Key EU medicinal product legislation and communications from May 2004 to date

Year enacted	Enabler	Effect
2004	Directive 2004/27/EC	• Updated the definition of medicinal product. • Updated the definition of risk related to the use of a medicinal product. • The ordering of information in the summary product characteristics. • Obliges Competent Authorities to publish assessment reports and reasons for the opinion marketing authorisations and Summary Product Characteristics • Amended the time limits on authorisations and provided guidance on borderline substances. • Permits Member States to seek to market a product on public health grounds even if the Marketing Authorisation Holder has not sought marketing authorisation
2004	**Regulation 726/2004**	• **Overhauled the authorisation and supervision procedures, replacing EEC/2309/93.** • **Morphed the EMEA into the European Medicines Agency (EMA)** • **Created the CHMP (replacing the 'new' CPMP).**
2006	Regulations 1901/2006 and 1902/2006	Modified 2001/83/EC provisions on medicinal products for paediatric use.
2007	Regulation 1394/2007	Modified 2001/83/EC provisions on advanced therapy medicinal products.
2008	Directive 2008/29/EC	Modified 2001/83/EC provisions on comitology procedures.

As is abundantly clear from the preceding sections, the regulation of medicinal products within the EU has (as would be expected) undergone considerable change in the last 50-odd years.

ii. Current EU Structures and Procedures for Regulating Medicinal Products

The EMA is responsible for producing scientific advice and safety evaluations, evaluating quality and efficacy, and supervision of and pharmacovigiliance for medicine products (human and animal), as well as more niche roles in paediatric investigation plans, designating orphan status and assignment to small or medium-sized enterprises (SMEs). Seven committees act to assist the EMA by providing expert scientific input and opinions. The EMA provides the secretariat and acts to coordinate these seven committees. Figure 2.1 provides an overview of the current EMA and committee structure. Each committee has members from each Member State and usually also has non-voting members from the EEA–EFTA states. Each committee has a chair and deputy chair, who are elected by committee members on a fixed-term basis. Adoption of Scientific Opinions usually requires a quorum[32] and a majority vote in favour.[33]

Figure 2.1 Organisation of the EMA and expert committees

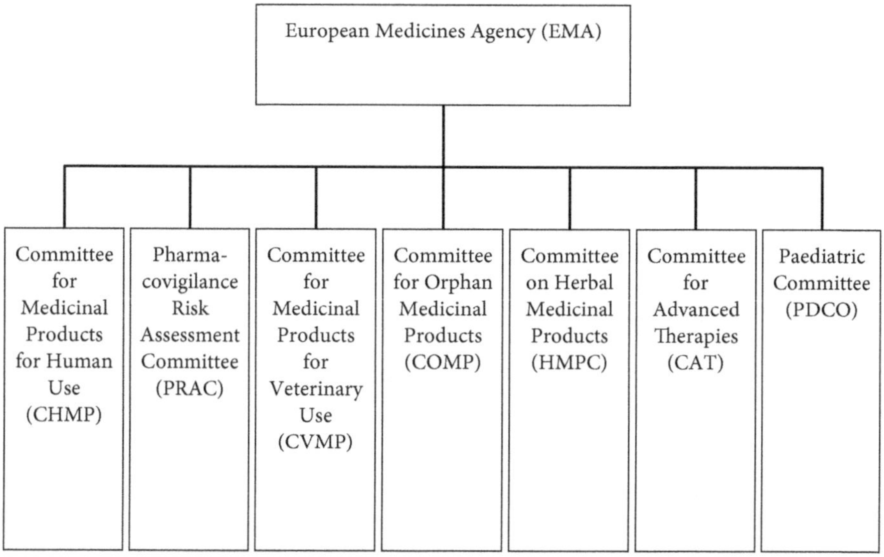

a. Marketing Authorisations within the EU

In relation to medicinal products, two parallel approval systems for marketing exist, a centralised system and a decentralised system. The decentralised mutual recognition system began in 1975,[34] with the centralised system coming into operation many years later in 1987.[35]

A key component of both systems was the CPMP. Figure 2.2 illustrates the various incarnations of the EMA and CPMP/CHMP.

1. Decentralised or Mutual Recognition Systems

Under the *decentralised* or *mutual recognition system*, marketing authorisations valid only for individual Member States are granted by national competent authorities.[36]

[32] Generally, a quorum is achieved when two-thirds of the voting committee members are present.

[33] Votes are usually a straight positive or negative, the except being if a member declares a conflict of interest. A simple majority operates for most committees, with COMP being the exception as a two thirds majority in favour is required in order for COMP to adopt and Opinion.

[34] Created by Directive 75/319/EEC.

[35] Created by Directive 87/22/EEC.

[36] In the UK the Competent Authority is the Licensing Authority, which originally comprised the Ministers of Health for England and Wales, Scotland and Northern Ireland, whose functions were assisted by the Medicines Control Agency and who were advised by expert committees such as the CSM: see Medicines Act 1968, ss 1–4. Nowadays delegated powers enable the MHRA to be the Competent Authority.

Figure 2.2 The evolution of the EMA and CPMP/CHMP

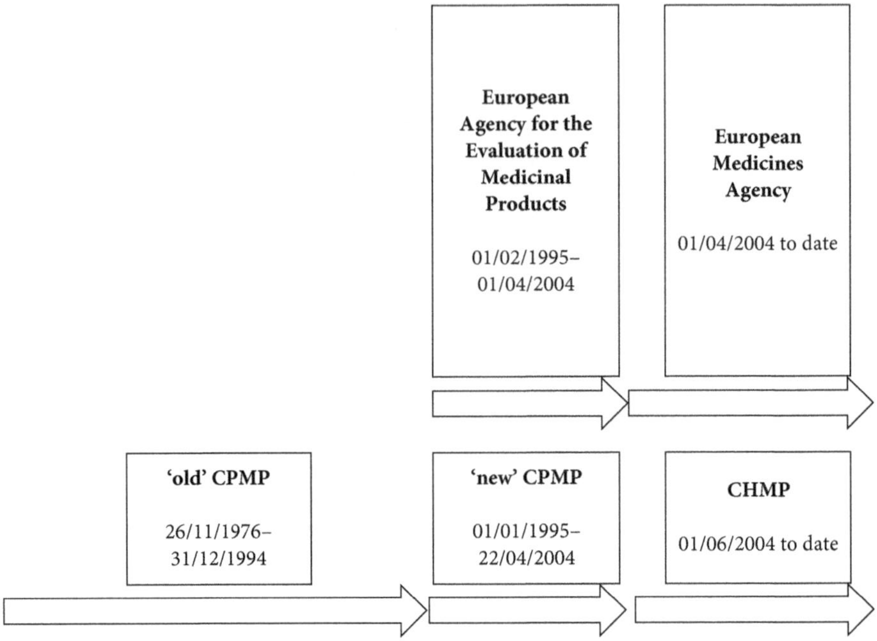

Applications in second and subsequent states can be subject to abbreviated procedures of cross-referencing to the first state's assessment and approval. This can be achieved in two ways: if an applicant already holds a marketing authorisation in a Member State then the mutual recognition process can be used to expedite a marketing authorisation for another EU state; if no marketing authorisation is held then the applicant can simultaneously apply for a marketing authorisation that is valid in multiple (named) EU states using the decentralised system. Under the decentralised system a Member State is chosen as the Reference Member State (RMS) and the marketing authorisation application is processed by agencies in that country. All other Member States to whom the application pertains are termed Concerned Member States (CMSs). Once a marketing authorisation application is approved by the RMS, the CMSs have 30 days to issue marketing authorisations for their countries.

2. Centralised System

Under the *centralised system*, a single marketing authorisation valid throughout the EU is granted by the European Commission, based on advice from the EMA.[37] The CHMP is responsible for formulating the opinions of the EMA on any question concerning the admissibility of the files submitted, the granting, variation, suspension or withdrawal of a marketing authorisation, and pharmacovigilance. The CHMP consists of representatives of the Member States and of the Commission and the EMA, and draws up its own rules of procedure.[38]

[37] Established under Regulation (EC) 726/2004, Art 5. Financial penalties for infringement of the centralised system are to be found in Commission Regulation (EC) 658/2007. The Eu

[38] Regulation (EC) 726/2004, Art 61.

Certain types of pharmaceutical have to go through the centralised process:[39] these include human medicines containing a new active substance to treat:

- Human Immunodeficiency Virus (HIV) or Acquired Immune Deficiency Syndrome (AIDS);
- cancer;
- diabetes;
- neurodegenerative diseases;
- auto-immune and other immune dysfunctions;
- viral diseases;

Certain types of medicines also have to go through the centralised procedure, regardless of the disease they are intended to treat. These include:

- medicines derived from biotechnology processes, such as genetic engineering;
- advanced-therapy medicines, such as gene-therapy, somatic cell-therapy or tissue-engineered medicines; and
- orphan medicines (medicines for rare diseases).

3. National Regulatory Architecture in Great Britain

In addition to the centralised agencies, the decentralised medicinal products marketing authorisation system relies upon a series of national agencies within Member States. In the UK the competent authority responsible for the grant, renewal, variation, suspension and revocation of authorisations initially is the Licensing Authority, which is a body consisting of the Ministers of Health and Agriculture.[40] Any function conferred on the Licensing Authority under the Medicines Act may be performed by one such Minister acting alone, or by two or more Ministers acting jointly.[41] Advice is given to Ministers by expert committees: prior to 2005 the principal committee was the Medicines Commission,[42] and since 2005 is has been the Commission on Human Medicines.[43] The administrative agency from 1971 to 2003 was the Medicines Control Agency (MCA); in 2003 it was merged with the Medical Devices Agency to form the Medicines and Healthcare products Regulatory Agency (MHRA).

b. Requirements for Developing and Marketing Medicinal Products

The EU controls on medicinal products are based on public authorities licensing virtually all activities that affect their safety. These controls apply throughout the lifespan of the medicinal product, from initial product development right through to post-marketing surveillance.

[39] Detailed at Annex 1 to Regulation EC/726/2004.

[40] Medicines Act 1968, ss 6 and 1(1), as amended by the Human Medicines Regulations 2012, SI 2012/1916.

[41] Medicines Act 1968, s 6(2).

[42] ibid, ss 2, 3 and 4.

[43] Established in 2005 under the Medicines Act 1968, s 3 and the Medicines (Advisory Bodies) Regulations 2005, SI 2005/1094, to replace the Committee of Safety of Medicines: see now the Human Medicines Regulations 2012, pt 2.

1. EU Product Development

The individuals, facilities and performance of animal experiments are regulated.[44] Laboratory experiments must be carried out in accordance with the Standards for Good Laboratory Practice (GLP) introduced in 2004.[45]

2. EU Clinical Trials

Clinical trials on medicinal products for human use require approval, from around 1990 under the Good Clinical Practice standard and later under more specific legislation.[46] A clinical trial may be conducted only where the following conditions are fulfilled:

> (a) the anticipated benefits to the subjects or to public health justify the foreseeable risks and inconveniences and compliance with this condition is constantly monitored;
> (b) the subjects or, when a subject is not able to give informed consent, his or her legally designated representative, have been informed of the information specified;
> (c) ...[47]

The 2014 Clinical Trials Regulation builds on the 2001 Clinical Trials Directive and requires prior approval of a clinical trial through scientific and ethical review and administrative authorisation as prescribed,[48] through a single application portal operated by the EMA.[49] This arrangement is designed to facilitate single centre or multi-centre studies, and those located in different Member States. The ethical review is undertaken by ethics committees that are independent bodies established in each Member State under its domestic law, empowered to give an opinion that takes into account the views of laypersons.[50]

3. EU Marketing Authorisation Applications

In order to place a medicinal product on the market, authorisations are required from the EMA or a national competent authority for the person(s) who perform(s) the activities of placing a medicinal product on the market, manufacturing it or arranging its wholesale distribution.

In order to obtain a marketing authorisation, the person responsible for placing the product on the market must submit an application to the relevant authority, accompanied by the required particulars and documents.[51] The list of particulars and documents now

[44] Directive (EEC) 86/609; the Animals (Scientific Procedures) Act 1986.

[45] Directives (EC) 2004/10 and (EC) 2004/9.

[46] Regulation (EU) No 536/2014. See previously Directive (EC) 2001/20, Art 22 and, in the UK, the Medicines for Human Use (Clinical Trials) Regulations 2004, SI 2004/1031, as amended. Practice was established from 1987 (Recommended basis for the conduct of clinical trials of medicinal products in the European Community, III/411/87-EN Rev) and developed in 1990 (Good Clinical Practice for trials on medicinal products in the European Community) and by Directive (EEC) 91/507. For further analysis and history, see CJS Hodges, 'Harmonisation of European Controls over Research' in A Goldberg and I Dodds-Smith (eds), *Pharmaceutical Medicine and the Law* (Royal College of Physicians, 1991).

[47] Regulation (EU) No 536/2014, Arts 2(11) and 4.

[48] Regulation (EU) No 536/2014, Arts 4 and 5.

[49] ibid, Art 80.

[50] ibid, Arts 2(11) and 4.

[51] The particulars and documents are specified in Art 8(3) of and Annex I to Directive (EC) 2001/83. See also Regulation 726/2004, Art 6; Medicines Act 1968, s 18; the Human Medicines Regulations 2012, pt 5.

required is extensive,[52] and the cost of product development is extremely high.[53] The central parts relevant to the current study are:

(a) Qualitative and quantitative particulars of all the constituents of the medicinal product in usual terminology, but excluding empirical chemical formulae, with mention of the international non-proprietary name recommended by the World Health Organization where such name exists or a reference to the relevant chemical name;
(b) Therapeutic indications, contra-indications, and adverse reactions;
(c) Posology, pharmaceutical form, method and route of administration, and expected shelf life;
(d) If applicable, reasons for any precautionary and safety measures to be taken for the storage of the medicinal product, its administration to patients and for the disposal of waste products, together with an indication of potential risks presented by the medicinal product for the environment;
(e) Description of the control methods employed by the manufacturer;
(f) Results of:[54]

    a. pharmaceutical (physico-chemical, biological, or microbiological) tests,
    b. pre-clinical (toxicological and pharmacological) tests,
    c. clinical trials;[55]

(g) A detailed description of the pharmacovigilance and, where appropriate, of the risk-management system which the applicant will introduce.

An application for a marketing authorisation must also include reports from experts in analysis, pharmacology and similar experimental sciences, and clinical trials must be submitted

[52] First introduced by Directive (EEC) 75/318, then significantly amended by Directive (EEC) 91/507, later by Directive (EC) 2001/83, Annex I, and amplified in the Commission's Notice to Applicants Amended by Directive (EC) 2003/63. Available in EudraLex – Volume 2 – Pharmaceutical legislation on notice to applicants and regulatory guidelines for medicinal products for human use, at ec.europa.eu/health/documents/eudralex/vol-2/index_en.htm.

[53] By the mid-2000s, this cost was said to be over $800 million, and rising at an annual rate of 7.4% above general price inflation: Boston Consulting Group, *A Revolution in R&D: How Genomics and Genetics are Transforming the Biopharmaceutical Industry* (Boston Consulting Group, 2001); J DiMasi, RW Hanson and H G Grabowski, 'The Price of Innovation: New Estimates of Drug Development Costs' (2003) 22 *Journal of Health Economics* 151; DW Light and RN Warburton, 'Extraordinary Claims Require Extraordinary Evidence' (2005) 24(5) *Journal of Health Economics* 1030.

[54] There are certain exceptions to the provision of pre-clinical tests and clinical trials, notably where an applicant can demonstrate: (i) that the product is a generic (ie the same qualitative and quantitative composition in active substances and the same pharmaceutical form, whose bioequivalence has been demonstrated in bioavailability studies) of a reference medicinal product which has been authorised for not less than eight years in a Member State or the Community, in which case the applicant's medicinal product may not be placed on the market for 10 years after the authorisation of the reference product, although the period is extended to 11 years if the original authorisation holder has obtained in the first eight years an authorisation for one or more new indications that are held to bring a significant clinical benefit in comparison with existing therapies; or (ii) that the active substances have been in well-established medicinal use within the Community for at least 10 years, with recognised efficacy and an acceptable level of safety: in the latter case the test and trial results shall be replaced by appropriate scientific literature: Directive (EC) 2001/83, Arts 10 and 10a and Annex I, pt II, ss 1–3, as amended by Directive (EC) 2004/27. In relation to the second exception, under which the scientific literature in the public domain must be complete, see Case C-440/93 *R v Licensing Authority of the Department of Health and Norgine Ltd, ex p Scotia Pharmaceuticals Ltd* [1995] ECR I-2851: 'the abridged procedure in no way relaxes the requirements of safety and efficacy which must be met'. See also Case C-368/96 *R v The Licensing Authority established by the Medicines Act 1968 (acting by The Medicines Control Agency), ex p Generics (UK) Ltd* [1999] ECR I-7967, which affirmed the same point.

[55] Regulation (EC) 536/2014 introduced new rules on clinical trials from June 2016, replacing Directive (EC) 2001/20.

with the application,[56] in order to provide verification that the experts have carried out the relevant tasks and have described the results objectively, and to describe their observations in accordance with the requirements.

Authorisation shall be refused if, after verification of the required information and particulars submitted, 'it appears that the applicant has not properly or sufficiently demonstrated the quality, safety or efficacy of the medicinal product'.[57] Authorisation shall likewise be refused if the particulars and documents provided by the applicant are incorrect, or if the labelling and package leaflets proposed by the applicant are not in accordance with the requirements.[58]

An authorisation for the manufacture of medicinal products[59] includes requirements that the applicant shall:

i. have at his disposal for the manufacture or import suitable and sufficient premises, technical equipment and control facilities complying with the legal requirements which the Member State concerned lays down as regards both manufacture and control and the storage of products;[60]
ii. have permanently and continuously at his disposal the services of at least one qualified person who is responsible for securing[61] that the manufacturer or importer is able to carry out manufacture in accordance with the particulars supplied pursuant to the application for marketing authorisation[62] and/or to carry out controls according to the methods described in the particulars accompanying the application.[63]

The qualified person must fulfil specified minimum conditions of qualification, including a four-year university course, or its equivalent, in one of the scientific disciplines of pharmacy, medicine, veterinary medicine, chemistry, pharmaceutical chemistry, and technology or biology, plus at least two years' practical experience in one or more undertakings authorised to manufacture medicines, in qualitative and quantitative analysis of and quality testing and checking of medicinal products.[64] Principles and guidelines of good manufacturing practice are to be applied by a manufacturer in the manufacture of medicinal products.[65]

[56] Directive (EC) 2001/83, Art 12 (first introduced by Directive (EEC) 75/319, Art 2); Regulation (EC) 726/2004, Art 6.

[57] Regulation (EC) 726/2004, Art 12; see earlier Regulation (EEC) 2309/93, Art 11 and Directive (EEC) 65/65, Art 5.

[58] Regulation (EC) 726/2004, Art 12; see earlier Regulation (EEC) 2309/93, Art 11 and Directive (EEC) 65/65, Art 5.

[59] Directive (EC) 2001/83, Art 40, first introduced by Directive (EEC) 75/319, Art 16; Medicines Act 1968, s 8(2). There are exceptions in relation to certain activities of doctors, dentists and pharmacists, notably in relation to a product specially prepared by or to the order of a doctor or dentist for administration to a particular patient (Medicines Act 1968, s 9(1)), or in relation to preparing or dispensing a medicinal product in a registered pharmacy or a hospital or health centre in accordance with a prescription given by a practitioner, by or under the supervision of a pharmacist (Medicines Act 1968, s 10). For the national criteria, procedures and conditions, see Medicines Act 1968, ss 19(5) and 20–24; the Human Medicines Regulations 2012.

[60] Pursuant to Directive (EC) 2001/83, Art 20.

[61] ibid, Art 20, which empowers an authority to permit certain variations.

[62] ibid, Art 8(3)(d).

[63] ibid, Art 8(3)(h).

[64] ibid, Art 49.

[65] ibid, Art 47: these principles and guidelines are set out in Commission Directive 2003/94.

An authorisation for the wholesale distribution of medicinal products includes requirements to:[66]

(a) have suitable and adequate premises, installations and equipment, so as to ensure proper conservation or distribution of medicinal products;
(b) have a responsible, designated qualified person and other staff;
(c) keep records of products received or dispatched, with dates, quantities, and names and addresses of suppliers and consignees;
(d) have an emergency plan which ensures effective implementation of any recall from the market;
(e) comply with the principles and guidelines of good distribution practice for medicinal products (GDP) published by the Commission;[67]

subject to checks on the authorisation holder and its establishments and inspection of premises.[68]

When a marketing authorisation is granted, the competent authority must specify the classification of the medicinal product as one that is, or is not, subject to medical prescription.[69] The three basic categories are medicinal products that are (i) subject to medical prescription, (ii) only available from a pharmacy, or (iii) generally available for sale.

There are specific and detailed requirements and limitations on both the information provided with medicinal products[70] and the advertising of medicinal products.[71]

An application for a marketing authorisation must contain a summary of the product characteristics (SmPC),[72] which is approved by the authorities and is made public together with their assessment report.[73] The SmPC and assessment report (which the authorities must update) fulfil the dual function of a public, transparent rationale for the grant of an authorisation and an official, uniform, approved statement of those product characteristics that are thought to be important prescribing information for users. The SmPC must contain the information specified.[74]

[66] Directive (EU) 2011/62, Arts 79–80.

[67] See European Commission, Guidelines on Good Distribution Practice of Medicinal Products for Human Use 2013/C343/01.

[68] Directive (EU) 2011/62, Art 77, first introduced by Directive (EEC) 92/25, Art 3. In the UK, see Medicines Act 1968, s 8(3) and the Human Medicines Regulations 2012, regs 18 and 42–45. There are exemptions for certain activities of doctors and dentists, notably in relation to products specially prepared for administration to a particular patient: Medicines Act 1968, s 9(1).

[69] Directive (EC) 2001/83, Art 70, first included in Directive (EEC) 92/26.

[70] These were first introduced by Directive (EEC) 92/27 and are now contained in the amended Directive (EC) 2001/83, Title V.

[71] First introduced by Directive (EEC) 92/28 and now contained in the amended Directive (EC) 2001/83, Titles VIII and VIIIa. A national prohibition on advertising that applies solely to foreign medicinal products not authorised in the Member State concerned is contrary to Art 30 of the EC Treaty: Case C-320/93 *Lucien Ortscheit GmbH v Eurim-Pharm Arznemittel GmbH* [1995] 2 CMLR 242. In the UK, see the Human Medicines Regulations 2012, pt 14.

[72] Directive (EC) 2001/83, Art 8(3)(j).

[73] ibid, Art 21, as amended by Directive (EC) 2004/27.

[74] Regulation (EC) 469/2009.

The following particulars are required to appear on the outer packaging of medicinal products or, where there is no outer packaging, on the immediate packaging:[75]

(a) the name of the medicinal product followed by its strength and pharmaceutical form, and, if appropriate, whether it is intended for babies, children or adults; where the product contains up to three active substances, the international non-proprietary name (INN) shall be included, or, if one does not exist, the common name;
(b) a statement of the active substances expressed qualitatively and quantitatively per dosage unit or according to the form of administration for a given volume or weight, using their common names;
(c) the pharmaceutical form and the contents by weight, by volume or by number of doses of the product;
(d) a list of those excipients known to have a recognized action or effect and included in the detailed guidance published pursuant to Article 65. However, if the product is injectable, or a topical or eye preparation, all excipients must be stated;
(e) the method of administration and, if necessary, the route of administration. Space shall be provided for the prescribed dose to be indicated;
(f) a special warning that the medicinal product must be stored out of the reach and sight of children;
(g) a special warning, if this is necessary for the medicinal product;
(h) the expiry date in clear terms (month/year);
(i) special storage precautions, if any;
(j) specific precautions relating to the disposal of unused medicinal products or waste derived from medicinal products, where appropriate, as well as reference to any appropriate collection system in place;
(k) the name and address of the marketing authorisation holder and, where applicable, the name of the representative appointed by the holder to represent him;
(l) the number of the authorization for placing the medicinal product on the market;
(m) the manufacturer's batch number;
(n) in the case of non-prescription medicinal products, instructions for use.

The inclusion in the packaging of all medicinal products of a package leaflet for the information of users is obligatory unless all the specified information required by Articles 59 and 62 of Directive (EC) 2001/83 is directly conveyed on the outer packaging or on the immediate packaging.[76] The package leaflet must be drawn up in accordance with the summary of the product characteristics,[77] and include specified details. Advertising of medicines is also regulated.

4. EU Human Tissues and Cells

The SANCO (Santé et Consommateurs) Directive regulates the donation, procurement, testing, processing, preservation, storage and distribution of human tissues and cells.[78]

[75] Directive (EC) 2001/83, Art 54; Medicines Act 1968, s 85; the Human Medicines Regulations 2012, pt 13 and schs 24 and 25.

[76] Directive (EC) 2001/83, Art 58; Medicines Act 1968, s 86; the Human Medicines Regulations 2012, pt 13 and schs 24 and 25.

[77] See n 75.

[78] Directive (EC) 2004/23 on setting standards of quality and safety for the donation, procurement, testing, processing, preservation, storage, and distribution of human tissues and cells became mandatory from 7 April 2007.

Under this Directive, the testing, processing, preservation, storage and distribution activities may only be undertaken by a 'tissue establishment' that has been accredited, designated, authorised or licensed.[79] A responsible person must be designated, and that person ensures that the requirements for quality management,[80] traceability, record-keeping, labelling, reporting of serious adverse events and reactions, import and export are met.[81]

Donations of tissues and cells must be voluntary and unpaid (compensating expenses and inconvenience is permitted), and all consent or authorisation requirements must be met before a donation is procured. The promotion and publicity of such donations is tightly controlled.[82] Some donations do not fall within the Directive, including blood, organs used for the same purpose in the human body and autologous grafts carried out within the same surgical procedure.[83] Tissues and cells intended for use in industrially manufactured products, including medical devices, are partially regulated by the SANCO Directive. The donation, procurement and testing of such cells are controlled by the SANCO Directive: other frameworks apply to other activities.[84]

5. EU Advanced Therapy Medicinal Products

Gene therapy medicinal products, somatic cell therapy medicinal products and tissue-engineered products[85] (collectively known as advanced therapy medicinal products (ATMPs)) have their own special regime.[86] These rules have been mandatory for gene therapy medicinal products and somatic cell therapy medicinal products from January 2012, and for tissue-engineered products from January 2013. Products containing or consisting exclusively of non-viable human or animal cells and/or tissues, and which do not act principally by pharmacological, immunological or metabolic action, are excluded from this definition.[87] These ATMPs are subject to more stringent marketing authorisation dossier requirements.[88] They fall within the EU's centralised procedure, and are subject to certain additional requirements, including on traceability, labelling, post-authorisation follow-up of efficacy and adverse reactions, and risk management.[89]

A medical device that forms part of a combined ATMP must also meet the standard requirements for medical devices.[90]

[79] ibid, Art 6.

[80] Quality and safety requirements are specified in Commission Directives (EC) 2006/17 and (EC) 2006/86. The Directives were implemented into UK law by the Human Fertilisation and Embryology (Quality and Safety) Regulations 2007, SI 2007/1522, in relation to human reproductive cells (gametes) and the Human Tissue (Quality and Safety for Human Application) Regulations 2007, SI 2007/1523, supplemented by many Human Tissue Act Directions.

[81] Directive (EC) 2004/23, Arts 8, 9, 11, 10, 16, 17, 22.

[82] ibid, Arts 13 and 12.

[83] ibid, Art 2(2).

[84] ibid, Art 2.

[85] A tissue-engineered product is one that contains or consists of engineered cells or tissues, and is presented as having properties for, or is used in or administered to human beings with a view to regenerating, repairing or replacing a human tissue. Regulation (EC) 1394/2007, Art 2(1).

[86] Regulation (EC) 1394/2007.

[87] ibid, Art 2(1).

[88] Annex I to Directive 2001/83 (the Community Code); Commission Directive (EC) 2009/120.

[89] Commission Directive (EC) 2009/120, Arts 4–15.

[90] ibid, Art 6; see Directive (EEC) 93/42 or, for active implantable medical devices, Directive 90/385/EEC.

6. EU Pharmacovigilance

The need for a pharmacovigilance system was recognised from the inception of modern regulation. The UK was a leader in this, developing the 'yellow card' scheme, a voluntary scheme for doctors to report ADRs to the regulatory authority. The EU system was reviewed in 2007, reforms were proposed in the first quarter of 2008,[91] and the system was amended in 2010 with effect from 2012 under legislation and a series of guidelines.[92] The underlying rationale is as follows:[93]

> It is recognized that the safe use of medicinal products is not simply a matter to be assessed at the time of marketing, but that there is a need for the continuous collection and re-evaluation of data relating to a product, throughout the time that its product type is marketed and/or remains on the market.[94] The legislation implicitly recognizes the limitations on the understanding of the level of safety which is possible at the time of authorizing its marketing that use of a product will present in normal, 'practical conditions of use'.[95]

The EU pharmacovigilance system relies on spontaneous reporting by healthcare professionals and others of adverse reactions in human beings,[96] and imposes:

(a) recording and reporting obligations on the commercial enterprises involved; and
(b) surveillance and other regulatory obligations on Member States, the Commission, the EMA and the CHMP.[97]

Different post-marketing obligations for medicinal products apply to the holders of marketing authorisations, the holders of manufacturing authorisations and the holders of wholesale distribution authorisations.

The EMA, in consultation with the Member States and the Commission, maintains a data-processing network (Eudra-vigilance database) to collate pharmacovigilance information regarding medicinal products, to which authorisation holders are required to send their reports.[98] The EMA also collaborates with the World Health Organization on international pharmacovigilance.[99]

[91] *Strategy to Better Protect Public Health by Strengthening and Rationalising EU Pharmacovigilance* (European Commission, 2007).

[92] Regulation (EU) 1235/2010 and Directive (EU) 2010/84. See vol 9A of the *Rules Governing Medicinal Products in the European Union: Guidelines on Pharmacovigilance for Medicinal Products for Human Use*, which includes guidelines for competent authorities and the EMA, at pt II.

[93] C Hodges, 'The Regulation of Medicinal Products and Medical Devices' in J Laing and J McHale (eds), *Principles of Medical Law*, 4th edn (Oxford University Press, 2017), para 17.97.

[94] See SM Roden, 'An Introduction to Drug Safety Surveillance' in Glaxo Group Research, *Drug Safety: A Shared Responsibility* (Churchill Livingstone, 1991).

[95] The phrase 'practical conditions of use' appeared in Directive (EEC) 93/39, recital 7, which justified the initial introduction into Community legislation of the pharmacovigilance system, but was not repeated in recital 54 to Directive (EC) 2001/83. Recital 15 to Regulation (EEC) 2309/93 only referred to the mechanistic 'intensive monitoring of adverse reactions', though it reappears in Art 57(1)(c) of Regulation (EC) 726/2004 in connection with the designation of the EMA's tasks.

[96] Directive (EC) 2001/83, Art 102, as amended: adapted from its first introduction in Directive (EEC) 93/39, Art 3(3).

[97] Centralised system: Regulation (EC) 726/2004, Art 25. Decentralised system: Directive (EC) 2001/83.

[98] Regulation (EC) 726/2004, Art 24; Directive (EC) 2001/83, Art 107. See also detailed provisions in Commission Implementing Regulation (EU) No 520/2012.

[99] Regulation (EC) 726/2004, Art 27.

Under the decentralised system, the Member States may impose specific requirements on doctors and other healthcare professionals, in respect of the reporting of suspected serious or unexpected adverse reactions.[100] However, the centralised system omits powers of reporting by doctors or other healthcare professionals, and only refers to suspected adverse reactions that are reported to the company that holds the marketing authorisation.[101] Neither the centralised nor decentralised/mutual recognition systems refers specifically to reports emanating from patients, nor imposes any reporting requirements on patients. Both systems envisage reports emanating essentially from healthcare professionals.[102] The system shall also take into account any available information on misuse and abuse[103] of medicinal products that may have an impact on the evaluation of their benefits and risks.

A marketing authorisation holder is required to have permanently and continuously at his disposal a 'qualified person' responsible for pharmacovigilance, who is responsible, inter alia, for:

- maintaining a system that collects all suspected adverse reactions reported to the personnel of the company, and to medical representatives;
- preparing reports on specified adverse reactions for the competent authorities;
- ensuring that any request from the competent authorities for the provision of additional information necessary for the evaluation of the benefits and risks afforded by a medicinal product is answered fully and promptly.[104]

The marketing authorisation holder must report all *suspected serious* adverse reactions occurring within the EU immediately to the Member State in whose territory the incident occurred, and in no case later than 15 days following receipt of the information.[105] Detailed records must be maintained of all *suspected* adverse reactions occurring within or outside the EU that are reported by a healthcare professional.[106] If a *suspected serious unexpected* adverse reaction to a centrally licensed product occurs in a non-EU country, a report must be made both to all Member States and to the Agency. Commission guidance covers the collection, verification and presentation of adverse reaction reports, including technical requirements for electronic exchange of pharmacovigilance information.[107]

Reports on suspected adverse reactions must be submitted by the marketing authorisation holder to the authorities immediately upon request, or at least every six months after authorisation until placing on the market. Periodic safety update reports must also be

[100] Directive (EC) 2001/83, Art 101.

[101] See, eg, Regulation (EC) 726/2004, Art 22.

[102] Regulation (EC) 726/2004, Arts 22 and 51; Directive (EC) 2001/83, Art 101.

[103] Defined in Directive (EC) 2001/83, Art 1(16) as persistent or sporadic, intentional excessive use of medicinal products which is accompanied by harmful physical or psychological effects.

[104] Directive (EC) 2001/83, Art 103; for the centralised procedure, see Regulation (EC) 726/2004, Art 23, which is almost identical. These provisions are supplemented by guidance in vol 9A of the *Rules Governing Medicinal Products in the European Union*, n 93.

[105] Under the centralised procedure, Regulation (EC) 726/2004, Art 24; under the Code, Directive (EC) 2001/83, Art 104: both provisions add that this applies to reactions brought to his attention by a healthcare professional and that separate guidance applies to the reporting and recording of other suspected serious adverse reactions.

[106] Directive (EC) 2001/83, Art 104; and Regulation (EC) 726/2004, Art 24.

[107] Directive (EC) 2001/83, Art 106 and Regulation (EC) 726/2004, Art 26. The suspension or revocation of a marketing authorisation may only be decided on the grounds laid down in the EU provisions: Case C-83/92 *Pierrel SpA v Ministerio della Sanita* [1993] ECR I-06419.

submitted immediately upon request, or at least every six months during the first two years following the initial placing on the EU market and once a year for the following two years. Thereafter, the reports shall be submitted at three-yearly intervals together with the application for renewal of the authorisation, or immediately upon request. These records shall be accompanied by a scientific evaluation particularly of the risk–benefit balance of the product. The Code sets out broadly equivalent requirements for products authorised nationally or under the decentralised/mutual recognition procedure.[108]

An authorisation holder must take into account technical and scientific progress and apply for approval of any necessary variations.[109] A marketing authorisation holder must forthwith inform the authorities of any new information that might entail the amendment of the particulars and documents that were supplied with the application for marketing approval, or amendment of the summary of product characteristics,[110] and, in particular, of any prohibition or restriction imposed by the competent authorities of any country in which the product is marketed and of any other new information that might influence the evaluation of the benefits and risks of the product.[111]

Central responsibility for initial analysis and prioritisation of signals of new risks or risks that change the risk–benefit balance rests with the EMA's Pharmacovigilance Risk Assessment Committee, which appoints a rapporteur to assess the periodic safety update reports on individual products.[112] Under the centralised system, that Committee may require a marketing authorisation holder to conduct post-authorisation studies on safety and efficacy, or to operate a risk management system.[113] The marketing authorisation holder and the competent authorities of the Member States shall ensure that all relevant information about suspected adverse reactions to medicinal products authorised in accordance with the Regulation are brought to the attention of the EMA also in accordance with the provisions of the Regulation. Patients shall be encouraged to communicate any adverse reaction to healthcare professionals.[114]

C. European Regulation of Medical Devices

Regulation of medical devices was introduced during the 1990s under EU legislation, having largely not existed before that time under national laws in Europe. In the UK, a certification regime existed before the EU regime was created, in which compliance with quality system requirements was required to trigger the ability to sell to the NHS.

The EU model was able to be customised on the pre-existing framework of regulation for engineered products,[115] originally known as the New Approach and from 2008 as the

[108] Regulation (EC) 726/2004, Art 24(3); Directive (EC) 2001/83, Art 104. The suspension or revocation of a marketing authorisation may only be decided on the grounds laid down in the EU provisions: *Pierrel SpA*, n 108.

[109] Regulation (EC) 726/2004, Art 16(1); Directive (EC) 2001/83, Art 23.

[110] Regulation (EC) 726/2004, Art 16(2); Directive (EC) 2001/83, Art 23.

[111] Regulation (EC) 726/2004, Art 16(2); Directive (EC) 2001/83, Art 23.

[112] Regulation (EC) 726/2004, Art 28a and 28(3); Directive (EC) 2001/83, Art 107.

[113] Regulation (EC) 726/2004, Arts 10a and 14(8).

[114] ibid, Art 22.

[115] Such as machinery, toys, personal protective equipment, low voltage equipment, electromagnetic compatibility requirements, and recreational craft.

New Legislative Framework (NLF).[116] The NLF was developed tor products that are typically designed and evolve through continuous iterative improvements in design (unlike chemical or pharmaceutical compounds, for which the concepts of design and improvement do not apply).

Three EU regimes were introduced for medical devices,[117] all implemented into UK law:[118]

- Active Implantable Medical Devices Directive (AIMDD), covering all powered implants or partial implants that are left in the human body, such as a heart pacemaker, in force from 1 January 1993 and mandatory from 1 January 1995;[119]
- Medical Devices Directive (MDD), covering a wide range of devices ranging from first aid bandages, tongue depressors and blood collection bags, to hip prostheses and active (powered) devices, in force from 1 January 1995 and mandatory from 14 June 1998.[120] The MDD was amended as of 13 June 2002,[121] but subject to further five- and seven-year transition periods, in relation to devices containing stable medicinal substances derived from human blood and plasma;
- In Vitro Diagnostics Directive (IVDD), covering such matters as pregnancy tests, blood glucose monitoring and tests for transmissible diseases, in force from 7 June 2000 and mandatory from 7 December 2003.[122]

Each Member State has designated a competent authority, which is the governmental authority responsible for implementing the Directive in that Member State. In the case of

[116] The basis of the NLF package is contained in three measures: Regulation (EC) No 765/2008 of the European Parliament and of the Council of 9 July 2008 setting out the requirements for accreditation and market surveillance relating to the marketing of products and repealing Regulation (EEC) No 339/93; Decision No 768/2008/EC of the European Parliament and of the Council of 9 July 2008 on a common framework for the marketing of products, and repealing Council Decision 93/465/EEC; and Regulation (EC) No 764/2008 of the European Parliament and of the Council of 9 July 2008, laying down procedures relating to the application of certain national technical rules to products lawfully marketed in another Member State, and repealing Decision No 3052/95/EC. These replaced Council Resolution of 7 May 1985 on a new approach to technical harmonization and standards [1985] OJ C136/1, 4 June 1985. The NLF applies to a large family of engineered products, all of which are subject to the 'CE' marking regime, albeit with significant differences in complexity between product families. The 2008 package extended the previous 'new approach' matrix in relation to obligations on distributors, on post-marketing surveillance, information and recall of products, strengthening the accreditation system for conformity assessment bodies, and strengthening the Community market surveillance system. Some of these aspects are already covered in the medical devices legislation. For general guidance see *The 'Blue Guide' on the implementation of EU product rules* (European Commission, 2014).

[117] The basic structure, concepts and terminology of the three Directives on AIMDs, MDs and IVDs are identical: such differences as exist between them arise out of the different nature of these products.

[118] All of these Directives were implemented into UK law as from 13 June 2002 by the Medical Devices Regulations 2002, SI 2002/618 (the Regulations), replacing earlier provisions including the Medical Devices Regulations 1994, SI 1994/3017. The Regulations deal with introductory provisions relating to all medical devices (pt i), general medical devices (pt ii), active implantable medical devices (pt iii), in vitro diagnostic medical devices (pt iv), notified bodies, conformity assessment bodies and marking of products (pt v), fees charged by the Secretary of State (pt VI), and general, enforcement and miscellaneous matters (pt VII). For reasons of space, the following discussion is largely limited to an overview of and references to the provisions that apply to general medical devices.

[119] Directive 90/385/EEC.

[120] Directive 93/42/EEC.

[121] Directive 2001/104/EC.

[122] Directive 98/79/EEC. The IVDD contained amendments to the two earlier Directives.

the UK, the competent authority is the MHRA,[123] an executive agency of the Department of Health.

The EU regulatory system for medical devices (like all products regulated under the NLF) places the onus for ensuring and declaring that a product has been designed and manufactured in accordance with the legal *essential requirements* on the *manufacturer* itself,[124] but in many instances this is subject to approval by an independent technical organisation (known as a *notified body*).[125] Thus, an authorisation by a competent authority, as is required for medicines, is not relevant.

For NLF products, a list of *essential requirements* is mandated, relating to the *safety* in use of the product, including labelling requirements, and principally expressed in terms of scientific and technical *performance* characteristics. Confirmation that a product conforms to the essential requirements must be made by the manufacturer through applying an appropriate *conformity assessment* procedure to the device, after which the manufacturer must certify this fact by signing a *declaration of conformity*. Medical devices may only be placed on the market and put into service if they comply with the requirements laid down in the Directive when duly supplied and properly installed, maintained and used in accordance with their intended purpose.[126] Conformity of a device with the essential requirements is denoted by affixing *'CE' marking* to the device.[127] This acts in effect as the passport that authorises the device to be placed on the market and to circulate freely within the EEA, and it must be marked on the device.

The essential requirements contained in Annex I to each NLF law specify the aspects of safety and performance that must be satisfied at the time at which a relevant product is placed on the market.[128] The essential requirements in the MDD fall under two headings: general requirements; and requirements regarding design and construction.[129] The general requirements in the 1993 MDD included the following provisions:

(i) The devices must be designed and manufactured in such a way that, when used under the conditions and for the purposes intended, they will not compromise the clinical condition or the safety of patients, or the safety and health of users or, where applicable, other persons, provided that any risks which may be associated with their use constitute acceptable risks when weighed against the benefits to the patient and are compatible with a high level of protection of health and safety.

(ii) The solutions adopted by the manufacturer for the design and construction of the devices must conform to safety principles, taking account of the generally acknowledged

[123] This Agency was created in 2003 on the merger of the Medicines Control Agency and the Medical Devices Agency. Before that, governmental regulatory functions were performed by the Medical Devices Directorate of the Department of Health.

[124] Regulation (EU) 2017/745, Art 10(1).

[125] For requirements and regulation of notified bodies, see now Regulation (EU) 2017/745, Arts 35–50. Upgrades following the Poly Implant Prothèse (PIP) breast implant saga were introduced in Commission Recommendation of 24 September 2013 on the audits and assessments performed by notified bodies in the field of medical devices; Commission Implementing Regulation (EU) No 920/2013 of 24 September 2013 on the designation and the supervision of notified bodies under Council Directive 90/385/EEC on active implantable medical devices and Council Directive 93/42/EEC on medical devices.

[126] eg Directive (EEC) 93/42, Art 2; the Regulations, reg 8.

[127] Regulation (EU) 2017/745, Arts 19 and 20.

[128] The Regulations, reg 8.

[129] The following paragraphs are taken from Directive (EEC) 93/42, Annex I.

state of the art. In selecting the most appropriate solutions, the manufacturer must apply the following principles in the following order:

— eliminate or reduce risks as far as possible (inherently safe design and construction),
— where appropriate take adequate protection measures including alarms if necessary, in relation to risks that cannot be eliminated,
— inform users of the residual risks due to any shortcomings of the protection measures adopted.

(iii) The devices must achieve the performances intended by the manufacturer and be designed, manufactured and packaged in such a way that they are suitable for one or more of the functions as specified by the manufacturer.

(iv) The characteristics and performances referred to in sections (i)–(iii) above must not be adversely affected to such a degree that the clinical conditions and safety of the patients and, where applicable, of other persons are compromised during the lifetime of the device as indicated by the manufacturer, when the device is subjected to the stresses which can occur during normal conditions of use.

(v) The devices must be designed, manufactured and packed in such a way that their characteristics and performances during their intended use will not be adversely affected during transport and storage taking account of the instructions and information provided by the manufacturer.

(vi) Any undesirable side-effect must constitute an acceptable risk when weighed against the performances intended.

Harmonised standard EN 14971 amplifies the methodology for risk analysis, elimination or reduction required by section (ii) in the list above.

The essential requirements in the 1993 MDD regarding design and construction covered the following headings:

i. Clinical, physical and biological properties;
ii. Infection and microbial contamination;
iii. Construction and environmental properties;
iv. Devices with a measuring function;
v. Protection against radiation;
vi. Requirements for medical devices connected to or equipped with an energy source;
vii. Information supplied by the manufacturer.

Confirmation of conformity must include *evaluation* of clinical data for many devices,[130] generated from either a compilation of scientific literature or the results of *clinical investigations* on the product,[131] for which prior ethical and regulatory approval is required.

Guidance was issued by the MHRA on clinical investigations in 2008.[132] If clinical evaluation is required, it must be subject to ethical approval in accordance with the principles of the Declaration of Helsinki.[133] Both the AIMDD[134] and the MDD[135] specified approval

[130] eg Regulation (EU) 2017/745, Arts 10(2), 61 and Annex XIV. Formerly Directive (EEC) 90/385, Art 10 and Annex 7; see also Annex 2, para 4.1 and Annex 3, para 3. Also, in general, implantable and long-term invasive devices falling within Classes IIa, IIb and all Class III devices: Directive (EEC) 93/42, Annex X and Art 15.

[131] Note, the concept of a 'clinical trial', relevant for medicinal products, does not apply for devices: the applicable concepts are clinical evaluation and clinical investigation.

[132] MHRA, *Guidance Notes for Manufacturers on Clinical Investigations to be carried out in the UK* (2008).

[133] Directive (EEC) 90/385, Annex 7, para 2.2; and Directive (EEC) 93/42, Annex X, para 2.2.

[134] Directive (EEC) 90/385, Art 10; the Regulations, reg 29.

[135] Directive (EEC) 93/42, Art 15; the Regulation, reg 16.

procedures for clinical investigations by the competent authority and relevant ethics committee(s).

Under the 2017 legislation, the manufacturer must have a 'person responsible for regulatory compliance who possesses the requisite expertise' and has specified professional qualifications and experience.[136] It also required a manufacturer of implantable and Class III devices to draw up a summary of safety and clinical performance.[137]

i. Classification and Standards

Since there is a wide range of medical devices, involving a wide range of risk (from very low-risk tongue depressors to higher-risk electrical implantable devices), a choice of conformity assessment procedures is usually open to a manufacturer, depending on a risk-based *classification* of the class into which the particular device falls.[138] The two main approaches to conformity assessment are based either on an approved total quality management system audited to ISO 9000 series standard, as customised for medical devices with EN 46000 series standard, or individual product assessment. The legal obligation is that a product must comply with the relevant essential requirements, but where the manufacturer chooses to apply a national standard that adopts a European *harmonised standard* (EN series) to an aspect of its product, conformity will be prima facie presumed in respect of the aspects of the essential requirements covered by that standard. Other national or international standards do not have this regulatory benefit.

Important harmonised standards[139] exist on the following:

- EN 13485 medical devices – quality management systems – requirements for regulatory purposes;
- EN 1041 information and labelling for medical devices;
- EN 980 graphical symbols;
- EN 10993 series biological evaluation of medical devices;
- EN 14155-1 clinical investigation of medical devices for human subjects – Part 1: general requirements;
- EN 14155-2 – clinical investigation of medical devices for human subjects – Part 2: clinical investigation plans;
- EN 60601 series medical electrical equipment;
- EN 14971 medical devices – application of risk management to medical devices.

[136] Regulation (EU) 2017/745, Art 15.

[137] Regulation (EU) 2017/745, Art 32.

[138] The classification rules are lengthy and intended to provide options for conformity assessment methods. See Regulation (EU) 2017/745, Art 51. Formerly Directive (EEC) 93/42, Annex IX. The classification system uses three basic criteria, in various combinations: duration of contact with the body, degree of invasiveness, and the anatomy affected by the use of the device. Class I covers those devices that do not enter or interact with the body; Classes IIa and IIb are invasive or implantable devices, or those which do interact with the body; Class III is for devices that affect the functions of vital organs. Implantables with an energy source are covered by the AIMDD.

[139] For the structure of collaboration between European standardisation organisations, national standardisation bodies, Member States and the Commission, see Regulation (EU) 1025/2012.

a. Conformity Assessment Procedures

Depending on the class of the device, a manufacturer may be able to choose between a number of alternative conformity assessment procedures in the assessment of whether a medical device conforms to the essential requirements. The basic options may be summarised as follows:[140]

(a) For all products in Classes IIa, IIb and III, and AIMDs, a *full quality assurance* system, audited periodically by a notified body (Annex II of the MDD), *which includes* examination and certification by the notified body of the design dossier of each product covered. The manufacturer must keep documentation on the quality system and the design dossier of each product plus other documentation. The quality system obligations include post-marketing and vigilance aspects. Compliance with Annex II may be achieved (this is not mandatory but is invariably adopted voluntarily) by compliance with the EN 29000 and 46000 series standards, which apply the ISO 9000 series.

(b) For products in Classes IIa, IIb and III, and AIMDs, examination and certification by a notified body of a specimen product (*type examination*: Annex III of the MDD) coupled with a varying degree (partially restricted by product class) of product or production quality assurance (MDD Annexes IV, V and VI), which ensures that the manufacturing process produces products that conform to the certified type and might involve a quality system for manufacture and final inspection (Annex V), or a quality system for final inspection and testing (Annex VI).

(c) For products in Class I, the manufacturer must have specified technical documentation on the design of the product, showing that it conforms to the essential requirements: manufacturing aspects are not covered and a notified body is not involved unless there is a measuring function and/or the product is sterilised (Annex VII: *EC declaration of conformity*).

Packs of items designed to be used in particular hospital procedures are subject to a specific declaration requirement.[141]

b. Adverse Event Reporting, Market Surveillance and Device Vigilance

The manufacturer is required to keep up to date the technical documentation for its devices.[142] Generic market surveillance and post-marketing requirements apply to all NLF products, in addition to which specific provisions exist in the relevant medical device legislation.[143] Manufacturers are subject to *post-marketing surveillance* and *vigilance* requirements. A Member State has *market surveillance* obligations and, if a marketed device is unsafe, its *competent authority* has power under a *safeguard clause* in each Medical Device Directive to take regulatory action to effect the withdrawal of the product from the market in its jurisdiction: the matter is then referred to the Commission and all Member States,

[140] See Regulation (EU) 2017/745, Arts 52–60.

[141] Regulation (EU) 2017/745, Arts 22, 14 and 5. Formerly Directive (EEC) 93/42, Art 12; the Regulations.

[142] Regulation (EU) 2017/745, Art 10(4).

[143] Regulation (EU) 2017/745, Arts 83–100. Formerly Regulation (EC) 765/2008, Art 15(2) and Decision (EC) 768/2008.

who then coordinate their actions. Specific general new approach obligations were applied to Member States from 1 January 2010, notably to organise and carry out market surveillance, to establish appropriate communication and coordination mechanisms, to perform appropriate checks on products, and to recall, withdraw or prohibit the marketing of products that present serious risks.[144] A series of surveillance and post-marketing obligations apply to manufacturers, importers and distributors that are not all found in the medical devices legislation (and so apply to medical devices).[145] All of these aspects were updated under the 2017 Regulation.

Reporting requirements were as follows under the 1993 MDD. A manufacturer must record all adverse events with its medical devices of which it becomes aware and must, in general,[146] report, and a Member State must record and evaluate:

(a) any malfunction or deterioration in the characteristics and performance of a device, or inadequacy in the labelling, which might lead to, or have led to, the death of a patient or user or to a serious deterioration in his state of health;
(b) any technical or medical reason in relation to the characteristics or performance of a device for the reasons referred to in (a) above, leading to systematic recall of devices of the same type by the manufacturer.

Guidance was issued by the European Commission on medical device vigilance[147] that included an explanation of the difficult concept of when a deterioration in state of health should be considered serious. That is:

(a) life-threatening illness or injury;
(b) permanent impairment of a body function or permanent damage to a body structure;
(c) a condition necessitating medical or surgical intervention to prevent permanent impairment of a body function or permanent damage to a body structure.

Guidance issued in the UK in 2008 stated that a manufacturer was expected to take relevant safety action in relation to devices that were on the market or in use, including corrective action (eg the return, modification, exchange, destruction or retrofit of a device), which covered in general terms the circumstances in which a recall might be appropriate and how it should best be implemented.[148]

In 2017, the Medical Device Regulations[149] modified several aspects of the vigilance and adverse events reporting for Medical Devices. Manufacturers must report:

(a) any serious incident involving devices made available on the Union market (except expected side-effects which are clearly documented in the product information and

[144] Regulation (EC) 765/2008, Arts 16–26.

[145] Decision (EC) 768/2008. These provisions were largely modelled on the General Product Safety (GPS) post-marketing provisions for consumer products, but updated: see section I.F of this chapter. It is mooted that future amendments of the medical devices legislation will introduce specific post-marketing and surveillance provisions, and thereby oust the new approach provisions.

[146] See, eg, Directive (EEC) 93/42, Annex II, para 3.1, seventh indent; these provisions match obligations imposed on Member States by Art 12.

[147] European Commission, MEDDEV, *Guidelines on a Medical Devices Vigilance System* (2009), 2.12-1 rev 6.

[148] Medical Devices Agency, Directives Bulletin no 3: *Guidance on the Operation of the EU Vigilance System in the UK* (MDA, 2008).

[149] Regulation (EU) 2017/745, Arts 87 and 88.

quantified in the technical documentation) to the Competent Authority in the country in which the incident occurred;

(b) any field safety corrective action in respect of devices made available on the Union market (including any field safety corrective action undertaken in a third country in relation to a device which is also legally made available on the Union market, if the reason for the field safety corrective action is not limited to the device made available in the third country) to the Competent Authority of Member States in which the corrective action is being or has been undertaken, and to the Competent Authority of Member States in which the manufacturer has its registered place of business.

Table 2.5 Medical device manufacturer reporting requirements by incident type

Incident type	**Timeframe for reporting**
Serious incident	Immediately after the manufacturer has established the causal relationship between that incident and its device, or that such causal relationship is reasonably possible, and not later than 15 days after it becomes aware of the incident.
Serious public health threat	Immediately, and not later than 2 days after the manufacturer becomes aware of that threat.
Death or an unanticipated serious deterioration in a person's state of health	Immediately after the manufacturer has established or as soon as it suspects a causal relationship between the device and the serious incident, but not later than 10 days after the date on which the manufacturer becomes aware of the serious incident.

The legislation is clear that reports must be submitted electronically, and to meet the deadlines a manufacturer may submit an incomplete initial report, which must be followed by a complete report.

Trend reporting of other adverse events is detailed at Article 88 of the 2017 Regulation. Manufacturers are obliged to report any statistically significant increase in the frequency or severity of incidents that are:

(a) not serious incidents; or
(b) expected undesirable side-effects that could have a significant impact on the benefit–risk analysis and which have led or may lead to risks to the health or safety of patients, users or other persons that are unacceptable when weighed against the intended benefits.

The significant increase is in comparison to the foreseeable frequency or severity of such incidents during a specific period, as specified in the technical documentation and product information.

The 2017 Regulation stipulates at Article 10:

> Manufacturers shall, in a manner that is proportionate to the risk class, type of device and the size of the enterprise, have measures in place to provide sufficient financial coverage in respect of their potential liability under Directive 85/374/EEC, without prejudice to more protective measures under national law.

The 2017 legislation introduced a Unique Device Identifier (UDI) system to facilitate the traceability of devices[150] and a European database of devices (Eudamed).[151]

D. General Product Safety Regulation in Europe

The preceding sections of this chapter deal with specific (vertical) regulatory rules for medicines and medical devices. In addition, general (horizontal) rules have been created to deal with the safety of consumer products of any type that are not subject to specific rules.

In the UK, the modern policy and introduction of legislation on consumer product safety only emerged from the 1960s or later.[152] Legislation was introduced from relatively limited beginnings, such as under the Consumer Protection Act 1961, the Consumer Safety Act 1978, the Consumer Protection Act 1961, the Consumer Protection Act 1987 and the Food Act 1984.

Under part 2 of the Consumer Protection Act 1987, trading standards officers were given powers to seize unsafe goods, but pre-marketing regulatory controls on general consumer products were rudimentary if not non-existent, and subject only to general principles that a product be 'safe'.

In the EU, GPS provisions were first passed in 1992 and extended in 2001.[153] The primary obligation was on producers simply to place only safe products on the market.[154] A sequence of obligations was also placed on distributors, principally:[155]

> Distributors shall be required to act with due care to help to ensure compliance with the applicable safety requirements, in particular by not supplying products which they know or should have presumed, on the basis of the information in their possession and as professionals, do not comply with those requirements. Moreover, within the limits of their respective activities, they shall participate in monitoring the safety of products placed on the market, especially by passing on information on product risks, keeping and providing the documentation necessary for tracing the origin of products, and cooperating in the action taken by producers and competent authorities to avoid the risks. Within the limits of their respective activities they shall take measures enabling them to cooperate efficiently.

E. Medicinal Product Regulation in the US

As with the historical summary of medicinal products in the UK and the EU, the following summary of the American history of medicinal product regulation is intended to provide a brief synopsis, rather than a detailed outline. The following sections on historical regulation are intended to provide context and background for the evolution of the regulatory system and for the products that were on the market at that time.

[150] Regulation (EU) 2017/745, Art 27.

[151] ibid, Art 33.

[152] See I Ramsay, *Consumer Protection. Text and Materials* (Weidenfeld & Nicholson, 1989) ch 11.

[153] Directive 2001/95/EEC. Implemented in the UK by the General Product Safety Regulations 2005, SI 2005/1803.

[154] Directive 2001/95, Art 3(1). There was a hierarchy of rules, standards and guidelines against which the safety of a product was to be presumed assessed: Art 3.

[155] ibid, Art 5(2).

The US had one of the earliest centralised pharmaceutical regulatory systems, commencing in earnest during the Progressive Era and expanding to this day. The Food and Drugs Administration (FDA) has an unusually broad remit. It includes core functions of protecting the public health by ensuring the safety, efficacy and security of human and veterinary drugs, biological products and medical devices. In addition, the FDA has a broader public good responsibility to advance the public health by helping to speed innovations that make medical products more effective, safer and more affordable, and by helping the public get the accurate, science-based information they need to use medical products and foods to maintain and improve their health.

The FDA's remit extends well beyond the scope of this book, and includes ensuring the safety of America's food supply, cosmetics and products that emit radiation, as well as regulating the manufacturing, marketing and distribution of tobacco products to protect the public health and to reduce tobacco use by minors. The FDA also plays a significant role in counterterrorism by ensuring the security of the food supply, and by fostering development of medical products to respond to deliberate and naturally emerging public health threats.

i. Historic Regulation of Medicinal Products in the US

In part the breadth of the FDA's remit can be explained by its early history and status.[156] The FDA started out within the US Department of Agriculture. When the Department of Agriculture was created in 1862 it incorporated the Patent Office's Agricultural Division, which then became the Division of Chemistry in 1890 and subsequently the Bureau of Chemistry in 1901. In 1927 the Bureau of Chemistry morphed into the United States Food, Drug and Insecticide Administration, which was renamed the US Food and Drug Administration in 1930.

In 1940 the FDA was transferred out of the US Department of Agriculture to the newly created Federal Security Agency,[157] now known as the Department of Health and Human Services. The synergy between pharmaceutical regulation and agriculture is not unique (for example, the UK medicinal products Licensing Agency comprises the Health and Agriculture Ministers), but the FDA is unusual in maintaining such a broad remit; most other pharmaceutical regulators have become more specialist over time.

a. 1800s–1930 – The Early Years

Arguably the earliest Act specifically concerned with medicinal consumer protection was the Vaccine Act of 1813.[158] The publicising of smallpox vaccination (as opposed to variolation) by Edward Jenner in 1796 led to a public interest in vaccination, and as a result there were fraudulent 'vaccines' circulating. The Vaccine Act created a federal agent responsible for maintaining genuine vaccine and authorised to distribute it free of charge. Although

[156] Details on the history of the FDA and of pharmaceutical legislation in the USA are taken from the FDA website at wayback.archive-it.org/7993/20180726152836/https://www.fda.gov/AboutFDA/History/FOrgsHistory/HistoryofFDAsCentersandOffices/ucm114470.htm and the United States Pharmacopoeia and National Formulary website at www.usp.org/.

[157] Between 1953 and 1979 it was known as the Department of Health, Education and Welfare.

[158] Act to Encourage Vaccination, ch 37, 2 Stat 806 (1813).

short-lived – the 1813 Act was repealed in 1822 due to a batch of contaminated vaccine supplied by the federal agent[159] – it is interesting to note that a centralised quality control and distribution system had been enacted this early.

The first pharmaceutical legislation was not enacted until the mid-nineteenth century. The high mortality rate among American soldiers during the Mexican–American War of 1846–48 was attributed to poor-quality adulterated drugs. This was combined with a perception that America had become a dumping ground for low-quality pharmaceuticals that would be considered substandard in Europe. In response Congress passed the 1848 Drug Importation Act,[160] which empowered the US Customs Service to carry out inspections and prevent the entry of adulterated drugs into the USA. Interestingly, it took another half a century before the next Congressional efforts to ensure the quality of medicinal products: the Biologics Control Act 1902[161] (also known as the Virus-Toxin Law) and the Pure Food and Drug Act 1906.[162]

The 1902 Act was precipitated by the deaths of 13 children from tetanus in St Louis after they received a diphtheria antitoxin that had been accidentally contaminated with tetanus. The 1902 Act contained detailed provisions on licensing of the manufacture of and the sale of biologics, though the biological products themselves were not licensed. The regulation of biologics fell to the Public Health and Marine Hospital Service (PH-MHS), a precursor of the National Institutes of Health.[163] The regulation of biologics and that of pharmaceuticals were treated separately, and – as in the UK – the licensing of biologics pre-dated that of pharmaceuticals. It took 70 years before biologicals joined pharmaceuticals to became part of the FDA's responsibility.

The 1906 Act concerned pharmaceuticals and set some minimum standards: it required that the presence and amount of specified dangerous or addicting substances (including alcohol, morphine, heroin and cocaine) had to be on the label; it identified the United States Pharmacopoeia and National Formulary[164] as the official standards for drugs; and it prohibited inter-state commerce in adulterated or misbranded drugs. However, it did not require the full list of ingredients to be included on the label, neither did it include any provisions on the therapeutic claims that could be made about a pharmaceutical. This latter deficit was highlighted by in 1911 by the Supreme Court in *US v Johnson*.[165] The Sherley Amendment was passed in 1912,[166] with the intention of preventing false claims being made about the efficacy of a pharmaceutical. However, under the Sherley Amendment, proof of an intent to defraud was still required, and this effectively substituted one problem for another as such intent was very difficult to prove.

Other laws passed in this period included the Harrison Narcotic Tax Act 1914,[167] which concerned better record-keeping for dispensing narcotics and mandated a prescription for products that exceeded the allowable limits of permissible narcotics.

[159] The 1813 Act was repealed by An Act to Repeal the Act to Encourage Vaccination, ch 50, 3 Stat 677 (1822).

[160] *Importations of Drugs and Medicines Act 1848*, Pub L no 30-70 (26 June 1848).

[161] Biologics Control Act 1902, Pub L no 57-228, ch 1378, 32 Stat 728 (1902).

[162] Pure Food and Drug Act 1906, Pub L no 59-384, ch 3915, 34 Stat 768 (1906).

[163] See at history.nih.gov/exhibits/history/index.html.

[164] See at www.usp.org/.

[165] *United States v Johnson* 221 US 488 (1911).

[166] Congressman Swagger Sherley's amendment to s 8 of the Pure Food and Drug Act was enacted on 23 August 1912. It prohibited 'false and fraudulent' labelling (but not advertising) of a product. Sherley Amendment (Food and Drugs) 1912, ch 352, 37 Stat 416.

[167] Harrison Narcotics Tax Act 1914, Pub L No 63-223, 38 Stat 785.

b. 1930–60

In 1933, well aware of the limitations of the 1906 Act, the FDA recommended a complete revision of the Act to rectify some of its defects, such as the lack of regulation of medical devices and cosmetics, the inability to conduct factory inspections, the inability to control the marketing of pharmaceuticals and the difficulty in proving that false therapeutic claims made about a drug were intended to defraud. The efforts to reform the 1906 statute languished until September 1937, when over 100 people were poisoned by an untested new formulation of sulfanilamide, sold as Elixir Sulfanilamide. The manufacturer, SE Massengill Company, had dissolved the sulfanilamide in diethylene glycol, and released the product without any safety testing on the new solvent. Despite considerable effort, over 100 people had died before the FDA managed to locate all of the remaining product and remove it from sale. The company claimed the deaths were due to idiosyncratic adverse reactions to the sulphanilamide. Despite the deaths, the only offence for which the FDA could prosecute the company was distributing a misbranded drug – an 'elixir' had to be dissolved in alcohol. Had the product been labelled a 'solution' rather than an 'elixir', the FDA would have had no power whatsoever to recover the drug as no law would have been broken. This was clearly deeply unsatisfactory, and this disaster proved the catalyst for the long-overdue revisions to medical product regulation. On 25 June 1938, the Food, Drug and Cosmetic Act[168] was signed by President Roosevelt.

The 1938 Act contained the underpinnings of the modern FDA regulatory structure and, as well as remedying the defect in the 1906 Act, included provisions requiring new drugs to be safe prior to marketing, providing that safe tolerances be set for unavoidable poisonous substances, and adding court injunctions to the previous penalties of seizures and prosecutions.

Although the 1938 Act formalised a lot of elements of pharmaceutical regulation, there were still gaps within the framework. Within months of the 1938 Act's being passed, it became clear that there were some pharmaceuticals that could not be safely used on the basis of a generic product label; these drugs required individualised directions and medical supervision. In 1938 the FDA determined that such drugs should be labelled as 'prescription only'. Although the concept of prescriptions pre-dated the 1938 Act, and prescriptions were referred to in the Act, the references were vague. Surprisingly there was no clarity on what a prescription was and, crucially, who was responsible for determining which medicines should be prescription only rather than for general sale. By 1941[169] the FDA had identified over 20 drugs or drug groups[170] it felt were too dangerous to be on general sale and that needed to be appropriately labelled, and which should only be available on a physician's or dentist's prescription. The conflict that arose from ambiguities over what ought be a prescription only medicine, and who was responsible for determining this, was addressed in the 1951 Durham-Humphrey Amendment[171] to the 1938 Act. It identified and clarified what constituted a prescription drug (those unsafe for self-medication) and what constituted an over-the-counter medicine, who would be responsible for the

[168] Food, Drug and Cosmetics Act 1938, n 8.

[169] See at wayback.archive-it.org/7993/20180726152836/https://www.fda.gov/AboutFDA/History/FOrgsHistory/HistoryofFDAsCentersandOffices/ucm114470.htm.

[170] Such as sulfas, barbiturates and amphetamines.

[171] Durham-Humphrey Amendment 1951, Pub L No 82-215, 65 Stat 648.

identification of prescription only drugs, and the conditions under which a prescription could be fulfilled.

c. 1961–79

There had been pressure for reform of the existing pharmaceutical legislation following the Kefauver hearings. These hearings, overseen by Senator Estes Kefauver of Tennessee, began in 1959 as an examination into the cost of pharmaceuticals in the USA. However, the hearings soon encompassed other issues, such as the lack of regulation of drug efficacy and advertising irregularities. Kefauver's bill to improve drug regulation stalled in Congress. As in Europe, the major impetus for change came from the drug thalidomide. In 1960 William S Merrell Company, Cincinnati, applied for a licence for thalidomide, under the brand name Kevadon. Thalidomide had been available in Germany since 1956, initially as an over-the-counter drug. The application was assigned to Frances Kelsey, who, despite widespread European use, felt that there were insufficient safety data to approve the licence.[172] William S Merrell continued to push for Kevadon to be approved, including conducting a study in the USA in which over 20,000 Americans were given thalidomide, over 600 of these recipients being pregnant women, and there were 17 known babies born with *in utero* thalidomide damage. Although a large-scale disaster had been averted, it was widely recognised that this was due to Kelsey's vigilance and that reform was necessary. The Thalidomide tragedy re-energized the drug regulation legislation, and the Kefauver-Harris Amendments (also known as the Drug Efficacy Amendments) were signed into law on 10 October 1962.[173] This was the first time that manufacturers were required to prove to the FDA that their drugs were efficacious and safe before they would be approved for the market. The Amendments expanded the FDA's regulatory powers over the control of clinical investigations, the advertising of prescription medicines, the promotion of quality assurance through good manufacturing process and manufacturers' record-keeping. The Amendments also required that all drugs that had been placed on the market between 1938 and 1962 had to demonstrate efficacy. In the resulting studies, almost 40% of these drugs were found to be ineffective. A comparable review of over-the-counter medicines began a decade later.

The basic backbone of modern drug regulation to achieve consumer protection was completed with the Kefauver-Harris Amendments, but this framework has been subject to constant refinement ever since. One area that has undergone considerable evolution is the provision of patient information leaflets. These were only started for prescription drugs in 1970, when the FDA required information leaflets to be included in packets of oral contraceptives. Over time, the inclusion of patient information leaflets spread from just this small class of medicines to become ubiquitous.

d. 1980–2000

The requirements for pre-market approval were well established: pre-clinical testing, including animal studies; phase one small-scale clinical studies on toxicity and pharmacology on

[172] Kelsey was awarded the President's Award for Distinguished Federal Civilian Service in 1961 in recognition of her actions.

[173] Kefauver-Harris Amendments 1962, Pub L No 87-781, 76 Stat 780.

health volunteers; phase two medium-scale, short-term studies on patients; and, finally, larger-scale, longer, phase three studies on patients. This process was acknowledged to be slow. During the 1980s and 1990s the majority of FDA reforms concerned alterations to the established drug approval pathways to improve access to medicines. In particular the advent of the AIDS crisis created a public health imperative to improve the speed of the approval system. It was clear that in a situation where there was no available treatment, the notion of making a patient with a very limited life expectancy wait for several years for a promising new treatment to be approved was unconscionable.

In 1987, Investigational New Drug applications (INDs)[174] were created to increase access to experimental drugs for patients who had serious diseases that had no alternative treatments. These were promptly followed by the accelerated approval mechanisms in 1988. These enabled early-stage medicines with promising clinical benefit profiles to be approved for treating life-threatening diseases when a surrogate endpoint had been met, while the clinical studies remained ongoing. The surrogate endpoint is a marker that is thought to predict clinical benefit, but is not itself a measure of clinical benefit; the surrogate endpoint could be a laboratory measurement, radiographic image, a physical sign or other measure. Likewise, an intermediate clinical endpoint is a measure of a therapeutic effect that is considered reasonably likely to predict the clinical benefit of a drug, such as an effect on irreversible morbidity and mortality.[175]

Parallel track investigations were brought in in 1990,[176] specifically to make experimental drugs more widely available to those infected with HIV. The parallel track allowed patients with AIDS, whose condition prevented them from participating in controlled clinical trials, to receive investigational drugs that had demonstrated promising results in preliminary studies. The 'standard' clinical trials procedure carried on in parallel to this 'parallel' use.

In 1992 the FDA was authorised to charge user fees under the Prescription Drug User Fee Act 1992,[177] to fund the drug approval process. The fees were used, in part, to provide additional drug review staff. This, in combination with revised review procedures, significantly reduced new drug application approval times. Typical approval times for drugs for serious and life-threatening diseases such as cancer and AIDS were reduced to less than six months, and sometimes to as little as a few weeks. Rightly, the FDA's drug review improvements were recognised in October 1997 by the John F Kennedy School of Government of Harvard University, with the Innovations in American Government Award.

As well as examining procedure the FDA also had a focus on process during the 1990s. A paperless approval system was instigated. This uses a harmonised format that is shared by the FDA and other regulatory agencies in the EU and Japan, which improves efficiency for the applicants in an increasingly global market, while allowing each jurisdiction to make individual approval decisions.

Although the majority of legislation and reforms during this period related to the drug approvals, a quiet revolution occurred in patient information. The standardised,

[174] IND regulations are contained in Title 21, Code of Federal Regulations, pt 312.

[175] See at www.fda.gov/ForPatients/Approvals/Fast/ucm405447.htm.

[176] *Federal Register* of 21 May 1990.

[177] Prescription Drug User Fee Act 1992, Pub L no 102-571, 106 Stat 4491.

easy-to-read labels for over-the-counter medicines were rolled out from 1994 onwards. In 1995 the FDA launched a program to improve patient awareness of the risks associated with certain prescription drugs. Pharmacists were required to provide patients with standardised literature, known as 'medguides'.

e. The Twenty-first Century

The FDA's intention to increase patient safety and drive down risk continued. In 1999 an FDA task force advised the Agency to make more systematic use of the principles of risk management in the way the FDA oversaw drug development and marketing. In light of the task force report, the FDA implemented a new model for risk management. The model aims to identify the risks associated with using a drug, to find strategies to minimise these risks, to communicate more effectively with those affected and to oversee how effectively risks are being contained.

The FDA recognised that there had been significant changes in the pharmaceutical industry during the decade between 1994 and 2004: a 70% increase in research and development funding was seen, but a 40% drop in new drug entities occurred.[178] Developing new medicines had become increasingly costly and slow. In response, in 2004 the FDA launched its Critical Path Initiative with the aim of reducing the time, cost and uncertainty of product development. The FDA aimed to address the need for up-to-date scientific means of evaluating the safety, efficacy and quality of medicines.

ii. Current Regulation of Medicinal Products in the US

The FDA is organised into six centres, which are responsible for:

- drug evaluation and research;
- medical and radiological devices;
- food and cosmetics;
- biologics;
- veterinary drugs; and
- tobacco products.

The largest centre within the FDA is the Center for Drug Evaluation and Research (CDER). Although the FDA has been in existence for years, the pharmaceutical regulatory process, particularly the drug approval process, has evolved considerably, giving CDER a key role in consumer protection. In recognition of the difficulties inherent in bringing a new drug to market, efforts have been made to make the approval process more collaborative, particularly to encourage FDA involvement early in the pre-application stages (see Figure 2.3).

[178] R Mahajan and K Gupta, 'Food and Drug Administration's Critical Path Initiative and Innovations in Drug Development Paradigm: Challenges, Progress and Controversies' (2010) 2(4) *J Pharm Bioallied Sci* 307, doi: 10.4103/0975-7406.72130.

Figure 2.3 Schematic of the FDA New Drug Application Pathway

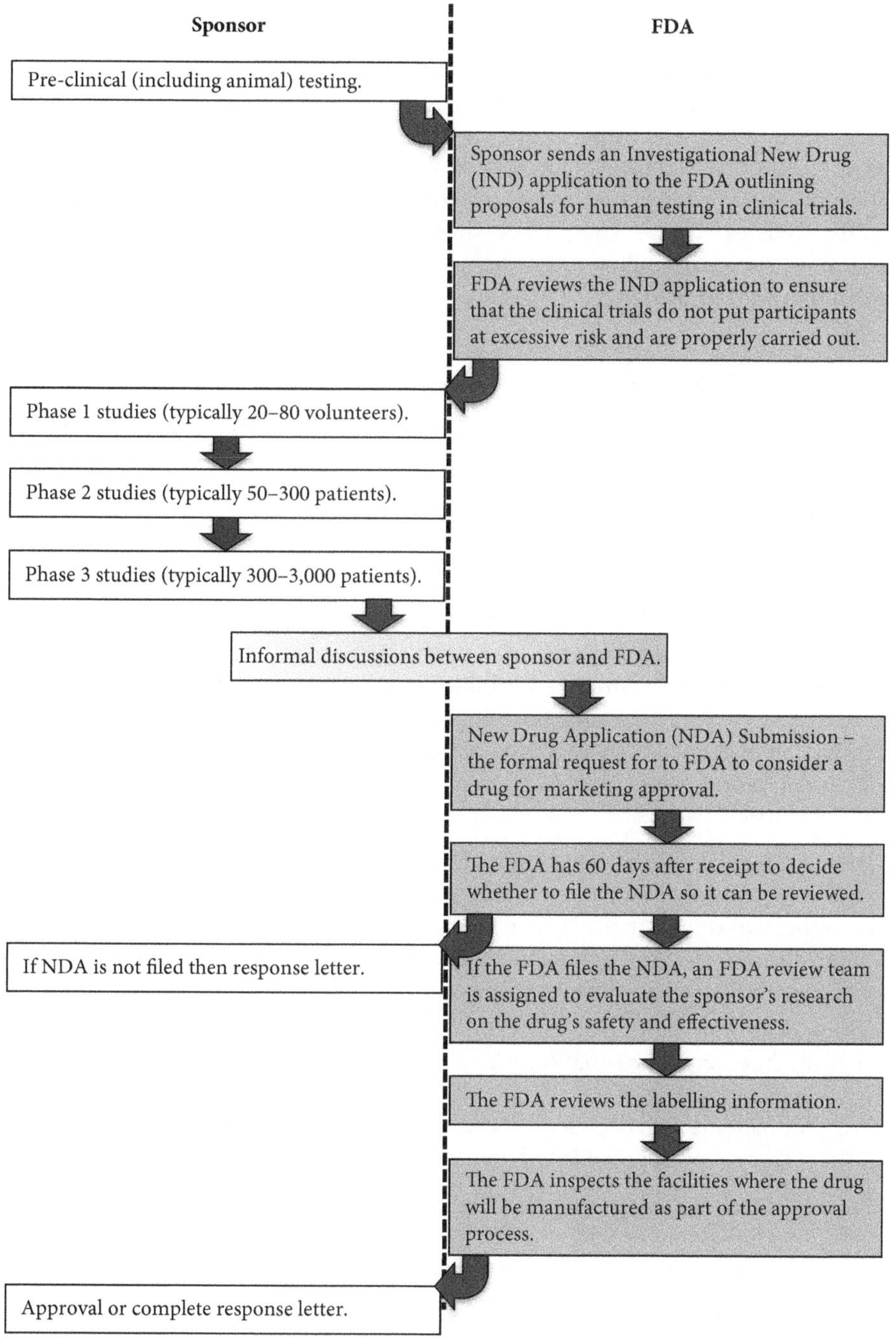

The CDER carries out pre-market evaluations of prescription, non-prescription and over-the-counter drugs (proprietary and generic), to ensure efficacy and a favourable risk–benefit profile. The risk–benefit profile will vary according to the severity of the condition being treated and the availability of other treatments; for example, a far higher risk profile is acceptable for a treatment for a life-threatening disorder, where there is no other available treatment, than would be permitted for a medicine intended to treat a relatively trivial illness which already has effective low-risk treatments available.

The application process is heavily structured, and all of the governing legislation is codified in the Code of Federal Regulations. There are several different application routes for marketing approval, depending upon the nature of the medicine. These are examined in more detail in section II.A.iii.[179]

iii. Marketing Authorisations within the US

In relation to medicinal products, a range of marketing authorisation application options exists, depending upon the nature of the particular product and its purpose.

a. US Investigational New Drug Applications

Investigational New Drug (IND) applications apply to pharmaceuticals that have undergone pre-clinical testing and which are now ready for testing in humans. An IND application has two key functions. First, to allow the FDA to assess the pre-clinical safety data on the new drug to look for risks to volunteers. Secondly, to overcome a technical legal requirement: under federal law a drug may not pass over State borders unless it has marketing authorisation; an IND application provides exemption from this legal requirement, allowing clinical trials to be conducted across State boundaries.

Three types of IND exist:

(a) *Investigator INDs*. These are submitted by a clinician who both initiates and conducts an investigation, and who is personally responsible for the way the investigational drug is administered and/or dispensed. A physician might submit a research IND application to propose studying an unapproved drug or an approved product for a new indication, or in a new patient population.
(b) *Emergency Use INDs*. These allow the FDA to authorise use of an experimental drug:
    (i) in an emergency situation where there is not enough time for a standard IND application,
    (ii) for patients who do not meet the criteria of an existing study protocol, or
    (iii) if there is no approved study protocol in existence.
(c) *Treatment INDs*. These permit experimental drugs showing promise in clinical testing to be used for serious or immediately life-threatening conditions while the final clinical work is conducted and the FDA review is ongoing.

An IND application can be either Commercial or Research (non-commercial).

[179] See further at www.fda.gov/Drugs/DevelopmentApprovalProcess/HowDrugsareDevelopedandApproved/ApprovalApplications/default.htm.

The IND application is much shorter and less detailed than a standard New Drug Application, but it must contain information on the following:

- Animal Pharmacology and Toxicology Studies;
- Manufacturing Information and Clinical Protocols; and
- Investigator Information.

The applicant must wait 30 calendar days after the IND application is submitted before initiating any clinical trials. During this time, the FDA can review the IND for safety to assure that participants will not be subjected to unreasonable risk.

b. US New Drug Application

The New Drug Application (NDA) has been the standard marketing authorisation pathway for new drugs since the FDA was created. The process is described in more detail section II.A.iv.

c. US Over-the-Counter Drugs

Over-the-counter drugs ('OTC', non-prescription) are defined as drugs that are safe and effective for use by the general public without seeking treatment by a health professional. The review of OTC drugs is undertaken by CDER's Office of Drug Evaluation IV, which is advised by the Non-prescription Drug Advisory Committee.

For each category of drugs, an OTC drug monograph[180] is developed and published in the Federal Register. Final OTC drug monographs define acceptable ingredients, doses, formulations and labelling.

Once a final monograph is implemented, companies can make and market an OTC product that conforms with the monograph without the need for FDA pre-approval. Even final monographs are not rigidly fixed, though, and drug companies may petition to change a final monograph to include additional ingredients or to modify labelling.

Products that do not conform to a final monograph must be reviewed under the NDA process.

d. US Abbreviated New Drug Application

The Abbreviated New Drug Application (ANDA) process allows generics to be approved on the basis of bioequivalence to an innovator drug that is already on the market. No preclinical or clinical data are required in an ANDA; instead the applicant must demonstrate bioequivalence with the innovator drug. Approval requires that the FDA is satisfied that the generic version delivers the same amount of active ingredients into a patient's bloodstream in the same amount of time as the innovator drug.

[180] Many of these monographs are found in s 300 of the Code of Federal Regulations.

iv. Requirements for Developing and Marketing Medicinal Products in the US

The US controls on medicinal products are based on the licensing by the FDA of virtually all activities that affect their safety. These controls apply throughout the lifespan of the medicinal product, from the initial product development right through to post-marketing surveillance.

a. US Product Development

Laboratory experiments must be carried out in accordance with the Standards for Good Laboratory Practice (GLP), which are regulated and enforced by the FDA.[181] The rules govern a substantial number of aspects of GLP, including controls on individuals, facilities and the performance of animal experiments.

b. US Clinical Trials

Clinical trials on new medicinal products for human use are overseen centrally and require prior approval by the FDA. Once pre-clinical studies have been completed, the sponsor is required to submit an IND application detailing proposals for conducting clinical trials in human volunteers. A granted IND application has the advantage that it exempts a sponsor from the usual federal law requirement that only drugs which have marketing approval can be transported or distributed across State boundaries, enabling clinical trials on investigational drugs to take place in many different States.

Since 1981 there have been strict provisions concerning the safeguarding of human volunteers, particularly children, and the obtaining of informed consent,[182] which have been subject to periodic review and updating.

The FDA is also charged with:

(a) ensuring that eligible clinical trials register on and submit results to the ClinicalTrials.gov databank;[183]
(b) ensuring that certain human drug, biological product and device applications and submissions to the FDA are accompanied by a certificate of compliance[184] with ClinicalTrials.gov requirements;[185] and
(c) undertaking compliance and enforcing proceedings if these actions are not completed.[186]

In order to verify the quality and integrity of data submitted, and to protect the rights and welfare of people in clinical trials, the FDA's Division of Scientific Investigations (DSI)

[181] See at www.fda.gov/ScienceResearch/SpecialTopics/RunningClinicalTrials/ucm155713.htm.

[182] Title 21 of the Code of Federal Regulations, pts 50 and 56.

[183] The operation and development of the ClinicalTrials.gov databank and the drafting of regulations related to the databank are the responsibility of the National Institutes of Health (NIH)/National Library of Medicine (NLM).

[184] To be supplied on Form FDA 3674, OMB Control No 0910-0616.

[185] Title VIII of the Food and Drug Administration Amendments Act 2007, Pub L no 110-85, 121 Stat 823.

[186] Title 42 of the Code of Federal Regulations, pt 11.

conducts inspections of clinical investigators' study facilities. The aim of these investigations is to establish whether the study was conducted properly and according to the investigational plan, whether all adverse events were recorded and whether the subjects met the inclusion/exclusion criteria outlined in the study protocol. Information supplied by clinical investigators to sponsors on case report forms is compared with information in primary source documents, such as medical records and lab results. If numerous or serious deviations are found, the DSI classifies the inspection as 'official action indicated' and sends a warning letter or Notice of Initiation of Disqualification Proceedings and Opportunity to Explain (NIDPOE) to the clinical investigator, specifying the deviations that were found. The issuing of a NIDPOE begins an administrative process to determine whether the clinical investigator should remain eligible to receive investigational products and conduct clinical studies.

The DSI also reviews the records of institutional review boards to be sure the boards are fulfilling their role in patient protection, and produces a report summarising any deficiencies.

c. US Marketing Authorisation Applications

In order to place a medicinal product on the market, authorisations are required from the FDA. Application is made online. The electronic Common Technical Document (eCTD) is the standard, accepted electronic format for the following types of submission:

- New Drug Application (NDA);
- Abbreviated New Drug Application (ANDA);
- Investigational New Drug Application (IND);
- Biologics License Application (BLA);
- Master Files: Drug Master File (DMF) and Biologics Master File (BMF);
- Emergency Use Authorization (EUA).

All IND and NDA applications are considered in accordance with the practices and procedures detailed in the Manual of Policies and Procedures (MAPP),[187] to help CDER staff standardise the IND and NDA review process.

The NDA and IND forms themselves are very short, just a few pages. However, the sponsor must submit an application to the FDA that provides enough information to enable a FDA reviewer to determine:

(a) whether the drug is safe and effective in its proposed use(s), and whether the benefits of the drug outweigh the risks;
(b) whether the drug's proposed labelling (package insert) is appropriate, and what it should contain;
(c) whether the methods used in manufacturing the drug and the controls used to maintain the drug's quality are adequate to preserve the drug's identity, strength, quality and purity.

[187] Available at www.fda.gov/AboutFDA/CentersOffices/OfficeofMedicalProductsandTobacco/CDER/ManualofPoliciesProcedures/default.htm.

The required particulars and documents that accompany the application form are extensive,[188] and the cost and complexity of product development are extremely high.[189] In recognition of the particular burden this places on small pharmaceutical businesses, the CDER has created the CDER Small Business and Industry Assistance (SBIA),[190] in order to help small pharmaceutical companies navigate the wealth of information the FDA offers, and to assist them in understanding the regulation of human drug products and the financial incentives and assistance that are available to them.

As shown in Figure 2.3, safety and efficacy are reviewed first, then labelling is examined and finally manufacturing facilities are inspected. Provided the application is considered satisfactory then the marketing authorisation will be granted, and approval will follow the complete review. If the product is not being authorised then a complete response letter will be sent to the sponsor by the FDA. This may reflect deficits in the safety and efficacy data, the labelling or other elements of the application. It indicates that the FDA will not approve the application in its current state, but it is not a bar to future approval if the defects in the application can be corrected.

d. US Risk Evaluation and Mitigation Strategy

Since 2007,[191] if the FDA considers that a medicine carries serious risk then a Risk Evaluation and Mitigation Strategy (REMS) can be required to help ensure that the benefits of the medication outweigh its risks. They are designed to reinforce medication use, behaviours and actions that support the safe use of that medication. While all medications have labelling that informs healthcare stakeholders about medication risks, only a few medications require a REMS. The Food and Drug Administration Amendments Act of 2007 gave the FDA the authority to require a REMS from manufacturers to ensure that the benefits of a drug or biological product outweigh its risks.

e. US Priority Review, Breakthrough Therapy, Accelerated Approval and Fast Track Designation

In order to facilitate the prompt availability of drug treatments for serious diseases, particularly when there are no existing treatments or if the new medication is an improvement over existing medications, four pathways have been developed by the FDA. These are:

- Priority Review;
- Breakthrough Therapy;

[188] The exact specification varies according to the type of drug, see Title 21 of the Code of Federal Regulations, pt 314.50, 'Content and Format of an NDA'.

[189] By the mid-2000s, this cost was said to be over $800 million, and rising at an annual rate of 7.4% above general price inflation: Boston Consulting Group, *A Revolution in R&D: How Genomics and Genetics are Transforming the Biopharmaceutical Industry* (Boston Consulting Group, 2001); J DiMasi, RW Hanson and HG Grabowski, 'The Price of Innovation: New Estimates of Drug Development Costs' (2003) 22 *Journal of Health Economics* 151; DW Light and RN Warburton, 'Extraordinary Claims Require Extraordinary Evidence' (2005) 24(5) *Journal of Health Economics* 1030.

[190] See at www.fda.gov/Drugs/DevelopmentApprovalProcess/SmallBusinessAssistance/ucm053133.htm.

[191] Food and Drug Administration Amendments Act 2007, n 184.

- Accelerated Approval; and
- Fast Track.

All of these reduce the approval time or the time before patients can receive the drug. The pathways are different, and the route chosen will depend upon the medication and the disease it is indicated for. Further detail on the difference between the pathways can be obtained from the FDA website.[192]

f. US Therapeutic Biologics Applications

The Center for Biologics Evaluation and Research (CBER) regulates biologics. The legislative situation for biologics is more complex than for drugs, with a variety of statutes governing biological products, including the Public Health Service Act 1944[193] and the Food, Drug and Cosmetic Act 1938. A biological product is defined under the Public Health Service Act[194] as a

> virus, therapeutic serum, toxin, antitoxin, vaccine, blood, blood component or derivative, allergenic product, or analogous product, … applicable to the prevention, treatment, or cure of a disease or condition of human beings.

While all 'biological products' also meet the definition of 'drugs' under the Food, Drug and Cosmetic Act, the converse is not true: hormones, for example insulin, glucagon and human growth hormone, are classified and regulated as drugs under the Food, Drug and Cosmetic Act, but not as biological products under the Public Health Service Act. Regulations and policies of the FDA have established that biological products include blood-derived products, vaccines, *in vivo* diagnostic allergenic products, immunoglobulin products, products containing cells or microorganisms, and most protein products.

The approval process for a biologic begins in the same was as for any other drug, with pre-clinical studies, and then an IND is submitted.[195] Once the clinical trials are completed the pathways for drugs and biological products diverge: drugs require an NDA, but biological products need a BLA.[196] As for drugs, the data from the pre-clinical and IND phases go into the BLA: the same form and electronic submission are used for both applications.

The criteria applied when licensing biologics varies slightly from those used for drugs. For a biologics licence to be issued, the FDA must be satisfied that the product, the manufacturing process and the manufacturing facilities meet applicable requirements to ensure the continued safety, purity and potency of the product.[197] Amongst other things, safety

[192] At www.fda.gov/ForPatients/Approvals/Fast/default.htm.

[193] The Public Health Service Act 1944, Pub L no 78-410, 58 Stat 682, ch 373.

[194] ibid, s 351.

[195] Title 21 of the Code of Federal Regulations, pt 312.

[196] Title 21 of the Code of Federal Regulations, pts 600–680; and the Public Health Service Act 1944, n 192.

[197] In this context: (i) 'safety' means the relative freedom from harmful effects, direct or indirect, when a product is prudently administered, taking into consideration the character of the product in relation to the condition of the recipient at the time; (ii) 'purity' means relative freedom from extraneous matter in the finished product, whether or not harmful to the recipient or deleterious to the product. Purity includes but is not limited to relative freedom from residual moisture or other volatile substances and pyrogenic substances; (iii) 'potency' is interpreted to mean the specific ability or capacity of the product, as indicated by appropriate laboratory tests, to yield a given result.

and purity assessments must consider the storage and testing of cell substrates that are often used to manufacture biologics. A potency assay is required due to the complexity and heterogeneity of biologics.

Any biologic that forms part of a combined biologic device product must also fulfil the standard requirements for medical devices.

g. US Expanded Use to Experimental Biologics

The CBER will consider applications to provide experimental biologics to some patients who are unable to enroll in clinical trials under an expanded access, or compassionate use, program.[198] This type of usage has allowed tens of thousands of patients with HIV/AIDS, cancer and other conditions to receive promising therapies when no approved alternative is available.

h. US Biosimilar Applications

Biosimilars are biological products that have no clinically meaningful differences in safety, purity and potency from an existing FDA-approved product – the reference product. Since 2010 an abbreviated pathway for biosimilar approval has existed.[199] The approval of a biosimilar requires that the biosimilarity between the proposed biosimilar product and the reference product be demonstrated; there is then no need to independently establish the safety and effectiveness of the biosimilar product.

i. US Cellular, Tissue and Gene Therapies

Depending upon the exact nature of the product, the regulation of cellular, tissue and gene therapy products varies. A detailed description is unfortunately outside the scope of this work.[200] This type of application is assisted by contributions from the Cellular, Tissue and Gene Therapies Advisory Committee. The Committee is a statutory entity[201] that reviews and evaluates available data relating to the safety, effectiveness and appropriate use of human cells, human tissues, gene transfer therapies and xenotransplantation products that are intended for transplantation, implantation, infusion and transfer in the prevention and treatment of a broad spectrum of human diseases, and in the reconstruction, repair or replacement of tissues for various conditions.

[198] See www.fda.gov/BiologicsBloodVaccines/DevelopmentApprovalProcess/ExpandedAccess/default.htm.

[199] Public Health Service Act 1944, n 192, s 351(k), as amended by the Biologics Price Competition and Innovation Act 2009 (BPCI Act), Pub L no 111-148, 124 Stat 119 (note that the BCPI Act is an amendment law contained within Title VII, Subtitle A, Sect 7001-7003 of the Patient Protection and Affordable Care Act).

[200] For example, mitochondrial donation has particular, specific rules.

[201] The Cellular, Tissue and Gene Therapies Advisory Committee was established under 15 USC 1451 et seq; 21 USC 321, 341, 342, 343, 343-1, 344, 345, 346, 348, 349, 350, 350a, 351, 352, 353(f), 355, 360b, 360c-j, 371, 375, 376, 378, 379e, 381, 393, 394, 881(b); 42 USC 217a, 241, 242, 242a, 262, 264; 21 CFR pt 14, 330.10(a); Pub L 92-463 (5 USC App), the Federal Advisory Committee Act, which sets forth standards for the formation and use of advisory committees.

j. US Pharmacovigilance

The need for a pharmacovigilance system was recognised from the inception of modern regulation, and the FDA has long had a facility to report adverse events: the FDA Adverse Events Reporting System (FAERS) is the latest incarnation.[202]

Two forms of adverse event reporting occur: (i) mandatory reporting by manufacturers, distributors and packers; and (ii) voluntary reporting by healthcare providers and consumers (and their representatives). As with almost all adverse event reporting systems, there is no guarantee that the adverse event that has been reported is connected to the regulated product. Additionally, the voluntary filing of adverse event reports via MedWatch is open to patients and their representatives, including claimant lawyers, who may be litigating about the very product about which they are complaining on behalf of their clients.

1. Mandatory Reporting

The requirements and procedures for reporting adverse drug events vary according to whether the drug in question is an investigational new drug,[203] a marketed prescription drug for human use without an approved NDA[204] or an approved drug.[205] The guidance for industry on what ADRs should be reported is extensive and detailed.[206]

The requirements and procedures for reporting adverse events associated with the use of biologics also vary. If the biologic is an investigational new drug then it us under the same regime as a medicine (see '(a) Investigational new drug reporting' below). The post-marketing reporting of adverse experiences with biologics has its own regime,[207] and there are separate provisions for reporting adverse events associated with human cells, tissues, and cellular and tissue-based products.[208]

(a) Investigational new drug reporting. The provisions set out in Table 2.6 apply to the sponsor.

Table 2.6 Reporting requirements for investigational new drugs

Reporter	What to report	To whom	Time limits
Sponsor	IND safety reports of potential serious risks from clinical trials.	FDA and all participating investigators	Within 15 calendar days of becoming aware of an event.
Sponsor	Unexpected fatal or life-threatening suspect adverse reaction reports.	FDA	Within 7 calendar days of becoming aware of an event.

[202] Before 10 September 2012 the system was known as Adverse Event Reporting System (AERS).
[203] Title 21 of the Code of Federal Regulations, pt 312.32.
[204] ibid, pt 310.305.
[205] ibid, pt 314.80.
[206] *Guidance for Industry Postmarketing Adverse Experience Reporting for Human Drug and Licensed Biological Products: Clarification of What to Report*, US Department of Health and Human Services, Food and Drug Administration, Center for Drug Evaluation and Research (CDER), Center for Biologics Evaluation and Research (CBER), August 1997, at www.fda.gov/downloads/Drugs/GuidanceComplianceRegulatoryInformation/Guidances/UCM071981.pdf.
[207] Title 21 of the Code of Federal Regulations, pt 600.800.
[208] ibid, pt 1217.350.

For the purposes of mandatory reporting in investigational new drugs *serious adverse events* or *serious suspected adverse reactions* and *unexpected adverse event* or *unexpected suspected adverse reaction* are defined as follows:[209]

> *Serious adverse event* or *serious suspected adverse reaction.* An adverse event or suspected adverse reaction is considered 'serious' if, in the view of either the investigator or sponsor, it results in any of the following outcomes: Death, a life-threatening adverse event, inpatient hospitalization or prolongation of existing hospitalization, a persistent or significant incapacity or substantial disruption of the ability to conduct normal life functions, or a congenital anomaly/birth defect. Important medical events that may not result in death, be life-threatening, or require hospitalization may be considered serious when, based upon appropriate medical judgment, they may jeopardize the patient or subject and may require medical or surgical intervention to prevent one of the outcomes listed in this definition. Examples of such medical events include allergic bronchospasm requiring intensive treatment in an emergency room or at home, blood dyscrasias or convulsions that do not result in inpatient hospitalization, or the development of drug dependency or drug abuse.
>
> *Suspected adverse reaction* means any adverse event for which there is a reasonable possibility that the drug caused the adverse event. For the purposes of IND safety reporting, 'reasonable possibility' means there is evidence to suggest a causal relationship between the drug and the adverse event. Suspected adverse reaction implies a lesser degree of certainty about causality than adverse reaction, which means any adverse event caused by a drug.
>
> *Unexpected adverse event* or *unexpected suspected adverse reaction.* An adverse event or suspected adverse reaction is considered 'unexpected' if it is not listed in the investigator brochure or is not listed at the specificity or severity that has been observed; or, if an investigator brochure is not required or available, is not consistent with the risk information described in the general investigational plan or elsewhere in the current application, as amended. For example, under this definition, hepatic necrosis would be unexpected (by virtue of greater severity) if the investigator brochure referred only to elevated hepatic enzymes or hepatitis. Similarly, cerebral thromboembolism and cerebral vasculitis would be unexpected (by virtue of greater specificity) if the investigator brochure listed only cerebral vascular accidents. 'Unexpected,' as used in this definition, also refers to adverse events or suspected adverse reactions that are mentioned in the investigator brochure as occurring with a class of drugs or as anticipated from the pharmacological properties of the drug, but are not specifically mentioned as occurring with the particular drug under investigation.

The issue of causality is explored further. The legislation specifies:[210]

> (i) *Serious and unexpected suspected adverse reaction.* The sponsor must report any suspected adverse reaction that is both serious and unexpected. The sponsor must report an adverse event as a suspected adverse reaction only if there is evidence to suggest a causal relationship between the drug and the adverse event, such as:
>
> (A) A single occurrence of an event that is uncommon and known to be strongly associated with drug exposure (eg, angioedema, hepatic injury, Stevens-Johnson Syndrome);
>
> (B) One or more occurrences of an event that is not commonly associated with drug exposure, but is otherwise uncommon in the population exposed to the drug (eg, tendon rupture);
>
> (C) An aggregate analysis of specific events observed in a clinical trial (such as known consequences of the underlying disease or condition under investigation or other

[209] ibid, pt 312.32(a).

[210] ibid, pt 310.305(c)(1)(i)(A),(B) and (C).

events that commonly occur in the study population independent of drug therapy) that indicates those events occur more frequently in the drug treatment group than in a concurrent or historical control group.

Trial sponsors have additional requirements to report other factors that may impact on the safety of an investigational drug on human participants, such as findings from other types of study (including epidemiological and preclinical studies) and increased occurrence of serious suspected adverse reactions.[211] This information can be reported to the FDA either in narrative format or on a specified form.

(b) Reporting requirements for marketed prescription drug for human use without an approved new drug application. Any person whose name appears on the label of a prescription drug as a manufacturer, packer or distributor of the product,[212] must establish and maintain records and make reports to the FDA of all serious, unexpected adverse drug experiences associated with the use of their drug product, according to the requirements detailed in Table 2.7.

Table 2.7 Reporting requirements for manufacturers, packers and distributors of a marketed prescription drug for human use without an approved new drug application

Reporter	What to report	To whom	Time limits
Manufacturer	15-day alert reports of adverse drug reactions that are both serious and unexpected.	FDA	Within 15 calendar days of becoming aware of an event.
Packer	15-day alert reports of adverse drug reactions that are both serious and unexpected.	Manufacturer	Within 5 calendar days of becoming aware of an event.
Distributor	15-day alert reports of adverse drug reactions that are both serious and unexpected.	Manufacturer	Within 5 calendar days of becoming aware of an event.
Manufacturer	15-day alert report follow-up data.	FDA	Within 15 calendar days of receipt of new information or as requested by the FDA.

For the purposes of mandatory reporting, *serious adverse drug experience* and *unexpected adverse drug experience* are defined as follows:[213]

Serious adverse drug experience. Any adverse drug experience occurring at any dose that results in any of the following outcomes: Death, a life-threatening adverse drug experience, inpatient hospitalization or prolongation of existing hospitalization, a persistent or significant disability/incapacity, or a congenital anomaly/birth defect. Important medical events that may not result in death, be life-threatening, or require hospitalization may be considered a serious adverse drug experience when, based upon appropriate medical judgment, they may jeopardize the patient or subject and may require medical or surgical intervention to prevent one of the outcomes listed in this definition. Examples of such medical events include allergic bronchospasm requiring

[211] ibid, pt 310.305(c)(1)(ii), (iii) and (iv).
[212] ibid, parts 310.305(c)(1).
[213] ibid, pt 310.305(b).

intensive treatment in an emergency room or at home, blood dyscrasias or convulsions that do not result in inpatient hospitalization, or the development of drug dependency or drug abuse.

Unexpected adverse drug experience. Any adverse drug experience that is not listed in the current labeling for the drug product. This includes events that may be symptomatically and pathophysiologically related to an event listed in the labeling, but differ from the event because of greater severity or specificity. For example, under this definition, hepatic necrosis would be unexpected (by virtue of greater severity) if the labeling only referred to elevated hepatic enzymes or hepatitis. Similarly, cerebral thromboembolism and cerebral vasculitis would be unexpected (by virtue of greater specificity) if the labeling only listed cerebral vascular accidents. 'Unexpected,' as used in this definition, refers to an adverse drug experience that has not been previously observed (*ie*, included in the labeling) rather than from the perspective of such experience not being anticipated from the pharmacological properties of the pharmaceutical product.

Reporting is electronic using specified forms.[214] Follow-up information should include individual case safety reports (ICSRs), the content of which is defined in the Regulations.[215]

(c) Post-marketing reporting of adverse drug experience. The applicant in this section is the person who holds the approved application for marketing the drug. A non-applicant is defined as anyone, such as a manufacturer, distributor or packer, whose name appears on the label of the approved drug product.[216] The definitions of serious and unexpected adverse drug experiences are the same as for marketed prescription drugs for human use without an approved NDA (see *(b)*).[217] The post-marketing reporting requirements in this section as are set out in Table 2.8.

Table 2.8 Post-marketing reporting requirements for applicants and non-applicants of an approved marketed prescription drug for human use

Reporter	What to report	To whom	Time limits
Applicant (licence holder)	15-day alert reports of adverse drug reactions that are both serious and unexpected (whether foreign or domestic).	FDA	Within 15 calendar days of becoming aware of an event.
Non-applicant	15-day alert reports of adverse drug reactions that are both serious and unexpected.	Applicant	Within 5 calendar days of becoming aware of an event.
Applicant	15-day alert report follow-up data.	FDA	Within 15 calendar days of receipt of new information or as requested by the FDA.

Again, reporting is electronic and in a prescribed format.[218]

Applicants are also required to submit periodic safety updates detailing, amongst other things, any actions taken in response to ADRs and any unreported ADRs. Periodic reports are quarterly for the first three years of marketing, then annual thereafter.

[214] ibid, pt 310.305(e).
[215] ibid, pt 310.305(c)(5)(d).
[216] ibid, pt 314.80(c)(1)(3).
[217] ibid, pt 314.80(a).
[218] ibid, pt 314.80(c), (d), (e) and (f).

(d) *Post-marketing reporting of adverse experiences with biological products.* The applicant in this section is the person who holds the approved application for marketing the biological product.[219] Others whose name appears on the label of the approved biologic product, such as a manufacturer, distributor or packer, also have reporting requirements.[220] See Table 2.9.

Table 2.9 Post-marketing reporting requirements for applicants and non-applicants of an approved marketed prescription drug for human use

Reporter	What to report	To whom	Time limits
Applicant (licence holder)	15-day alert reports of adverse reactions that are both serious and unexpected (whether foreign or domestic).	FDA	Within 15 calendar days of becoming aware of an event.
Others	15-day alert reports of adverse biologics reactions that are both serious and unexpected.	Applicant	Within 5 calendar days of becoming aware of an event.
Applicant	15 day alert report follow-up data.	FDA	Within 15 calendar days of receipt of new information or as requested by the FDA.

The definitions of serious and unexpected adverse biologic experiences are:[221]

> *Serious adverse experience.* Any adverse experience occurring at any dose that results in any of the following outcomes: Death, a life-threatening adverse experience, inpatient hospitalization or prolongation of existing hospitalization, a persistent or significant disability/incapacity, or a congenital anomaly/birth defect. Important medical events that may not result in death, be life-threatening, or require hospitalization may be considered a serious adverse experience when, based upon appropriate medical judgment, they may jeopardize the patient or subject and may require medical or surgical intervention to prevent one of the outcomes listed in this definition. Examples of such medical events include allergic bronchospasm requiring intensive treatment in an emergency room or at home, blood dyscrasias or convulsions that do not result in inpatient hospitalization, or the development of drug dependency or drug abuse.
>
> *Unexpected adverse experience.* Any adverse experience that is not listed in the current labeling for the biological product. This includes events that may be symptomatically and pathophysiologically related to an event listed in the labeling, but differ from the event because of greater severity or specificity. For example, under this definition, hepatic necrosis would be unexpected (by virtue of greater severity) if the labeling only referred to elevated hepatic enzymes or hepatitis. Similarly, cerebral thromboembolism and cerebral vasculitis would be unexpected (by virtue of greater specificity) if the labeling only listed cerebral vascular accidents. 'Unexpected,' as used in this definition, refers to an adverse experience that has not been previously observed (ie, included in the labeling) rather than from the perspective of such experience not being anticipated from the pharmacological properties of the pharmaceutical product.

Again, reporting is electronic and in a prescribed format.[222]

[219] ibid, pt 1217.350(b).
[220] ibid, pt 1217.350(c)(1)(iii).
[221] ibid, pt 1217.350(a).
[222] ibid, pt 1217.350(c), (d), (e) and (f).

Applicants are also required to submit periodic safety updates detailing, amongst other things, any actions taken in response to ADRs and any unreported ADRs. Periodic reports are quarterly for the first three years of marketing, then annual thereafter.[223]

(e) Reporting adverse events associated with human cells, tissues and cellular and tissue-based products. The legislation on reporting adverse events associated with human cells, tissues, and cellular and tissue-based products[224] provides as follows:

> (a) *Adverse reaction reports.*
>
> (1) You must investigate any adverse reaction involving a communicable disease related to an HCT/P that you made available for distribution. You must report to FDA an adverse reaction involving a communicable disease if it:
>
> (i) Is fatal;
> (ii) Is life-threatening;
> (iii) Results in permanent impairment of a body function or permanent damage to body structure; or
> (iv) Necessitates medical or surgical intervention, including hospitalization.
>
> (2) You must submit each report on a Form FDA-3500A to the address in paragraph (a)(5) of this section within 15 calendar days of initial receipt of the information.
>
> (3) You must, as soon as practical, investigate all adverse reactions that are the subject of these 15-day reports and must submit follow-up reports within 15 calendar days of the receipt of new information or as requested by FDA. If additional information is not obtainable, a follow-up report may be required that describes briefly the steps taken to seek additional information and the reasons why it could not be obtained.
>
> (4) You may obtain copies of the reporting form (FDA-3500A) from the Center for Biologics Evaluation and Research (see address in paragraph (a)(5) of this section). Electronic Form FDA-3500A may be obtained at http://www.fda.gov/medwatch or at http://www.hhs.gov/forms.
>
> (5) You must submit two copies of each report described in this paragraph to the Food and Drug Administration, Center for Biologics Evaluation and Research, Document Control Center, 10903 New Hampshire Ave, Bldg 71, Rm G112, Silver Spring, MD 20993-0002. FDA may waive the requirement for the second copy in appropriate circumstances.
>
> (b) *Reports of HCT/P deviations.*
>
> (1) You must investigate all HCT/P deviations related to a distributed HCT/P for which you performed a manufacturing step.
>
> (2) You must report any such HCT/P deviation relating to the core CGTP requirements, if the HCT/P deviation occurred in your facility or in a facility that performed a manufacturing step for you under contract, agreement, or other arrangement. Each report must contain a description of the HCT/P deviation, information relevant to the event and the manufacture of the HCT/P involved, and information on all follow-up actions that have been or will be taken in response to the HCT/P deviation (eg, recalls).
>
> (3) You must report each such HCT/P deviation that relates to a core CGTP requirement on Form FDA 3486 within 45 days of the discovery of the event either electronically using the Center for Biologics Evaluation and Research electronic Web-based application or by mail to the Food and Drug Administration, Center for Biologics Evaluation and Research, Document Control Center, 10903 New Hampshire Ave, Bldg 71, Rm G112, Silver Spring, MD 20993-0002.

[223] ibid, pt 1217.350(2).
[224] ibid, pt 1271.350.

2. Voluntary Reporting

MedWatch is a web-based platform[225] that enables any member of the medical professional not subject to mandatory reporting requirements or members of the public (or their chosen representatives, including their lawyers) to report directly to the FDA:

- a serious adverse event;
- a product quality problem;
- a medication error;
- a therapeutic inequivalence/failure; or
- counterfeit medical products;

that they believe to be associated with the use of an FDA-regulated medical product.

Reports are on specified forms, with different forms for consumers and healthcare professionals.

Healthcare professionals and consumers may also choose to report to the manufacturer. If they chose that option, the manufacturer has to forward the information to the FDA in accordance with the Regulations.[226]

3. FAERS

All adverse reports that are reported under the mandatory reporting regime are automatically added to the FAERS database. MedWatch reports are added manually. This allows for analysis of adverse event reports.

MedWatch provides a voluntary reporting system for healthcare professionals and consumers. All MedWatch reports are put into FAERS.

The reports in FAERS are monitored by clinical reviewers from the CDER and the CBER to look for potential safety signals. If a potential safety signal is identified then further analysis, such as undertaking studies using other large databases, is performed. If a safety concern is identified, regulatory action may follow. This could involve updating a product's labelling information, restricting the use of the drug, communicating new safety information to the public or, in rare cases, removing a product from the market.

4. Post-market Safety Evaluations

The FDA conducts a post-market safety evaluation on any product approved under an NDA and BLA after 27 September 2007.[227] These post-market evaluations are performed either 18 months after approval, or once the product has been used by 10,000 individuals, whichever is later. These evaluations aim to:

(a) identify any new serious adverse events that were not apparent during product development;
(b) establish if reports of known side-effects have occurred in an unusual or unexpected way; or

[225] Available at www.fda.gov/Safety/MedWatch/HowToReport/default.htm.

[226] See sections on 'Investigational new drug reporting', 'Reporting requirements for marketed prescription drug for human use without an approved new drug application', 'Post-marketing reporting of adverse drug experiences' and 'Post-marketing reporting of adverse experiences with biological products'.

[227] Title 21 of the Code of Federal Regulations, pt 355(r).

(c) identify any potential new safety concerns now that the products are being used in the general population.

The CDER and the CBER, carry out evaluations on the medical products they regulate. Each evaluation is jointly conducted by scientists from two different offices within the regulator, as detailed in Table 2.10.

Table 2.10 Bodies responsible for evaluations on medical products

Product	**Body responsible for carrying out the evaluation**	**Offices jointly carrying out the evaluation**	
Drug	CDER	Office of Surveillance & Epidemiology	Office of New Drugs
Biologic[228]	CBER	Office of Biostatistics & Epidemiology	The most relevant of: – Office of Blood Research and Review – Office of Cellular, Tissue and Gene Therapies – Office of Vaccine Research and Review

The scientists jointly review the relevant data, summarise findings and, if required, develop a plan to further investigate potential new safety issues for the products under evaluation. They rely on a variety of data sources, including:

- the product's pre-approval safety profile;
- the product's current FDA-approved label;
- reports made to the FAERS;
- reports made to the Vaccine Adverse Event Reporting System (VAERS);
- manufacturer-submitted periodic safety reports;
- medical literature;
- drug utilisation databases;
- data from post-approval clinical trials and other studies, when applicable.

The FDA compiles the post-market safety evaluations, and each quarter a report is published detailing the drug or biological identifiers, with a summary of evaluation findings, actions taken and ongoing surveillance activities.

5. Alerts, Healthcare Provider Letters and Recall

An alert can be issued by the FDA on the FDA website to provide the public and healthcare providers with information about the safe use of a drug on the market. A 'Dear Healthcare Provider' letter can also be issued regarding the safe use of a drug within a clinical setting.

[228] Assuming the biologic is regulated by CBER; if it is regulated by CDER then CDER is responsible for carrying out the evaluation.

The last-resort option, when there are serious concerns about drug safety, is to recall the drug from the market. The vast majority of drug recalls have been voluntarily undertaken by manufacturers,[229] but the FDA does have the power to mandate a drug's recall from the market if necessary.[230] Human biologics[231] and human tissues[232] fall under different statutory provisions, but the same general premise applies, that the majority of recalls have been undertaken voluntarily.

F. US Regulation of Medical Devices

Devices have been regulated in the US since May 1976,[233] though some earlier devices were regulated as 'drugs' so subject to FDA approval.[234] Medical device regulation is the responsibility of the Center for Devices and Radiological Health (CDRH).

i. US Classification and Standards

As in the EU, the wide range of medical devices, involving a wide range of risk (from very low-risk tongue depressors to higher-risk electrical implantable devices), means that medical devices are classified based on the risks associated with the use of the particular device. The classification system in the US differs from the EU one. In the USA, devices are classified as Class I, Class II or Class III,[235] with Class I being the lowest risk and Class III the highest risk.[236] Class I devices are considered sufficiently safe that general controls can provide reasonable assurance that the device is safe and effective for its intended use. Class II device safety can be reasonably managed by applying performance standards. Class III devices are devices where neither general controls nor performance standards are sufficient to provide reasonable assurance that the particular device is safe and effective for its intended use, and more information is required to verity this:

- Class I – These devices present minimal potential for harm to the user. Examples include enema kits and elastic bandages. Of medical device types, 35% are Class I and 93% of these are exempt from pre-market review.
- Class II – These are devices that generally present a moderate risk of harm to the user. Examples of Class II devices include powered wheelchairs and some pregnancy test kits. Of device types, 53% are Class II, most of which require FDA review through pre-market notification.
- Class III – These are devices that sustain or support life, are implanted, or present potential high risk of illness or injury. Examples of Class III devices include implantable

[229] Title 21 of the Code of Federal Regulations, subpt C, pts 7.40–7.59.
[230] ibid, subpt C, pt 7.40(b).
[231] Title 42 of the Code of Federal Regulations, pt 262.
[232] Title 21 of the Code of Federal Regulations, pt 1270, subpt D.
[233] The Medical Device Amendments 1976, Pub L no 94-295, 90 Stat 539.
[234] See the case study on the Gravigard or Copper7 IUD Chapter 3, II, A.
[235] Food, Drug and Cosmetics Act 1938, n 8, s 201(h).
[236] Taken from www.fda.gov/MedicalDevices/ResourcesforYou/Consumers/default.htm.

pacemakers and breast implants. Of device types, 9% are Class III and require FDA review through pre-market approval (PMA) or humanitarian device exemption (HDE).

- Unclassified/not classified – These are device types that the FDA has not yet classified. Of device types, 3% are unclassified/not classified.

To assist manufacturers and sponsors with classification, the majority of medical devices can be classified by finding the matching description of the device in question in Title 21 of the Code of Federal Regulations, parts 862–892. The FDA has classified and described over 1,700 distinct types of devices, and has organised them in the Code into 16 medical speciality 'panels', such as 'Cardiovascular' devices or 'Ear, Nose, and Throat' devices. For each of the devices classified by the FDA, the Code gives a general description, including the intended use, the class to which the device belongs (ie Class I, II or III) and information about marketing requirements.

a. Clearance or Approval

There are two potential routes to market a medical device in the USA. It must be either cleared, or approved for sale.

Cleared medical devices have been determined to be substantially equivalent to another marketed device that is already being legally marketed and which is not the subject of a pre-marketing approval requirement. A pre-market notification submission is referred to as a 510(k) and must be submitted to the FDA to review and provide clearance.

Approved medical devices have been approved by the FDA after a PMA application or an HDE application has been considered. This review and approval process is mandatory for Class III medical devices and involves a more rigorous review than the 510(k) review process.

The FDA website houses databases of 510(k) and PMA approvals, which can be searched freely to find more information on a medical device.

Some devices may be considered 'exempt'.[237] If a device is considered 'exempt', the manufacturer would not be required to submit a pre-market notification submission (a 510(k) submission) or to obtain FDA clearance before marketing the device in the US (exemptions include 'grandfathering', where a device was on the market before 28 May 1976 and has not been significantly changed or modified in design, components, method of manufacture or intended use). The manufacturer of an exempt device is still required to register its establishment and list its devices with the FDA.

b. Pre-Market Notification 510(k) Procedures

There are three types of pre-market notification 510(k)s: traditional, special and abbreviated. The special and abbreviated 510(k) methods were developed in 1998s under the 'New 510(k) Paradigm' in order to streamline the 510(k) review process.

[237] The exemptions are listed at Title 21 of the Code of Federal Regulations, pts 862.9 and 864.9.

1. Traditional 510(k) Notification

If a PMA application is required then the applicant cannot use the 510(k) route. The marketing of all other Class I, II or III devices intended for human use requires that a 510(k) application is submitted to the FDA, unless the device is exempt.[238] There is no set 510(k) form, but there are detailed requirements for a 510(k) submission.[239] A device must not be placed on the market until the submitter has received an order (in the form of a letter) from the FDA that finds the device to be substantially equivalent (SE) and states that the device can be marketed in the US. This order 'clears' the device for commercial distribution.

The purpose of the 510(k) pre-market submission is to demonstrate to the FDA that the device to be marketed is substantially equivalent to a legally marketed device[240] that is not subject to PMA. The legally marketed device(s) to which equivalence is applied is usually referred to as the 'predicate'. The predicate device can be any legally marketed device, including:

- a pre-amendments device (a device that was legally marketed prior to 28 May 1976);
- a device that has been reclassified from Class III to Class II or I;
- a device that has been found to be substantially equivalent under the 510(k) process; or
- a device that was granted marketing authorisation via the de novo classification process,[241] and which is not exempt from pre-market notification requirements.

Submitters must compare their device to one or more similar legally marketed device, and must make and support their substantial equivalence claims. Substantial equivalence does not require that the new device is a carbon copy of the predicate device; it means that the new device is at least as safe and effective as the predicate.

Various factors are taken into account when determining substantial equivalence, including whether the new device:

(a) has the same intended use as the predicate; *and*
(b) has the same technological characteristics as the predicate; *or*
(c) has the same intended use as the predicate; *and*
(d) has different technological characteristics and does not raise different questions of safety and effectiveness; *and*
(e) the information submitted to FDA demonstrates that the device is at least as safe and effective as the legally marketed device.

Substantial equivalence is established with respect to intended use, design, energy used or delivered, materials, chemical composition, manufacturing process, performance, safety, effectiveness, labelling, biocompatibility, standards and other characteristics, as applicable.

If the FDA determines that a device is *not* substantially equivalent, the applicant may chose to:

(a) resubmit another 510(k) application with new data;
(b) request a Class I or II designation through the de novo classification process;

[238] For the full 510(k) requirements, see the Food, Drug and Cosmetics Act 1938, n 8.
[239] Title 21 of the Code of Federal Regulations, pt 807.
[240] ibid, pt 807.92(a)(3).
[241] Food, Drug and Cosmetics Act 1938, n 8, s 513(f)(2).

(c) file a reclassification petition; or
(d) submit a PMA application.

The intention is that the 510(k) process will be completed within 90 days. If the FDA determines that the device is substantially equivalent then it can be placed on the market immediately after 510(k) clearance is granted. The FDA does not perform any 510(k) pre-clearance facility inspections, but it is empowered to perform an FDA quality system[242] inspection at any time after 510(k) clearance has been granted.

2. Special 510(k) Notification

The special 510(k) notification is used for device modifications. It is a less intensive notification, which relies upon the design controls aspect of the Quality System (QS) regulation.[243] Special 510(k)s may be used when a modification is proposed to a device that has already been cleared under the 510(k) process. If a new 510(k) is needed for the modification, and if the modification does not affect the intended use of the device or alter the fundamental scientific technology of the device, then a special 510(k) notification containing summary information that results from the design control process can submitted.

The Quality System regulation mandates that all Class II and III devices and certain Class I devices must be designed in conformity with section 820.30 Design Controls.[244] The Special 510(k) allows the manufacturer to declare conformity with design controls without providing the data. A 'Special 510(k): Device Modification' has broadly the same basic content requirements as a traditional 510(k),[245] but this type of submission must also reference the cleared 510(k) number and contain a 'Declaration of Conformity' with design control requirements.

Manufacturers of Class I devices requiring a 510(k) may elect to comply with the design control provisions of the QS regulation and submit a special 510(k).

To make this an attractive option for obtaining FDA clearance where applicable, the intention is to process special 510(k)s within 30 days of receipt by the FDA's Document Mail Center.

3. Abbreviated 510(k) Notification

Device manufacturers may choose to submit an abbreviated 510(k) when:

(a) a guidance documents exists;
(b) a special control has been established; or
(c) the FDA has recognised a relevant consensus standard.

An abbreviated 510(k) submission must include certain specific required elements.[246] However, in an abbreviated 510(k) submission, firms elect to provide summary reports on the use of guidance documents and/or special controls or declarations of conformity with FDA recognised standards to expedite the review of a submission.

[242] Title 21 of the Code of Federal Regulations, pt 820.
[243] ibid, pt 820.30.
[244] ibid.
[245] ibid, pt 807.87.
[246] ibid.

4. Third Party 510(k) Review Procedures

Manufacturers of certain devices have the choice to submit their traditional 510(k) notification either to the CDRH, or to certain private parties ('Recognized Third Parties') accredited by the FDA for the purpose.[247] The accredited person will review the application and make a recommendation to the FDA. The FDA then has 30 days to respond.

c. PMA Procedures

1. PMA for pre-amendment devices, post-amendment devices, and transitional and 'new' devices

From 28 May 1976,[248] a Class III device has been defined as one that supports or sustains human life, or which is of substantial importance in preventing impairment of human health or a potential, unreasonable risk of illness or injury. All Class III devices are subject to PMA requirements.[249] Pre-market approval by the FDA is required to ensure the safety and effectiveness of Class III devices before they are placed on the market.

Pre-market approval applications can be required in several circumstances, not just before a product is marketed. The circumstances in which a PMA may be sought relate to pre-amendment devices, post-amendment devices, and transitional and 'new' Class III devices. Pre-market approval requirements apply differently to these three categories.

A pre-amendment device is one that was legally in commercial distribution before the Medical Device Amendments were enacted on 28 May 1976. If either a promulgation of a final classification regulation or a final regulation requiring the submission of a PMA is issued then manufacturers are required to submit a PMA.[250] Eventually all Class III pre-amendment devices will have a PMA.

A post-amendment device is one that was first distributed commercially on or after 28 May 1976. If the FDA determines that a post-amendment device is substantially equivalent to a pre-amendment Class III device then the post-amendment device is subject to the same requirements as a pre-amendment device. Substantial equivalence is determined after reviewing an applicant's 510(k) pre-market notification. If the FDA determines that a post-amendment devices is not substantially equivalent to any legally marketed device (either pre-amendment or post-amendment) in Class I or II then that device will be classed as a 'new' device and falls automatically into Class III.

Class III transitional devices and 'new' devices require PMA by the FDA before they may be commercially distributed. Transitional devices are devices that were regulated by the FDA as new drugs before 28 May 1976. Any Class III device that was approved by an NDA is now governed by the PMA regulations.

Applicants may submit either a PMA or Product Development Protocol (PDP),[251] or may petition the FDA to reclassify the device as Class I or Class II.

[247] Food and Drug Administration Modernization Act 1997, Pub L no 105-115, 111 Stat 2296.

[248] Medical Device Amendments 1976, n 234.

[249] ibid, s 515.

[250] The PMA must be submitted within 30 months or the promulgation of a final classification regulation, or within 90 days after the publication of a final regulation requiring the submission of a PMA, whichever period is later. The FDA may choose to extend the 90-day timeframe.

[251] Under Title 21 of the Code of Federal Regulations, pt 814.19, a Class III device for which a PDP has been declared completed by FDA is considered to have an approved PMA.

The required elements of a PMA are detailed at Title 21 of the Code of Federal Regulations, part 814.20, and are substantial and technical. Further guidance can be found on the FDA website.[252]

Clinical studies in support of a PMA, PDP or a reclassification petition are subject to the investigational device exemption (IDE) regulations.[253]

Pre-market approval supplements are required for all changes that affect safety and effectiveness, unless such changes involve modifications to manufacturing procedures or methods of manufacture. These types of manufacturing changes require a 30-day notice, or, where FDA finds such notice inadequate, a 135-day PMA supplement.[254]

A Class III device that fails to meet PMA requirements cannot be marketed.

Any interested person is entitled to petition for administrative review of the CDRH's decision to approve a PMA application.

2. Humanitarian Device Exemption

The Humanitarian Device Exemption (HDE) approval is a niche process and was designed to balance protection of public health and safety with ethical standards, while encouraging the discovery and use of devices intended to benefit patients in the treatment or diagnosis of diseases or conditions that affect or are manifested in not more than 8,000 individuals in the US each year.

Obtaining marketing approval for a humanitarian device (HUD) involves two steps:[255]

(a) obtaining designation of the device as a HUD from the FDA's Office of Orphan Products Development; and
(b) submitting an HDE to the Office of Device Evaluation (ODE), CDRH, CBER or CDER, as applicable.

The process for obtaining an HDU is detailed under Title 21 of the Code of Federal Regulations, part 814, subpart H, and differs from the standard PMA in several ways.

d. Post-marketing Requirements including Vigilance

Post-marketing requirements for medical devices include such things as:

- tracking systems;
- reporting of device malfunctions, serious injuries or deaths; and
- registering the establishments where devices are produced or distributed.

Post-marketing requirements may also include any post-approval studies stipulated at the time the device was approved for market, as well as any studies required under section 522 of Title 21 of the Code of Federal Regulations. Manufacturers, importers and device user facilities are required to report certain device-related adverse events and product problems to the FDA in a specified electronic format.[256]

[252] At www.fda.gov/MedicalDevices/DeviceRegulationandGuidance/HowtoMarketYourDevice/PremarketSubmissions/PremarketApprovalPMA/ucm050289.htm.

[253] Title 21 of the Code of Federal Regulations, pts 812 and 813.

[254] ibid, pt 814.39.

[255] ibid, pt 814.100.

[256] The Medical Device Reporting Regulation, ibid, pt 803.

Post-marketing adverse event reports for medical devices come from two sources: mandatory reports from specified groups and spontaneous voluntary reports from the public.

1. Mandatory Reporting

Manufacturers must report to the FDA within 30 days of learning that any of their devices may have caused or contributed to a death or serious injury.[257] Manufacturers are also required to report to the FDA within five days of becoming aware that their device has malfunctioned and that remedial action is required to prevent an unreasonable risk of substantial harm to public health.

Importers who learn that one of their devices may have caused or contributed to a death or serious injury must report this fact to the FDA and the manufacturer within 30 days of becoming aware of it. The importer must report only to the manufacturer (or the FDA in circumstances where the manufacturer is unknown) when one of its imported devices has malfunctioned and if, were the malfunction to recur, it would be likely to cause or contribute to a death or serious injury.

A 'device user facility' is defined as a hospital, ambulatory surgical facility, nursing home, outpatient diagnostic facility or outpatient treatment facility that is not a physician's office. User facilities must report a suspected medical device-related death to both the FDA and the manufacturer. User facilities must report a medical device-related serious injury to the manufacturer, or to the FDA if the medical device manufacturer is unknown.

User facilities are also obliged to submit an annual report to the FDA on 1 January, detailing any device-related deaths and serious injuries in the preceding year.[258] Curiously, under the User Facility Reporting Requirements,[259] there is no obligation on device user facilities to report a device malfunction where the malfunction would likely cause or contribute to death or serious injury if the malfunction were to recur. A voluntary report can be made by the user facility to the FDA via MedWatch.

The specific statutory reporting requirements imposed on manufacturers, importers and user facilities are detailed in Table 2.11.

Table 2.11 Device vigilance reporting requirements on manufacturers, importers and user facilities

Reporter	What to report	To whom	Time limits
Manufacturer	30-day reports of deaths, serious injuries and malfunctions	FDA	Within 30 calendar days of becoming aware of an event
Manufacturer	5-day reports for an event designated by the FDA, or an event that requires remedial action to prevent an unreasonable risk of substantial harm to the public health	FDA	Within 5 work days of becoming aware of an event
Importers	Reports of deaths and serious injuries		Within 30 calendar days of becoming aware of an event

(continued)

[257] As defined ibid, pt 803.3.
[258] ibid, pt 803.33.
[259] ibid, pt 803.30.

Table 2.11 *(Continued)*

Reporter	What to report	To whom	Time limits
Importers	Reports of malfunctions	Manufacturer	Within 30 calendar days of becoming aware of an event
User Facility	Device-related death	FDA and Manufacturer	Within 10 work days of becoming aware
User Facility	Device-related serious injury	Manufacturer. FDA only if manufacturer unknown	Within 10 work days of becoming aware
User Facility	Annual summary of death and serious injury reports	FDA	1 January for the preceding year

2. Spontaneous Reporting

MedWatch is a web-based platform[260] that enables any member of the medical professional not in one of the preceding categories, or a member of the public (or his or her chosen representative, including his or her lawyer), to report directly to the FDA:

- a serious adverse event;
- a product quality problem;
- a product use error; or
- a therapeutic inequivalence/failure

that that person believes to be associated with the use of an FDA-regulated medical device. Reports are on specified forms, with different forms for consumers and healthcare professionals.

Healthcare professionals and consumers may also choose to report to the device manufacturer. If they chose that option, the manufacturer has to forward the information to the FDA in accordance with the regulations.[261]

e. MAUDE

All adverse reports that are reported under mandatory reporting are automatically added to the MAUDE database. MedWatch reports are added manually. This allows for analysis of adverse event reports.

1. Section 522 Studies

Where there are concerns about the safety of a medical device that is on the market, the FDA has powers under section 522 of the Federal Food, Drug, and Cosmetic Act[262] to order that manufacturers carry out post-marketing safety and efficacy studies. This only applies to

[260] Available at www.fda.gov/Safety/MedWatch/HowToReport/default.htm.
[261] Title 21 of the Code of Federal Regulations, pt 803.50.
[262] Food, Drug, and Cosmetic Act, 21 USC § 360l, s 522.

products that are on the market, so if a manufacturer decides to cease marketing the device in question, the safety study cannot be enforced.

2. Reclassification

Devices are not fixed within one class forever; they can be moved either up or down the classification schema as new safety data come to light. For example, in January 2016, transvaginal mesh for pelvic organ prolapse repair was reclassified as a Class III device,[263] which required PMA.[264] All new products required a PMA, and the manufacturers of products already on the market had 30 months from the notice date to submit a PMA.

3. Alerts, Healthcare Provider Letters and Recall

An alert can be issued by the FDA on the FDA website to provide the public and healthcare providers with information about the safe use of a device on the market. A 'Dear Healthcare Provider' letter can also be issued regarding the safe use of a medical device within a clinical setting.

The last-resort option, when there are serious concerns about a device's safety, is to recall the device from the market.[265] The vast majority of recalls have been voluntarily undertaken by manufacturers,[266] but the FDA does have the power to mandate a device's recall from the market if necessary.[267]

[263] Federal Register 21 CFR 884, effective date 5 January 2016, available at www.federalregister.gov/documents/2016/01/05/2015-33163/effective-date-of-requirement-for-premarket-approval-for-surgical-mesh-for-transvaginal-pelvic-organ.

[264] Federal Register 81 FR 363 effective date 5 January 2016, available at https://www.federalregister.gov/documents/2016/01/05/2015-33163/effective-date-of-requirement-for-premarket-approval-for-surgical-mesh-for-transvaginal-pelvic-organ

[265] See further at www.fda.gov/MedicalDevices/DeviceRegulationandGuidance/PostmarketRequirements/RecallsCorrectionsAndRemovals/default.htm.

[266] Title 21 of the Code of Federal Regulations, pt 807.

[267] ibid, pt 810.

3

Detailed Case Descriptions and Regulatory Histories

I. Teratogens and Foetal Damage

A. Thalidomide (alpha-phthalimido-glutarimide)

i. Description

Thalidomide, the progenitor of the thalidomide class of drugs, was first patented by Chemie Grünenthal in West Germany in May 1954.[1] It was used as sleeping tablet and sedative, and was marketed as being safer than other products available on the market, as it was non-habit forming and overdose caused prolonged sleep rather than death.

Later, compound preparations that combined thalidomide with other drugs were created and marketed. These compound formulations were indicated for a wide variety of conditions, including Asmaval for asthma, Tensival for hypertension and Valgraine for migraine. Marketing materials for these products stressed the safety of thalidomide based on the overdose profile.

Subsequent studies have found it has an immunomodulatory effect, and it is still used in some parts of the world for the treatment of certain cancers, such as myeloma, and some complications arising from leprosy.

The thalidomide molecule occurs as one of two optical isomers, an R(+) isomer and an S(-) isomer. Optical isomers are molecules made of the same components, but are mirror images of each other – the easiest analogy is to think of them as a left and a right hand – the same, but not superimposable. Standard chemical manufacturing usually produces an equal proportion of each of the two isomers, known as a racemix.

ii. Safety Issue

Thalidomide is a teratogen: maternal ingestion of thalidomide while pregnant could cause malformations of the foetus, foetal death and death shortly after birth. The exact pattern of damage depended upon the stage of gestation at which the drug was taken. The most obvious sign of thalidomide damage was phocomelia (literally seal-limbs) – a bilateral malformation

[1] Patent number DE00000107584 (process number 5 produces thalidomide), available at depatisnet.dpma.de/DepatisNet/depatisnet?action=pdf&docid=DE000001074584A and depatisnet.dpma.de/DepatisNet/depatisnet?action=bibdat&docid=DE000001074584B.

where the hands and/or feet are close to the trunk, with significant shortening or absence of the limbs. A number of associated malformations were also seen in children exposed *in utero*, including congenital heart disease, microphthalmos and coloborna, intestinal atresis, renal malformations, abnormal pinnae and facial nacvus. These conditions were often life-limiting – one-year survival data for children born with thalidomide-induced damage are stark, with reports that only 60% of affected children survived to one year old.[2]

The first animal model confirmation of thalidomide as a teratogen came from testing New Zealand White Rabbits in 1962.[3]

Animal testing after the thalidomide disaster showed that the S(-) isomer was the teratogen, and the R(+) isomer was the sedative. However, even if the drugs supplied had only contained the R(+) isomer, the disaster would not have been prevented. Even if just one isomer is present in the formulation, once the drug enters the body this single isomer form is converted into a racemix, with both forms present in equal proportions.

iii. *Marketing and Regulatory History*

Thalidomide was marketed over the counter as Contergan in Germany from 1957. In 1959, reports of irreversible peripheral neuritis (nerve damage to the hands and feet), usually in the elderly, were raised. These findings led to the package insert's being amended to include details of peripheral neuritis, and in May 1961 Chemie Gruüenthal applied to have the status of Contergan upgraded to a prescription-only medicine in Germany.

In the UK, thalidomide was available on prescription from April 1958, where it was known as Distaval. Later compound preparations, which combined it with other drugs, were marketed for a wide variety of indications.

Contergan was never licensed in the US. Since 1938,[4] the FDA had overseen a centralised pre-marketing pharmaceutical safety assessment procedure. The licensing decision for thalidomide was the responsibility of one FDA worker, Dr Frances Kelsey. She steadfastly delayed approving the licensing of Contergan because she was not prepared to accept that the widespread Europe usage provided adequate safety data. Because of this, thalidomide was only available in the USA as part of a clinical trial.

In the late 1950s and early 1960s, German doctors began to see children with gross limb malformations of a novel and unusual pattern. In October 1960, Kosenow and Pfeiffer presented two case studies at a paediatric meeting in Kassel;[5] at this point in time this patterns of defects was very unusual. In the following months a substantial increase in case numbers was seen. In 1961, Wiedemann described 13 affected infants who had been referred to him within 10 months.[6] The wide availability of thalidomide in Germany meant that many more cases were seen there.

[2] W Lenz, 'A Short History of Thalidomide Embryopathy' (1988) 38 *Teratology* 203.

[3] GF Somers, 'Thalidomide and Congenital Abnormalities' (1962) 279(7235) *Lancet* 912.

[4] The Food, Drug and Cosmetic Act 1938.

[5] W Kosenow and RA Pfeiffer (1961) 109 *Monatsschrift Kinderheilkunde* 227.

[6] HR Wiedemann, 'Indications of a Current Increase of Hypoplastic and Aplastic Deformities of the Extremities' (1961) 37 Die *Medizinische Welt* 1863.

Dr Widukind Lenz wrote to Chemie Grünenthal on 16 November 1961, suggesting that these deformities resulted from maternal ingestion of thalidomide during pregnancy.[7] Simultaneously, the Australian clinician Dr William McBride made the same suggestion to Distillers, the distributer of thalidomide in Australia and the UK.[8] These two independent reports prompted Chemie Grünenthal to withdraw thalidomide from the West German market on 27 November 1961. Distillers took action to curtail the availability of thalidomide in the UK: in December 1961,[9] thalidomide use was restricted to hospitals, where its administration could be closely supervised. In May 1962, the UK Government sent a letter to all doctors warning of the dangers of the use of thalidomide, and instructing that all stocks be destroyed.

Nine months after thalidomide was removed from the market there was a substantial drop in the numbers of affected births, confirming the causal relationship between thalidomide and congenital malformations. A very small number of affected births were seen in the UK after September 1962, but these could usually be attributed to the mothers' taking old medications containing thalidomide.

There were significant changes to the UK pharmaceutical regulatory structures in the wake of the thalidomide disaster. In 1967 a White Paper was brought forward, which went on to form the basis of the Medicines Act 1968. The Medicines Act formalised and centralised drug regulation, which had previously been covered in a piecemeal fashion by various statutes. The 1968 Act introduced licensing, with requirements that licence holders demonstrate the safety and efficacy of their products before they were placed on the market.[10] However, there was a transitional period between 1968 and 1971 where this requirement was voluntary. Between 1968 and 1971, the Committee for the Safety of Drugs (CSD) oversaw all applications. The CSD had no legal powers to prevent drugs from being placed on the market, but pharmaceutical firms and members of the Association of British Pharmaceutical Industries (ABPI) voluntarily undertook not to place drugs on the market unless they had CSD approval.

In 1971 new powers were obtained by the Licensing Authority, which was responsible for the regulation of drug safety, efficacy and quality. The Licensing Authority had the legal powers necessary to approve drugs and to remove drugs from the market. In order to assist the Licensing Authority, the Committee for the Safety of Medicines (CSM) was formed to take over the function of assessing pre-marketing applications, previously undertaken by the CSD.

[7] Lenz wrote to Grünenthal suggesting a link between thalidomide and birth defects on 16 November 1961. On 18 November 1961, Lenz raised the possibility that thalidomide was a teratogen at a conference: see RA Pfeiffer and W Kosenow 'On the problem of exogenous causes of severe malformations of the extremities' (1962) 104 *Munchener Medizinische Wochenschrift* 68. These concerns were more widely expressed in a letter to *The Lancet* published on 6 January 1962 (in vol 279(7219) 45; originally published as vol 1(7219)), available at ac.els-cdn.com/S014067366292665X/1-s2.0-S014067366292665X-main.pdf?_tid=23f49fbc-5b5a-11e3-a104-00000aab0f6c&acdnat=1385993026_86f7746f0ecf4bf36b3d1ebefb684a1f.

[8] Letter to *The Lancet* ((1961) 278(7216) 1358) (originally published as 2(7216)), available at ac.els-cdn.com/S0140673661909278/1-s2.0-S0140673661909278-main.pdf?_tid=e0f771d2-5b52-11e3-9d6f-00000aacb35e&acdnat=1385989907_95275eb90cb730827b30a0070cea9e39.

[9] DJ Hayman, Managing Director of Distillers Company (Biochemicals) Ltd, in a letter to *The Lancet*, published vol 279(7219) 45 (originally published as vol 1, issue 7219), available at ac.els-cdn.com/S014067366292665X/1-s2.0-S014067366292665X-main.pdf?_tid=23f49fbc-5b5a-11e3-a104-00000aab0f6c&acdnat=1385993026_86f7746f0ecf4bf36b3d1ebefb684a1f.

[10] The transitional period was to allow for consultation with the pharmaceutical industry and to allow time to adjust to the new regime.

As part of the new regulatory regime the 'yellow card system' of reporting adverse drug reactions (ADRs) was devised. Doctors and manufactures were mandated to report cases of suspected ADRs to the CSM using the yellow card system.

iv. Litigation

Litigation about thalidomide was undertaken in many different jurisdictions on various legal bases. The litigation in Germany and England and Wales is summarised here.

a. Germany

Litigation was undertaken in Germany to sue Chemie Grünenthal, but this trial has subsequently become mired in controversy.[11] Briefly, civil claims for compensation for damage caused by Thalidomide in Germany could not be brought until a criminal trial of Chemie Grünenthal employees had taken place. The trial commenced in Alsdorf on 27 May 1968. It never ran to a full legal conclusion; the trial was closed down on 18 December 1970. The nine men on trial were released, the closing statements of the judge indicating that this was done with the explicit consent of the prosecution. Shortly afterwards a law was passed providing Chemie Grünenthal with immunity from prosecution. The recent discovery of various documents has raised suspicions that the criminal trial was halted in a way that was procedurally highly irregular at best and illegal at worst. Chemie Grünenthal has consistently denied any liability, but has contributed to a voluntary scheme. The voluntary scheme, the Contergan Foundation, received around 10% of the sums claimed by the families in their civil proceedings from Chemie Grünenthal at the time of the settlement. Chemie Grünenthal has paid a very low percentage of the compensation awarded to Contergan victims, the German Government funding most of the compensation. There has been considerable criticism both of the level of compensation paid to Contergan victims and of Chemie Grünenthal's response to the scandal.

b. England and Wales

The children affected by thalidomide sued the UK distributor Distillers in negligence for personal injuries. There was no precedent for this litigation. There had not been a collective action for children, nor a claim where the cause of action was for damages accrued before birth. Some contemporaneous commentators questioned whether a claim could be brought in negligence for cause of action accrued before birth.

The litigation was settled in several waves, without progressing to a full trial. The eventual outcome of the litigation, establishment of the Thalidomide Trust, was groundbreaking, as it was one of the first structured settlements, and the first settlement established solely for children.

[11] For a more detailed analysis of the Contergan trial, see M Johnson, RG Stokes and T Arndt, *The Thalidomide Catastrophe: How it happened, who was responsible, and why the search for justice continues after more than six decades. Onwards and Upwards* (N Lenhard-Schramm, 2018) [*Das Land Nordrhein-Westfalen und der Contergan-Skandal – Gesundheitsaufsicht und Strafjustiz in end lagen sechziger Jahren* (Vandenhoeck & Ruprecht, 2016) (in German)]; or H Evans, 'Thalidomide: How men who blighted lives of thousands evaded justice' *Guardian* (14 November 2014).

1. The 1968 Settlement

This initial settlement[12] was for 65 children and their parents who had existing individual cases filed against Distillers. They were awarded settlements that varied from £5,000 to £45,000. The quantum of the awards was 40% of the value of their successful claims, with 33% of the award value added on to cover inflation. Three representative cases were used to assess quantum, featuring one child with severe impairment (DJ) and two other children with mid-range injuries. Settlements made for children required the approval of the High Court, which was obtained on 19 February 1968.[13]

This settlement had been recommended to the parents by Desmond Ackner QC, the barrister acting for the children, as he was concerned that taking the case to court could result in obtaining absolutely nothing, as negligence might not be proved. Questions were raised at the time as to whether it was sufficient.

2. The 1973 Settlement and Establishment of the Thalidomide Trust

The second settlement for the remaining 389 children occurred five years later in 1973. Since the first settlement, Distillers had maintained that it was aiming to reach a settlement, but an offer the families were prepared to accept was slow to materialise. A high-profile campaign for a just settlement for all the affected children (aided by the *Sunday Times* from 1972 onwards) maintained the pressure on Distillers, and in 1973 a settlement was reached.

3. Collective Redress – The Thalidomide Children's Trust

The 1973 offer of settlement contained both individual awards and a collective settlement, which became the Thalidomide Children's Trust.[14] Payments are calculated annually: an assessment is made of the amount the Trust has available for beneficiaries and the number of surviving beneficiaries. Every beneficiary's injuries are known and the severity of each injury is ranked according to the 1968 personal injury tariffs. Payments are tiered according to the severity of injury.

The original funding of the Trust, of £14,000,000, came from seven £2,000,000 contributions made by Distillers: the initial payment was made upon acceptance of the settlement offer, with a further six made at annual intervals. When the settlement was made it was thought that payments to the thalidomiders could be made solely from the interest. By the mid-1990s it became clear that this was not the case, and the Deed of Trust was varied to allow the trustees to make payments from the capital. Although there was no legal imperative to do so, the funding was continued by Guinness Plc (who had purchased Distillers), providing an additional £37.5 million, and then by Diageo (who had purchased Guinness Plc), which agreed to make contributions to fund the Trust until 2022.

[12] Reached on 19 February 1968.

[13] *S and Another v Distillers Company (Biochemicals) Ltd J* and *Another v Same* [1970] 1 WLR 114, [1969] 3 All ER 1412, (1969) 113 SJ 672, *The Times* (31 July 1969).

[14] The Thalidomide Children's Trust is a charitable trust fund established on 10 August 1973 under court order. It holds funds for the benefit of individuals affected by thalidomide exposure *in utero*. Eligibility is determined by the trustees. To qualify, individuals must meet the Trust's eligibility criteria for residence and demonstrate, to the satisfaction of the trustees, that the congenital disability sustained was caused by maternal ingestion of thalidomide while pregnant. This was never a fixed class: initially it included all of the 454 children under the 1963 settlement and the 1973 settlement, but other eligible individuals have been added since it was created. New applications are still being made and considered 45 years on.

The UK Government did not wish to benefit from the thalidomide tragedy, so various funds and grants have been given to ensure that the Trust remains tax neutral. In addition, the UK Government provides millions in health grants, required because thalidomiders face additional health needs as they age, which the Trust distributes.

The Thalidomide Trust that resulted from the 1973 settlement has been ground-breaking in many ways. It is arguable that it has had a more positive impact on the beneficiaries than individual litigation settlements would have done. The beneficiaries have a forum, it allowed greater campaigning in an age before social media, and it provided a hub of expertise and understanding. Potentially the most important feature is the collective bargaining position, which has provided greater leverage when asking for tax breaks, health grants and, most importantly, increased payments to the Trust.

Although a determination on liability for thalidomide damage was not been made by the UK courts, it is pertinent to consider what might have been. If the England and Wales Thalidomide litigation had concluded with liability being either admitted or proved, the settlements made in 1968 and 1973 would have constituted individual full and final settlements. As the predictions were that the thalidomiders would have much shorter life expectancies than they have enjoyed, this would potentially have been problematic for them. Any increase would have been entirely discretionary and applicable to only the individual concerned, and more than likely confidential.

v. Conclusion

The safety signal from thalidomide came from observations by the international medical community, with a voluntary product withdrawal following. The regulatory response to thalidomide was substantial: the scandal led to a hugely improved testing and regulatory regime for pharmaceuticals in many jurisdictions. Interestingly, in both Germany and in England and Wales there have been no formal findings of legal liability for the birth defects attributable to thalidomide. All the resulting regulatory changes have been a response to the situation, rather than to a court judgment. These changes preceded, rather than followed, the Thalidomide litigation. In the UK the way was paved for the formalisation of the regulation of pharmaceuticals, in the shape of the Medicines Act 1968, including the development of the yellow card ADR reporting system.

B. Hormonal Pregnancy Tests – Including Primodos

i. Description

Oral administration of a product containing a combination of the sex hormones estrogen and progestogen was recognised in the mid-1950s as an indicator of pregnancy and/or treatment of short duration secondary amenhorrea (missed periods). Primodos, the most commonly used formulation, contained the progestogen norethisterone acetate (10mg per tablet) and the synthetic estrogen ethinylestradiol (0.02mg per tablet). One tablet was taken per day on two consecutive days. If the woman was not pregnant, a withdrawal bleed followed up to a few days later. In pregnant women there was no withdrawal bleed because the pregnancy naturally increased circulating level of hormones, which meant that the increase and decrease in the hormone level caused by the administration of Primodos were small in comparison and so did not trigger a withdrawal bleed.[15] The reliability of this method was comparable to existing biological tests, but it was much quicker.[16] Primodos was, therefore, widely prescribed as a pregnancy test.[17]

ii. Safety Issue

For many years doctors prescribed Primodos based on the belief that it was harmless. This was based on the knowledge that a percentage of pregnancies result in miscarriage, as a natural mechanism of expelling fertilised eggs that carry risks of malformations. It was widely thought that Primodos did not raise hormone levels significantly, in comparison to levels prevailing in the pregnant women.

In 1967, Dr Isabel Gal, of the Queen Mary's Hospital for Children at Carshalton, reported the examination of the children of 100 women who had taken the drug as a pregnancy test, and the children of 100 women who had not. She suggested that the statistics indicated that the children of the women who had taken the drug were more likely to have some congenital malformations than the children of those who had not.[18] This sparked much controversy and research work in many countries investigating Dr Gal's studies. Over the following years various epidemiological studies were published, some of which found a statistical association between ingestion of sex hormones and a higher incidence of congenital malformations and some of which did not.

In the intervening 50 years since the initial findings by Dr Gal, the controversy over the link between hormonal pregnancy tests and birth defects and miscarriages has remained. In October 2017 the Report of the Commission on Human Medicines Expert Working Group on Hormone Pregnancy Tests[19] reviewed the available evidence and found that there was, on balance, insufficient evidence to support a causal association between the use of

[15] (1958) 108 *The Practitioner* 1080.

[16] GD Matthew, 'Simple Clinical Test for the Diagnosis of Early Pregnancy' (1956) 2 *British Medical Journal* 979.

[17] Primodos brochure, 'For the early diagnosis of pregnancy and treatment of amenorrhoea' (Schering AG Berlin, Germany, 1967).

[18] I Gal, B Kirman and I Stern, 'Hormonal Pregnancy Tests and Congenital Malformation' (1967) 216 *Nature* 83.

[19] Available at www.gov.uk/government/publications/report-of-the-commission-on-human-medicines-expert-working-group-on-hormone-pregnancy-tests.

hormone pregnancy tests, such as Primodos, by the mother during early pregnancy and congenital anomalies in the child. The Report also concluded that there was no evidence that the administration of hormones in the doses present in Primodos was linked to an increased risk of miscarriage. This Report was quickly dismissed as flawed by campaigners from the Association for Children Damaged by Hormone Pregnancy Tests.[20]

iii. Marketing and Regulatory History

The German company Schering, which has long been known for its specialisation in hormonal products, first marketed hormonal pregnancy tests, including Primodos, in the UK and elsewhere in Europe in the 1950s. Primodos was granted a product licence of right in the UK in the early 1970s. Other manufacturers, such as Roussel, marketed similar products.

Table 3.1 Hormone pregnancy test products available in the UK[21]

Estrogen/progestogen combination	Products	Dates available in UK
Ethinylestradiol and ethisterone	Amenorone Amenorone Forte Disecron Menstrogen Orasecron Paralut tablets Paralut Forte tablets Pregornot	1950 to 1977 Until 1977** Pre-1952* to 1969 1951 to 1975 1950 to 1975 NA NA 1973
Ethinylestradiol and norethisterone acetate	Norlestrin Norlutin-A Primodos oral	1961 to 1975 1961 to 1975 1958 to 1978
Ethinylestradiol and dimethisterone	Secrodyl	1961 to 1975
Estradiol benzoate and progesterone	Paralut injection Paralut Forte injection Primodos injectable	NA NA NA
Norethisterone	Norone	1965 to 1969

NA information not available
* exact date not known
** withdrawal date only known

On 17 February 1970, the McGregor Committee wrote to all manufacturers suggesting the deletion of the indication pregnancy testing from the hormone preparations previously recommended for this use.[22] The McGregor Committee, a Standing Joint Committee on

[20] Available at www.theguardian.com/society/2017/nov/15/1960s-hormone-pregnancy-test-did-not-cause-birth-defects-review-finds.

[21] Table taken from the 2017 CHM Report of the Expert Working Group on Hormone Pregnancy Tests, available at www.gov.uk/government/publications/report-of-the-commission-on-human-medicines-expert-working-group-on-hormone-pregnancy-tests.

[22] PropList (February 1970), 'Products Classified by the Standing Joint Committee on the Classification of Proprietary Preparations'.

the Classification of Proprietary Preparations, functioned between 1967 and 1970 to help doctors decide which preparations should be used in treatment and to identify those preparations for which prescriptions needed special justification. It sent a regular booklet to prescribers, called the Proplist. In 1970, the functions of the Committee were taken over by the Medicines Commission (formed under the Medicines Act 1968) to advise the UK Minister of Health, and the Committee was disbanded.

The manufacturers, including Schering, accepted this suggestion, and in the UK the product information for Primodos was amended so that its only indication was now the treatment of secondary amenorrhoea of short duration, not due to pregnancy. On this basis the McGregor Committee supported the continued use of the product. Evidence suggests such products were being used as pregnancy tests after 1970.

In early 1975, Dr Inman of the CSM made known the preliminary results of an epidemiological study of which he had been an author,[23] and which he considered supported a possible link between the use of hormone pregnancy tests and congenital abnormalities. In June 1975, the CSM issued a warning to doctors about this possible link.[24] The CSM's warning stated:

> Hormonal Pregnancy Tests: A possible association with congenital abnormalities … On the present evidence the committee believe that it is possible that the use of these preparations for the diagnosis of pregnancy could on occasion lead to abnormalities in the fetus. There are other means of diagnosing pregnancy which do not require the administration of hormones, and the committee consider that in view of this possible hazard this method should not now normally be used.

As a result Schering amended its product information for Primodos to make pregnancy a contraindication. It is of interest that when Schering inserted a contraindication of pregnancy in the entry for the product in MIMS (the Monthly Index of Medical Specialities), the editors of that prescribing guide felt it was unnecessary in view of the fact that the indication itself excluded use in pregnancy.[25] However, Schering's position ultimately prevailed.

A further warning notice was issued by the CSM in November 1977 that the product had either been removed from the market or contraindicated for use in pregnant women,[26] and the product was withdrawn in 1978.

The product was discontinued on commercial grounds in 1978.

[23] Full results were published later in G Greenberg, WHW Inman, JAC Weatherall, AM Adelstein and JC Haskey, 'Maternal drug histories and congenital abnormalities' (1977) 2 *British Medical Journal* 853.

[24] Committee on Safety of Medicines, Adverse Reaction Series no 13, June 1975, 'Hormonal Pregnancy Tests: a possible association with congenital abnormalities', available at data.parliament.uk/DepositedPapers/files/DEP2010-1878/DEP2010-1878.pdf.

[25] Monthly Index of Medical Specialities (Haymarket Publishing Ltd, Medical Division (publisher Alfred E Morgan)) and the MIMS Annual Compendium, ed EN Pullom.

[26] Committee on Safety of Medicines, Adverse Reaction Series no 13, June 1975, 'Hormonal Pregnancy Tests: a possible association with congenital abnormalities' and Committee on Safety of Medicines, Adverse Reaction Series no 16, November 1977, 'Hormonal Pregnancy Tests and Congenital Abnormalities: a Further Statement'.

iv. Litigation

In 1977, following the regulatory initiatives taken by the CSM in 1975, various claims were made against Schering and other companies manufacturing hormone pregnancy tests. However, in the event only claims in respect of Primodos (which was the market leader) were actively pursued. A group action was begun that ran until 1982 when, after an exchange of expert reports on issues of causation, the claimants' own counsel advised the legal aid authorities that the cases should be discontinued. The claimants obtained the permission of the court to discontinue the claims, saying that in the light of the expert evidence presented in the case there was no reasonable prospect of establishing as probable the existence of a causal association between Primodos and congenital malformations.[27]

v. Conclusion

The first suggestion of a safety issue came from a doctor in 1967, and there followed several years of medical research in order to test its validity. The regulatory response to the potential safety signal preceded litigation. The regulatory response was to restrict the uses of the product on the basis of the suggestion of the possibility of a link between use of the product and an increased incidence of malformations, rather than on proof of causation between the product and the safety issue. The effectiveness of the initial regulatory action is questionable. Litigation arose out of a regulatory response in 1975, but was discontinued due to lack of evidence of causation. In the 50 years since the question of a safety issue was raised, no causative link between the product and the alleged safety issue has been satisfactorily proved. The collapse of the Primodos litigation demonstrates that a different, and lower, evidential threshold was needed to trigger regulatory action than was required to prove causation in law.

[27] *'D' and others v Schering Chemicals Ltd and 'R' and another v Schering Chemicals Ltd*, Judgment of Mr Justice Bingham (QBD, 2 July 1982).

C. Diethylstilboestrol (DES)

i. Description

Diethylstilbestrol (DES) is a synthetic form of the female hormone estrogen. It was sometimes known as 'stilboestrol', before 'diethylstilbestrol' was adopted as the British approved name (and branded as Apstil and Tampovagan).

It has been indicated for a variety of conditions, the most contentious being its (ineffective) use in pregnant women with the aim of preventing miscarriage, premature labour and related complications of pregnancy, which occurred between 1940 and 1971.[28]

ii. Safety Issue

In 1971, researchers linked pre-natal (before birth) DES exposure in a small group of women to a type of cancer of the cervix and vagina called clear cell adenocarcinoma, which was also found in their daughters.[29] Daughters exposed to DES also showed higher rates of reproductive tract abnormalities, including both epithelial and structural changes. Subsequent studies have found that *in utero* exposure to DES can impact on sons too, with higher rates of cyrpotorchidism (absence of one or both testicles from the scrotum) found in DES sons.[30]

iii. Marketing and Regulatory History

DES was the first synthetic estrogen to be synthesised by a team led by Sir Charles Dodds in Britain in 1938. At that time, as a matter of policy, research funded by the Medical Research Council was not patented, as it was felt that government-funded research should be freely available for the public benefit. Therefore, the product had no patent restrictions and was made and marketed by a number of different companies in various countries.

DES was approved by the US FDA for marketing by several manufacturers: for example, on 19 September 1941 it was indicated for gonorrheal vaginitis (this indication was dropped when antibiotic penicillin became available for widespread use in 1943), atrophic vaginitis, menopausal symptoms and postpartum lactation suppression to prevent breast engorgement.[31] Indications were quickly extended to preventing miscarriages and premature labour. The FDA originally considered DES effective and safe for both the pregnant woman and the developing baby. It was marketed for this purpose from about 1940 to 1970. No pre-marketing controlled studies were ever conducted to determine the effectiveness or safety of DES for use during pregnancy.[32] The supposed efficacy of DES in

[28] Professional and Public Relations Committee of the DESAD (Diethylstilbestrol and Adenosis) Project of the Division of Cancer Control and Rehabilitation, 'Exposure in utero to diethylstilbestrol and related synthetic hormones. Association with vaginal and cervical cancers and other abnormalities' (1976) 236(10) *Journal of the American Medical Association* 1109.

[29] AL Herbst, H Ulfelder and DC Poskanzer, 'Adenocarcinoma of the vagina. Association of maternal stilbestrol therapy with tumor appearance in young women' (1971) 284(15) *New England Journal of Medicine* 878.

[30] HE Virtanen and A Adamsson, 'Cryptorchidism and endocrine disrupting chemicals' (2012) 355(2) *Molecular and Cellular Endocrinology* 208, doi:10.1016/j.mce.2011.11.015.

[31] R Meyers, *D.E.S.: The Bitter Pill* (Putnam, 1983).

[32] *Annual Report 2010* (Society of Apothecaries of London, 2011).

preventing miscarriage and the dosing schedule were largely based on the flawed work of Olive Watkins Smith and her husband George Van Siclen Smith. Their studies were neither appropriately controlled nor blinded.[33] Despite this, DES was aggressively marketed and routinely prescribed. Sales in the US peaked in 1953. Usage for this indication declined after a double-blinded study in the 1953 demonstrated that DES was not effective in preventing miscarriage.[34] By the late 1960s, the prevailing wisdom in obstetrics agreed that it was ineffective in that regard.[35] Despite the absence of evidence supporting the use of DES to prevent adverse pregnancy outcomes, however, it continued to be given to pregnant women through the 1960s, albeit at lower frequency than previously.

Table 3.2[36] shows the availability and estimated DES prescriptions (where known) for pregnancy complications by country. DES was clearly most heavily used in the USA. Usage in Europe varied considerably by country. In Europe, UCB[37] and Novartis were the market leaders. The Netherlands, which had a far higher per capita rate of prescribing DES in pregnancy than other European nations (see Table 3.2) had around a dozen companies selling the product. In the UK, DES usage was relatively light. Various factors could explain this – for example, cultural factors surrounding NHS prescribing. While DES was never actually authorised for use in pre-menopausal women in the UK, it should be remembered that stilboestrol tablets were on the UK market before the licensing system began in the early 1970s.

Table 3.2 Availability and estimated DES prescriptions to prevent miscarriage by country

Country	**Years prescribed to prevent miscarriage**	**Estimated numbers of pregnancies**	**Source**[38]
Belgium	1950–65		Direcks et al, 1991
Czechoslovakia	1958–76	63 000	Direcks et al, 1991
France	1950–77	200 000 60 000–240 000	Pons et al, 1988 Direcks et al, 1991
Germany	?–1977	200 000	Direcks et al, 1991
Ireland	1950–76		Wingfield, 1992

(continued)

[33] O Watkins Smith, 'Diethylstilbestrol in the Prevention and Treatment of Complications of Pregnancy' (1948) 56 *American Journal of Obstetrics and Gynecology* 821.

[34] WJ Dieckmann, ME Davis, LM Rynkiewicz and RE Pottinger, 'Does the administration of diethylstilbestrol during pregnancy have therapeutic value?' (1953) 66(5) *American Journal of Obstetrics and Gynecology* 1062, doi:10.1016/S0002-9378(16)38617-3.

[35] DB Dutton, *Worse than the disease: pitfalls of medical progress* (Cambridge University Press, 1988); and RJ Apfel and SM Fisher, *To do no harm: DES and the dilemmas of modern medicine* (Yale University Press, 1984).

[36] Taken from D Ibarreta and SH Swan, 'The DES story: long-term consequences of prenatal exposure' in *Late lessons from early warnings: the precautionary principle 1896–2000*, European Environment Agency, Report No 22/2001 (9 January 2002), available at www.eea.europa.eu/publications/environmental_issue_report_2001_22.

[37] Union Chemique Belge, a biopharmaceutical manufacturer based in Brussels, Belgium.

[38] A Direcks, S Figueroa, B Mintzes, and D Banta, Report from DES Action the Netherlands for the European Commission Programme Europe Against Cancer (DES Action the Netherlands, Utrecht, 1991) 69; F Garcia-Alonso, E Rodriguez-Pinilla and ML Martinez-Frias 1988, 'The use of diethylstilbestrol in Spain' (1988) 91(11) *Medicina Clinica* 436; JM Goldberg and T Falcone, 'Effect of diethylstilbestrol on reproductive function' (1999) 72(1) *Fertility and Sterility* 1; AG Hanselaar, ND Van Leusen, PC De Wilde and GP Vooijs, 'Clear cell adenocarcinoma of the vagina and cervix. A report of the Central Netherlands Registry with emphasis on early detection and prognosis' (1991) 67(7) *Cancer* 1971; LJ Kinlen, MA Badaracco, J Moffett and MP Vessey, 'A survey of the use of oestrogens during pregnancy in the United Kingdom and of the genito-urinary cancer mortality and incidence

Table 3.2 *(Continued)*

Country	Years prescribed to prevent miscarriage	Estimated numbers of pregnancies	Source
Italy	– 1960 (?)		Direcks et al, 1991
Netherlands	1947–75	189 000–378 000	Hanselaar et al, 1991
Norway	1948–72		Palmlund et al, 1993
Portugal	1960–70		Direcks et al, 1991
Spain	1953–77 (1983?)	25 000	Garcia-Alonso et al, 1988
United Kingdom	1940–71 (1973?)	7 000–8 000	Kinlen et al, 1974
United States	1943–71	2–6 million	Goldberg and Falcone, 1999

The product has been used for a variety of other indications. One of its original uses was as a treatment for prostate cancer; it had been used for this condition since 1941.[39] It is still used in the UK for this indication.[40]

From the 1950s through to the early 1970s, DES was also prescribed to tall prepubescent girls to limit their height. It acted by starting puberty, which triggered the closing of the growth plates in the bones, thus stopping growth. Despite DES being a known carcinogen, doctors continued to prescribe it for 'excess height'.[41]

In 1960 a new indication was added – the treatment of advanced breast cancer in postmenopausal women.[42] DES remained the first-line hormonal treatment option until it was replace by tamoxifen, a selective estrogen receptor modulator with efficacy similar to DES but with fewer side-effects,[43] which the FDA approved in 1977.

In 1970 a cluster of hitherto rare vaginal clear cell adenocarcinoma cases in girls and young women (ages 14 to 22) was reported: prior to these cases, this type of cancer had never been reported in women of this age.[44] In April 1971 these cases were linked to *in utero*

rates in young people in England and Wales' (1974) 81(11) *Journal of Obstetrics and Gynaecology of the British Commonwealth* 849; I Palmlund, R Apfel, S Buitendijk, A Cabau and JG Forsberg, 'Effects of diethylstilbestrol (DES) medication during pregnancy: Report from a symposium at the 10th international congress of ISPOG' (1993) 14(1) *J Psychosom Obstet Gynaecol* 71; JC Pons, J Goujard, C Derbanne and M Tournaire, 'Outcome of pregnancy in patients exposed in utero to diethylstilbestrol. Survey by the National College of French Gynecologists and Obstetricians' (1988) 17(3) *Journal de Gynecologie Obstetrique et Biologie de la Reproduction, Paris* 307; M Wingfield, VS Donnelly, P Kelehan, JM Stronge, J Murph, and P Boylan, 'DES clinic – the first six months' (1992) 85(2) *Irish Medical Journal* 56.

[39] C Huggins, 'Endocrine Control of Prostatic Cancer' (1943) 97(2529) *Science* 541; C Huggins, 'The Treatment of Cancer of the Prostate: The 1943 Address in Surgery before the Royal College of Physicians and Surgeons of Canada' (1944) 50(4) *Journal of the Canadian Medical Association* 301.

[40] UK licence number PL 44710/0016, www.mhra.gov.uk/home/groups/par/documents/websiteresources/con816085.pdf.

[41] S Cohen and C Cosgrove, *Normal at Any Cost: Tall Girls, Short Boys and the Medical Industry's Quest to Manipulate Height* (Jeremy P Tarcher/Penguin, 2009).

[42] Council on Drugs, 'Androgens and estrogens in the treatment of disseminated mammary carcinoma: retrospective study of nine hundred forty-four patients' (1960) 172(12) *Journal of the American Medical Association* 1271.

[43] JN Ingle et al, 'Randomized clinical trial of diethylstilbestrol versus tamoxifen in postmenopausal women with advanced breast cancer' (1981) 304(1) *New England Journal of Medicine* 16.

[44] AL Herbst and RE Scully, 'Adenocarcinoma of the vagina in adolescence. A report of 7 cases including 6 clear-cell carcinomas (so-called mesonephromas)' (1970) 25(4) *Cancer* 745.

DES exposure: an article by Herbst et al in the *New England Journal of Medicine* gave the first indications of dangers of pre-natal exposure to DES.[45] This was corroborated later that year by a second study.[46] The FDA responded in November 1971 by sending out an *FDA Drug Bulletin* to all US physicians advising against the use of DES in pregnant women. The FDA added pregnancy as a contraindication for DES use and removed prevention of miscarriage as an indication for its use.

In the UK at this time there were no known cases of vaginal adenocarcinoma resulting from mothers' use of DES during pregnancy. However, in 1973 the CSM wrote a 'Dear Doctor' letter to doctors to inform them about the research into DES (known as stilboestrol in the UK at that time) in pregnant and pre-menopausal women.[47]

In the early 1970s, DES was being used off-label by many university health services as a post-coital contraceptive: this usage was primarily driven by an influential study in 1971 published in the *Journal of the American Medical Association*.[48] In 1973, it was reported that an *FDA Drug Bulletin* that was sent to all US physicians and pharmacists said that the FDA had approved a change in labelling to restrict off-label post-coital contraceptive use of DES to emergency situations such as rape and incest.[49] However, in 1975 the FDA said that DES had never been approved as a post-coital contraceptive, but that an indication for post-coital contraception in emergency situations, such as rape or incest, would be approved, subject to specific labelling and packaging requirements.[50]

In February 1975, to discourage off-label use of DES as a post-coital contraceptive, the FDA withdrew 25 mg and 100 mg tablets of DES and amended the package insert of lower doses (5 mg and lower) of DES to state 'THIS DRUG PRODUCT SHOULD NOT BE USED AS A POST-COITAL CONTRACEPTIVE'.[51] In the 1980s, off-label use of DES as a post-coital contraceptive was superseded by newer contraceptives.[52]

The principal European manufacturer, UCB, applied to the French regulatory agency in 1976 to change the labelling, and it took 14 months for the agency to consider the application and respond. In 1977, UCB voluntarily withdrew the product in France.

In 1978, approval for the use of DES for postpartum lactation suppression to prevent breast engorgement was withdrawn by the FDA.[53]

By the 1990s, the treatment of advanced cancers was the only remaining FDA approved indication for DES in the US: respectively, advanced prostate cancer in men and advanced breast cancer in post-menopausal women.

[45] Herbst et al, n 30.

[46] P Greenwald, JJ Barlow, PC Nasca and WS Burnett, 'Vaginal cancer after maternal treatment with synthetic estrogens' (1971) 285(7) *New England Journal of Medicine* 390.

[47] Committee on Safety of Medicines (May 1973), Ref CSM/AR/18C – 'Dear Doctor' letter.

[48] LK Kuchera, 'Postcoital contraception with diethylstilbestrol' (1971) 218 (4) *Journal of the American Medical Association* 562.

[49] (1973) 224(12) *Journal of the American Medical Association* 1581, available at jamanetwork.com/journals/jama/issue/224/12.

[50] FDA, 'Diethylstilbestrol as postcoital oral contraceptive; patient labeling' (1975) 40(25) *Federal Register* 5451.

[51] FDA, 'Certain estrogens for oral use. Notice of withdrawal of approval of new drug applications' (1975) 40(25) *Federal Register* 5384; and FDA, 'Estrogens for oral or parenteral use. Drugs for human use; drug efficacy study; amended notice' (1975) 40(39) *Federal Register* 8242.

[52] RA Hatcher et al, *Contraceptive Technology 1982–1983* (Irvington Publishers, 1982) 152–57.

[53] FDA, 'Estrogens for postpartum breast engorgement' (1978) 43(206) *Federal Register* 49564.

On 30 September 2000, the FDA withdrew the licence for DES for human use[54] at the request of the licence holders, as DES was no longer being marketed in the US.

DES is hardly unique in being a carcinogen, but it is the only confirmed transplacental carcinogen in humans. Over the last half century a consistent finding has been a substantial (approximate 40-fold) increased risk of vaginal/cervical clear cell adenocarcinoma in women who were exposed to DES *in utero*. Figure 3.1, taken from Dolores Ibarreta and Shanna H Swan's chapter, 'The DES story: long-term consequences of prenatal exposure' in EEA Report No 22/2001,[55] illustrates US market sales of 25 mg DES tablets and cases of clear cell cancer. While this is a substantially increased risk, vaginal clear cell adenocarcinoma fortunately remain a relatively rare cancer even in DES-exposed daughters; fewer than 0.1% of DES-exposed daughters go on to develop this cancer.[56] However, these women may also have an increased risk of moderate/severe cervical squamous cell dysplasia and of developing and of dying from breast cancer.[57] Research is ongoing to investigate whether epigenetic changes are passed to DES grandchildren.[58]

Figure 3.1 USA market sales of 25 mg of DES and cases of clear cell cancers

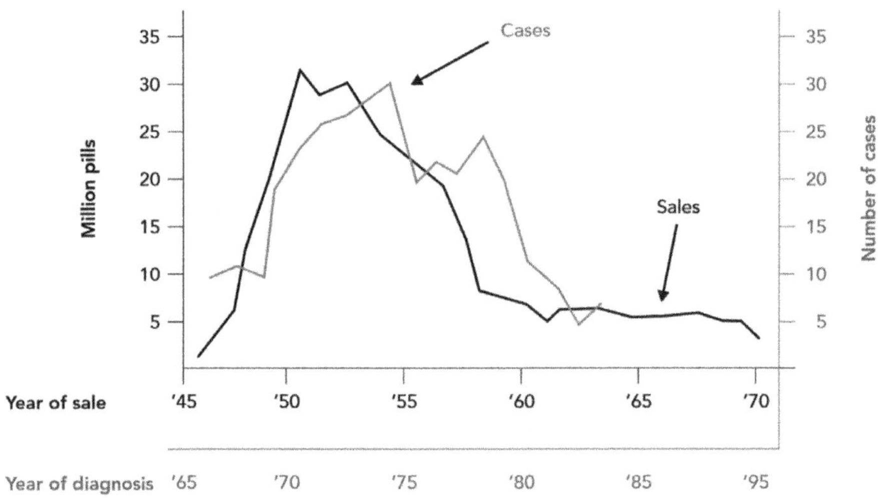

As well as being a carcinogen, in 1995 DES was confirmed as a teratogen – a substance that can cause malformations in both daughters and sons who were exposed *in utero*.[59] Daughters exposed to DES are at an increased risk of several reproductive tract abnormalities,

[54] See NDA 004014 at www.accessdata.fda.gov/scripts/cder/daf/index.cfm?event=overview.process&ApplNo=004041.

[55] Ibarreta and Swan, n 37, Figure 8.1. (Data source: S Melnick, P Cole, D Anderson and A Herbst, 'Rates and risks of diethylstilbestrol-related clear-cell adenocarcinoma of the vagina and cervix: An update' (1987) 316(9) *New England Journal of Medicine* 514; and Market Share Litigation Exhibit, Graph (EEA, 2001).)

[56] Melnick et al, n 55.

[57] R Mittendorf, 'Teratogen update: carcinogenesis and teratogenesis associated with exposure to diethylstilbestrol (DES) in utero' (1995) 51(6) *Teratology* 435.

[58] See at www.desfollowupstudy.org/index.asp.

[59] Mittendorf, n 57.

such as vaginal epithelial changes, a larger cervical transformational zone (the most common place in the cervix for abnormal cells to develop), and other structural changes to the cervix and uterus. These women may also be at an increased risk of infertility and adverse pregnancy outcomes. Sons exposed to DES *in utero* also have reproductive organ issues, including higher incidences of testicular abnormalities.

The last remaining US manufacturer of DES, Eli Lilly, stopped making and marketing it in 1997, and it was finally withdrawn by the FDA in 2000. Usage continues in other countries for non-pregnancy indications, with increased warnings.

The number of persons exposed to DES during pregnancy or *in utero* during 1940–71 is unknown but may be as high as 6 million in the US (see Table 3.2). Usage in Europe varied by country, but at least half a million pregnancies are thought to have been exposed to DES. Although the FDA contraindicated DES for use during pregnancy in 1971, Table 3.2 shows that other countries were nowhere near as prompt to act. This raises questions about the effectiveness of the sharing of information between countries and the relative prioritisations of patient safety and economic interests during the second half of the twentieth century.

iv. Litigation

In the 1970s, the negative publicity surrounding the discovery of DES's long-term effects resulted in a huge wave of lawsuits in the US against its manufacturers. There was litigation against the principal manufacturer, Bayer, which Bayer won. Each claimant faced the considerable difficulty of establishing which manufacturer had produced the DES her mother had ingested. Medical records tended to record the drug and dose, but not the specific manufacturer. This was compounded by the fact that the DES had been prescribed many years earlier to the claimants' mothers. In order to found liability, the claimant had to prove that her injuries were caused by the defendant's product. In the majority of DES cases this evidential burden was too high for claimants to overcome; although they knew that their mothers had been given DES many years beforehand, they could seldom establish exactly which manufacturer had produced the specific product taken.

The manifest unfairness of this culminated in a landmark 1980 decision of the Supreme Court of California, in *Sindell v Abbott Laboratories*. Sindell listed 11 of the largest DES manufacturers as defendants and claimed that her mother's ingestion of DES caused her bladder, vaginal, cervical and breast cancers. Her case had previously been dismissed at the County and Appeal Court level, as she could not demonstrate which manufacturer had produced the drug her mother took. The Supreme Court of California adopted a different approach to liability and imposed a rebuttable presumption of market share liability upon any DES manufacturer, not merely the five of the original 11 listed in the claim. Manufacturers of DES were liable to pay a share of the damage, which was directly proportional to their share of the market at the time the drug was consumed by the mother of a particular claimant.[60] In effect, the burden of proof was reversed. Prior to this, claimants had been required to prove that the defendant had manufactured the product that caused their damage. The decision in *Sindell v Abbott* moved the burden of proof on to the defendants, to prove that they did not manufacture the product that caused the damage.

[60] *Sindell v Abbott Laboratories* 26 Cal 3d 588 (1980).

This groundbreaking arrangement helped alleviate the dual issues of the latency of the damage suffered by DES daughters and the evidential difficulties in accurately establishing which manufacturer produced the product that had harmed them. However, the evaluation of market share liability was not straightforward: one of the major problems was the practical problem of defining market share liability. The *Sindell* case stated that a manufacturer could not be liable for a DES daughter's injuries if the manufacturer was not producing DES at the time when the claimant was *in utero*. However, no further guidance was given, leaving various issues open. For example: Should market share be determined on a national or local basis? How could DES supplies from generic manufacturers be accounted for? These issues fell to local courts to determine. However, *Sindell* provided compensation for DES daughters, and in doing so moved US tort liability for pharmaceuticals forward.

The first liability case in Europe was brought in the Netherlands in 1987. Claimants faced the same difficulties of identifying the correct manufacturer as in the US. In the mid-1990s, the Dutch Supreme Court established that any manufacturer placing a product on the market would be jointly and severally liable for the whole damage, with the market share of any manufacturer used to determine recourse among the defendants.[61] This reasoning is more aligned with the 'alternative causation' approach and forms a slightly different approach from that of market share liability taken in *Sindell v Abbott*, but both cases enabled compensation and arrived at broadly similar outcomes.[62]

A settlement was then negotiated between Dutch claimants and UCB that led to a highly innovative solution on how to make the agreement binding on all (or most) of the class members. The Class Action Settlement Act was passed in 2005, under which the Amsterdam Court of Appeal was empowered to approve a settlement, which would then be binding on all class members unless they chose to opt out (see chapter 1, section I.E).

In France, long-running litigation by DES daughters eventually resulted in two cases that reversed of the burden of proof.[63] These cases established that the defendants were jointly and severally liable, unless the particular defendant could prove that the damage was not caused by its product. Given that the two named defendants were UCB, who had 98% of the market share of DES in France, and Novartis, who had just 2% of the market share of DES, joint and several liability appears difficult and their relative responsibility is likely to be questioned.

Under UK law there is no equivalent to either the market share liability seen in the US, or the alternative causation model seen in the Netherlands. Thus, the usual legal principles of causation and damage apply. Unfortunately for the DES children and grandchildren, they will not benefit from the Congenital Disabilities (Civil Liabilities) Act 1976 as the Act was not retrospective. This Act only applies to children born from 22 July 1976, by which point DES should not have been prescribed to pregnant women in the UK. As such, no collective litigation has ensued, probably due to the difficulties of establishing manufacturer liability. The situation for DES grandchildren is even more legally complex in England and Wales, making the prospect of litigation very difficult.[64]

[61] *Van Ballegooijen v Bayer Nederland BV* (Rvdw 1992, No 219).

[62] See JG Teulings, 'DES and Market Share Liability in the Netherlands' (1994) 110 *LQR* 228 for a more detailed discussion.

[63] Cass civ 1ère 24 September 2009 no 08-16305; and Cass civ 1ère 28 January 2010 no 08-18837.

[64] R Goldberg, 'Causation and Drugs: The Legacy of Diethylstilbestrol' (1996) 25 *Anglo-American Law Review* 286 (1996).

Interestingly, cases have been brought in the USA by 53 DES daughters against manufacturers, claiming that their breast cancers were caused by pre-natal exposure to DES.[65] These cases were settled before full trial was completed, and hence before liability was established.

v. Conclusion

The safety signal came from medical monitoring, but given the scarcity of the vaginal clear cell adenocarcinomas resulting from DES exposure, it is partly down to luck that this signal was noticed. The introduction of DES on to the market generally preceded the introduction of regulation in Europe during the 1960s. Regulatory action in response to the adverse findings was piecemeal and varied by country. The FDA was relatively quick to contraindicate DES use in pregnancy, and litigation in the US followed this regulatory action. In order to allow recovery of damages, the courts had to modify the test for establishing liability and a special settlement procedure was invented in the Netherlands. Litigation in Europe grew out of litigation in the US rather than after regulatory action in Europe. Litigation has had varying degrees of success in different countries: in general, where litigants have received compensation, a change in approach to establishing liability has been required.

[65] *Fecho et al v Eli Lilley and Company et al* Civil Action no 11-10152-MBB (2013) on 20 January 2012 in the Massachusetts District Court. Magistrate Judge Marianne Bowler ordered the parties to attend mediation, where settlement was reached.

D. Epilim/Depakote/Depakene (sodium valproate, valproic acid, magnesium valproate, valproate semisodium or valpromide)

i. Description

Sodium valproate is an anticonvulsant used in the treatment of epilepsy; it is also used for the treatment of bipolar disorder[66] and in some countries for migraine. Various formulations exist, including gastro-resistance and intravenous formulations.

ii. Safety Issue

From 1968, evidence accumulated from epidemiological surveys from various parts of the world reporting an increase in the incidence of congenital malformations in children born to women with epilepsy.[67] While most of the early surveys have shown that the incidence of malformations has been higher in women with epilepsy receiving drug treatment during pregnancy than in those untreated, those who do not require anti-epileptic treatment for their epilepsy during pregnancy are likely to have different or less severe epilepsy than patients who do require such treatment.[68] Children of mothers who took valproate during pregnancy had a higher incidence of congenital malformations than the general population. However, some epilepsy can only be controlled by valproate, and seizures also pose grave risks to mother and child. Valproate therefore tended to be prescribed to women with more severe epilepsy, or with epilepsy refractory to other treatment. For this reason, for many years it was considered difficult to ascertain whether the severity of the disease itself or the medicine used in its treatment was responsible for the increased malformation rates: see, for example, the 1991 review by Roy Meadows on the question of attribution.[69]

Reports of congenital abnormalities in children born to mothers taking valproate (rather than more general warnings of anti-epileptics) were surprisingly slow to arise, with published case reports surfacing in the early 1980s.[70] More recent studies have indicated that while anti-epileptics as a class are linked with birth defects, valproate is associated with higher levels of adverse outcomes for children exposed *in utero*.[71] Some studies have

[66] This use is off-label in UK, but such usage is approved by the National Institute for Health and Care Excellence (NICE) in their Clinical Guideline [CG185], 'Bipolar Disorder: assessment and management', published in September 2014, available at www.nice.org.uk/guidance/cg185.

[67] J Elshove and JHM van Eck, 'Congenital malformations particularly cleft lip with or without cleft palate in children with epileptic mothers' (1971) 115 *Ned Tijdsch Geneesk* 1371; SR Meadow, 'Congenital abnormalities and anticonvulsant drugs' (1970) 63 *Proceedings of the Royal Society of Medicine* 48; J Fredrik, 'Epilepsy and pregnancy. A report from the Oxford Record Linkage Study' (1973) 2 *British Medical Journal* 442; FM Sullivan, (1979) 'The teratogenic and other toxic effects of drugs on reproduction' in PF D'Arcy and JP Griffin (eds), *Latrogenic Diseases*, 2nd edn (Oxford University Press, 1979) 445.

[68] BD Spiedel and RS Meadow, Maternal epilepsy and abnormalities of the foetus and new-born' (1972) 2 *The Lancet* 839; RM Hill, 'Teratogenesis and antiepileptic drugs' (1973) 289: *New England Journal of Medicine* 1089.

[69] R Meadows, 'Anticonvulsants in pregnancy' (1991) 66 *Archives of Disease in Childhood* 62.

[70] B Dalens, EJ Raynaud and J Gaulme, 'Teratogenicity of valproic acid' (1980) 97 *Pediatrics* 332; MR Gomez, 'Possible teratogenicity of valproic acid' (1981) 98 *Journal of Pediatrics* 508; E Robert and P Guibaud, 'Maternal valproic acid and congenital neural tube defects' (1982) 2 *The Lancet* 937.

[71] KJ Meador et al, 'Fetal antiepileptic drug exposure and cognitive outcomes at age 6 years (NEAD study): a prospective observational study' (2013) 12(3) *Lancet Neurology* 244; KJ Meador et al, 'Cognitive function at 3 years of age after fetal exposure to antiepileptic drugs' (2009) 360(16) *New England Journal of Medicine* 1597.

indicated that there may be a dose-response profile, in that the children of mothers on lower doses of valproate have lower levels of congenital malformations than mothers on higher doses.[72] However, other studies have found no discernible difference in adverse events due to maternal doses.[73] Inevitably these studies all have methodological limitations, but the weight of evidence tends to support the conclusion that valproate is a more potent teratogen than other anti-epileptics.

In the past decade studies have also indicated that there may be an increased risk of autistic spectrum disorders.[74] Although these studies are methodologically difficult because of the confounding factors, they indicate an increased risk.

iii. Marketing and Regulatory History

a. Europe

The anti-epileptic activity of valproate was an accidental discovery.[75] Dipropylacetic acid (as valproate was originally known) had long been used as an organic solvent. In 1962, a small Grenoble-based pharmaceutical company, La Laboratoire Berthier, in collaboration with George Carraz from the University of Grenoble, started testing a series of potential tranquiliser compounds in rats. The test compounds were dissolved in dipropylacetic acid; all of the test compounds demonstrated anti-epileptic activity. Further testing demonstrated that dipropylacetic acid alone possessed an anti-epileptic effect. La Laboratoire Berthier began to develop valproate in-house, but drug development required considerable resources. By the mid-1960s the drug was sold on to Sanofi-Labaz. Valproate was promptly licensed in various European countries. It has been marketed in France since 1967. Marketing in Spain commenced in 1970; Belgium and Holland followed in 1971. In 1972 it was brought to market in Switzerland, Italy and Britain.

The marketing of valproate products in Britain pre-dated the UK's accession to the Common Market in 1973. The initial UK product licence was under the UK licensing regime, which was then superceded by the EU rules. In the UK it was indicated only for the treatment of epilepsy. From the outset, the data sheet advised doctors that sodium valproate had been shown to be teratogenic in animals, and that any benefit that might be expected from its use should be weighed against the hazard suggested by these findings. Doctors were advised that in women of child-bearing age the products should only be used in severe cases or those resistant to other treatment. Three case reports specifically linking valproate

[72] FJ Vajda et al, 'Foetal malformations and seizure control: 52 months data of the Australian Pregnancy Registry' (2006) 13(6) *European Journal of Neurology* 645.

[73] J Christensen et al, 'Prenatal valproate exposure and risk of autism spectrum disorders and childhood autism' (2013) 309(16) *Journal of the American Medical Association* 1696.

[74] RL Bromley et al, 'Early cognitive development in children born to women with epilepsy: a prospective report' (2010) 51(10) *Epilepsia* 2058, doi:10.1111/j.1528-1167.2010.02668.x; C Cummings et al, 'Neurodevelopment of children exposed in utero to lamotrigine, sodium valproate and carbamazepine' (2011) 96(7) *Archives of Disease in Childhood* 643; Meador et al, 'Cognitive function at 3 years of age', n 72; SV Thomas et al, 'Motor and mental development of infants exposed to antiepileptic drugs in utero' (2008) 13(1) *Epilepsy & Behaviour* 229, available at www.sciencedirect.com/science/article/pii/S1525505008000115; Meador et al, 'Fetal antiepileptic drug exposure', n 72; Christensen et al, n 74.

[75] SD Shorvon, 'Drug treatment of epilepsy in the century of the ILAE: The second 50 years, 1959–2009' (2009) 50 *Epilepsia* 93, doi:10.1111/j.1528-1167.2009.02042.x.

and developmental abnormalities were published in 1980, 1981 and 1982 respectively.[76] In January 1983, warnings about the risk of congenital abnormalities in babies born to epileptic mothers were published by the CSM in *Current Problems in Pharmacovigilance*.[77] Product information for prescribers recommended that doctors should assess the risks and benefits when prescribing for women of child-bearing age. A reminder to doctors was published in June 1993.

The advice was revised upon review of two retrospective epidemiological studies from 2001 and 2002, which suggested an association between *in utero* exposure to sodium valproate and a risk of developmental delay.[78] Following review of these data and including data from the UK Pregnancy and Epilepsy Register,[79] warnings were issued in September 2003.[80]

Progressively more detailed warnings were added to the UK product information by the manufacturer, reflecting developing scientific knowledge.[81]

A European Medicines Agency (EMA) reassessment of the risk–benefit ratio of valproate use in women of childbearing age was published in November 2014.[82] The report advised that doctors in the EU should not prescribe valproate for epilepsy or bipolar disorder:

(a) in pregnant women;
(b) in women who can become pregnant; or
(c) in girls;

unless other treatments are ineffective or not tolerated. Those for whom valproate is the only option for epilepsy or bipolar disorder should be advised on the use of effective contraception, and treatment should be under the supervision of a doctor experienced in treating these conditions. The report also concluded that valproate must not be used as a preventive treatment for migraine in pregnant women. Doctors should exclude pregnancy before starting women on valproate treatment for migraine, and should not prescribe valproate for this purpose unless the woman is on effective contraception.

When treating epilepsy and biopolar disorder in women of childbearing age, valproate should be a last resort therapeutic, but it still has a therapeutic function in women and girls who are refractory to other treatments, even during pregnancy.

[76] Dalens, Raynaud and Gaulme, n 71; Gomez, n 71; Robert and Guibaud, n 71.

[77] See at webarchive.nationalarchives.gov.uk/20141206140254/http://www.mhra.gov.uk/home/groups/pl-p/documents/websiteresources/con2024416.pdf.

[78] N Adab et al, 'Additional educational needs in children born to mothers with epilepsy' (2001) 70(1) *Journal of Neurology, Neurosurgery and Psychiatry* 15, dx.doi.org/10.1136/jnnp.70.1.15; and JCS Dean et al, 'Long term health and neurodevelopment in children exposed to antiepileptic drugs before birth' (2002) 39 *Journal of Medical Genetics* 251.

[79] Craig et al (2002) 43 (Suppl 8) *Epilepsia* 079 JSC Dean et al 'Long term health and neurodevelopment in children exposed to antiepileptic drugs before birth' (2002) 39 *Journal of Medical Genetics* 251, dx.doi.org/10.1136/jmg.39.4.251.

[80] See CSM *Current Problems in Pharmacovigilance* (September 2003) 29, 'Sodium valproate and prescribing in pregnancy' 6, available at webarchive.nationalarchives.gov.uk/20141206183805/http://www.mhra.gov.uk/home/groups/pl-p/documents/websiteresources/con007450.pdf

[81] Product information relating to warnings about use in pregnancy was updated by the manufacturer, Sanofi, in 1993, 1996, 1997, 2003 and 2010.

[82] 'CMDh [Coordination Group for Mutual Recognition and Decentralised Procedures – Human] agrees to strengthen warnings on the use of valproate medicines in women and girls', EMA/709243/2014, 21 November 2014, available at www.ema.europa.eu/docs/en_GB/document_library/Referrals_document/Valproate_and_related_substances_31/Position_provided_by_CMDh/WC500177637.pdf.

In 2015, the Medicines and Healthcare Products Regulatory Agency (MHRA) produced the valproate toolkit, a resource bank for patients, clinicians and pharmacists. Despite this, a survey in 2016 indicated that one in five of the women taking valproate were unaware of the risks it posed in pregnancy, and fewer than one in five had seen any of the educational materials from the toolkit. A further UK safety alert was issued in April 2017.[83] This included the risk of neurodevelopmental disabilities including lower intelligence and autistic spectrum disorder, as well as the risk of birth defects

Following the 2014 EMA assessment, on 26 May 2015 changes to the way valproate was prescribed in France were announced by the French regulator, Agence nationale de sécurité du medicament et des produits de santé (ANSM). Essentially valproate should only be used where there was no alternative therapy in women of childbearing potential and girls. Initial prescriptions were limited to doctors specialising in neurology, psychiatry or paediatrics, with annual reviews thereafter conducted by a doctor.[84] In addition, in June 2015 the French Minister of Social Affairs and Health commissioned the Inspection générale des affaires sociales (IGAS) to undertake a fact-finding report on valproate use in France. It was to focus on what information had been provided to patients and prescribers. When examining the timing and regulatory decisions that had been made in determining the risk–benefit balance of the use of valproate during pregnancy, two factors were to be taken into account:

(a) the state of knowledge at the time;
(b) any relevant decisions made by other countries (particularly in Europe), particularly focusing on the state of knowledge.

When it was published in February 2016, the IGAS report[85] was highly critical of the slow response of the French regulator AFSSAPS and of Sanofi. In August that year, IGAS concluded that over 14,000 women in France took valproate while pregnant between 2007 and 2014, when the risks of exposure were widely known, and estimated that 425–450 children would have been affected.

The French drug regulator ANSM took two key actions after the IGAS report. First, on 9 March 2017 ANSM requested, under Article 31 of Directive 2001/83/EC, that the EMA review the use of valproate containing medicines within the EU.

Secondly, in July 2017 the ANSM wrote a 'Dear Doctor' letter to all French healthcare providers, saying that valproate should only be used to treat bipolar disorder in women and girls of childbearing age if they were taking effective contraception. When treating epilepsy, valproate should only be used in girls, adolescents, women of childbearing age and pregnant women when all other treatments had proved ineffective.[86]

The Article 31 review requested by France eventually resulted in a legally binding pan-European package of measures to avoid valproate exposure in pregnancy, which was launched by the EMA in March 2018.[87]

[83] Alert number NHS/PSA/RE/2017/002, issued 6 April 2017 and available at improvement.nhs.uk/documents/911/Patient_Safety_Alert_-_Resources_to_support_safe_use_of_valproate.pdf.

[84] See at www.ansm.sante.fr/Dossiers/Valproate-et-derives/Valproate-et-derives/(offset)/0.

[85] Inspection générale des affaires sociales, Rapport *Enquête relative aux spécialités pharmaceutiques contenant du valproate de sodium*, February 2016, IGAS Rapport No2015-094R, available at www.igas.gouv.fr/IMG/pdf/2015-094R.pdf (in French).

[86] See at ansm.sante.fr/Dossiers/Valproate-et-derives/Valproate-et-derives/(offset)/0.

[87] See at www.ema.europa.eu/docs/en_GB/document_library/Press_release/2018/03/WC500246391.pdf.

Later in March, the MHRA issued a restriction on the prescription of valproate to women and girls of childbearing age, unless they were on a pregnancy prevention programme.[88]

b. USA

The US licence for valproate was held by Abbott, which was ambivalent about launching the product there during the early 1970s as the existing European data were insufficient to pass a licensing application. It would possibly have remained unavailable in the US had it not been for the actions of Kiffin Penry in combination with considerable public outcry. Penry conducted a campaign to the US Senate,[89] seeking access to various anti-epileptics that were already available in Europe, including valproate. He founded the Antiepileptic Drug Development Program in 1969 as a mechanism to improve access to anti-epileptic drugs. Usually the clinical trials submitted to the FDA for marketing approval are conducted by the pharmaceutical company. Unusually, the additional trials needed for valproate to obtain approval in the US[90] were conducted using National Institutes of Health (NIH) contracts at medical universities and a state hospital under the auspices of the Antiepileptic Drug Development program.[91] The initial application decision in December 1977 was to reject the application as there were insufficient clinical data. This caused a public outcry. New evidence was presented to the FDA early in 1978, and on 28 February 1978 Abbott were granted a licence to market valproic acid under the brand name Depakene.[92] Further formulations and indications were subsequently added, including Depakote for the treatment of bipolar disorder.

As the state of knowledge changed, the labelling on valproate-containing products changed. Some of the key changes are outlined below. In October 2006 a black-box warning was added to the outside of packages, alerting to the risk of birth defects for all valproate-containing medicines.[93] On 3 December 2009 a reminder was sent to healthcare providers about the risk of neural tube defects following pre-natal exposure to valproate.[94]

The FDA issued a safety alert on 30 June 2011, warning that children born to mothers taking valproate had an increased risk of lower cognitive test scores than children exposed to other anti-seizure medications during pregnancy.[95] This decrease in cognitive ability led to a subsequent safety alert on 6 May 2013,[96] which contraindicated valproate use for migraine in pregnant women. Valproate had been a category D drug, which meant that the

[88] Alert CEM/CMO/2018/001, issued 24 March 2018 and available at www.cas.mhra.gov.uk/ViewandAcknowledgment/ViewAlert.aspx?AlertID=102736; www.gov.uk/drug-safety-update/valproate-medicines-epilim-depakote-contraindicated-in-women-and-girls-of-childbearing-potential-unless-conditions-of-pregnancy-prevention-programme-are-met.

[89] W Loscher, 'Foreword' in *Valproate (Milestones in Drug Therapy)* (Birkhauser, 1999); and Shorvon, n 76, doi:10.1111/j.1528-1167.2009.02042.x.

[90] And other anti-epileptics that were already licensed outside the US.

[91] Shorvon, n 76, doi:10.1111/j.1528-1167.2009.02042.x.

[92] NDA 018081, available at www.accessdata.fda.gov/scripts/cder/daf/index.cfm?event=overview.process&ApplNo=018081.

[93] ibid.

[94] Available at wayback.archive-it.org/7993/20170112032650/http://www.fda.gov/Drugs/DrugSafety/PostmarketDrugSafetyInformationforPatientsandProviders/DrugSafetyInformationforHeathcareProfessionals/ucm192649.htm.

[95] Drug Safety Alert, available at www.fda.gov/Drugs/DrugSafety/ucm261543.htm.

[96] Available at www.fda.gov/Drugs/DrugSafety/ucm350684.htm.

benefit obtained from use in pregnancy might outweigh the risks of use in pregnancy. It remained a category D drug for treatment of seizures and bipolar disorder, but became a category X drug (the potential risks clearly outweigh any benefit when used in pregnancy) for the treatment of migraine. The 2013 FDA Safety Alert provides some interesting data on the predominant indication for valproate use in the US. In women of reproductive potential age in 2012, the predominant indication for valproate prescription was in episodic mood disorder (57%): schizophrenia accounted for 10% of prescriptions within this cohort; migraine accounted for just 9% of the valproate use in this cohort; similarly, epilepsy and/or seizures accounted for just 9% of the valproate use in this cohort.

iv. Litigation

a. England and Wales

Some claims were made against clinicians, and the Medical Defence Union[97] is believed to have settled some of them. It was the changes in advice upon review of two retrospective epidemiological studies from 2001 and 2002, which suggested that the product was associated with an increased risk of developmental delay in exposed children, that resulted in the commencement of litigation. Group action involving approximately 100 claimants began in England and Wales in 2003 against manufacturers of a range of anti-epileptic drugs. Litigation was dropped against most manufacturers but continued against Sanofi, the leading manufacturer of sodium valproate. The case collapsed when, after spending £4 million on legal aid, the Legal Services Commission withdrew funding 10 days before the trial in November 2010, following a negative assessment of the prospects of success by independent counsel.

b. France

Valproate campaigning and litigation in France crystallised upon the formation of the Association d'Aide aux Parents d'Enfants souffrant du Syndrome de l'Anti-Convulsivant (APESAC) in 2011. The litigation regarding valproate in France is complex and ongoing, so only an outline will be presented here. Since 2012 both civil and criminal cases have been initiated, with around 2,000 families involved in the various trials.

A criminal complaint with associated *partie civile* claims (explained in chapter 1, section I.E) was filed by APESAC to the Vice-Prosecutor for Public Health, which resulted in the opening of a full judicial investigation in September 2016. The outcome of this investigation could take years, and any civil cases would have to be stayed until the outcome of the criminal investigation was clear.

In December 2016, APESAC attempted to launch a class action against Sanofi. This was the first such attempt at a group action in health, and was only possible because of a change in the law in January 2016, which extended the existing French class action procedures to include health.[98] The case was thrown out by the Court of Appeal in Paris

[97] One of the insurers of medics.

[98] Loi no 2016-41 de modernisation du système de santé.

on 14 March 2017 as APESAC lacked the appropriate standing.[99] Undeterred, in May 2017 APESAC launched an *action de groupe*, *APESAC v Sanofi*, on behalf of 2,000–4,000 affected individuals. Fourteen families are involved in this litigation as test cases. The preliminary hearings were heard in the Paris High Court of First Instance in October 2017. Pre-trial requests to have Sanofi pay €400 million into court in case it was found liable to provide compensation were rejected in November 2017. Cases are ongoing, and a final judgment is expected at the end of 2018.

Individual cases have also been filed. The number of families opting for this route is far lower than the numbers involved in the group action, with tens of cases commenced rather than hundreds. The first one that resulted in a claimant win is the case of Camille C and his family. A €3 million verdict issued by the High Court of Tours in 2015 was upheld by the Orléans Court of Appeal on 20 November 2017.[100] Other cases are ongoing.

The French Government announced in 2016 that a compensation fund would be set up for those affected by *in utero* valproate exposure. In November 2016, the French Government set aside an initial €10 million from the 2017 budget to create a valproate compensation fund. Health Minister Marisol Touraine told the lower house of parliament that the €10 million were a starting point, and that in future years the sums should be much higher. Touraine later told the parliament that compensation would ultimately be paid by 'those deemed responsible'. Sanofi has stated that it will pay into the fund if a court requires it. The fund, which is administered by the Office national d'indemnisation des accidents médicaux (ONIAM), commenced on 1 June 2017.

c. USA

There have been both individual actions and a class action against Abbott Laboratories. The majority of cases became part of an MDL. In May 2010, around 40 individuals filed a lawsuit in the Southern District of Illinois against Abbot Laboratories, claiming that Abbott failed to fully research the potential side-effects of Depakote and failed to adequately warn about the risk of birth defects. The claim alleged that the Abbott knew of the potential birth defect risks prior to marketing Depakote, but failed to inform either the medical community or patients about it. The cases were consolidated into an MDL on 18 January 2012. Further cases were added, and by 27 August 2017 the Depakote litigation had 129 pending cases, involving approximately 698 plaintiffs.[101] The Court opted for a 'bellwether' approach, with three representative cases selected for fast-track trials. The aim of this approach is to allow the parties to assess the relative strengths and weaknesses of the evidence and the value of the remaining claims. Attempts at a global settlement took place in parallel to the bellwether approach. The first bellwether trial was the case of Danny Kaleta,[102] which was heard in March 2015. At the conclusion of the three-week trial the jury reached a verdict that Abbott was not liable for Danny's injuries, as the warnings had been adequate. By contrast, two

[99] Court of Appeal Paris, 14 March 2017, no 16/17958.

[100] Court of Appeal Orléans, ch civ, 20 November 2017, no 16/00141.

[101] *In Re Depakote*, Case no 12-CV-52-NJR-SCW Memorandum and Order of 28 August 2017.

[102] *DWK, a Minor by Mary Kaleta and Daniel Kaleta, Individually and as Parents and Next Friends of DWK v Abbott Laboratories, Inc*, Case no 14-cv-847 (SD Ill 2014).

months later, in May 2015, $38 million was awarded to Maddison Schmidt and her family for failure to warn. The Schmidt decision was subsequently appealed by the defendant. In September 2017 the Missouri Supreme Court upheld the award of $15 million in compensatory damages and $23 million in punitive damages, stating that the original jury trial had been fair.[103]

By July 2016[104] it was clear that both the bellwether process and global settlement efforts had failed. Three 'bellwether' cases were set for trial later in 2016,[105] but these were vacated to allow the court to hold joint trials as to common issues of fact and law to the maximum extent possible.[106] Eight months later an order[107] was issued staying all pending Depakote cases while the court pursued an aggressive settlement attempt. As at August 2018 talks are ongoing.

v. Conclusion

The same safety issue has essentially remained constant throughout, namely that the risks, especially of teratogenicity, are inherent in use of the product as a beneficial treatment for epilepsy. This is a risk–benefit issue, which should be considered by doctors when making prescribing decisions and should be made clear to patients so that they can make informed choices.[108] Throughout the lifespan of the product there has been ongoing updating of the recommendations for prescribers in an attempt to minimise associated risks. In some instances, it has been concluded that the regulatory response was slow to adapt to the increases in knowledge at the time.

[103] *Barron v Abbott Labs, Inc*, 2017 BL 320656, Mo en banc, Case no SC96151, 9/12/17.

[104] *In Re Depakote*, Case no 12-CV-52-NJR-SCW Court noted in its Order dated 6 July 2016 (Doc 485).

[105] (1) *HB and parent Stacy Bartolini*, 12-cv-0053; (2) *TC and parent Kayla Rose McGuinness-Colon*, 12-cv-0694; and (3) *ERG and parent Christina Raquel*, 12-cv-0055).

[106] *In Re Depakote*, Case no 12-CV-52-NJR-SCW Memorandum and Order of 28 August 2017.

[107] *In Re Depakote*, Case no 12-CV-52-NJR-SCW Order of 23 April 2018.

[108] H Angus-Leppan and RSN Liu, 'Weighing the risks of valproate in women who could become pregnant' (2018) 361 *British Medical Journal* k1596.

E. Accutane/Roaccutane (isotretinoin)

i. Description

Isotretinoin is used for the treatment of severe skin conditions (predominantly severe acne where there is a risk of scarring) and a number of cancers. It was first developed to be used as a chemotherapy medication for the treatment of brain cancer, pancreatic cancer, etc. It is still used in the treatment of these cancers because of its ability to kill rapidly dividing cells; however, its effects are systemic and non-selective.

ii. Safety Issue

Isotretinoin is a teratogen if taken by the mother in the month prior to conception or during pregnancy. This is due to the molecule's close resemblance to retinoic acid, a vitamin A derivative found in small quantities naturally in the body, which regulates patterning in normal embryonic development. Isotretinoin can lead to a variety of birth defects, including facial dysmorphism, missing or malformed external ears, auditory and visual impairments, and cognitive impairment.[109]

In addition to reports of teratogenicity, ADR reports arose from 1982 onwards covering defects ranging from skin disorders, musculoskeletal disorders, gastrointestinal disorders, eye disorders, neurological disorders and psychiatric disorders.[110] A review of the Roche global safety database up to 27 April 2010 determined that 66 cases of severe skin reactions have been reported worldwide in association with isotretinoin,[111] and updated safety information has been disseminated through the regulators.

This case study will focus on the teratogenic, depressive and irritable bowel syndrome adverse events.

iii. Marketing and Regulatory History

Isotretinoin's potential to cause birth defects was recognised from the outset, and has resulted in stringent restrictions that make isotretinoin difficult to obtain. It was licensed by Hoffman-La Roche in 1982 in many parts of the world, often subject to prescription being restricted to dermatologists. For example, it was licensed in the UK on 30 June 1983, with

[109] JS Choi, G Koren and I Nulman, 'Pregnancy and isotretinoin therapy' (2013) 185(5) *Canadian Medical Association Journal* 411, doi:10.1503/cmaj.120729.

[110] For example, see CSM, 'In Focus Isotretinoin (Roaccutane)' 24 (August 1998) *Current Problems in Pharmacovigilance* 12, available at webarchive.nationalarchives.gov.uk/20141206135347/http://www.mhra.gov.uk/home/groups/pl-p/documents/websiteresources/con2023231.pdf. For a review, see JJ Leyden, JQ Del Rosso and EW Baum, 'The Use of Isotretinoin in the Treatment of Acne Vulgaris – Clinical Considerations and Future Directions' (2014) 7(2 Suppl) *Journal of Clinical and Aesthetic Dermatology* S3–S21.

[111] Available at webarchive.nationalarchives.gov.uk/20141206120551/http://www.mhra.gov.uk/home/groups/pl-p/documents/websiteresources/con099719.pdf.

prescribing restricted to consultant dermatologists.[112] In New South Wales and Victoria, the prescriber must be a Fellow of the Australasian College of Dermatologists (FACD).[113] Interestingly, restricting prescribing to specialist dermatologists does not apply in the USA.[114]

a. USA

1. Teratogenicity

Although the teratogenicity of isotretinoin was known from the outset, there have been incidents of women becoming pregnant while taking it. It was launched as category X, with the following warning on the package insert:[115]

> Because teratogenicity has been observed in animals given isotretinoin, patients who are pregnant or intend to become pregnant while undergoing treatment should not receive Accutane. Women of childbearing potential should not be given Accutane unless an effective form of contraception is used, and they should be fully counseled on the potential risks to the fetus should they become pregnant while undergoing treatment. Should pregnancy occur during treatment, the physician and patient should discuss the desirability of continuing the pregnancy.

Even with this warning pregnancies occurred,[116] and in July 1983 a 'Dear Doctor' letter was sent out highlighting the teratogenicity and recommending pregnancy testing before commencing isotretinoin treatment. By 1985 a black-box warning had been added to the label. Over the years there were further attempts to minimise the number of pregnancies occurring among women taking this medication. In April 1988, a voluntary Pregnancy Prevention Program was launched by the manufacturer Hoffman-La Roche, including new packaging.[117] Despite these efforts the Accutane Survey, which was commissioned by Hoffman-La Roche and carried out by the Slone Epidemiology Unit, Boston University School of Public Health, found that the rate of pregnancy remained at around 1 woman per 1,000 enrolled in the study throughout the 1990s.[118] The majority of these pregnancies ended in miscarriage or were terminated, but a number of children were born with birth defects.

[112] Joint Formulary Committee, *British National Formulary*, 47th edn (2004, British Medical Association and Royal Pharmaceutical Society of Great Britain).

[113] Pharmaceutical Services Branch, *Guide to poisons and therapeutic goods legislation for medical practitioners and dentists* (NSW Department of Health, 2006).

[114] Where the product was marketed as Accutane prior to July 2009.

[115] Center for Disease Control, 'Epidemiologic Notes and Reports Isotretinoin – A Newly Recognized Human Teratogen' (1984) 33(13) *Morbidity and Mortality Weekly Reporter* 171, available at www.cdc.gov/mmwr/preview/mmwrhtml/00000310.htm.

[116] ibid.

[117] See the presentation of Dr Colonel Evans in Dermatologic Drugs Advisory Committee, 37 Open Session (8 May 1989), available at wayback.archive-it.org/7993/20180125041216/https://www.fda.gov/ohrms/dockets/ac/accutane/29t1.pdf.

[118] Survey of Accutane Use in Women, conducted by the Slone Epidemiology Unit, Boston University School of Public Health, Allen A Mitchell, MD, Principal Investigator, Carla Van Bennekom, RN, MPH, Epidemiologist, 28 August 2000, available at wayback.archive-it.org/7993/20180126002209/https://www.fda.gov/ohrms/dockets/ac/00/backgrd/3639b1c_24.pdf; AA Mitchell, CM Van Bennekom, C Louik, *An assessment of the*

As there were still women in the US who were taking isotretinoin while pregnant, the availability of isotretinoin was further tightened in April 2002 with Hoffman-La Roche's launch of a new voluntary risk management program, System to Manage Accutane Related Teratogenicity (or 'SMART'). The novel feature of the SMART program was the requirement on prescribers to fill in and affix a yellow 'qualification' sticker to all isotretinoin prescriptions issued. The 'qualification' stickers were intended to remind prescribers that they had a responsibility to ensure that female patients 'qualified' for isotretinoin. To 'qualify' female patients had to have had two negative pregnancy tests and to have agreed to two specified contraception measures. In order to obtain qualifications stickers, prescribers had to sign and return a detailed description of the qualification requirements. Pharmacists were required to supply Accutane only when the prescriptions had a sticker affixed to them.[119]

From 2002 onwards, generic versions of isotretinoin became available,[120] and these were not automatically covered by the SMART program.[121] Although rates of pregnancy were not increasing, a background of rising isotretinoin prescription numbers (including many 'off-label' prescriptions where the condition being treated was not as severe as the indication) meant that there were isotretinoin-exposed pregnancies. In an attempt to minimise such pregnancies, since April 2006 the dispensing of isotretinoin has been further controlled by an FDA-mandated website called iPLEDGE, where clinicians are required to register their patients before prescribing and pharmacists are required to check the website before dispensing the drug, and various other controls are observed.[122] The introduction of iPLEDGE has not had the impact that would have been hoped on the rate of pregnancy among isotretinoin users.[123]

2. Depression and/or Suicidal Ideations

Several other adverse events have been reported, most notably depression and suicidal ideations. The first reports of psychological changes including depression were received very shortly after the product was initially marketed.[124] Other contemporaneous reports included improvements in depression scores when patients were taking isotretinoin.[125]

Accutane (isotretinoin) Pregnancy Prevention Program, FDA Dermatologic Drugs Advisory Committee Meeting, 18 September 2000, Gaithersburg MD, available at wayback.archive-it.org/7993/20170404134301/https://www.fda.gov/ohrms/dockets/ac/00/backgrd/3639b1c_03.pdf.

[119] A Brinker, C Kornegay, P Nourjah, 'Trends in adherence to a revised risk management program designed to decrease or eliminate isotretinoin-exposed pregnancies: evaluation of the accutane SMART program' (2005) 141(5) *Archives of Dermatology* 563; and L Abroms, E Maibach, K Lyon-Daniel and SR Feldman, 'What is the best approach to reducing birth defects associated with isotretinoin?' 2006 Nov 3(11) Public Library of Science Medicine: e483. Published online 21 Nov. 2006 doi:10.1371/journal.pmed.0030483.

[120] Amnesteem® 8 November 2002; Claravis® 11 April 2003; Myorisan® 19 January 2012; Zenatane™ 1 April 2013.

[121] Generic manufacturers did put in place safety measures, eg Amnesteem prescriptions for isotretinoin were governed by SPIRIT (System to Prevent Isotretinoin-Related Issues of Teratogenicity).

[122] See at www.ipledgeprogram.com/AboutiPLEDGE.aspx.

[123] J Shin et al, 'The impact of the iPLEDGE program on isotretinoin fetal exposure in an integrated healthcare system' (2011) 65(6) *Journal of the American Academy of Dermatology* 1117.

[124] FL Meyskens 'Short clinical reports' (1982) 6(4 Pt 2 Suppl) *Journal of the American Academy of Dermatology* 732, doi.org/10.1016/S0190-9622(82)80054-6.

[125] GL Peck, 'Short clinical reports' (1982) 6(4 Pt 2 Suppl) *Journal of the American Academy of Dermatology* 732, doi.org/10.1016/S0190-9622(82)80054-6.

Depression was added to the adverse reactions portion of label in 1985. Further cases were reported over the years, including cases of suicidal ideations.[126] In February 1998 a 'Dear Doctor' letter was sent out strengthening the warning as follows:[127]

> [T]he WARNINGS section will now begin with the following paragraph in bold type:
>
> > **Psychiatric disorders: Accutane may cause depression, psychosis and, rarely, suicidal ideation, suicide attempts and suicide. Discontinuation of Accutane therapy may be insufficient; further evaluation may be necessary. No mechanism of action has been established for these events.**
>
> the paragraph on depression in the ADVERSE REACTIONS section will become paragraph 5 of that section and will be revised as follows:
>
> > In the post-marketing period, a number of patients treated with Accutane have reported depression, psychosis and, rarely, suicide ideation, suicide attempts and suicide. Of the patients reporting depression, some reported that the depression subsided with discontinuation of therapy and recurred with reinstitution of therapy.

At the time it was noted that there was a 'possible connection' but not conclusive evidence.[128]

In January 2001 another 'Dear Doctor' letter was sent out, stating that all Accutane prescriptions must be accompanied by an informed consent form signed by the patient and that all prescriptions of Accutane must be dispensed with a copy of the Medication Guide for Accutane, which summarised key product information for patients.[129] Later that year, in October, an FDA paper was published in the *Journal of the American Academy of Dermatology* indicating that there had been adverse event reports of depression in patients taking Accutane, but further research was needed to establish if the drug was a causal factor.[130]

There had been a growing groundswell of publicity linking Accutane use and depression/suicide, which was reflected in a Congressional Hearing, *Accutane – Is this acne drug treatment linked to depression and suicide?*, that took place on 5 December 2001.[131] A safety alert was issued in 2002, adding to the warning the fact that aggressive and violent

[126] For reviews, see VP Kontaxakis et al, 'Isotretinoin and psychopatology: a review' (2009) 8:2 *Annals of General Psychiatry*, published online 20 January 2009, doi: 10.1186/1744-859X-8-2; and P Magin, D Pond and W Smith, 'Isotretinoin, depression and suicide: a review of the evidence' (2005) 55(511) *British Journal of General Practice* 134. For individual case reports, see PG Hazen et al, 'Depression – a side effect of 13-cis-retinoic acid therapy' (1983) 9 *Journal of the American Academy of Dermatology* 278; H Lindemayr, 'Isotretinoin intoxication in attempted suicide' (1986) 66 *Acta Dermato-Venereologica* 452; PL Scheinman et al, 'Acute depression from isotretinoin' (1990) 22(6)(1) *Journal of the American Academy of Dermatology* 1112, doi.org/10.1016/S0190-9622(08)81018-3; NC Hepburn, 'Deliberate self-poisoning with isotretinoin' (1990) 122 *British Journal of Dermatology* 840, doi:10.1111/j.1365-2133.1990.tb06279.x.; S Gatti and F Serri, 'Acute depression from isotretinoin' (1991) 25 *Journal of the American Academy of Dermatology* 132, doi:10.1016/S0190-9622(08)80509-9.

[127] Available from the MedWatch archive 1996–2008, at www.fda.gov/Safety/MedWatch/SafetyInformation/default.htm.

[128] A Ault, 'Isotretinoin use may be linked with depression' (1998) 351(9104) *The Lancet* 730.

[129] Available from the MedWatch archive 1996–2008, at www.fda.gov/Safety/MedWatch/SafetyInformation/default.htm.

[130] DK Wysowski, M Pitts and J Beitz, 'An analysis of reports of depression and suicide in patients treated with isotretinoin' (2001) 45 *Journal of the American Academy of Dermatology* 515, doi.org/10.1067/mjd.2001.117730.

[131] House Hearing, 106th Congress, 'Accutane – is this acne drug treatment linked to depression and suicide?', available at www.gpo.gov/fdsys/pkg/chrg-106hhrg73924/content-detail.html.

behaviours had been observed in patients receiving Accutane.[132] A second hearing, *Issues relating to the safety of Accutane*, took place on 11 December 2002.[133]

In July 2005 the FDA issued an alert, and a further labelling revision was undertaken on 12 August 2005 to ensure that patients on Accutane were monitored for suicidal ideations.[134] The debate on whether isotretinoin is causal in depression and suicidal ideations has continued for many years. Published articles have appeared that strongly correlate isotretinoin use and psychopathology, particularly when compared to other acne treatments.[135] However, in 2017 a meta-analysis did not find a causal link between depression and isotretinoin; in fact an amelioration of depressive symptoms was noted.[136]

3. Irritable Bowel Syndrome and Ulcerative Colitis

Case reports of irritable bowel syndrome (IBS) or ulcerative colitis (UC) after taking isotretinoin surfaced within a couple of years of the product's launch. In response, in March 1984 a 'Dear Doctor' letter was sent out detailing 10 patients who had developed bowel symptoms while taking Accutane, and the manufacturer added to the 'Warnings' section of the Accutane package insert provided to physicians that 'Accutane has been temporally associated with [IBD] in patients without a prior history of intestinal disorders' and that patients 'experiencing abdominal pain, rectal bleeding or severe diarrhea should discontinue Accutane immediately'.[137]

Cases continued to arise at a fairly low level in the decade after the product's launch.[138] It was initially thought that these cases resolved upon the cessation of the Accutane treatment. In May 2000[139] the warning was amended to remove the reference to bowel conditions being temporary:

> Accutane has been associated with inflammatory bowel disease (including regional iletis) in patients without a prior history of intestinal disorders. In some instances, symptoms have been reported to persist after Accutane treatment has been stopped. Patients experiencing abdominal pain, rectal bleeding or severe diarrhea should discontinue Accutane immediately (see ADVERSE REACTIONS: Gastrointestinal).

According to Reddy et al, there were 85 cases of IBD associated with isotretinoin use reported to the FDA in the five years between 1997 and 2002.[140] The headline from the

[132] Available from the MedWatch archive 1996–2008, at www.fda.gov/Safety/MedWatch/SafetyInformation/default.htm.

[133] See at www.gpo.gov/fdsys/pkg/CHRG-107hhrg85967/pdf/CHRG-107hhrg85967.pdf.

[134] Available at www.fda.gov/Drugs/DrugSafety/PostmarketDrugSafetyInformationforPatientsandProviders/ucm094305.htm.

[135] Kontaxakis et al, n 127.

[136] Yu-Chen Huang and Ying-Chih Cheng, 'Isotretinoin treatment for acne and risk of depression: A systematic review and meta-analysis' (2017) 76(6) *Journal of the American Academy of Dermatology* 1068.

[137] *In re Accutane Litigation*, 2017 NJ Docket no A-2717-11T2.

[138] For examples of case reports, see P Martin et al, 'Isotretinoin-associated proctosigmoiditis' (1987) 93 *Gastroenterology* 606; T McGinn and C Bewira, 'Isoretinoin (Accutane) associated pancolitis' (1997) 92 *American Journal of Gastroenterology* 1682; D Reniers and J Howard, 'Isotretinoin-induced inflammatory bowel disease in an adolescent' (2001) 35 *Annals of Pharmacotherapy* 1214; LD Prokop, 'Isotretinoin: possible component cause of IBD' (1999) 94 *American Journal of Gastroenterology* 2568.

[139] See at www.accessdata.fda.gov/drugsatfda_docs/nda/2000/018662_S038_ACCUTANE_AP.pdf.

[140] D Reddy et al, 'Possible Association between Isotretinoin and Inflammatory Bowel Disease' (2006) 101 *The American Journal of Gastroenterology* 1569, doi:10.1111/j.1572-0241.2006.00632.x.

Reddy et al article was that they concluded that isotretinoin use precipitated IBS in some patients and was 'probably' or 'highly probably' causal. However, the article was more nuanced and balanced than the headline suggests: the authors stated they could not confirm that there was a causal relationship, and noted that the age of onset of IBS coincided with the average age of isotretinoin treatment.

The Food and Drug Administration Adverse Event Reporting System (FAERS) received 2,214 reports of isotretinoin-associated IBS between 2003 and 2011.[141] This was a substantial increase in report numbers over the previous five years.

A further potentially confounding factor in establishing the nature of the relationship between isotretinoin and IBS/UC is the role of attorneys. Stobaugh et al examined the extent of attorney-initiated reporting of isotretinoin-associated IBD on FAERS between 2003 and 2011. Their findings are striking. Attorneys reported 87.8% of the isotretinoin-associated IBS cases. By way of comparison, just 3.6% of the total adverse events reported to FAERS are reported by attorneys. This shows that attorney behaviour can have a significant impact on the strength of a pharmacovigilance signal.

The preferred option for establishing a causal link between a pharmaceutical and an adverse event is an epidemiological study. The first epidemiological studies into Accutane and IBD were published in 2009,[142] and in 2010 the first positive association between isotretinoin and UC was demonstrated in a population-based case control study by Crocket et al.[143] Further studies were published that were inconsistent in their findings.[144] A causal link between isotretinoin and IBS and UC has yet to be confirmed.[145] There has been criticism of the way in which lawyers have used the pharmacovigilance data in litigation.[146]

Roche ceased marketing Accutane in the USA in 2009. The FDA website states that there was a Federal Register determination that the product was not discontinued or withdrawn for safety or efficacy reasons.[147] Roche stated that the withdrawal was in the

[141] DJ Stobaugh, P Deepak and ED Ehrenpreis, 'Alleged isotretinoin-associated inflammatory bowel disease: disproportionate reporting by attorneys to the Food and Drug Administration Adverse Event Reporting System' (2013) 69(3) *Journal of American Academy of Dermatology* 393, doi: 10.1016/j.jaad.2013.04.031.

[142] CN Bernstein et al, 'Isotretinoin is not associated with inflammatory bowel disease: a population-based case-control study' (2009) 104(11) *American Journal of Gastroenterology* 2774; SD Crockett et al, 'A causal association between isotretinoin and inflammatory bowel disease has yet to be established' (2009) 104(10) *American Journal of Gastroenterology* 2387.

[143] SD Crockett et al, 'Isotretinoin use and the risk of inflammatory bowel disease: a case-control study' (2010) 105(9) *American Journal of Gastroenterology* 1986.

[144] A Racine et al, 'Isotretinoin and risk of inflammatory bowel disease: a case control study from the French National Health Insurance System' (2012) 142(5) (Suppl 1) *Gastroenterology* S88; RO Alhusayen et al, 'Isotretinoin use and the risk of inflammatory bowel disease: a population-based cohort study' (2013) 133(4) *Journal of Investigative Dermatology* 907; M Etminan et al, 'Isotretinoin and risk for inflammatory bowel disease. A nested case-control study and meta-analysis of published and unpublished data' (2013) 149(2) *Journal of the American Medical Association Dermatology* 216; A Racine et al, 'Isotretinoin and risk of inflammatory bowel disease: a French nationwide study' (2014) 109(4) *American Journal of Gastroenterology* 563; S Rashtak et al, 'Isotretinoin exposure and risk of inflammatory bowel disease' (2014) 150(12) *Journal of the American Medical Association Dermatology* 1322.

[145] SS Coughlin, 'Clarifying the Purported Association between Isotretinoin and Inflammatory Bowel Disease' (2015) 1(2) *Journal of Environment and Health Sciences* 110.15436/2378–6841.15.007; B Lindsey Bauer et al, 'Isotretinoin: controversies, facts, and recommendations' (2016) 9:11 *Expert Review of Clinical Pharmacology* 1435, doi:10.1080/17512433.2016.1213629.

[146] S Tenner, 'Editorial: Isotretinoin and Inflammatory Bowel Disease: Trial Lawyer Misuse of Science and FDA Warnings' (2014) 109 *The American Journal of Gastroenterology* 570.

[147] See at www.accessdata.fda.gov/scripts/cder/daf/index.cfm?event=overview.process&ApplNo=018662.

light of competition from generic manufacturers and the 'high costs from personal injury lawsuits'. Generic versions remain available in the USA.

b. Europe

Isotretinoin was licensed in the UK on 30 June 1983, with availability in all other EU states (except Sweden), based on mutual recognition, following shortly thereafter. Isotretinion is currently available as Roaccutane (the European brand name for Accutane) and as generic version.[148]

1. Teratogenicity

The teratogenicity of isotretinoin has been recognised from the outset, with several states restricting the ability to prescribe it. For example, only dermatologists can prescribe isotretinoin in the UK. However, such restrictions were not consistent between different states. As isotretinoin had been approved using the mutual recognition procedure, the actions taken to prevent pregnancies being exposed to isotretinoin had been dealt with on a state-by-state basis.

A marketing authorisation was granted to Schering Health Care Ltd on 16 August 2001 for a generic isotretinoin. This then triggered an application for mutual recognition to approve the generic across the EU. France received the application for mutual recognition on 4 February 2002, and in response, on 29 May 2002, France made a referral under Article 30 of Directive 2001/83/EC to the EMA. The Article 30 referral was due to the fact that isotretinoin did not have the same summary of product characteristics across Member States.

Given the teratogenicity of isotretinoin, this seemed a potential risk to public health. The Committee for Proprietary Medicinal Products (CPMP) issued an opinion (converted to a decision on 17 October 2003), stating that the summary of product characteristics should be amended. It recommended that isotretinoin should only be prescribed to women of childbearing potential within a Pregnancy Prevention Programme.[149] Also included was a restriction on who could prescribe isotretinoin, which was now only available for 'physicians with expertise in the systemic use of retinoids'.

This effectively set the minimum standards for pregnancy prevention while taking isotretinoin across the whole EU, but there was nothing to prevent states from exceeding these standards. These prescribing conditions were far more restrictive than those in the US.

Interestingly, there seem to be far fewer isotretinoin-exposed pregnancies. For example, up to January 2010 just 105 pregnancies were spontaneously reported to the MHRA.[150]

[148] A list of nationally authorised medicinal products containing isotretinoin available in the EU (correct as at 19 July 2017) can be found at www.ema.europa.eu/docs/en_GB/document_library/Periodic_safety_update_single_assessment/2017/08/WC500234072.pdf.

[149] See at www.ema.europa.eu/ema/index.jsp?curl=pages/medicines/human/referrals/Roaccutane/human_referral_000085.jsp.

[150] MJD Goodfield et al, 'Advice on the safe introduction and continued use of isotretinoin in acne in the UK (2010) 162 *British Journal of Dermatology* 1172.

The British Association of Dermatologists issued guidelines for isotretinoin use in 2010,[151] and carried out audits in 2012[152] and 2014[153] to assess compliance with the guidelines. These indicated that the levels of pregnancy while taking isotretinoin were very low: one pregnancy was reported in the 2012 audit and three pregnancies were reported in the audit from 2013–14. The conclusion is that in the UK, compliance with the guidelines is good. However, there are indicators that the implementation of the Pregnancy Prevention Programme has not been as successful across the EU as a whole.[154]

In 2018 it was recommended that the use of topical retiniods also be subject to a Pregnancy Prevention Programme.[155]

2. Depression and/or Suicidal Ideations

Warnings about the possible occurrence of depression and other psychiatric symptoms were first added to the Summary of Product Characteristics (SmPC) for isotretinoin in 1998. Since 1998 these warnings have been expanded, and they now include further guidelines.[156]

In June 2005, an Expert Working Group of the Committee on Safety of Medicines met to consider all available data relating to psychiatric reactions with isotretinoin, including non-clinical data, clinical trials, published literature, spontaneous reports and epidemiological studies. The Expert Working Group concluded that the product information reflected the currently available evidence.[157]

In June 2014, the MHRA carried out a *Review of isotretinoin and adverse psychiatric reactions*.[158] The review concluded that there were insufficient data to establish a causal association, but an association between isotretinoin and psychiatric disorders could not be ruled out. The warnings in the SmPC were considered appropriate and it was concluded that there no further regulatory action was required, either to amend the warnings regarding psychiatric disorders or to introduce new risk minimisation measures. The review noted that patients should be regularly and routinely screened and monitored for psychiatric disorders.

On 8 July 2016, the UK requested a review of the use of retinoids under Article 31 of Directive 2001/83/EC.[159] The initial review was carried out by the Pharmacovigilance Risk

[151] ibid.

[152] Available at www.bad.org.uk/healthcare-professionals/clinical-standards/clinical-audits/isotretinoin/isotretinoin-2012.

[153] LS Exton et al, 'Compliance with national guidelines on isotretinoin: where are we 2 years since the last audit? Results of the National Isotretinoin Re-Audit 2014' *Clinical and Experimental Dermatology* (20 February 2017), doi:10.1111/ced.13068.

[154] HJ Crijns et al, 'Compliance with pregnancy prevention programmes of isotretinoin in Europe: a systematic review' (2011) 164(2) *British Journal of Dermatology* 238, doi:10.1111/j.1365-2133.2010.09976.x.

[155] See at www.ema.europa.eu/docs/en_GB/document_library/Press_release/2018/03/WC500246349.pdf.

[156] Including warnings about depression, worsening depression in those with a history of depression, anxiety, aggressive tendencies, mood alterations, psychotic symptoms, abnormal behaviour, suicidal thoughts and behaviour, including attempts and accomplished suicide occurring in patients treated with isotretinoin: see 'Isotretinoin (Roaccutane): psychiatric adverse reactions' in (2006) 31 *Current Problems in Pharmacovigilance* 8, available at www.mhra.gov.uk/home/groups/pl-p/documents/websiteresources/con2023860.pdf.

[157] ibid.

[158] Available at assets.publishing.service.gov.uk/media/5492db7ce5274a42900002f2/DSU2.pdf.

[159] EMA/165360/2018.

Assessment Committee (PRAC) and was later endorsed by the Committee for Medicinal Products for Human Use (CHMP),[160] being sent to the European Commission where it became the foundation of a legally binding decision. The review concluded that the limitations of the available data meant that they could not clearly establish whether the risk of neuropsychiatric disorders was due to the use of retinoids. However, the review concluded that as patients with severe skin conditions may be more vulnerable to neuropsychiatric disorders, the prescribing information for oral retinoids should be updated to include a warning about this possible risk. This additional warning applied to oral retinoids but not to topical retinoids, based on the available data.

Despite the lack of conclusive evidence of a causal link between isotretinoin and psychiatric disorders, there have been numerous reports in the press.[161]

iv. Litigation

a. In the USA

The majority of Accutane cases have been related to claims of IBS and UC, and there were several multi-million dollar Accutane awards made by juries. High-profile IBS/UC cases have included:

- Andrew McCarrell, who was awarded $2.6 million in July 2007, award overturned in March 2017;[162]
- Kamie Kendall-Rees, awarded $10.5 million in 2008, reduced to $.5 million at a retrial in March 2017;[163] and
- the four cases of Katheleen Rossitto, Riley Dean Wilkinson, Rebecca Ree Wilkins Reynolds and Jason Young, which were heard together. The jury found for Roche in the cases of Reynolds and Young, and found in favour of Rossitto and Wilkinson, who were awarded $9 million each in June 2012, but the verdicts were vacated and remanded for a new trial in July 2016.[164]

These cases demonstrate the evidential difficulties with asserting a causal relationship between IBS and/or UC and Accutane. The four cases of Rossitto et al, were part of the New Jersey MCL. Interestingly, one (of several) of the reasons that the verdicts in Rossitto and Wilkinson were vacated was because the first instance court was felt to have erred by wrongly excluding some of the defence experts, necessitating a retrial. This demonstrates that the exclusion of experts is not solely a claimant concern.

[160] See at www.ema.europa.eu/ema/index.jsp?curl=pages/medicines/human/referrals/Retinoids_containing_medicinal_products/human_referral_prac_000061.jsp&mid=WC0b01ac05805c516f.

[161] For example, see 'Dying for Clear Skin', the BBC3 documentary first broadcast on 26 November 2012; and H Dixon, 'Controversial acne drug blamed for a number of suicides' *Telegraph* (4 July 2013), available at www.telegraph.co.uk/news/health/10160484/Controversial-acne-drug-blamed-for-a-number-of-suicides.html.

[162] *Andrew McCarrell v Hoffmann-La Roche, Inc. and Roche Laboratories*, Case no A-4481-12T1 (NJ Appellate Division, 2 May 2017).

[163] *Kamie Kendall Rees v Hoffman-La Rochel Inc*, Case no 008213-05 (NJ Super, Atlantic Co).

[164] *Kathleen Rossitto v. Hoffman-La Roche Inc, et al*, Case no A-1236-13T1, *Riley Dean Wilkinson v. Hoffman-La Roche Inc, et al*, Case no A-1237-13T1 (NJ Super, App Div; 22 July 2016).

Despite these evidential issues, over 7,000 claims for damage from Accutane have been filed. The majority of these claims were consolidated into two group actions, an MDL[165] consolidated through the Middle District of Florida and an MCL in New Jersey.

The MDL centralised seven constituent actions in the Middle District of Florida in November 2004.[166] The litigation ran for several years, with various toing and froing. One of the key moments was in June 2007 when Judge Moody, who was overseeing the MDL, granted the defendants' motion to exclude the testimony of the claimants' expert, Dr Ronald Fogel, on general causation.[167] The claimants did not put forward any more persuasive evidence of causation, and the eventual result of the exclusion of Dr Fogel's evidence was that summary judgment was entered for the defendants, effectively dismissing the cases, on 25 July 2012.[168] The litigation had lasted the best part of a decade, and was hardly a resounding success for the claimants.

The MCL commenced in 2003, and at May 2018 was still live. Again, this litigation has had a very long and difficult history with regard to causation and evidential strength. Similar to the MDL, in the MCL the trial judge had banned evidence from two of the plaintiffs' experts in April 2007, only to have it reinstated on appeal.[169] Around 2,000 claimants had been excluded from the MCL as they had been reliant upon the expert testimony, so when the Appellate Division decided to take a more 'relaxed' view of admissibility of expert testimony,[170] this reinstated these plaintiffs. The application of this more 'relaxed' standard caused considerable disquiet: Hoffman-La Roche's appeal was supported by 21 amicus briefs from some of New Jersey's largest employers, including Roche competitors, the New Jersey Chamber of Commerce, the HealthCare Institute of New Jersey, the American Medical Association, and eight notable legal scholars and law professors. Another issue raised was the role of a rebuttable presumption under New Jersey law that an FDA warning is sufficient to trigger the running of any relevant limitation time period. Again, this was contentious and heavily supported by amicus briefs on both sides of the argument.

On 23 April 2018, the defendants in the MCL, Hoffman-La Roche, asked the New Jersey Supreme Court to reinstate the dismissals of the 2,000 cases, and a decision about whether these cases was reached on 1 August 2018.[171] The Court unanimously overturned the decision of the Appellate Division and clarified that the State's required standard for scientific evidence was the four core factors from *Daubert*. This may prove the final act in a very long-running litigation saga.

Litigation over generic isotretinoin is undertaken by several US law firms for various conditions.

[165] *Re Accutane (Isotretinoin) Products Liability Litigation*, MDL no 1626 in the Middle District of Florida.

[166] *Re Accutane (Isotretinoin) Products Liability Litigation*, MDL no 1626 (MD Fla, 343 F Supp 2d 1382, 1383) (JPML, 2004).

[167] *In re Accutane Products Liability Litigation*, MDL 1626 (MD Fla, 15 June 2007).

[168] *In re Accutane Products Liability Litigation*, MDL 1626 at 10 (MD Fla, 24 July 2012).

[169] *In re Accutane Litigation*, 2017 NJ Super LEXIS 116 (App Div, 28 Jul 2017).

[170] Essentially applying the standard from *Rubanick v Witco Chemical Corp*, 125 NJ 421, 449 (1991), whereby evidence is admissible if it is 'based on a sound, adequately-founded scientific methodology involving data and information of the type reasonably relied on by experts in the scientific field', even if it is not generally accepted. This is in contrast to the more stringent *Daubert* standard with which tort lawyers will be familiar: see *Daubert v Merrell Dow Pharmaceuticals, Inc*, 509 US 579, 597 (1993).

[171] *In re Accutane Litigation*, no 079958, 2018 WL 3636867 (NJ, 1 August 2018).

b. In the UK

Reports of potential claims in the UK began as early as 1998[172] but foundered soon after, seemingly on economic grounds.[173] Threats of further claims in UK followed in 1999 when the CSM published amendments to warnings to note the risk of depression, psychotic symptoms and, in rare cases, suicidal ideation.[174] While there have been a number of coroners' cases linking isotretinoin use and psychiatric symptoms, this has not translated to litigation. To date there has been no large-scale litigation over isotretinoin in the UK.

v. Conclusion

Regulatory actions reflected ADR reports and resulted in stricter warnings and access to the drug. The US Accutane litigation has been protracted and complex, and has raised various questions over the status of different evidence types in assessing causation. Of particular interest is the use of FAERS data by claimant lawyers, when the majority of the bowel related adverse incidence reports made to FAERS were by claimant lawyers.

[172] See at news.bbc.co.uk/1/hi/health/218028.stm.

[173] Richard Girling, 'Scarred for life: Does the drug that cures acne have devastating side effects?' *Sunday Times* (30 June 2002).

[174] See *Current Problems in Pharmacovigilance*, August 1998, available at webarchive.nationalarchives.gov.uk/20141206135347/http://www.mhra.gov.uk/home/groups/pl-p/documents/websiteresources/con2023231.pdf.

II. Contraceptives and Hormone Replacement Therapy

A. Gravigard or Copper 7 Intrauterine Device

i. Description

Gravigard or Copper 7 was an intrauterine device (IUD) consisting of a copper wire wound around a plastic frame shaped like the figure 7 with tail string to facilitate removal. It was inserted into the uterus, where it acted to prevent pregnancy. It was marketed as 'Gravigard' in the UK and as 'Copper 7' in the US.

ii. Safety Issue

An association between IUD use and pelvic inflammatory disease (PID) had been noted from the mid-1970s onwards. Pelvic inflammatory disease is an infection of the female upper genital tract. It is caused by bacteria migrating from the cervix and vagina into the upper genital tract, the uterus, fallopian tubes and ovaries. If untreated, PID can cause scarring, which can block the fallopian tubes, leading to infertility.

The Gravigard safety issues followed the Dalkon Shield controversy. Dalkon Shield was an IUD manufactured by AH Robbins, with a different design. The Dalkon shield had a relatively large 'crab'-shaped plastic and copper inter-uterine portion, with a multi-filament tail for extraction. It was thought that the multi-filament design of the tail string acted as a 'wick' to enable bacteria to travel from the vagina through the cervix into the uterus. From 1971 onwards, when there were reports of mid-trimester septic abortions being associated with the Dalkon Shield,[175] considerable controversy arose. The Dalkon Shield was removed from the market in June 1974 and substantial litigation followed in USA.[176]

Despite the fact that the products were very different in their design, Gravigard and all other IUDs were tainted by association. Medical literature in the 1970s indicated that there was an association, presumed to be causal, between IUD use and PID.[177]

The assumption of a causal link between IUD use and PID was overthrown upon the discovery of a link between bacterial infections, commonly chlamydia trachomatis and neisseria gonorrhoeae, and PID.[178] Pelvic inflammatory disease can be caused both by sexually transmitted infections, such as chlamydia and gonorrhoeae, and from bacteria that naturally occur in the female lower reproductive tract. From the late 1980s it was considered that the lifestyle of the woman (and her partner(s)) was more likely to be the determining factor both in her choice of an IUD as a method of contraception and in her risk of developing PID.

[175] JS Templeton, 'Letter: Septic abortion and the Dalkon Shield' (1974) 2 *British Medical Journal* 612.

[176] KR Feinberg, 'The Dalkon Shield Claimants Trust' (1990) 53 *Law and Contemporary Problems* 79, available at scholarship.law.duke.edu/cgi/viewcontent.cgi?article=4073&context=lcp.

[177] For example, see WL Faulkner and HW Ory, 'Intrauterine Devices and Acute Pelvic Inflammatory Disease' (1976) 235(17) *Journal of the American Medical Association* 1851, doi:10.1001/jama.1976.03260430021016.

[178] J Hare, 'Pelvic inflammatory disease: current approaches and ideas' (1990) 1(6) *International Journal of STD & AIDS* 393.

Current medical opinion asserts that the use of IUDs is safe, and PID is rare even in younger women using IUDs.[179]

iii. Marketing and Regulatory History

Commercially available intrauterine contraceptive devices began to be marketed from the start of the twentieth century. The advent of plastic and the addition of a tail string for easy removal increased the popularity and availability of IUDs. By the late 1960s, 'second generation' devices were appearing, which contained both plastic and copper (an effective spermicide) within the frames.

The company GD Searle & Co developed and tested Copper 7 in the US, based on prototypes created by a Chilean clinician Dr Jaime Zipper.[180] There were ongoing clinical studies on the product throughout the early 1970s. There were various changes to the labelling and product information throughout the product's lifespan, and these usually were national and were not consistently applied across the jurisdictions in which the product was marketed.

a. In the USA

Copper 7 was sent to the FDA for approval in 1971. At that time there was no formal framework for medical device approval,[181] but the copper component of the IUD meant that when it was submitted to the FDA in 1971 it was classified it as a 'drug'.[182] Further research data were required, which were then considered by the FDA. Following FDA approval, marketing commenced in 1974.

On 7 November 1977 there was a label change, and the FDA required warnings specifically citing the risk of PID to be supplied to patients and doctors.

In 1986 Searle was acquired by Monsanto, and subsequently the Copper 7 IUD was voluntarily removed from the US market due to what Searle referred to as 'unwarranted' product liability claims.[183] Searle were very clear that the removal from the US market was a business decision, not a regulatory one, and the device remained available in the UK, Europe and elsewhere.

b. In the UK

In the UK there was also no separate medical device regulatory system, so the device was considered under the Medicines Act 1968. After considering the available data, a product

[179] CB Sufrin et al, 'Neisseria gonorrhea and Chlamydia trachomatis screening at intrauterine device insertion and pelvic inflammatory disease' (2012) 120(6) *Obstetrics and Gynecology* 1314, doi:10.1097/AOG.0b013e318273364c; TC Jatlaoui, HE Riley and KM Curtis, 'The Safety of intrauterine devices among young women: a systematic review' (2017) 95(1) *Contraception* 17, doi:10.1016/j.contraception.2016.10.006.

[180] J Zipper et al, 'Metallic copper as an intrauterine contraceptive adjunct to the "T" device' (1969) 105(8) *American Journal of Obstetrics and Gynecology* 1274, doi:doi.org/10.1016/0002-9378(69)90302-0.

[181] Device regulation was first enacted by Congress in 1976 in Pub L no 94-295, 90 Stat 539 (codified at 21 USC 360–360K (1976)).

[182] NDA 017408, which lists the active ingredient as copper.

[183] Taymar Lewin, 'Searle, Assailing Lawsuits, Halts Us Sales of Intrauterine Devices' *New York Times* (National Edition) (1 February 1986), available at www.nytimes.com/1986/02/01/us/searle-assailing-lawsuits-halts-us-sales-of-intrauterine-devices.html.

licence was granted in November 1973. In 1980 the UK data sheet was amended to indicate that there was an association between IUD use and PID, and that PID could lead to infertility. In 1990 the product was removed from the UK market as part of the worldwide product withdrawal.

c. In Australia

Interestingly, Australia had a more codified regulatory system for IUDs at this point in time. This framework was found in the Therapeutic Goods Act 1966. This statute was intended to cover 'goods for therapeutic use', so was not restricted to 'medicines' or 'substances', and defined therapeutic use as including 'use in, or in connection with, testing for pregnancy, contraception, prosthetics or orthotics'. Late in 1984 an application was made to the Australian Drug Evaluation Committee for approval for the importation and general marketing of the Gravigard-Cu-7 device. This was granted and marketing began in 1985. Gravigard was removed from the Australian market in the 1990 worldwide withdrawal.

iv. Litigation

a. In the US

The Copper 7 litigation started in earnest in the US in 1985/86, when several hundred claims were launched against Searle. The timing may have been partially driven by events in the Dalkon Shield litigation. First, the Dalkon Shield cases raised public awareness of adverse events associated with IUD use. Secondly, in August 1985 the Dalkon Shield defendant, HA Robbins, filed for Chapter 11 bankruptcy. Suddenly, claimant lawyers with expertise in IUD claims had a gap where Dalkon Shield claims had been. For the claimant lawyers, similar IUD claims with defendants with deeper pockets would have been an ideal substitute for the Dalkon Shield claims. In September 1985, Johnson & Johnson removed their Lippes Loop IUD from the US market after couple of hundred lawsuits were launched against it. Copper 7 claims appeared, and by the end of January 1986 nearly 800 claims had been made.[184]

One firm in particular was vigorous in its pursuit of Copper 7 claims – Robins, Zelle, Larson & Kaplan of Minneapolis. This firm handled the case that was pivotal in the Copper 7 litigation, *Kociemba v GD Searle & Co.*[185] Ester Kociemba had a Copper 7 IUD inserted by her physician, Dr Timothy Scanlan on 6 June 1977. At this point in time,[186] GD Searle produced a patient information leaflet, which was supposed to be given to patients, which stated:

> Pelvic infections have been reported following insertion of the Copper 7. These can occur anyway, but it is certainly possible for the Copper 7 to pick up germs in the vagina and carry them into the uterus on insertion. Even though the Copper 7 was packaged sterile, the vagina is not sterile. Most infections can be eliminated by antibiotic therapy, but if not, the Copper 7 should be removed.

[184] ibid.

[185] *Kociemba v GD Searle & Co*, USDC, District of Minnesota, Third Division, Civ no 3-85-1599.

[186] The FDA labelling change that required GD Searle to inform of the risk of PID and infertility did not come into effect until 7 November 1977.

This does not mention either the possibility of PID or the risk of infertility. In any case, Ester Kociemba's doctor, Dr Scanlan, stated that he did not believe he had received the brochure and, therefore, had not given it to Mrs Kociemba.

Mrs Kociemba suffered a pelvic infection 12 days after the IUD was inserted. Dr Scanlan prescribed antibiotics, which seemed to resolve the situation. Her IUD remained in place until November 1978, when she had it removed as she and her husband wanted to start a family. She did not get pregnant, and it was subsequently discovered that her fallopian tubes were blocked. Her husband also had a low sperm count.

On 9 September 1988 the jury found for Mrs Kociemba and stated that Searle was negligent in testing the IUD and in failing to warn Mrs Kociemba and her doctor. Mrs Kociemba was awarded $8.75 million,[187] of which $750,000 was compensation and the remainder punitive damages. This case had a substantial impact, generating a lot of publicity and interest from other women in suing Searle. This alone damaged Monsanto's stock price,[188] but it was the impact of a second case, *Daher v GD Searle & Co*,[189] that proved decisive. Monsanto had claimed that a veil existed between Monsanto and Searle, and that Monsanto was only liable to the value of the Searle subsidiary, which was estimated at less than $1 billion. However, in the *Daher* case the notion of a veil was dismissed, as Monsanto was included as a co-defendant and was tried alongside Searle. This had a dire effect on Monsanto's share price, and it pushed the firm to settle the remaining Copper 7 cases without trial. These were generally settled promptly and, where compensation was awarded, for relatively low sums.

Over the course of the Copper 7 litigation only 24 cases went to full trial, and the defendant prevailed in 19 of these. Just five cases were won by claimants. In total, Searle paid just under $700,000 in combined damages for four of these cases, and $8.15 million for the *Kociemba* case. *Kociemba* was a total outlier, in terms both of the quantum awarded and the general pattern of litigation verdicts, which tended to find for the defendant. Despite this, that one outlier case dictated the way in which Copper 7 claims were handled by Monsanto/Searle.

b. In England and Wales

The impact of the *Kociemba* case stretched across the Atlantic.[190] In 1986, a user group, the Cu-7 Association, had formed, and in January 1988 the first letter of claim was sent to the UK product licence holder, GD Searle & Co Ltd. The *Kociemba* verdict in September 1988, combined with national media coverage, led to an increased interest in litigation from affected women. The women considered issuing proceedings in the US, but were advised against it.

The claim then proceeded in the English courts. By January 1989 there were 32 women who each had a legal aid certificate to proceed. One case had been designated as the lead

[187] Later reduced by the judge to $8.15 million.

[188] Julia Flynn, 'Siler Monsanto Stock Plunges on Copper-7 Case' *New York Times* (National Edition) (13 September 1988), available at www.nytimes.com/1988/09/13/business/monsanto-stock-plunges-on-copper-7-case.html.

[189] *Daher v GD Searle & Co*, USDC, District of Minnesota, Third Division, Civ no 3-88-0099.

[190] Information taken from C Hodges, 'Gravigard IUD' in C Hodges (ed), *Multi-Party Actions* (Oxford University Press, 2001) ch 20.

file. There were several applications for extensive pre-trial disclosure, with a considerable volume of information disclosed that took some time to consider. In November 1991 the solicitors firm Pannone Napier stated that it was in a position to proceed, and it requested that the case be transferred to the Central Office of the High Court and managed in accordance with the Supreme Court Procedure Committee's *Guide for Group Action*. This request was granted.

Despite indications from the claimants' counsel that there were around 70 women who were expected to proceed, including over 40 who had legal aid, very few proceedings were issued. A draft Master Statement of Claim was served in May 1993, a substantial document which contained generic allegations, without details of individual claims. By the end of 1994, seven years after the start of the litigation, only 17 women had actually issued proceedings, and only 15 of those had supplied draft individual statements of claim.

In February 1995, the defendants served their Commentary on the draft Master Statement of Claim. They also wrote to the Legal Aid Board with responses to the generic allegations in the draft Master Statement of Claim and with responses to the individual claims that had been filed, and suggesting that legal aid funding should be withdrawn. The Legal Aid Board considered the available evidence, and in June 1996 the legal aid funding was withdrawn. Nine women appealed against this decision to the Legal Aid Board's Area Committee, but their appeals were dismissed in October 1996.

The main issue in the case was of causation. While the popular press was certain that the IUD was causing injuries, the state of scientific knowledge did not support that certainty. This placed the claimants in an unenviable position. The conviction they held that they had been damaged by the product appeared to be upheld everywhere except for the one place they needed it to be – the courtroom. Likewise, the defendants were vilified in the popular press and forced into expensive litigation to defend a product that the available evidence suggested was not defective.

c. In Australia

Australia was also home to a long-running litigation on Gravigard.[191] Proceedings were issued there in 1987, but not served until 1991. Various statements of claim were issued throughout the litigation: as in the UK, the number of claimants in the action fluctuated up to a maximum of 300. The case proceeded to an extremely lengthy trial of nine cases, which commenced on 19 January 1996 and ran for almost nine months, with final submissions presented on 23 December 1997. On 22 February 1999, over a decade since the litigation was initiated, the court found for the defendant on the issue of general causation. What had been, according to the judge, Bruce J, 'the longest and most complex product liability litigation in Australian legal history' seemed finally to have concluded. However, the nine lead claimants appeal to the New South Wales Court of Appeal, where the judges found that Bruce J had erred in determining liability based on issues of general causation and that individual causation should have been established, and a retrial was ordered.[192]

[191] *Denzin v The Nutrasweet Co* [1999] NSWSC 106 (Bruce J, 22 February 1999), available at www.austlii.edu.au/cgi-bin/viewdoc/au/cases/nsw/NSWSC/1999/106.html.

[192] *Moylan v Nutrasweet Co* [2000] NSWCA 337, available at www.austlii.edu.au/cgi-bin/viewdoc/au/cases/nsw/NSWCA/2000/337.html.

After this judgment in August 2001, a confidential out-of-court settlement was finally reached between the parties.

v. Conclusion

The safety signal with the product was complex and highlights the difficulty in establishing whether the association between a product and an adverse event is causal or not. The regulatory position for Gravigard/Copper 7 remained unchanged. The product was removed from the market for commercial reasons. Claimants have won a handful of cases in the US, where the jury system judges the complex, and sometimes contradictory, scientific evidence. In England and Wales, where judges determine these cases, with exception the defendants have prevailed. The Australian litigation ran for many years, and cost many millions of dollars, finally resulting in an out-of-court settlement rather than a retrial. One single high-value case American case, *Kociemba*, had a major impact and drove the defendant into settlements in the US, and seemingly encouraged litigation in other jurisdictions.

B. Third-Generation Oral Contraceptives

i. Description

The first oral contraceptives (OCs) were approved for human use in the USA in 1959, and prescriptions for women in the UK began during the 1960s. Oral contraceptives became known as 'the pill' and took hold of a significant share of the contraceptives market. The pill became a very popular form of birth control; if taken correctly, once a day, it is highly effective in preventing pregnancy.

The original, or 'first-generation', combined oral contraceptives (COCs) contained a combination of two distinct constituents: synthetic estrogens and synthetic progestogens (progestins). Estrogens used in COCs have remained fairly constant, with the vast majority of pills containing either ethinylestradiol or estradiol. Over the years the dose of both constituents and the progestogens used have changed. The progestins in the first-generation pills included norethynodrel, norethindrone, lynestrenol and ethynodiol diacetate. The first-generation COCs contained higher doses of both hormones than subsequent iterations. Second-generation COCs were produced from the 1970s onwards and contained progestins such as lefonorgestrel and norethisterone. The third-generation products appeared in the 1980s and contained progestins such as norgestimate, desogestrel, gestodene and cyproterone acetate. Fourth-generation COCs contain the progestogin drospirenone.

ii. Safety Issue

On 18 October 1995, the UK CSM wrote a 'Dear Doctor' letter to all relevant prescribers stating that there were three unpublished studies concerning the safety of COCs in relation to venous-thromboembolism (VTE). The most common forms of VTE are deep vein thrombosis (DVT) and pulmonary embolism (PE). The studies alleged 'around a 2-fold increase in the risk' of VTE in comparison to the second generation of COCs.

iii. Marketing and Regulatory History

In 1982 and 1989, Organon introduced two COCs to the UK market, branded Marvelon and Mercilon.[193] These products contained the progestogin desogestrel (DSG), and an estrogen. In 1987, Schering introduced their new COC to the UK market, under the name Femodene[194] (known in Germany as Femovan), which contained the progestogin gestodene (GSD). An identical product was licensed to Wyeth, who marketed it under the name Minulet.[195]

Chemically, DSG and GSD are distinct products but are designed to achieve the same biological result. Collectively they are consistently referred to as 'third-generation' progestogens, and the COCs (of which they are constituent parts) have been referred to as 'third-generation COCs'.

[193] Marvelon and Mercilon were grated UK licences on 4 November 1981 and 12 February 1986 respectively.
[194] Femodene was granted a UK licence on 12 July 1986.
[195] Minulet was granted a UK licence on 27 August 1987.

From 1 February 1987, ADR reporting relating to OCs became compulsory in Germany. Shortly after Femovan's launch by Schering in May 1987, in November 1988 the medicines agency in Germany[196] requested Schering to make a reassessment of the risks and benefits of the drug, and to produce data on its ADRs and sales. In December 1988, Schering submitted the requested data and sent out a 'Dear Doctor' letter. By the end of 1988, sales of Femovan had reached the relatively high market share of 14%. The number of thrombolic events reported to the BGA amounted to 20. In February 1989, the BGA issued a 'Drug Information Sheet' (ASI) in which the medical profession was asked to pay particular attention to cardiovascular complications with OC preparations containing GSD and to report them to the BGA. From 21 February 1989, negative publicity ensued. From 1 March 1989, a graduated plan procedure, under section 63 of the German Law on Medicines, was initiated, requiring all manufacturers to report ADRs to all monophasic OCs containing ethinyl-estradiol.

In September 1989, there was a meeting between Schering and the Medicines Committee of the German Medical Association. The Committee asked for an epidemiological study into safety of modern OCs. In May 1991, the BGA sent Schering a letter with questions arising from the Hannover meeting. In August 1991, Schering received a list of ADRs on file at the authority pertaining to Femovan, Minulet, Marvelon and Cilest. Organon had also started reporting ADRs after reporting of individual cases became obligatory on 1 February 1987. The BGA had included in its list more than 50 reports originating from the large phase IV Gestodene-F trial.

In January 1992, the BGA included all low-dose OCs into the graduated step plan to report ADRs. In March of that year, all relevant manufacturing companies met to coordinate a joint approach to the step plan through the Federal Association of Pharmaceutical Manufacturers (BPI). Class labelling was agreed upon for OCs. In May 1992, the BGA entered phase two of the step plan and proposed a stricter thrombosis warning and the inclusion of a warning for breast cancer in the label. In July 1992, companies involved in Germany, with the exception of Organon and Ortho, agreed to alter the labels of the OCs concerned and submit applications to vary marketing authorisations in due course.

On 18 October 1995, the UK CSM circulated a 'Dear Doctor' letter, entitled 'Combined Oral Contraceptives and Thromboembolism', to all doctors and pharmacists in the UK, stating that there were three unpublished studies concerning the safety of COCs in relation to VTE.

On 6 November 1995, a letter was sent to manufacturers by the *Bundesinstitut für Arzneimittel und Medizinprodukte* (BfArM), the German Federal Institute for Drugs and Medical Devices, stating that OCs should not to be prescribed to those under 30 for the next six months. It also required manufacturers in Germany to make changes to labelling and package inserts by 11 December 1995. Claimants applauded the letter and said the warnings should still be attached to third-generation COCs, but the defendants said that the letter was precipitate and led to a public health disaster.[197]

[196] The *BundesGesundheitsAmt* (or BGA).

[197] A 1997 Office for National Statistics report estimated that in eight months alone following the letter's pronouncement, there were 30,000 conceptions in the UK beyond the number that might have been the case prior to the pronouncement, and 10,000 of these were aborted.

The European CPMP took a different approach from the CSM in the UK. In a statement on 27 October 1996, the CPMP asked the three companies manufacturing OCs for more data. The statement made clear that it would not be withdrawing third-generation COCs on the basis of the evidence then available. On 3 December 1996, after having considered the additional data provided, the CPMP reached a preliminary conclusion that users of third-generation COCs should be warned of an excess absolute risk of about 10 cases per 100,000 woman years. In light of this information, it was recommended that women without recognised risk factors for VTE, and who might be intolerant of other COCs, should take third-generation COCs if they were prepared to accept an increased risk of VTE.

On 20 January 1999, the UK Licensing Authority accepted the advice of the Medicines Commission that the SmPC for the third-generation COCs should be amended. The Medicines Commission maintained the view that there was an increased relative risk 'of about 1.7 to 1.8 after adjustment', which was 'not fully explained by bias or confounding'. New warnings were required to appear on the SmPCs, that an increased risk of VTE associated with COCs was generally well established but was smaller than that associated with pregnancy (60 cases per 100,000 pregnancies).[198] In healthy, non-pregnant women who were not taking any COCs the figure was about five cases per 100,000 woman years; in those taking second-generation COCs the figure was about 15 cases; and in those taking third-generation COCs the figure was about 25 cases. It was also stated that the risk for VTE increases with age and other known risk factors, such as obesity.

The Medicines Commission pointed out that the risk for VTE was so small that, so long as prescribers and patients had all the relevant information, there was no point in restricting third-generation COCs to those intolerant of second-generation COCs, or to 'second-line' prescription only.

Meanwhile, the CPMP completed its assessment on 28 September 2001. It viewed the risk of VTE posed by second-generation COCs to be about 20 per 100,000 woman years, which increased by 1.5–2% for third-generation COCs. The CPMP concluded that this risk was highest in the first year of use, and therefore should mainly be taken into consideration by first-time users. This view was incorporated into the proposed changes to the SmPCs of the relevant products, as well as in the European equivalent of the 'Dear Doctor' letter. The CPMP concluded that there was no reason for a woman using any brand of COC to stop taking it on the basis of its findings.

The situation continued to be monitored by the regulatory agencies. In May 2004, the CPMP had been replaced by the EMA's CHMP. In October 2013, the PRAC of the EMA concluded that the benefits of COCs continued to outweigh their risks.[199] On 31 January 2014, CHMP completed a review,[200] which concluded that the benefits of COCs outweighed

[198] (1999) 25 *Current Problems in Pharmacovigilance* 12, available at webarchive.nationalarchives.gov.uk/20080907001210/http://www.mhra.gov.uk/Publications/Safetyguidance/CurrentProblemsinPharmacovigilance/CON007465. Changes to product information were notified to doctors on 8 April 1999.

[199] See at www.ema.europa.eu/docs/en_GB/document_library/Minutes/2013/11/WC500154424.pdf and http://www.ema.europa.eu/docs/en_GB/document_library/Referrals_document/Combined_hormonal_contraceptives/Recommendation_provided_by_Pharmacovigilance_Risk_Assessment_Committee/WC500151959.pdf.

[200] Available at www.ema.europa.eu/ema/index.jsp?curl=pages/medicines/human/referrals/Combined_hormonal_contraceptives/human_referral_prac_000016.jsp&mid=WC0b01ac05805c516f.

the risks. The CHMP opinion and the previous PRAC recommendation were sent to the European Commission. The Commission then made a legally binding decision to update the product information on all COCs throughout the EU to include more information on the risks of VTEs; this decision was adopted on 16 January 2014.

Various national agencies, including the MHRA in the UK,[201] responded to this change by issuing alerts to prescribers on the updated product information and by issuing guidance such as prescribing checklists,

iv. Litigation

Litigation in the UK commenced after the 1995 'Dear Doctor' letter. Claimants' lawyers said that proper consideration of the three unpublished studies described in the letter would support their claims. Claimants alleged that they had suffered various cardio-vascular injuries, commonly described as VTE, as a result of use of third-generation products. Deep vein thrombosis and PE were the commonest cases, but some patients claimed to have suffered cerebral venous thrombosis and strokes. Claims were based on the strict liability legislation. A trial of seven lead claims in 2003, taken from a group of 99 claims (40 against Schering, 46 against Organon, and 13 against Wyeth) resulted in judgment for the defendants, based on absence of proof of general causation.[202]

v. Conclusion

The potential safety issue was identified by the regulatory authorities by 1988, shortly after third-generation products were introduced, and was subject to continuous scrutiny through studies and coordinated ADR reporting. The German authorities played a lead role (since the major manufacturers were German companies). The European central authorities were also involved, and some differences of expert view emerged between the authorities, which sharpened debate between them. Group litigation arose in the UK in 1995, and failed following an exhaustive analysis of the scientific evidence on general causation.

[201] See at www.gov.uk/drug-safety-update/combined-hormonal-contraceptives-and-venous-thromboembolism-review-confirms-risk-is-small.

[202] *XYZ and Others v Schering Health Care Ltd, Organon Laboratories Ltd and John Wyeth and Brother Ltd* [2002] EWHC 1420 (QB), Mackey J.

C. Norplant (levonorgestrel)

i. Description

Norplant[203] is a contraceptive device that is implanted under the skin and can remain effective for up to five years. The original Norplant implants consisted of a set of six small (2.4 mm × 34 mm) silicone capsules, each filled with 36 mg of levonorgestrel, a synthetic progestogen used in many birth control pills. Norplant was manufactured between 1990 and 2008.

The original implant should not be confused with the second-generation implant, Norplant II (Norplant-2, Jadelle); the following information relates to the original Norplant implant.

ii. Safety Issue

Shortly following the drug's introduction to the US market in 1991, ADR reports began to surface on unexpected side-effects, such as irregular menstrual bleeding, headaches, nausea and depression.[204] Between February 1991 and December 1993 the FDA received 5,800 reports of adverse health events involving Norplant use, through its Medwatch Reporting System. Concerns were also raised over the implantation and explantation of the device, with some patients reporting that practitioners were unable to remove the device when requested as it could not be located. Questions were raised as to whether the device had never actually been implanted, had been misplaced within the tissue during implantation or had migrated after implantation.

iii. Marketing and Regulatory History

Norplant was developed by Sheldon Segal, an American embryologist and biochemist, who was director of Population Control, an international non-governmental organisation. It was the first major advancement in contraception since the birth control pill. The device was first approved in 1983 in Finland, where it was manufactured by Leiras Oy Pharmaceuticals.

Norplant was approved by the US FDA in 1990, and was marketed in the US in 1991 by Wyeth Pharmaceuticals. Roussel Laboratories Ltd was granted a UK marketing authorisation for the product as a prescription only medicine on 17 May 1993.

Norplant was withdrawn from the UK market in 1999.[205] Hoechst Marion Roussel cited dwindling demand for the product, which made it no longer commercially viable. The company blamed adverse media coverage, and legal action by women who claimed that they had suffered serious side-effects after using the contraceptive.[206] Wyeth also announced that due to limitations in product component supplies, it did not plan to

[203] See A McDougall, 'Norplant Litigation' in Hodges (ed), n 191, ch 31.

[204] 'Contraceptive Maker Wins Woman's Suit Over Side Effects' *New York Times* (5 September 1998), available at query.nytimes.com/gst/fullpage.html?sec=health&res=9500E5D7163EF936A3575AC0A96E958260.

[205] 'Contraceptive implant withdrawn' *BBC News* (30 April 1999), available at news.bbc.co.uk/1/hi/health/331618.stm.

[206] See news.bbc.co.uk/2/hi/health/331618.stm.

resume marketing the original formulation of Norplant system in the US.[207] The UK licence for Norplant was cancelled on 7 August 2007.

iv. Litigation

Claims were brought in the US from the early 1990s onwards, based on various allegations of a wide range of side-effects, failure to warn of potential side-effects, and lack of sufficient training and information for doctors using the product. The litigation was substantial, with over 40,000 claimants reported to have sued Wyeth nationwide.[208] The majority of the cases were in the MDL, but there were also relatively small-scale actions in State courts in Chigaco, Texas, Illinois and Indiana.[209]

The largest Norplant litigation was the MDL in Texas, which comprised almost 3,000 lawsuits and around 30,000 claimants. In August 1995, MDL 1038 was certified to be heard in the District Court for the Eastern District of Texas by Chief Judge Richard Schell. In an unusual move, Judge Schell decided that the class certification might not have been appropriate at that stage of proceedings, and he ordered that three bellwether trials should be conducted to allow the court to explore the issues at stake and to decide if certification into a federal action was an appropriate route for the Norplant cases. The court applied the learned intermediary principle, and found that as Wyeth had properly prepared and manufactured Norplant, including selling it with proper directions and warnings to the prescribing physician, Wyeth was not liable for any resulting damages, nor was there any requirement for Wyeth to warn patients directly. Wyeth therefore won the first of the three bellwether trials convincingly.[210] The litigation carried on, and over the next two years Wyeth won another two jury trials and had granted various applications for summary judgment, which almost halved the claimant cohort. Despite this success in court, by the end of August 1999 Wyeth made an offer of $54 million to settle the remaining claims. It said that although it had not lost a trial, the cost of defending the claims was too high, and that the offer of settlement was a commercial decision.[211] The settlement was relatively modest in comparison to the sums sought, with the remaining plaintiffs receiving around $1,500 each. By August 2002, around 32,000 plaintiffs had accepted the settlement offer, with a remaining 2,970 either refusing the offer or failing to respond. On 14 August 2002, Wyeth had the remaining 2,970 cases dismissed.[212]

[207] See Shari Roan, 'Maker of Norplant Decides to Take Product Off the Market' *LA Times* (5 August 2002).

[208] 10-k Filing for American Home Products Corporation for the year ending December 1999.

[209] *Mealey's Litigation Report. Drugs and Medical Devices.* American Home updates pending Norplant suits. 18 April 1997.

[210] *In Re Norplant Contraceptive Products Liability Litigation*, 955 F Supp 700 (ED Tex 1997) RA Schell, Memorandum Opinion and Order Granting Defendant's Motion for Summary Judgment, US District Court for the Eastern District of Texas, Beaumont Division, 4 March 1997, available at law.justia.com/cases/federal/district-courts/FSupp/955/700/1516035/.

[211] For a more detailed analysis, see S Garber, *Economic Effects of Product Liability and Other Litigation involving the Safety of Pharmaceuticals* (RAND Institute for Civil Justice, 2013) ch 4.

[212] *In Re Norplant Contraceptive Products Liability Litigation*, 215 F Supp 2d 795 (ED Tex 2002) RA Schell, Memorandum Opinion and Order (1) Granting in part and denying in part Wyeth's Motion for Partial Summary Judgment Re the Learned Intermediary Doctring/Causation and (2) Granting Wyeth's Motion for Partial Summary Judgment Re Conditions for which there is no Evidence of Causation, US District Court for the Eastern District of Texas, Beaumont Division, 4 March 1997, available at law.justia.com/cases/federal/district-courts/FSupp2/215/795/2503637/.

This did not end the US litigation over Norplant. A relatively small cohort, around 3,500–4,000, women had launched litigation in Louisiana, first filed in 1994 and 1995. This was then certified as a class in 2001, confirmed on appeal.[213] These lawsuits were on a different basis, alleging that the Norplant implant was defective because it released too much active ingredient in the first year and a half after implantation. This litigation continued for 17 years until it finally ended in a settlement offer, reported to be $29.5 million, which was made by Pfizer (which had acquired Wyeth in 2009) to settle the matter. There was no admission of liability.

A Norplant Action Group was formed in the UK in May 1995, which coordinated a media campaign and obtained legal aid for about 10 claimants to bring claims. During the case preparation it became clear that the focus of the litigation was shifting, from adverse events and side-effects to implantation and explantation, in particular whether sufficient training had been provided by Rousell. Proceedings were started in 1996, but after exchange of witness statements and experts' reports, the claimants' counsel advised the Legal Aid Board that the cases could not succeed, and funding was withdrawn in 1999.

Although the case was withdrawn there were unanswered questions on the fairness of the way in which liability for costs had been allocated,[214] and the impact this could have on future collective litigation.

v. Conclusion

Hoechst Marion Roussel withdrew Norplant from the UK market, citing negative media coverage and the commencement of litigation. No admission of liability or payments were made in the England and Wales. Wyeth ended distribution of Norplant in the US in 2002 for reasons allegedly unrelated to safety allegations. Despite not losing a trial in the MDL, substantial settlements were paid to end various Norplant claims.

[213] Louisiana: *Davis v American Home Products Corp*, 844 So 2d 242 (La App 2003) (affirming certification of class of patients implanted with Norplant device).

[214] See McDougall, n 204.

D. Hormone Replacement Therapy

i. Description

Hormone replacement therapy (HRT) is a system of medical treatment for surgically menopausal, pre-menopausal and some post-menopausal women. It involves the use of one or more of a group of medications designed to artificially boost hormone levels for the purpose of preventing discomfort caused by diminished circulating estrogen and progesterone hormones, or, in the case of the surgically or prematurely menopausal, to prolong life and reduce incidence of dementia.

ii. Safety Issue

Three papers published in *The Lancet* on 12 October 1996[215] all showed an increased risk of DVT and/or PE in women currently taking HRT. These studies contributed to five in total,[216] which cumulatively resulted in the launch of a regulatory investigation.

The link to DVT/PE is not the only condition risk of which HRT appears to increase. There have been reports of increased risks of certain cancers for women taking HRT.[217]

iii. Marketing and Regulatory History

There are two main forms of HRT: a combined estrogen and progestogen preparation for women who have their wombs; and estrogen only HRT for women who have had a hysterectomy. The treatment is available in many different formulations, including tablets, transdermal patches, skin gels and implants.

A third type of HRT is tibolone, a synthetic steroid taken as a tablet, which is broken down to metabolites with estrogenic, progestational and androgenic properties. Tibolone has been available in the UK since March 1991, but it is not widely used.[218]

a. In the USA

Diethylstilboestrol (DES) was launched in 1941 as the first synthetic estrogen and was indicated for the treatment of menopausal symptoms. The DES case study provides details of the regulatory and litigation history of the product.

[215] E Daly et al, 'Risk of venous thromboembolism in users of hormone replacement therapy' (1996) 348 *The Lancet* 977; H Jick et al, 'Risk of hospital admission for idopathic venous thromboembolism among users of postmenopausal oestrogens' (1996) 348 *The Lancet* 981; F Grodstein et al, 'Prospective study of exogenous hormones and risk of pulmonary embolism in women' (1996) 348 *The Lancet* 983.

[216] Daly et al, n 216, 1027; SP Gutthann et al, 'Hormonal Replacement Therapy and the Risk of Venous Thromboembolic Events: A Population-Based Case-Control Study' (1995) 4 *Pharmacoepidemiology & Drug Safety* S118.

[217] For example, see N Wentzensen and B Trabert, 'Hormone Therapy: short-term relief, long-term consequences' (2015) 385(9980) *The Lancet* 1806, doi.org/10.1016/S0140-6736(14)62458-2.

[218] MHRA, Public Assessment Report, Decentralised Procedure, Tibolone 2.5mg tablets (PL 34096/0012 UK/H/5924/001/DC), available at www.mhra.gov.uk/home/groups/par/documents/websiteresources/con809941.pdf.

The first conjugated natural estrogen product to be licensed in the USA was Premarin.[219] This was made from pregnant mares' urine, and was launched by Wyeth in May 1942. It was originally marketed for estrogen depletion. From the 1950s onwards there were concerns about a possible association between Premarin use and uterine cancer. In 1962, a small study by gynaecologist Robert A Wilson was published in *Journal of the American Medical Association*; it was based on an uncontrolled study of just 304 women and asserted that exogenous estrogen treatment reduced the risk of breast and genital cancers.[220] The sales of Premarin increased substantially after Wilson's subsequent book, *Feminine Forever*. *Feminine Forever* essentially medicalised the menopause and suggested that all undesirable 'symptoms' could be resolved by treatment with estrogens. Most concerning, *Forever Feminine* repeated and widely publicised Wilson's 1962 assertion that exogenous estrogen treatment reduced the risk of breast and genital cancers.[221] This became the prevalent view, despite being unfounded. There have been suggestions that Wilson was being paid (indirectly) by Wyeth.

The controversy over cancer risks was finally resolved by two articles in the *New England Journal of Medicine* in December 1975, which confirmed the long-suspected link between endometrial cancer and estrogen use.[222] A dip in sales was seen, but Premarin remained on the market. In response the pharmaceutical companies devised combined HRT, which contained both estrogen and progesterone. Many different companies developed many brands, but Provera and Prempro were the market leaders. Provera comprised a progestogen, which was used in combination with an estrogen (such as Premarin), so the two active ingredients were in two different products. Prempro had both active ingredients in one tablet. Premarin and Prempro were made by Wyeth, Provera was manufactured by Pfizer/Pharmacia/Upjohn. Between them these companies had more than 85% of the market share of HRT.

There were claims that HRT was cardio-protective: these were largely based on the epidemiological findings that pre-menopausal women have lower incidences of heart attacks and strokes (note this is not based on women taking HRT). By the late 1970s reports doubting this cardio-protective claim and indicating that HRT could increase the risk of such events started to be published. The Heart and Estrogen-Progestin Replacement Study (HERS) was the first placebo-controlled trial of HRT and examined this question. In 1998 the preliminary results of the HERS were published,[223] indicating that combined HRT slightly increased the risk of heart attack and stroke.

[219] NDA 004782, available at www.accessdata.fda.gov/scripts/cder/daf/index.cfm?event=overview.process&ApplNo=004782.

[220] RA Wilson, 'The Roles of Estrogen and Progesterone in Breast and Genital Cancer' (1962) 182(4) *Journal of the American Medical Association* 327, doi:10.1001/jama.1962.03050430001001.

[221] ibid.

[222] DC Smith et al, 'Association of Exogenous Estrogen and Endometrial Carcinoma' (1975) 293 *New England Journal of Medicine* 1164, doi:10.1056/NEJM197512042932302; HK Ziel and WD Finkle, 'Increased Risk of Endometrial Carcinoma among Users of Conjugated Estrogens' (1975) 293 *New England Journal of Medicine* 1167, doi:10.1056/NEJM197512042932303.

[223] D Grady et al, 'Heart and Estrogen/progestin Replacement Study (HERS): design, methods, and baseline characteristics'(1998) 19(4) *Controlled Clinical Trials* 314.

Further confirmation of the link between HRT and adverse events came in 2002 from the publication of data from the Women's Health Initiative.[224] This was a large-scale, long-term double-blinded clinical trial. It was a government-sponsored trial launched in 1993, which involved almost 162,000 women. Both the estrogen only and the combined HRT arms of the trial were stopped early; both interventions were judged to be more harmful than beneficial. The estrogen only HRT findings included trends for beneficial effects on breast cancer and heart disease risk but a small increased risk of stroke. The combined HRT findings included a small increase in the risk of breast cancer, heart disease, stroke and blood clots. The increased risks were small, but caused a substantial reaction, with some patients stopping treatment. There was a drop off in HRT usage rates.

In January 2003, the FDA mandated that the labels on all estrogen and estrogen-progestin replacement therapy should include a boxed warning, stating the increased risks for heart disease, heart attacks, strokes and breast cancer.

In 2004, the Women's Health Initiative published further analysis, indicating that the 2002 publication had overstated the increase in risk. Further publications have supported this conclusion.[225] Various reports have indicated that there is continuing professional support for the use of HRT to treat symptoms of menopause. A scientific statement by the Endocrine Society supported the use of HRT in the short-term treatment of menopausal symptoms.[226] The FDA's current position mirrors this.

b. In the UK

Various products were licensed in the UK from the early 1970s.

Following *The Lancet* studies in 1996, the MHRA has maintained its preliminary view from 1 October 1996,[227] based upon consideration of the data from the five studies available, that the new data emerging on the risk of VTE did not change the overall positive balance between the benefits and risks of short-term HRT treatment for most women. However, guidance issued by NICE in 2015 is clear that the relative risks have to be assessed and explained on a case-by-case basis. There appeared to be some differences between types or preparations of HRT in relation to allegations against the class of drugs. Oral (but not transdermal) estrogen is associated with a small increase in the risk of VTE and a small increase in the risk of a stroke.[228]

In April 2002, updated product information was disseminated by the MHRA following a *Current Problems in Pharmacovigilance* publication.[229] It described how the CSM and its

[224] Available at www.whi.org/; and The Writing Group for the WHI Investigators, 'Risks and benefits of estrogen plus progestin in healthy post-menopausal women: Principal results of the Women's Health Initiative randomized control' (2002) 288(3) *Journal of the American Medical Association* 321.

[225] JE Rossouw et al, 'Postmenopausal Hormone Therapy and Risk of Cardiovascular Disease by Age and Years Since Menopause' (2007) 297(13) *Journal of the American Medical Association* 1465, doi:10.1001/jama.297.13.1465.

[226] RJ Santen and WH Utian, 'Executive Summary: Postmenopausal Hormone Therapy: An Endocrine Society Scientific Statement' (2010) 95 (Suppl 1) *Journal of Clinical Endocrinology and Metabolism* S1–S66, doi:10.1210/jc.2009-2509.

[227] Available at www.mhra.gov.uk/home/groups/pl-p/documents/publication/con2023237.pdf.

[228] NICE guideline [NG23], Menopause: diagnosis and management (November 2015), available at www.nice.org.uk/guidance/ng23/chapter/Recommendations#long-term-benefits-and-risks-of-hormone-replacement-therapy.

[229] See at webarchive.nationalarchives.gov.uk/20141205223636tf_/http://www.mhra.gov.uk/Publications/Safetyguidance/CurrentProblemsinPharmacovigilance/CON007453.

Working Group on HRT formed in January 2001 reviewed various safety aspects of HRT, and how similar discussions occurred throughout other Member States within the EU. These discussions resulted in an agreement being reached to ensure that the information given to prescribers and patients was consistent within the EU.

The CSM and its Working Group continued to routinely review several ongoing studies,[230] including the Women's Health Initiative randomised placebo-controlled trial[231] and the large observational Million Women's Study in the UK.[232] Regular updates were published through *Current Problems*. Early termination of one part of the Women's Health Initiative trial in October 2002 prompted renewed considerations of the risks and benefits of long-term combined HRT.[233]

In December 2003, the Chairman of the CSM wrote to all healthcare professionals, advising them that for the prevention of osteoporosis, the risks from long-term use of HRT outweighed the benefits and that, in women over the age of 50, HRT should no longer be the therapy of first choice for this purpose. Subsequently, the estrogen-only arm of the Women's Health Initiative trial was stopped a year ahead of schedule.[234] In February 2004, the HABITS trial, a randomised, prospective follow-up study, which examined the risk of breast cancer recurrence with HRT use, was also stopped prematurely. A similar trial, the Stockholm Study, did not find such an increase but was stopped too, primarily on the grounds that recruitment would now be overwhelmingly difficult.[235]

Prescriptions for HRT and Tibolone in the UK were fairly stable between 1997 and 2001, but following the study outcomes and the changes in prescribing advice, a 50% reduction in HRT prescriptions was seen between 2002 and 2005. This may be partially driven by newer formulations of alternative treatments, for example availability of weekly formulations of bisphosphonates for treating osteoporosis. However, this clearly demonstrates that trends in prescribing behaviour can follow increased awareness and changes in advice.[236]

In the UK the NICE guideline [NG23] Menopause: diagnosis and management (November 2015) continues to recommend the short-term use of HRT, with risks assessed

[230] For example, see D Grady et al, 'Cardiovascular Disease Outcomes During 6.8 Years of Hormone Therapy Heart and Estrogen/Progestin Replacement Study Follow-up (HERS II)' (2002) 288 *Journal of the American Medical Association* 49, doi:10.1001/jama.288.1.49; and CM Viscoli et al, 'A Clinical Trial of Estrogen-Replacement Therapy after Ischemic Stroke' (2001) 345 *New England Journal of Medicine* 1243, doi:10.1056/NEJMoa010534.

[231] RT Chlebowski et al, 'Influence of Estrogen Plus Progestin on Breast Cancer and Mammography in Healthy Postmenopausal WomenThe Women's Health Initiative Randomized Trial' (2003) 289(24) *Journal of the American Medical Association* 3243, doi:10.1001/jama.289.24.3243.

[232] V Beral et al, 'Breast cancer and hormone-replacement therapy in the Million Women Study' (2003) 362 *The Lancet* 419.

[233] Writing Group, n 225.

[234] Women's Health Initiative Steering Committee, 'Effects of Conjugated Equine Estrogen in Postmenopausal Women With Hysterectomy: The Women's Health Initiative Randomized Controlled Trial' (2004) 291(14) *Journal of the American Medical Association* 1701, doi:10.1001/jama.291.14.1701.

[235] L Holmberg and H Anderson for the HABITS Steering and Data Monitoring Committees, 'HABITS (hormonal replacement therapy after breast cancer – is it safe?), a randomised comparison: trial stopped' (2004) 363 *The Lancet* 453, doi.org/10.1016/S0140-6736(04)15493-7.

[236] J Watson, L Wise and J Green, 'Prescribing of hormone therapy for menopause, tibolone, and bisphosphonates in women in the UK between 1991 and 2005' (2007) 63 *European Journal of Clinical Pharmacology* 843, doi:10.1007/s00228-007-0320-6.

on a case-by-case basis. Indeed, some professionals have questioned whether the benefits of HRT are being unduly undermined by the relatively small increase in risks, suggesting that the NICE guideline provides a more balanced assessment of the risks and benefits.[237]

iv. Litigation

a. In the USA

The litigation in the USA has been substantial, and so key highlights will be presented in this case study rather than a detailed description.

1. MDL Arkansas *In Re Prempro* Products Liability Litigation
This MDL[238] involved more than 9,000 plaintiffs and was heard by Judge William Wilson. Despite its name, it covered other types of HRT. It was certified as an MDL in 2003 and ran for 13 years until it was finally closed in March 2016. In the first trial (Linda Reeves) in 2006, the jury returned for the defendant (Wyeth). Over the next five years Pfizer won seven out of the 15 trials. Given that the results were mixed, both sides began to look towards settlement.

2. MCL and Class Actions
Over 1,000 cases were listed in Philadelphia, with just under 200 in New Jersey and fewer than 100 in New York and a handful of other individual cases. The Philadelphia litigation was heavily contested, with some significant sums awarded (on 6 December 2011 the jury awarded Susan Elfont $20 million, Bernadette Kalenkoski $27.85 million and Judy Mulderig $24.75 million),[239] and verdicts were routinely appealed.

3. Settlements
Early in 2011 it was reported that Pfizer was making active efforts to settle the remaining HRT lawsuits. It was reported that the company had agreed to pay $330 million to resolve 2,200 claims, averaging approximately $150,000 per woman. Later that year Pfizer was reportedly prepared to pay $772 million (including the previous $330 million settlement) to resolve the HRT lawsuits. Over the next five years or so, all the HRT claims were settled. This litigation was hugely costly: with damages, settlements and legal expenses it ran to over $1 billion.

b. In the UK

Fifteen claims were announced in March 1997, which were not pursued.

[237] 'HRT for menopause: a NICE treatment?' (2015) 386(10008) *The Lancet* 2030, dx.doi.org/10.1016/S0140-6736(15)01031-4.
[238] *In Re Prempro Products Liability Litigation*, MDL Docket no 1507, no 03-1507, ED Ark.
[239] *Susan Elfont et al v Wyeth et al*, Case no 040700924, Pa Comm Pls, Philadelphia Co.

v. Conclusion

Advice in the UK remains that for the majority of women with menopausal symptoms that affect their quality of life, the risk of short-term treatment is generally small and is outweighed by the benefits. Women should be counselled appropriately with respect to the benefits and possible risks, and HRT initiation should be determined on a case-by-case basis. Claims arose out of new medical literature concerning the possible risks and regulatory action was taken in the light of that literature. The subsequent drop in UK HRT prescriptions is likely to reflect the increased awareness of the risks from research and regulatory action, as well as improved treatment alternatives, such as new formulations of bisphosphonates for the treatment of/prevention of osteoporosis.

The difference between the USA and UK litigation is stark.

III. Vaccines

A. DTP Vaccine

i. Description

The DTP vaccine is a class of combination vaccines against three infectious diseases in humans: diphtheria, pertussis (whooping cough) and tetanus.

ii. Safety Issue

Pertussis vaccines had been developed as early as 1914.[240] The combined DTP vaccine was developed in the 1940s, and was widely used thereafter. It was manufactured by a number of companies. In the 1970s and 1980s, controversy arose over the question of whether the whole-cell pertussis component caused permanent brain injury in rare cases, called pertussis vaccine encephalopathy. Most of the reactions to whole-cell DPT injection are thought to be from the pertussis component.

Concerns about the risk of the vaccine should be balanced against the risks of the illness itself. As an illness, pertussis can cause encephalitis, which can lead to death or permanent sequelae. This risk is highest in children under two years old and in the developing world.[241]

A retrospective study published in 1974 (the Kulenkampff paper) described 36 children at Great Ormond Street Hospital, London, who apparently suffered neurological conditions following receipt of the DTP vaccine.[242] Following this study, it became widely accepted that in rare cases the pertussis vaccine could cause brain damage. This finding was controversial, with claims[243] and counterclaims[244] on both sides. British research in the 1980s into whole-cell DTP[245] (which is now rarely used in developed countries) suggested that such severe neurologic events occur after approximately 1 in 140,000 doses of the DPT vaccine (0.0007%). In fact, all scientific studies show pertussis (and measles) vaccines to be highly effective and safe, with only rare, moderate, adverse side-effects. The current World Health Organization guidance categorically states that there is no evidence that the DPT vaccine causes any serious neurological disorder such as encephalopathy.[246]

The reports that the DTP vaccine could cause brain damage were followed by a drop in vaccination rates. In the UK, for example, the vaccination rate in children was almost

[240] Pertussis vaccine is listed in American Medical Association, *New and Nonofficial Remedies* (Council on Pharmacy and Chemistry, 1914).

[241] G Gabutti et al, 'Pertussis: Current perspecitives on epidemiology and prevention' (2015) 11(1) *Human Vaccines and Immunotherapeutics* 108, published online 12 August 2014, doi: 10.4161/hv.34364.

[242] M Kulenkampff, JS Schwartzman and J Wilson, 'Neurological complications of pertussis inoculation' (1974) 49 *Archives of Disease in Childhood* 46.

[243] For example, see GT Stewart, 'Whooping cough and pertussis vaccine: a comparison of risks and benefits in Britain during the period 1968–83' (1985) 61 *Developments in Biological Standardization* 395.

[244] P Ray et al for the Vaccine Safety Datalink Group, 'Encephalopathy after whole-cell pertussis or measles vaccination: lack of evidence for a causal association in a retrospective case-control study' (2006) 25(9) *Pediatric Infectious Disease Journal* 768.

[245] D Miller et al, 'Pertussis vaccine and whooping cough as risk factors in acute neurological illness and death in young children' (1985) 61 *Developments in Biological Standardization* 389.

[246] See at www.who.int/immunization/topics/pertussis/en/index2.html.

80% at start of the 1970s, but by 1975 only 30% of children were vaccinated for pertussis.[247] Given that academic papers were also published that indicated that the purported risks posed by vaccination were greater than the dangers of the illness,[248] it is not surprising that vaccination rates dropped, even though such findings were contested.[249] The reduction in vaccination rates was followed by an observable increase of reports on the incidence of pertussis, particularly among infants and teenagers. In the UK the vaccination position stabilised, and since 1992 vaccination rates in children have remained about 94%, with additional vaccinations given to pregnant women.

In the US the current position is similar, with over 95% of children between 19–35 months now having had three DTP vaccinations.[250] In 1976, there were just over 1,000 reported cases of pertussis in the US; by 2012 the figures peaked at just over 48,000 cases (including 20 deaths). At the same time, studies and anecdotal reports from doctors nationwide reported an increase in the number of parents refusing to vaccinate their children against childhood diseases.[251] Much of this refusal had to do with perceived vaccine safety issues, such as purported associations between vaccines and autism, attention deficit disorder, seizures and epilepsy. None of these concerns has been upheld in research.

Figure 3.2 Reported pertussis cases in the United States 1922–2016[252]

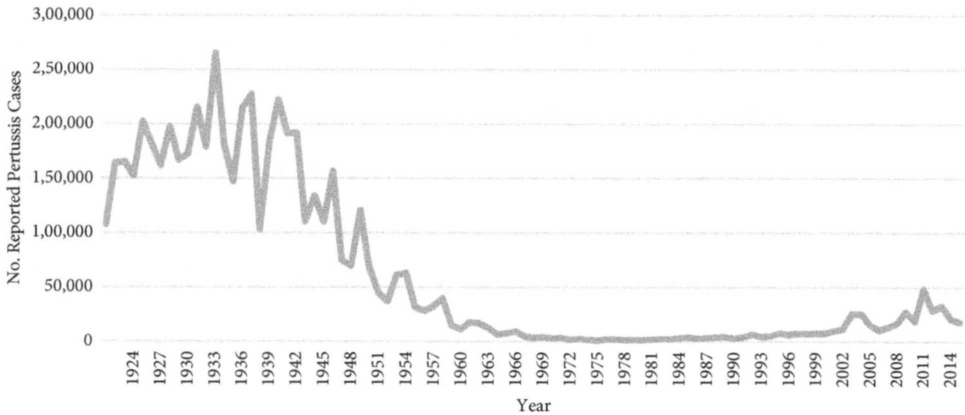

iii. Marketing and Regulatory History

Early evidence[253] was unable to confirm the presence or absence of a causal relationship between DPT and chronic nervous system dysfunction. At the request of the Department

[247] See at vk.ovg.ox.ac.uk/pertussis-whooping-cough.

[248] Stewart, n 244.

[249] AR Hinman and JP Koplan, 'Pertussis and pertussis vaccine: further analysis of benefits, risks and costs' (1985) 61 *Developments in Biological Standardization* 429.

[250] The current vaccinations consist of the acelluar DTP vaccine, DTaP.

[251] Pattie Neighmond, 'Is Vaccine Refusal Worth The Risk?', *NPR Radio*, available at www.npr.org/templates/story/story.php?storyId=104523437.

[252] Data taken from the CDC website information on pertussis at www.cdc.gov/pertussis/index.html.

[253] For example, see JM Berg, 'Neurological complications of pertussis immunization' (1958) 2 *British Medical Journal* 24; RK Byers and FC Moll, 'Encephalopathies following prophylactic pertussis vaccine' (1948) 1 *Pediatrics*

for Health and Social Security, three panels, the Dudgeon Panel, the Meade Panel and the North West Thames Study, were set up to retrospectively examine cases to study the issue of pertussis vaccination and brain damage. None of these studies could confirm causation and a larger-scale case-control study was recommended.

In 1976, the UK Government responded by funding the National Childhood Encephalopathy Study (NCES) – a three-year research program that systematically studied chronic nervous system dysfunctions after DPT, and which found a serious acute neurologic illness that occurred in children within seven days after receiving the vaccine.[254] The NCES concluded that acute neurologic reactions and permanent brain damage can follow both DPT and measles vaccines, but that the latter is a very rare complication. The attributable risk of serious neurologic illness in the seven days following pertussis vaccination was estimated to be 1 in 110,000 immunisations, and that of persistent neurologic damage after one year is estimated to be 1 in 310,000 immunisations. However, the NCES did not determine a causal connection, and later studies[255] showed no connection of any type between administration of the DPT vaccine and permanent brain injury. The alleged vaccine-induced brain damage often proved to be an unrelated condition – infantile epilepsy. Eventually evidence against the hypothesised existence of pertussis vaccine encephalopathy mounted to the point that in 1990, the *Journal of American Medical Association* called it a 'myth' and 'nonsense'.[256]

However, before that, criticism of the studies showing no connection, and a few well-publicised anecdotal reports of permanent disability that were blamed on the DTP vaccine, gave rise to anti-DTP movements in the 1970s.[257] The negative publicity and the fear that it aroused caused the immunisation rate to fall in several countries, including Great Britain, Sweden and Japan. In many cases, a dramatic increase in the incidence of pertussis followed.[258] For example, in Japan the childhood vaccination program was temporarily suspended for a few months in 1975 following concerns over deaths following the vaccination. In 1974, prior to the suspension, 70% of children were immunised and 393 pertussis cases were reported (with no deaths). Following the temporary withdrawal, vaccination rates varied between 20–40%, and by 1979 there were over 13,000 reported pertussis cases, including 41 deaths.[259]

437; JH Globus and JL Kohn, 'Encephalopathy following pertussis vaccine prophylaxis' (1949) 141 *Journal of the American Medical Association* 507; HG Miller and JB Stanton, 'Neurological sequelae of prophylactic inoculation' (1954) 23 *Quarterlv Journal of Medicine* 1; J Strom, 'Is universal vaccination against pertussis always justified?' (1960) 2 *British Medical Journal* 1184; J Strom, 'Further experience of reactions, especially of a cerebral nature, in conjunction with triple vaccination: a study based on vaccinations in Sweden, 1959–1965' (1967) 4 *British Medical Journal* 320; and JM Sutherland, 'Encephalopathy following diphtheriapertussis inoculation' (1953) 28 *Archives of Disease in Childhood* 149.

[254] R Alderslade et al, 'The National Childhood Encephalopathy Study: a report on 1000 cases of serious neurological disorders in infants and young children from the NCES research team' in *Whooping Cough: Reports from the Committee on the Safety of Medicines and the Joint Committee on Vaccination and Immunisation* (Department of Health and Social Security, 1981).

[255] Institute of Medicine, *DPT Vaccine and Chronic Nervous System Dysfunction: A New Analysis* (Washington, DC: National Academy Press, 1994), doi.org/10.17226/9814.

[256] JD Cherry, '"Pertussis vaccine encephalopathy": it is time to recognize it as the myth that it is' (1990) 263(12) *Journal of the American Medical Association* 1679.

[257] D Geier and M Geier, 'The true story of pertussis vaccination: a sordid legacy?' (2002) 57(3) *Journal of the History of Medicine and Allied Sciences* 249.

[258] EJ Gangarosa et al, 'Impact of anti-vaccine movements on pertussis control: the untold story' (1998) 351(9099) *The Lancet* 356.

[259] HL Coulter and BL Fisher, *DPT: A Shot in the Dark* (Harcourt Brace Jovanovich, 1985).

In the US, the Centers for Disease Control (CDC) formalised the Monitoring System for Illness Following Immunization (MSIFI) in 1978. The was an extension of the monitoring of adverse events system created following the cases of Guillain-Barre syndrome seen in the wake of the 1976 swine flu vaccination program.[260] The MSIFI system was initially piloted in a handful of States, but by late 1978 it was rolled out to cover all States. This system collected information on DTP vaccines for post-marketing analysis. The CDC, the FDA and the Bureau of Biologics maintain an ongoing interest in the safety of the DTP vaccine; the FDA also funded projects to assess adverse events and any linkage.[261] Various panels and commissions were formed to assess the safety of mass vaccination, including DTP vaccination, most notably the Advisory Commission on Childhood Vaccines, formed in 1989, and the Institute of Medicine Committee to Review the Adverse Consequences of Pertussis and Rubella Vaccines, formed in 1990.

The DTP vaccine was produced by culturing the pertussis bacterium and then killing it and suspending the dead cells in the vaccine, hence it is sometimes known as a 'whole cell vaccine'. As an alternative, specific antigenic components of the B. pertussis bacteria were isolated and used to produce a vaccine that contained only the specific antigen required. These acellular vaccines are known as DTaP.[262]

In Japan, following concern over the whole cell DTP vaccine, DTaP vaccines had been developed in the 1970 and used as the exclusive pertussis vaccination since 1979. On 17 December 1991, the US FDA licensed a DTaP vaccine, ACEL-IMUNE, manufactured by Lederle Praxis/Takeda, for use as the forth and fifth element of a five-shot vaccination dosing schedule.[263] A few months later, on 22 August 1992, a second DTaP vaccine, Tripedia, manufactured by Connaught (US) /BIKEN, was licensed for the same purpose.[264] At present there are two manufacturers that produce six different variants and combinations of the DTaP vaccine for the US market, Sanofi Pasteur Inc and GlaxoSmithKlein Biologicals.[265]

Despite the alleged associated risks of DTP and DTaP vaccines, it was recommended in the US that the vaccine continue to be administered due to the overwhelming public health benefit. In 1997 it was advised that the DTaP vaccine should be used rather than the DTP vaccine, as the latter was thought to have higher rates of adverse events. On 3 August 1999, Dr David Satcher, then Assistant Secretary for Health and Surgeon General, gave a statement on the risks versus benefits of vaccinations. He referred to a study published in the January 1998 issue of *The Lancet*, which provided empirical evidence of what happens when successful vaccination programs are halted.

The research compared countries in which immunisation with pertussis vaccines was disrupted to countries that maintained high coverage, including the US. The findings were clear and consistent. Pertussis incidence was 10 to 100 times lower in countries where high

[260] See SA Macleod and C Hodges, *Redress Schemes for Personal Injuries* (Hart Publishing, 2017) ch 15, 'Vaccine Injury Compensation Schemes'.

[261] CL Cody et al, 'Nature and rates of adverse reactions associated with DTP and DT immunizations in infants and children' (1981) 68 *Pediatrics* 650.

[262] Some research has concluded that the acellular vaccine is safer, with fewer reports of adverse effects: ME Pichichero et al, 'Combined tetanus, diphtheria, and 5-component pertussis vaccine for use in adolescents and adults' (2005) 293(24) *Journal of the American Medical Association* 3003.

[263] See at www.cdc.gov/mmwr/preview/mmwrhtml/00041836.htm.

[264] See at www.cdc.gov/mmwr/preview/mmwrhtml/00041801.htm.

[265] See at www.fda.gov/BiologicsBloodVaccines/Vaccines/ApprovedProducts/ucm093833.htm.

vaccination coverage was maintained, relative to those countries where unsubstantiated vaccine safety claims temporarily halted use of the vaccines. Australia, Ireland, Japan, the UK, Italy, the Russian Federation and the former West German Republic all experienced pertussis outbreaks following the suspension of successful pertussis vaccination programs. Each country also found it necessary to reinstate its pertussis immunisation recommendations.

Satcher stated:

> We know that vaccines have dramatically reduced the number of people who get infectious diseases. Without vaccines, epidemics of vaccine-preventable diseases would return, resulting in increased and unnecessary illness, disability, and death. History shows that in times of high vaccine coverage and very low incidence of vaccine-preventable diseases, it is common and very easy to shift attention away from the real benefits of vaccines to potential vaccine risks.[266]

The DTP vaccine is cheaper to produce than the purified DTaP vaccine. As a result, DTP is still used in the developing world. The current World Health Organization recommendation is that the DTP vaccine is safe and does not cause serious neurological disorders.

iv. Litigation

Publication of the Great Ormond Street study in 1974 attracted wide publicity in the media in UK, and coincided with the formation of the Association of Vaccine Damaged Children in 1973.[267] Some senior doctors supported the campaign, and even suggested that the risk of damage from vaccination was greater than the risk of the disease itself. The rate of immunisation in England fell from 79% in 1972 to 38% in 1976. A national state-funded compensation scheme was established under the Vaccine Damage Payments Act 1979, which paid compensation for any child assessed as 80% or greater disabled. However, awards under the scheme were capped (then at £10,000) at a level that was clearly insufficient to meet a lifetime's care needs for a seriously brain injured child, and so litigation was brought to seek increased sums.

A group of claims was brought in England and coordinated in 1985, supported by £2 million in legal aid, which resulted in a 1988 trial on causation as a preliminary issue that examined some 50 years of medical literature. In March 1986 a single test case was put forward to determine the issue of causation, with stays being put on all other pertussis litigation. Interestingly, the Wellcome Foundation had applied to join as a defendant[268] in the case as a necessary party to the action under Order 15, Rule 6(2)(a) of the Rules of the Supreme Court.[269] The Wellcome Foundation did this because it was, at this time, the only pertussis vaccine manufacturer in the UK, and as such wanted to protect the reputation of its pertussis vaccine. No allegations of negligence were ever made against the Wellcome

[266] Statement on Risk vs Benefit of Vaccinations by David Satcher, MD, PhD, before the House Committee on Government Reform, Dept of Health and Human Services (1999), available at www.govinfo.gov/content/pkg/CHRG-106hhrg62560/pdf/CHRG-106hhrg62560.pdf.

[267] S Pearl, 'Pertussis Vaccine Litigation' in Hodges (ed), n 191, ch 17; and AH Griffin, 'Permanent brain damage and pertussis vaccination: is the end of the saga in sight?' (1989) 7(3) *Vaccine* 199.

[268] See *Department of Health and Social Security v Kinnear & Others* [1984] 134 NLJ 886 for further background.

[269] *The Rules of the Supreme Court, 1965* (HM Stationery Office) (as amended) (SI 1965/1776).

Foundation. The initial (unreported) case that was chosen as a test case was that of Jonnie Kinnear.[270] However, inconsistencies in the evidence given by his mother and the medical records led to case collapsing.

After the collapse of *Kinnear*, a replacement test case was needed for the pertussis litigation. The replacement case selected was *Loveday v Renton*.[271] The *Loveday* case had originally been pleaded as a straight clinical negligence case against the vaccinating doctor only; it was not known which manufacturer had produced the vaccine that had been given to Susan Loveday. However, the Wellcome Foundation was permitted to join as a defendant on the general issue of causation, on the basis that it paid its own costs regardless of the outcome of the trial. This joining proved crucial. The trial commenced on 2 October 1978. The most significant action in the trial was the interlocutory hearing, where an application under Order 24, Rule 7A[272] was granted for discovery of the raw data from the Kulenkampff paper and the NCES Study. This application was made by the Wellcome Foundation and proved to be a cornerstone of the case.

Upon re-examination of the NCES data, it became clear that the permanent brain damage suffered by these children did not occur within the 48 hours following vaccination in any child in England, Scotland and Wales in the two years from mid-1976 to mid-1978. This ran contrary to the other previously published case studies, particularly the Kulenkampff paper, which placed considerable emphasis on brain damage occurring in the initial hours post-vaccination. The NCES data for this period included 2 million doses of the vaccine.

This trial had taken 63 days, with over 18 world-leading experts giving evidence, and had cost over £2 million in legal aid. The judge stated that the widely held belief that the pertussis vaccine could occasionally cause brain damage was genuinely held, but that the evidence presented had rebuffed this view and led him to conclude that the plaintiff had failed to prove on balance that the pertussis vaccine causes brain damage in young children. The judge laid down a framework for any future attempt to prove causation and also expressed the view, obiter, that even if causation had been established, the plaintiff would still have faced the almost insuperable difficulty of establishing negligent liability under the *Bolam* principle.[273]

After the *Loveday* case was concluded, the stays on all the other pertussis cases were lifted, but the legal aid certificates were discharged. There was a judicial review of the blanket refusal by the Legal Aid Board to issue any further legal aid for pertussis cases, but although the application for judicial review was successful, this did not result in any further

[270] There is no report of the Kinnear case, but a first-hand account of (some of) the evidence presented can be found in GT Stewart, 'The law tries to decide whether the whooping cough vaccine causes brain damage: Professor Gordon Stewart gives evidence' (1986) 293 *British Medical Journal* (Clinical Research Edition) 203, doi.org/10.1136/bmj.293.6540.203-a.

[271] *Loveday v Renton and the Wellcome Foundation Ltd* [1990] 1 MLR 117.

[272] Rules of the Supreme Court, n 271.

[273] *Bolam v Friern Hospital Management Committee* [1957] 1 WLR 582. The *Bolam* principle was that a doctor's conduct would not be negligent if a responsible body of medical opinion would support that conduct. The *Bolam* principle does not apply to the issue of consent. The judgment set out in *Montgomery v Lanarkshire Health Board* [2015] UKSC 11 requires a doctor to take 'reasonable care to ensure that the patient is aware of any material risks involved in any recommended treatment, and of any reasonable alternative or variant treatments'.

legal aid being granted. The failure of the single test case to demonstrate causation effectively resolved all the pertussis litigation in England and Wales.

Extensive litigation in the US in the 1970s and 1980s resulted in several jury findings of negligence against manufacturers.[274] Interestingly, the issue of causation and whether the DTP vaccine had actually caused the injuries was seldom tested in court. Adverse judgments, unscientific claims about the vaccine and increases in insurance rates, all steadily pushed suppliers of the vaccines out of the market by the early 1980s;[275] by 1984 there was only one DTP vaccine manufacturer operating in the USA. This led to the US introducing a vaccine damage compensation scheme in 1988 so as to ensure the continued supply of production.[276] This established the Vaccine Courts, and also provided compensation retrospectively for vaccinations that occurred before the inception of the Vaccine Injury Compensation Program.

A 1985 claim in Scotland failed on its particular facts. Litigation in Ireland resulted in rejection of a single claim at trial in 1991, which was upheld by the Supreme Court in 1993.[277] However, this is a case based on a particular batch of pertussis vaccine (batch 3741 manufactured by the Wellcome Foundation) that was found to be eight times more potent than the recommended strength. Therefore, this case is not really a reflection of the standard pertussis vaccine but a 'hot batch' case. No regulatory action was taken following these judgments.

v. Conclusion

Medical review of the DTP vaccine in 1974 led to widespread publicity about risk. The interpretation of these findings was complex. Studies were commissioned by the UK and US Governments, and surveillance programs were put in place, but no conclusive link between the vaccine and brain damage was proved. Concerned parents ceased to have children immunised, which led to major public health issues. Compensation schemes were set up in both the UK and the US. A group action in England failed as causation could not be proved; this case re-examined the original data that had triggered the publicity of the risk and found it to be wanting. Cases have succeeded in the US, where the jury system judges the complex, and sometimes contradictory, scientific evidence. The regulatory position remains unchanged – that the benefits associated with vaccination outweigh the risks and that there is no proven causative link between pertussis vaccination and brain damage.

[274] G Evans, 'Update on Vaccine Liability in the United States: Presentation at the National Vaccine Program Office Workshop on Strengthening the Supply of Routinely Recommended Vaccines in the United States, 12 February 2002' (2006) 42 *Clinical Infectious Diseases* S130, available at https://doi.org/10.1086/499592.

[275] Peter Huber, 'Junk Science in the Courtroom' *Forbes* (8 July 1991), available at www.overlawyered.com/articles/huber/junksci.html.

[276] The US National Childhood Vaccine Injury Act was passed in 1968, and Vaccine Injury Compensation Program created in 1988. See Macleod and Hodges, n 261, for more detail.

[277] *Kenneth Best v The Wellcome Foundation Ltd &Others* (1994) 5 Med LR 81 (Supreme Court of Ireland).

B. MMR Vaccine

i. Description

The MMR vaccine is an immunisation against the triple diseases of measles, mumps and rubella. The vaccine is a mixture of three live attenuated viruses, administered via a single injection. Two doses are required for immunity. The standard UK protocol is to vaccinate at around 12 months old and then again at 3 years, 4 months. However, this schedule can be altered if a baby is at high risk of measles, for example due to a local measles outbreak, when an additional vaccination can be given between 6–9 months of age.[278]

Measles, mumps and rubella (MMR) are all highly contagious diseases, which were common before the advent of vaccination.

Measles is an unpleasant illness, including cold-like symptoms, sore red eyes, light sensitivity, a fever, and small greyish-white spots on the inside of the cheeks, followed by a characteristic red-brown blotchy rash that normally radiates out from the head and neck to the rest of the body. While the vast majority of people make a full recovery from measles, it can have serious complications, including infections of the eye, middle ear, airways and lungs, febrile convulsions, diarrhoea and vomiting (potentially causing dehydration), hepatitis, a squint, meningitis and/or encephalitis, blindness and death. Measles also has implications for the foetus if contracted by a pregnant mother, which can include stillbirth, miscarriage, premature delivery and low birth weight.[279]

Mumps is a viral infection. While it is asymptomatic in around a third of cases, mumps can cause swelling of the parotid glands, headache, joint pain, nausea, abdominal pain, dry mouth, loss of appetite, tiredness and a fever. Complications of mumps are usually temporary and not too serious, but they can include swelling of the testicles in post-pubertal males (occasionally leading to infertility), swelling of the ovaries in post-pubertal females, acute pancreatitis, hearing loss, viral meningitis and encephalitis.[280]

Rubella, or German measles, is generally a mild illness with symptoms including a red-pink rash of small spots, swollen head and neck glands, fever, cold-like symptoms and (usually only in adults) aching joints. The major concern with rubella is the risk it poses to unborn babies. If a mother catches rubella in the first 20 weeks of pregnancy, there is a risk of her unborn child developing Congenital Rubella Syndrome.[281]

Table 3.3 Congenital Rubella Syndrome critical periods and observed birth defects

Infection period	CRS risk	Possible birth defects
0–10 weeks pregnant	90%	Multiple birth defects including eye defects, deafness, congenital heart disease, proportionally small head, decreased inter-uterine growth rate and damage to the brain, liver lungs or bone marrow.
10–17 weeks pregnant	10–20%	Fewer birth defects including eye defects, deafness, congenital heart disease, proportionally small head, decreased inter-uterine growth rate and damage to the brain, liver lungs or bone marrow.
17–20 weeks pregnant	≤10%	Deafness.

[278] See at www.nhs.uk/conditions/vaccinations/mmr-vaccine/.
[279] See at www.nhs.uk/conditions/measles/.
[280] See at www.nhs.uk/conditions/mumps/.
[281] See at www.nhs.uk/conditions/rubella/.

The individual vaccinations for MMR have proved to be extremely effective at preventing relevant outbreaks. The rationale behind the combined MMR vaccine was that a single injection is less painful than three separate injections, and immunity is acquired more quickly and more efficiently from a single injection than from three injections given on different dates.

The MMR vaccine is so effective that measles had been declared eliminated from the US in 2000. However, MMR are still endemic in countries with less developed vaccination programs, and high rates of vaccination are required to maintain the prevention of outbreaks and to sustain the elimination of measles.

Scares about potential links between the MMR vaccine and autism were first circulated in early 1998. This had a significant impact on vaccination rate (see Figure 3.3).[282]

Figure 3.3 The percentage of children in England receiving the first dose of MMR vaccine before the age of 2: 1988–2016

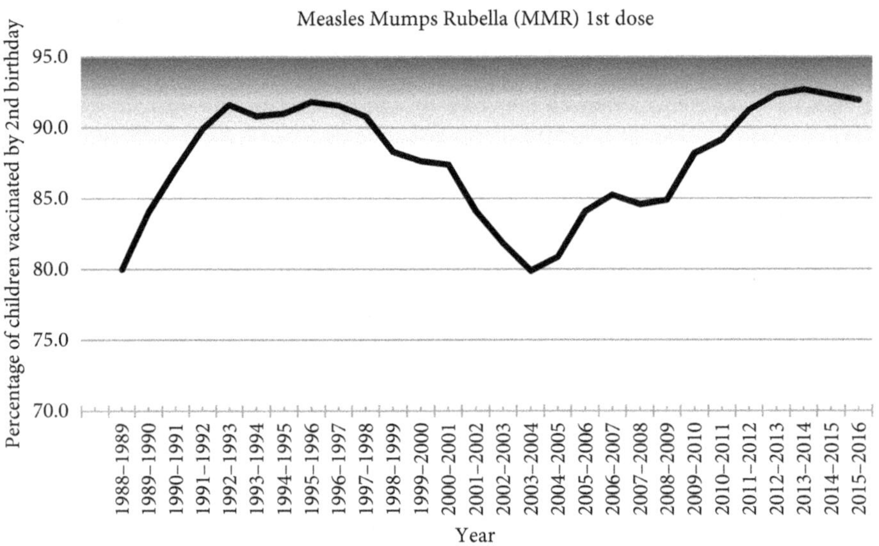

Figure 3.3 shows that MMR vaccination rates in England fell to a record low of just under 80% in 2003–04. The recommended rate is 95%. Any rate below 90%–95% does not give 'herd immunity'.[283]

In 2005, the Cochrane Library published a review of 31 scientific studies. Its authors concluded, 'Existing evidence on the safety and effectiveness of MMR vaccine supports current policies of mass immunisation aimed at global measles eradication in order to reduce morbidity and mortality associated with mumps and rubella.'[284]

[282] Data taken from Childhood Vaccination Coverage Statistics England 2016–2017, available at digital.nhs.uk/catalogue/PUB30085.

[283] 'Blair Signals Support for MMR' *BBC News* (2002), available at news.bbc.co.uk/2/hi/health/1803609.stm; and Dr Manish Sadarangani for the Oxford Vaccine Group, 'Herd Immunity: How does it work' (26 April 2016) at https://www.ovg.ox.ac.uk/news/herd-immunity-how-does-it-work.

[284] V Demicheli et al, 'Vaccines for measles, mumps and rubella in children' (2005) 19(4) *Cochrane Database Systematic Review* CD004407.

ii. Safety Issue

In February 1998, *The Lancet* published an Early Report on 12 children, in eight of whom parents had linked the onset of behavioural symptoms to the triple vaccine given for immunisation against MMR.[285] The author, Dr Andrew Wakefield of the Royal Free Hospital, London, was a former surgeon with an interest in adult gastroenterology. He was known to be interested in whether the measles virus might have a causal role in Crohn's disease. His paper suggested that there was a causal association between MMR and autism.

iii. Marketing and Regulatory History

The MMR vaccine was first developed by Maurice Hilleman while at Merck in the late 1960s.[286] The vaccine was licensed in 1971 in the US and in 1972 in the UK. A second formulation was introduced in 1989.[287] Since its worldwide introduction from the early 1970s, over 500 million doses have been used in over 60 countries.[288] Triple vaccines have continued to be sold by Merck (or its joint venture with Sanofi-Pasteur called Sanofi-Pasteur MSD) as MMR II,[289] by GlaxoSmithKline as Priorix,[290] by the Serum Institute of India as Tresivac and by Sanofi Pasteur as Trimovax. Pluserix MMR was authorised between 17 June 1988 and 1998 (to SmithKline & French and later Smithkline Beecham).

After Dr Wakefield's report in June 1999, the CSM published an article in *Current Problems*.[291] The article described the formation of a MMR Working Party, including relevant experts, to assess the evidence to date. In agreement with several other worldwide reports, it was concluded that the benefits of the MMR vaccine far outweigh any risks and no further regulatory action was required.

On 28 January 2010, after a long and complex fitness to practice hearing, Dr Wakefield was struck off by the General Medical Council (GMC).[292] The GMC did not make any judgment on any potential linkage between MMR and autism, but only sought to examine the conduct of the research leading to *The Lancet* paper. It was found that Dr Wakefield had behaved 'dishonestly and irresponsibly'.

a. Vaccine Composition Changes

Over the years there had been changes in the use of the mumps element of the triple vaccine. For example, the UK NHS stopped using the Urabe mumps strain in the early 1990s due

[285] A Wakefield et al, 'Ileal-lymphoid-nodular hyperplasia, non-specific colitis, and pervasive developmental disorder in children' (1998) 351(9103) *The Lancet* 637.

[286] PA Offit, *Vaccinated: One Man's Quest to Defeat the World's Deadliest Diseases* (Smithsonian, 2007).

[287] JE Banatvala and DW Brown, 'Rubella' (2004) 363(9415) *The Lancet* 1127.

[288] 'MMR's Global Success' *BBC News* (2002), available at news.bbc.co.uk/1/hi/health/1804509.stm.

[289] MMR II (Merck Sharp & Dohme) was first authorised on 17 August 1972. Immravax (Aventis Pasteur) was authorised between 18 October 1993 and 2004.

[290] Priorix (Smithkline Beecham) was first authorised on 4 December 1997 and is still authorised.

[291] See at webarchive.nationalarchives.gov.uk/20141206135254/http://www.mhra.gov.uk/home/groups/pl-p/documents/websiteresources/con2023234.pdf

[292] See at www.nhs.uk/news/2010/01January/Documents/FACTS%20WWSM%20280110%20final%20complete%20corrected.pdf

to cases of transient mild viral meningitis, and switched to a form using the Jeryl Lynn mumps strain instead.[293] The Urabe strain remains in use in a number of countries as it is less expensive to manufacture than vaccine with the Jeryl Lynn strain.[294] Despite what was sometimes claimed, these changes to the mumps component of the vaccine were unrelated to the subsequent controversy created by Andrew Wakefield and to any possible link between the MMR vaccine and autism.

iv. Litigation

Considerable media publicity was given to Dr Wakefield's 1999 assertion that the MMR vaccine could case autism, and to the developments in litigation, and this led to a major public health scare. Many parents decided not to get their children vaccinated, and this led to an increase in the constituent diseases.

Prior to *The Lancet* article and the accompanying public health scare, solicitors acting for potential claimants helped facilitate the referral to Dr Wakefield of children whose parents thought the vaccine might have caused an inflammatory bowel disorder as well as autism. In August 1996, the Legal Aid Board granted £55,000 for Dr Wakefield's medical research into a possible link between the MMR vaccine and autism. This use of a public litigation support fund to finance speculative medical research was unique, and subsequently much criticised. There are clear difficulties in lawyers being involved in prospective scientific research – the credibility and objectivity of the scientific research is instantly debatable, not to mention the ethical issues about referring vulnerable patients into such arrangements.

In 1998, the first claims were issued against three pharmaceutical companies: two manufacturers, SmithKline Beecham and Merck Co Inc, and a marketing authorisation holder, Aventis Pasteur MSD. The claims were based on the strict liability rules of the Consumer Protection Act, which had come into effect in 1988, the same year the MMR vaccination was first routinely administered to children in the UK.

The claimants in the MMR litigation were almost all children, whose claims alleged that the vaccine caused autism and other disorders. It was said that the claimants were developing normally until usually their second year, when they were given the MMR vaccination, and within a few weeks or months they became ill and/or their development regressed, leaving them with continuing serious disorders. The claimants said that this was not a coincidence but attributable to the MMR vaccine.

The group of claimants was constituted in July 1999, under a Practice Direction from the Lord Chief Justice. Although this was before the Group Litigation Order (GLO) procedure came into effect, for all practical purposes the litigation was conducted under the GLO procedures in Part 19 of the Civil Procedure Rules 1999. The claimants were funded by the Legal Aid Board (later known as the Legal Services Commission (LSC)).

The defendants said that there was no medical or scientific evidence that the vaccine caused such disorders in any group of children so as to render it defective within the meaning of the Consumer Protection Act, nor was there any evidence that it had caused such a

[293] A Colville et al, 'Withdrawal of a mumps vaccine' (1994) 153(6) *European Journal of Pediatrics* 467.

[294] KE Fullerton and SE Reef, 'Commentary: Ongoing debate over the safety of the different mumps vaccine strains impacts mumps disease control' (2002) 31(5) *International Journal Epidemiology* 983.

disorder in any of the claimants. It was well established that autism commonly manifested itself during the second year of an affected child's life, at a time shortly after most children in this country received their routine MMR immunisation. This timing was the same prior to the introduction of MMR in 1988.

The case proceeded with eight illustrative lead cases, four chosen by the claimants and four by the defendants from a cohort of over 1,000 cases. The trial of these lead cases, which was due to have started in April 2004, was to have been restricted to the issue of whether the vaccines were defective and, if so, whether the defects caused the conditions complained of by the eight lead claimants.

The litigation effectively collapsed in the Summer of 2003, when the LSC withdrew funding, having spent at least £15 million. This occurred on review of advice from the claimants' leading counsel that the action had no reasonable prospect of success after exchange of expert reports (28 from the claimants and 32 from the defendants), from which it became apparent that the claimants' case was not properly supported by the scientific evidence.

v. Conclusion

The allegation of a safety issue with MMR vaccines was made by a single doctor, and achieved wide currency and media attention, also associated with the four years of litigation. The doctor was subsequently discredited and struck off, and no causal link was ever established between the product and autism. The group action was discontinued. No regulatory action resulted, save for an increase in individual 'yellow card' reports made by defendants when claims were notified to them.[295] Public concern over the supposed risk led to significant fall in child vaccination, leading to an increase in incidence of measles in particular, and to additional deaths.

[295] Presentations by J Meltzer of Lovells LLP, and also J Stuart-Smith, QC, at a conference at the Centre for Socio-Legal Studies, Oxford University, in December 2006.

IV. Neuromodulators

A. Benzodiazepines

i. Description

Benzodiazepines form a class of drugs that function as minor tranquillisers by enhancing the effect of the inhibitory neurotransmitter gamma-aminobutyric acid (GABA) at $GABA_A$ receptors. They are most frequently used for the treatment of anxiety and insomnia, and have hypnotic, sedative, anxiolytic, anticonvulsant and muscle relaxant effects.

ii. Safety Issue

Prior to the introduction of benzodiazepines in 1960, barbiturates were the most commonly prescribed anxiolytics and hypnotics in the UK. The risk–benefit balance of benzodiazepines was considered to be superior to barbiturates. In particular, benzodiazepines were considered safe in acute over-dosage as compared to barbiturates, which had serious side-effects and could prove potentially lethal in over-dosage. However, even 10 times the recommended therapeutic dose with benzodiazepines was found only to induce sleep, from which the patient could be easily roused.

Benzodiazepines had been in widespread clinical practice without any apparent problems throughout the 1960s. Safety issues began to be raised from 1980 through medical literature, concerning a potential for long-term dependency and withdrawal symptoms upon therapy cessation.[296]

iii. Marketing and Regulatory History

The first benzodiazepine, chlordiazepoxide (branded as Librium), was introduced in the US in 1959 and then to the UK market a year later by Roche Products Ltd (Roche). Roche launched a second benzodiazepine, diazepam (Valium), three years later.[297] In the meantime, other companies were conducting research on the class of drugs, which resulted in the introduction of oxazepam (Serenid)[298] and lorazepam (Ativan)[299] into the UK market in 1966 and 1972 respectively by John Wyeth & Brother Ltd (now Pfizer).

Many of these products were on the UK market before licensing began in the early 1970s. Others, including lorazepam, had to satisfy the criteria of safety, efficacy and quality as judged by the CSD or its successor under the Medicines Act, the CSM, by reference to the results of substantial pre-clinical and clinical data. However, the full marketing authorisation for Ativan was not granted in the UK until 6 June 1985.

[296] Committee on the Review of Medicines (CRM), 'Systematic Review of the Benzodiazepines, Guideline for Data Sheets' (1980) 280 *British Medical Journal* 910.

[297] C Medawar, *Power and dependence: Social audit on the safety of medicines* (Social Audit Ltd, 1992).

[298] This product had been introduced in the US as Serax in 1965.

[299] Wyeth introduced Ativan in the US in 1977.

A third company, Upjohn Ltd (now Pfizer), introduced the sedative Halcion (first authorised in the UK on 26 September 1978). Several additional generic and branded products were introduced to the market by various companies, making a considerable range of benzodiazepines available from the end of the 1970s.

Many medical papers accumulated from around the 1980s[300] onwards discussing the issues of dependency and withdrawal symptoms. In 1980, the Committee on Review of Medicines (CRM) published a detailed statement on benzodiazepines, which concluded that the risk of dependence was very low.[301] An alert about Halcion was published by the CSM in *Current Problems* in February 1981.[302] This alert stemmed from the Dutch Regulatory Authority's ban on Halcion in the Netherlands from early 1980. Increased reports of adverse events associated with Halcion were attributed by the CSM to being dose related. Higher doses of Halcion were generally used in the Netherlands, and so similar adverse event reports were not common in the UK.

Shortly following the CSM publication, and following up on a paper describing benzodiazepines as the 'opium of the masses',[303] Professor Malcolm Lader reported that he and his co-workers had identified significant withdrawal effects on abrupt discontinuation of benzodiazepines in a series of long-term users.[304] From 1982 to 1983, informal communications and publication of Lader's findings (which included patients using Ativan) suggested that the CRM had underestimated the hazard posed by benzodiazepines. From 1983 onwards there was considerable media coverage and successive tightening of the authorised recommendations and labelling information for benzodiazepines.[305]

The growing publication of medical papers from 1980[306] gave rise to widespread press comment and concern over the use of benzodiazepines. Further detailed advice on their prescription only for short-term use was published by the CSM in *Current Problems* in January 1988.[307]

A 'Dear Doctor' letter was sent by the CSM to doctors, dentists and pharmacists on 1 October 1991, informing them of the withdrawal of Halcion (triazolam) due to the risk of psychiatric side-effects.

iv. Litigation

Claims were made in Scotland and the Republic of Ireland, but the most extensive litigation was brought in England and Wales, where claims were brought against several manufacturers but ultimately were focused upon the market leaders, Wyeth and Roche.[308]

[300] For examples see H Peturrson and M Lader,. 'Benzodiazepine dependence' (1981) 76 *British Journal of Addiction* 133; and F Kaupl-Taylor, 'Benzodiazepines on trial' (1984) 288 *British Medical Journal* 1379.

[301] CRM, n 297.

[302] See at www.mhra.gov.uk/home/groups/pl-p/documents/publication/con2024412.pdf.

[303] MH Lader, 'Benzodiazepine – The opium of the masses?' (1978) 3 *Neuroscience* 159.

[304] MH Lader, 'Benzodiazepine withdrawal phenomena' (1981) 16 *International Pharmacopsychiatry* 235.

[305] For example, see JY Wick, 'The History of Benzodiazepines' (2013) 28(9) *The Consultant Pharmacist* 538, doi:10.4140/TCP.n.2013.538.

[306] For examples see J Calalan and D Gath, 'Benzodiazepines in general practice: time for a decision' (1985) 290 *British Medical Journal* 1374; and SI Cohen, 'Are benzodiazepines useful in anxiety?' (1987) 330(8572) *The Lancet* 1080.

[307] See at www.mhra.gov.uk/home/groups/pl-p/documents/websiteresources/con2024428.pdf.

[308] See G Hickinbottom, 'Benzodiazepine Litigation' in Hodges (ed), n 191, ch 22.

Manufacturers received their first claims in 1987. In that year the Benzodiazepine Solicitors Group (BSG) was formed to coordinate the large number of solicitors who had been approached by potential claimants. A Steering Committee was created to head the BSG, which varied over time between five and eight firms. In May 1988, letters before action were sent by the Steering Committee's correspondent firm, Pannone Napier, to the primary target manufacturer companies, Wyeth and Roche. At this initial stage it was clear to those advising the claimants that 'even by recent standards the scale of the litigation [would] be vast'.[309]

During the next three years, over 17,000 potential claimants came forward, instructing approximately 3,000 firms of solicitors and 40 counsel. Of these claims, approximately 5,000 resulted in proceedings, with Wyeth and Roche facing over 3,500 and 2,000 actions respectively (some plaintiffs suing more than one manufacturer). Fifty sets of proceedings were served on other manufacturers, the vast majority on Upjohn in regard to Halcion.

In addition to the manufacturers, a substantial number of healthcare professionals (general practitioners and hospital authorities) were also included in the litigation. In the initial stages of the proceedings, a number of plaintiffs also sued the various regulatory bodies, although these claims were never actively pursued.

Claims against manufacturers were made primarily in negligence, as product supply often pre-dated the Consumer Protection Act of 1987. The plaintiffs made broad allegations of negligent research and marketing (the Master Statement of Claim was nearly 100 pages long). However, the plaintiffs' primary case against benzodiazepines, except for Halcion, was that the manufacturer should have included a warning in the product literature that the product should not be used for more than two to four weeks. Their argument asserted that had such a warning been included, the product would not have been prescribed for longer than four weeks, thereby preventing the patient from becoming dependent and suffering injury.

The case against Halcion differed, in that plaintiffs alleged that Halcion was inherently unsafe and no extent of warning would have made the product safe to market. For this reason, it was alleged that the product should never have made it to market. These claims were not pursued.

The group litigation collapsed in 1994 when the Legal Aid Board withdrew funding, after spending £30–35million in legal and expert costs. This followed service of defences in individual cases showing that most were inherently flawed, in particular because the symptoms and injuries alleged to be due to use of the products in question were indistinguishable from the underlying conditions of patients before they began taking the products. Claims were discontinued and the defendants made no payments to any plaintiffs. Some individuals continued claims as litigants in person, but these claims were struck out by the court as an abuse of process.[310]

[309] ibid.

[310] See Hickinbottom, n 309, section I, 'Striking Out'.

v. *Conclusion*

The safety issues were identified by the medical community and regularly evaluated. The authorities regularly updated product warnings. The CSM's *Current Problems* publication in January 1988,[311] describing regulatory labelling changes based upon new medical literature, sparked extensive litigation, which was associated with widespread media concern. Claims were discontinued in 1994 after several years of litigation, with no consequential regulatory change. This litigation led to changes in the way group litigation was handled by the courts, and to the parameters for providing legal aid funding for group litigation.[312]

[311] See at webarchive.nationalarchives.gov.uk/20141205224504/http://www.mhra.gov.uk/Publications/Safetyguidance/CurrentProblemsinPharmacovigilance/CON2024486.

[312] Memorandum by Dr Reg Peart, Minutes of Evidence, Select Committee on Health, House of Commons, UK Parliament (1999), available at publications.parliament.uk/pa/cm199899/cmselect/cmhealth/549/99072723.htm.

B. Merital (nomifensine)

i. Description

Merital's active ingredient nomifensine is an isoquinoline. Nomifensine acts as a potent noradrenalin[313] and dopamine reuptake inhibitor, with little impact on serotonin levels.[314] Dopamine and noradrenalin reuptake transporters are membrane-spanning proteins, which usually clear the dopamine and noradrenalin out of the synaptic cleft back into the axon terminal for re-use. Nomifensine's inhibition of the reuptake of dopamine and noradrenalin increases the synaptic availability of dopamine and noradrenalin, potentiating their signalling.

ii. Safety Issue

There was an association with kidney and liver toxicity and haemolytic anaemia, possibly causing death. It was known that nomifensine had a short half-life and lack of accumulation, and was rapidly metabolised, predominantly by the kidneys. This was why it was administered as a divided dose spaced throughout the day.

iii. Marketing and Regulatory History

Nomifensine was test marketed in the US by Hoechst AG (now Sanofi-Aventis) and was found to be a useful antidepressant at doses of 50–225 mg per day. A UK marketing authorisation for Merital was first granted on 29 November 1976.

In the 1970s, nomifensine offered a unique pharmacological profile. It was found to be as effective as other available antidepressants, with relatively few side-effects (mainly dry mouth, headache, nausea). Minimal anticholinergic effects, sedation or impairment of psychomotor performance were reported, and nomifensine did not interact significantly with alcohol. Overdose did not result in serious toxicity; this contrasted with the available tricyclic antidepressants and was important, as 70% of suicides are linked to depression, with a substantial number of these deaths due to self-poisoning with antidepressants.[315] Withdrawal symptoms were not documented when treatment was discontinued after six months of treatment. It was recommended for treating depression, but was not recommended as a sole treatment for schizoaffective disorder or patients with agitated depression.

Later case reports in the 1980s concluded that there was potential for dependence and abuse of nomifensine.[316] The dependence and abuse typically arose in patients with a history

[313] Noradrenalin is the British term; it is known as norepinephrine in the US.

[314] JL Kinney, 'Nomifensine maleate – A new 2nd-generation antidepressant' (1985) 4 *Clinical Pharmacology* 62.

[315] Relative overdose safety was not part of the Licensing Authority's considerations in the UK when nomifensine was licensed. Subsequently it was established that overdose safety could form part of the Licensing Authority's considerations when determining a licence application: see D Brahams, 'Medicine and the Law: Mianserin Product License' (1999) 333(8635) *The Lancet* 452; and D Brahams, 'Medicine and the Law: Safety in overdose and drug licensing' (1990) 335(8685) *The Lancet* 343. This might have helped nomifensine, as the overdose profile would have had a positive impact on the overall risk–benefit assessment.

[316] J Boning and G Fuchs, 'Nomifensine and psychological dependence-a case report' (1986) 19 *Pharmacopsychiatry* 386.

of stimulant addiction, or when the drug was used in very high doses (400–600mg per day). Warnings were published by the CSM in *Current Problems* in 1985 about dependence and abuse of nomifensine.[317] These issues justified changes in the warnings in the labelling, but not more.

The more serious adverse events were the cases of haemolytic anaemia, hepatic cases and fever cases. Although the exact mechanism still remains unclear, it is likely that the toxicity is due to the aromatic amine group; other compounds containing aromatic amine groups produce toxic metabolites. The first UK reports of haemolytic anaemia were three cases recorded by Hoechst UK in 1978. There was an increase in nomifensine prescriptions from 1977–85, accompanied by an increase in cases of haemolytic anaemia, hepatic cases and fever cases. Nomifensine withdrawal often cured these disorders, but there were some fatalities (eight in the UK).[318] In October 1984 the product data sheet was amended to state:

> In rare cases, haemolytic anaemia and abnormal liver function tests with or without clinical jaundice have been observed. These reactions subside within a short time of discontinuing Merital (nomifensine) but may recur if it is taken again.

Ongoing discussions were held. The CSM highlighted issues associated with newer antidepressants in *Current Problems*, including nomifensine, and presented a summary of the ADRs.[319] By late 1985, a number of adverse reaction reports were received concerning kidney and liver toxicity and haemolytic anaemia associated with use of the product. In response, on 30 September, the company issued a 'Dear Doctor' letter in the UK, warning of the serious adverse reactions with nomifensine reported internationally; concurrently a 'Red Hand' letter was issued by the parent company in Germany. On 16 December 1985, the *Drug and Therapeutics Bulletin* published an article, 'Trouble with nomifensine',[320] and this was followed by several newspaper reports on the product. Further cases of haemolytic anaemia were reported to the company in January 1986. Upon analysis and on reviewing the safety reports in the medical literature and follow-up inquiries, the manufacturer Hoechst issued a voluntary worldwide withdrawal of nomifensine on 23 January 1986,[321] shortly before a US licence was likely to have been issued.[322] The product is still used in scientific research.

Nomifensine was an effective option for some patients who did not respond to other available antidepressants. Withdrawal from the market removed all risks associated with this drug, but also removed this treatment option. Subsequent discovery of new antidepressant medications will have helped some of these treatment-refractive patients, but there may still be some who potentially could have benefitted from nomifensine, had they had

[317] See CSM, 'Dangers of Newer Antidepressants.' (July 1985) 15 *Current Problems in Pharmacovigilance* 2, available at webarchive.nationalarchives.gov.uk/20150110191938/http://www.mhra.gov.uk/Publications/Safetyguidance/CurrentProblemsinPharmacovigilance/CON2024496.

[318] For a detailed description written by a Hoechst employee, see PD Stonier, 'Nomifensine and hemolytic anemia – experience of a post-marketing alert' (1992) 1 *Pharmacoepidemiology and Drug Safety* 177, doi:10.1002/pds.2630010404.

[319] CSM, n 318.

[320] 'Trouble with nomifensine' (1985) 23 *Drug and Therapeutics Bulletin* 98.

[321] See (1986) 51(116) *Federal Register*, available at cdn.loc.gov/service/ll/fedreg/fr051/fr051116/fr051116.pdf; and CSM Update, 'Withdrawal of nomifensine' (1986) 293 *British Medical Journal* 41.

[322] Information from CJS Hodges, who advised Hoechst UK Limited at the time of the withdrawal.

the option. The balance of potential risks and benefits for such medications are complex and often do not have simple answers.

iv. Litigation

It appears that no litigation claims were made before the withdrawal. Ostensibly this appeared to be a straightforward case of post-marketing surveillance detecting a previously unknown relatively rare ADR. Subsequently questions have been raised over whether Hoechst were aware of adverse events and did not report them to the relevant national regulators. Litigation has been undertaken by the regulators in the USA and in Germany for not reporting adverse events and withholding information. Interestingly, in April 1991 the FDA took out a criminal prosecution of the German parent company of Hoechst, which pleaded guilty to failing to inform its own US subsidiary of the adverse events, resulting in omissions from the US label.[323] This was one of the first cases where the American authority exercised its power to take action concerning misleading information supplied on American products, despite the activities that led to this misinformation having occurred entirely outside of the USA.

v. Conclusion

The safety issue was identified through the ADR reporting system, and the company voluntarily withdrew the product worldwide. Questions have been raised as to the integrity of the company in reporting ADRs to the relevant regulators and the tardiness of the withdrawal. Litigation has followed the withdrawal, but had no role in the detection of the nomifensine safety signal or in its removal from the market; the FDA prosecution commenced five years after the drug had been withdrawn voluntarily.

[323] See Trade and Government Memos, 52 (51) F-D-C Reports, 'The Pink Sheet' 9 (17 December 1990).

C. Selective Serotonin Reuptake Inhibitors

i. Description

Selective Serotonin Reuptake Inhibitors (SSRIs) are a class of compounds primarily used as antidepressants and also in the treatment of other psychiatric disorders, including, but not exclusive to, anxiety disorders and some personality disorders. Their mechanism of action is on reuptake transporters, membrane-spanning proteins that clear the serotonin out of the synaptic cleft back into the axon terminal for re-use. As the name suggests, SSRIs' inhibition of the reuptake of serotonin increases the synaptic availability of serotonin, potentiating serotonergic signalling.

ii. Safety Issues

a. Suicidal Ideations, Self-harm and Aggressive Behaviour

Several studies[324] from the mid-2000s found that SSRIs can cause a higher risk of suicidal behaviour in children and adolescents.[325] For instance, a 2004 US FDA analysis of clinical trials on children with major depressive disorders found statistically significant increases of the risks of 'possible suicidal ideation and suicidal behavior' by about 80%, and of agitation and hostility by about 130%.[326] Some studies, however, have been inconclusive.[327] There is also evidence of a correlation between higher rates of SSRI prescriptions and lower rates of suicide in children, but a clear causal relationship cannot be determined.[328]

In 2004, the UK MHRA concluded that fluoxetine (Prozac) was the only antidepressant that offered a favourable risk–benefit ratio in children with depression, though it was also associated with a slight increase in the risk of self-harm and suicidal ideation.[329] Only two SSRIs are licensed for use with children in the UK – sertraline (Zoloft) and fluvoxamine (Luvox) – and only for the treatment of obsessive-compulsive disorder. Fluoxetine, despite having a favourable risk–benefit ratio for use with depression in adolescents and children, is not licensed for this use.[330]

[324] For examples see C Martinez et al, 'Antidepressant treatment and the risk of fatal and nonfatal self harm in first episode depression: nested case-control study' (2005) 330 *British Medical Journal* 389; and T Hammad et al, 'Suicidality in pediatric patients treated with antidepressant drugs' (2006) 63 *Archives of General Psychiatry* 332.

[325] MB Stone and ML Jones, 'Clinical review: relationship between antidepressant drugs and suicidal behavior in adults' (17 November 2006), Overview for December 13 Meeting of Psychopharmacologic Drugs Advisory Committee (PDAC), FDA 11–74; M Olfson et al, 'Antidepressant drug therapy and suicide in severely depressed children and adults: A case-control study' (2006) 63(8) *Archives of General Psychiatry* 865.

[326] TA Hammad, 'Review and evaluation of clinical data. Relationship between psychiatric drugs and pediatric suicidal behavior' (FDA, 2004) 42; 115.

[327] S Hetrick et al 'Selective serotonin reuptake inhibitors (SSRIs) for depressive disorders in children and adolescents' (2007) (3) *Cochrane Database Systematic Reviews* CD004851.

[328] RD Gibbons, 'The relationship between antidepressant prescription rates and rate of early adolescent suicide' (2006) 163(11) *The American Journal of Psychiatry* 1898.

[329] MHRA, *Report of the CSM expert working group on the safety of selective serotonin reuptake inhibitor antidepressants* (1 December 2004), available at webarchive.nationalarchives.gov.uk/20120424013641/http://www.mhra.gov.uk/PrintPreview/DefaultSP/CON1004259.

[330] MHRA, *Selective Serotonin Reuptake Inhibitors (SSRIs): Overview of regulatory status and CSM advice relating to major depressive disorder (MDD) in children and adolescents including a summary of available safety and efficacy data* (29 September 2009), available at webarchive.nationalarchives.gov.uk/20141206082100/http://www.mhra.gov.uk/Safetyinformation/Safetywarningsalertsandrecalls/Safetywarningsandmessagesformedicines/CON019494.

Studies conducted have not confirmed increased suicide rates in adults prescribed SSRIs.[331]

Shortly following allegations of increased suicide rates in children prescribed SSRIs, the effectiveness of SSRIs as a drug class was brought under scrutiny. A widely-reported 2008 meta-analysis combined 35 clinical trials submitted to the US FDA before licensing of four newer antidepressants (including the SSRIs paroxetine and fluoxetine, and two non-SSRI antidepressants nefazodone and venlafaxine).[332] The authors found that although the effect of antidepressants versus placebos was statistically significant, it did not exceed the NICE criteria for a clinically significant effect. In particular, they found that the effect size was very small for moderate depression but increased with severity, reaching 'clinical significance' for very severe depression. The relationship between severity and efficacy was attributed to a reduction of the placebo effect in severely depressed patients, rather than an increase in the effect of the medication.[333] Some researchers have questioned the statistical basis of this study, suggesting that it underestimates the effect size of antidepressants, but re-analysis of the data even with all results combined shows that it remains below the NICE threshold for 'clinical significance'. Individually, however, paroxetine and venflafaxine exceed this threshold.[334]

More recent data have brought the effectiveness of SSRIs into renewed dispute. A 2010 meta-analysis states that

> the magnitude of benefit of antidepressant medication compared with placebo ... may be minimal or nonexistent, on average, in patients with mild or moderate symptoms. For patients with very severe depression, the benefit of medications over placebo is substantial.[335]

However, this analysis discarded the great majority of FDA-approved antidepressant studies, including ones that used placebo washout periods (typically used as controls).[336] In 2018, Cipriani et al compared 21 antidepressants, including eight known SSRIs and three drugs

[331] M Levenson and C Holland (17 November 2006), 'Statistical Evaluation of Suicidality in Adults Treated with Antidepressants' (pdf), *Overview for December 13 Meeting of Psychopharmacologic Drugs Advisory Committee (PDAC)*, FDA 75, available at wayback.archive-it.org/7993/20170405070114/https://www.fda.gov/ohrms/dockets/ac/06/briefing/2006-4272b1-01-FDA.pdf; D Gunnell et al, 'Selective serotonin reuptake inhibitors (SSRIs) and suicide in adults: meta-analysis of drug company data from placebo controlled, randomised controlled trials submitted to the MHRA's safety review' (2005) 330(7488) *British Medical Journal* 385.

[332] I Kirsch et al, 'Initial severity and antidepressant benefits: a meta-analysis of data submitted to the Food and Drug Administration' (2008) 5(2) *Public Library of Science Medicine* e45.

[333] M Day, 'Prozac does not work in majority of depressed patients' *New Scientist* (26 February 2008), available at www.newscientist.com/article/dn13375-prozac-does-not-work-in-most-depressed-patients.html; 'Anti-depressants "no better than placebo"' *Nursing Times* (26 February 2008), available at www.nursingtimes.net/anti-depressants-no-better-than-placebo/817362.article; L Blue, 'Antidepressants Hardly Help' *Time* (6 February 2008), available at www.time.com/time/health/article/0,8599,1717306,00.html.

[334] J Horder et al, 'Placebo, Prozac and PloS: significant lessons for psychopharmacology' (2011) 25(10) *Journal of Psychopharmacology* 1277.

[335] JC Fournier et al, 'Antidepressant Drug Effects and Depression Severity' (2010) 303(1) *Journal of the American Medical Association* 47.

[336] PD Kramer, 'In Defense of Antidepressants' *New York Times* (9 July 2011), available at www.nytimes.com/2011/07/10/opinion/sunday/10antidepressants.html; KN Fountoulakis and HJ Moller, 'Efficacy of antidepressants: a re-analysis and re-interpretation of the Kirsch data' (2010) 14(03) *International Journal of Neuropsychopharmacology* 1.

with putative SSRI activity, and concluded that they all outperformed placebos for major depression, but with considerable differences between drugs in efficacy and acceptability.[337]

b. Withdrawal Symptoms

It has long been recognised by the FDA that SSRI-associated withdrawal symptoms can be severe.[338] Patients have reported a variety of symptoms, including suicidal and self-harm ideations, similar to those detailed in section IV.C.ii.a, and uncharacteristically aggressive behaviour. It has been claimed that the withdrawal symptoms were so severe that the only way to prevent them was to resume the individual patient's previous dose of medication. Claimants often assert that they were not informed of the potential severity of withdrawal symptoms.

iii. Marketing and Regulatory History

The first SSRI was zimelidine, developed in 1972 by Arvid Carlsson and colleagues. Zimelidine, indalpine, fluvoxaine and fluoxetine were the first four SSRIs to make it to market, but the first two were withdrawn due to side-effects.[339]

UK licence approvals included: fluoxetine (Prozac), granted on 25 November 1988; paroxetine (Seroxat) granted on 12 December 1990; citalopram (Cipramil) granted on 17 March 1995; escitalopram (Cipralex) granted on 10 June 2002; sertraline (Lustral) granted on 19 November 1990; and fluvoxamine (Faverin) granted on 17 December 1986.

In 2003, Professor Gordon Duff, chairman of the CSM, issued a message on the safety of antidepressants in children and adolescents.[340] He described the Expert Working Group's findings that only fluoxetine (Prozac) has been shown in clinical trials to have a favourable balance of risks and benefits for the treatment of Major Depressive Disorder (MDD) in children under 18. He also specifically advised against the use of Seroxat in children and adolescents.[341] In 2004, the UK MHRA issued a warning about increases in 'insomnia, agitation, weight loss, headache, tremor, loss of appetite, self-harm and suicidal thoughts' when the medications are used with children and adolescents.[342]

In 2003, GlaxoSmithKline (GSK) informed the FDA that a review of its pediatric clinical trials demonstrated an increased rate of suicidal thoughts and behaviour (there were no actual suicides). Following this there was extensive GSK and FDA review, culminating in

[337] A Cipriani et al, 'Comparative efficacy and acceptability of 21 antidepressant drugs for the acute treatment of adults with major depressive disorder: a systematic review and network meta-analysis' (2018) 391(10198) *The Lancet* 1357, doi:10.1016/s0140-6736(17)32802-7.

[338] A Tonks, 'Withdrawal from paroxetine can be severe, warns FDA' (2002) 324 *British Medical Journal* 260.

[339] A Carlsson and DT Wong, 'A note on the discovery of selective serotonin reuptake inhibitors' (1997) 61(12) *Life Sciences* 1203.

[340] Available at webarchive.nationalarchives.gov.uk/20141206131926/http://www.mhra.gov.uk/home/groups/pl-p/documents/websiteresources/con019492.pdf.

[341] Available at webarchive.nationalarchives.gov.uk/20141206132138/http://www.mhra.gov.uk/home/groups/pl-p/documents/websiteresources/con019507.pdf.

[342] MHRA, *Questions and answers: Advice on SSRIs in children from the Committee on Safety of Medicine* (pdf) (12 February 2004), available at webarchive.nationalarchives.gov.uk/20141206131928/http://www.mhra.gov.uk/home/groups/pl-p/documents/websiteresources/con019493.pdf.

label changes in April 2004 and a boxed warning on the US label in January 2005 for pediatric patients. The introduction of a warning regarding the association between SSRIs and suicide by the FDA in 2004 led to a dramatic decrease in prescriptions of these medications to young people. Originally, there were concerns that the decrease in prescriptions caused by the warnings could increase the number of teenage suicides in the US.[343] However, data from the US National Center for Health Statistics put these concerns to rest. The suicide rates for persons younger than 25 actually decreased between 2004 and 2007 in the USA.[344]

Starting in 2005, both the FDA and GSK conducted analyses in adult patients. An increased rate of suicidal thoughts and behaviour in young adults (not statistically significant) and in clinical trials of adults with major depressive disorder (statistically significant) was found by GSK, which changed its label based on this in May 2006. The FDA had similar findings for young adults for all antidepressants,[345] and implemented a black-box warning on SSRI and other antidepressant medications regarding the increased risk of suicidal behaviour in patients younger than 24[346] in August 2007. The label further states that short-term studies did not show an increase in the risk of suicidality with antidepressants compared to placebo in adults beyond age 24, and that there was a reduction with antidepressants compared to placebo in adults aged 65 or older.

In response to the FDA meta-analysis, it was agreed in 2008 to include the following wording on all patient information leaflets and summary product characteristics for all SSRIs and selective noradrenergic reuptake inhibitors (SNRIs) across all EU countries:[347]

> Thoughts of suicide and worsening of your depression or anxiety disorder
>
> If you are depressed and/or have anxiety disorders you can sometimes have thoughts of harming or killing yourself. These may be increased when first starting antidepressants, since these medicines all take time to work, usually about two weeks but sometimes longer. You may be more likely to think like this:
>
> - if you have previously had thoughts about killing or harming yourself
> - if you are a young adult; information from clinical trials has shown an increased risk of suicidal behaviour in adults aged less than 25 years with psychiatric conditions who were treated with an antidepressant
>
> If you have thoughts of harming or killing yourself at any time, contact your doctor or go to a hospital straight away. You may find it helpful to tell a relative or close friend that you are

[343] RD Gibbons et al, 'Early evidence on the effects of regulators' suicidality warnings on SSRI prescriptions and suicide in children and adolescents' (2007) 164(9) *The American Journal of Psychiatry* 1356.

[344] J Xu et al, 'Deaths: Preliminary Data for 2007' (pdf) (2009) 58(1) *National Vital Statistics Reports* 29, available at www.cdc.gov/nchs/data/nvsr/nvsr58/nvsr58_01.pdf.

[345] RA Friedman and AC Leon, 'Expanding the black box – depression, antidepressants, and the risk of suicide' (2007) 356(23) *New England Journal of Medicine* 2343; and TP Laughren for the Department of Health and Human Services, Public Health Service, Food and Drug Administration Center for Drug Evaluation and Research. Overview for 13 December meeting of Psychopharmacologic Drugs Advisory Committee.

[346] FDA, 'FDA Proposes New Warnings About Suicidal Thinking, Behavior in Young Adults Who Take Antidepressant Medications' (2 May 2007), available at wayback.archive-it.org/7993/20171114232308/https://www.fda.gov/Drugs/DrugSafety/InformationbyDrugClass/ucm096273.htm.

[347] MHRA Guidance, *Selective serotonin reuptake inhibitors (SSRIs) and serotonin and noradrenaline reuptake inhibitors (SNRIs): use and safety*, published 18 December 2014, available at www.gov.uk/government/publications/ssris-and-snris-use-and-safety/selective-serotonin-reuptake-inhibitors-ssris-and-serotonin-and-noradrenaline-reuptake-inhibitors-snris-use-and-safety.

depressed or have an anxiety disorder, and ask them to read this leaflet. You might ask them to tell you if they think your depression or anxiety is getting worse, or if they are worried about changes in your behaviour.

Similar precautionary notice revisions were implemented by the Japanese Ministry of Health.[348]

The controversy and linkage between SSRIs and suicide and violence have continued, with claims and counterclaims on the relative balance of the risks and benefits of SSRIs.[349]

iv. Litigation

a. Paxil Litigation in the US

GlaxoSmithKline has experienced litigation associated with its selective serotonin reuptake inhibitor Paxil. The litigation centres on allegations that Paxil caused patients to commit suicide and/or acts of violence, and that patients experienced problems when they try to discontinue taking Paxil. In May 2001, the first successful Paxil suicide/murder case, *Tobin*,[350] was tried in the federal court in Wyoming. Mr Donald Schell killed himself, his wife Rita, their daughter Deborah Tobin and granddaughter Alyssa Tobin. The trial ended in an $8 million verdict against GSK (reduced to $6.4 million by 20% comparative fault of the deceased). This was the first case a claimant had won against a manufacturer of an SSRI.

After the successful *Tobin* case, substantial litigation was brought in the US. The 'murder/suicide litigation' became common against manufacturers of all SSRIs, as well as other types of antidepressant. This tranche of 'murder/suicide' litigation mimicked the Prozac litigation against Eli Lilly that began in the 1990s (Eli Lilly won the majority of the cases). In many of these cases, plaintiffs alleged that the drugs were generally good, but that in a small number of individuals these drugs would cause suicidal/homicidal acts. After the *Tobin* case these claims were more rigorously defended by manufacturers, with considerable attention paid to the admissibility of evidence. A subset of lawyers and experts began to specialise in these cases. A handful of plaintiff lawyers, particularly Andy Vickery and Baum Hedlundbrought, have brought the majority of this type of case, with relatively few being been brought by other counsel. A consistent line of argument is generally taken, with the plaintiffs tending to rely upon the same publications in support of their allegations. Key experts have also emerged, with Dr David Healy and Dr Joseph Glenmullen frequently being called provide expert testimony on behalf of the plaintiffs.

Another body of litigation related to discontinuation symptoms and again affected a number of manufacturers. For example, GSK was served with purported class actions in California, alleging breaches of the Californian Unfair Trade Practices Act and seeking changes in the labelling and doctors to be informed. This and a purported class action in New Hampshire were dismissed. The company also received numerous lawsuits alleging

[348] Japanese Ministry of Health (in Japanese), available at www1.mhlw.go.jp/kinkyu/iyaku_j/iyaku_j/anzenseijyouhou/261.pdf.

[349] See I Torjesen, 'SSRIs double the risk of suicide and violence in healthy adults' (2016) 355 *British Medical Journal* i5504, doi.org/10.1136/bmj.i5504; G Adshead, 'Antidepressants and murder: case not closed' (2017) 358 *British Medical Journal* j3697; and Cipriani et al, n 338.

[350] *Estates of Tobin ex rel Tobin v SmithKline* Civil no 00-CV-0025-Bea, 2001 WL 36102161 (D Wyo, 8 May 2001).

individual personal injury, many of which were consolidated in federal MDL. The company and plaintiffs entered into a conditional agreement to settle the vast majority of the cases. The conditions were satisfied and at this time, virtually all pending US claims have been settled.

b. Seroxat Litigation in England and Wales

1. Introduction

In June 2002, GSK received a letter from Hugh James (HJ), solicitors, claiming that HJ represented 5,291 individuals who suffered from withdrawal symptoms, suicidal behaviour and aggression, which they attributed to Seroxat. The solicitors claimed that this meant that the products were defective within the meaning of the Consumer Protection Act 1987. No proceedings were issued at the time. In November 2004, HJ wrote to GSK stating that it represented 1,641 potential claimants who were pursuing claims against the manufacturer for injuries alleged to have been caused by Seroxat. It stated that there were 22 other firms representing approximately 400 further claimants.

When claims were issued, HJ represented the majority of claimants, with a handful of other firms representing a small number of claimants. The majority of the claimants lived in the UK or the Republic of Ireland, with a small number of claims from individuals resident in Australia, Spain and Guernsey. The claimants alleged that injuries were caused by a propensity of the product to cause suicide attempts and agitation and/or aggression, and to cause withdrawal reactions,

The case progressed slowly, and HJ confirmed in February 2007 that 'after taking expert advice' it would only be pursuing claims for 'those who have found it difficult or impossible to withdraw from the drug or have suffered adverse effects following withdrawal that has made it difficult for them to remain free of the drug'.

2. Group Litigation Order

On 29 June 2008, the court ordered that the group should proceed under a GLO. The court defined the issues under the GLO as:

> Does Seroxat have a capacity to cause adverse effects consequent upon or following discontinuance (withdrawal) such as to prevent or make more difficult the ability of users to discontinue, withdraw from or remain free from taking Seroxat to a greater extent than all other Selective Serotonin Re-uptake Inhibitors (SSRIs).

3. Legal Aid

In October 2010, HJ was required to produce 'show cause' letters to demonstrate to the LSC (the public body funding the generic case) why public funding should remain in place for this litigation. The funding was considered by a Special Controls Review Panel at the LSC. The public funding certificate was revoked late in 2010 and a substantial number of cases were discontinued. Proceedings were stayed while there were several (unsuccessful) challenges to the LSC's decision to withdraw funding.

4. The Revived Action

In August 2015, around 100 of the claimants revived the action, stating that they had secured third-party funding and after-the-event insurance. These claimants were represented by

Fortitude Law, which was 'created as a vehicle by which this litigation could be continued'.[351] The third-party funding of £1.2 million had been committed to the case by Managed Legal Solutions Ltd. £750,000 was said to be available in 'after the event' insurance.[352] The issue arose of whether this was sufficient to cover the defendant's legal expenses; GSK made an application for £6.8 million in security for costs. In December 2017 a judgment was handed down that awarded GSK £3.4 million in security for costs against a third-party litigation funder that had committed only £1.2 million to fund the litigation.[353] The impact this will have on the progress of the litigation is currently uncertain.

v. Conclusion

Medical studies triggered the regulatory responses. Meta-analysis by both the manufacturers and the regulators drove changes in labelling. Following the changes in regulation, an increase in cases was seen in the US. Some suicide/murder cases have been brought and have succeeded, but the majority of cases have focused on discontinuation or withdrawal symptoms. These have formed the class actions in the US, which were settled out of court. The majority of cases in England and Wales dropped out after the public funding was withdrawn due to low prospects of success. Third-party funding has enabled a reduced-scale group action to address the question of withdrawal symptoms, which is still being contested.

[351] See *Bailey and others v GlaxoSmithKline (UK) Ltd* [2016] EWHC 178 (QB), [2016] All ER (D) 44 (Feb) [64].
[352] ibid.
[353] *Bailey and others v GSK* [2017] EWHC 3195 (QB).

D. Sabril (vigabatrin)

i. Description

Sabril (vigabatrin) is an anti-epileptic drug that works by inhibiting the breakdown of the inhibitory neurotransmitter gamma-animobutyric acid (GABA) by preventing the activity of the enzyme GABA transaminase. It is prescribed as last-line adjunctive therapy to treat refractory (otherwise untreatable) seizures in adults, and as a monotherapy for West syndrome in infants (infantile spasms).

ii. Safety Issue

In January 1997, two consultants from Leicester, a neurologist and an ophthalmologist, published a paper in the *British Medical Journal* on three symptomatic patients who experienced peripheral visual field loss, measured by automated perimetry, which the authors attributed to Sabril.[354] Other case reports followed,[355] triggering a series of academic investigations into the pathogenesis of the drug, which failed to reach firm conclusions. In 1999, Lawden et al published a paper[356] suggesting that Sabril was responsible for visual field loss in around 29% of users. At that stage the data sheet stated that Vigabatrin-associated visual field loss (VAVFL) had been reported in about a third of users.[357] Subsequent research has supported the conclusion that Sabrin can lead to permanent loss of peripheral visual field.[358]

iii. Marketing and Regulatory History

Vigabatrin was developed in the 1970s and later owned by Aventis Pharma Ltd, now a part of Sanofi Aventis. The product was licensed in the UK on 22 September 1989. It was then rolled out in many other European countries, and is now marketed in 62 countries.

In 1997, Finland[359] initiated an Article 12 referral[360] related to the risk and safety profile of Sabril. The UK MHRA issued safety information in 1998.[361] In October 1999, the

[354] T Eke et al (1997) 314 *British Medical Journal* 180.

[355] G Harding et al, 'Elector oculography, E.R.Gs, multi-focal E.R.G's and VEP's in epileptic patients showing visual field disorders' (1997) 103:96 *Electroenceph Clin Neurophysiol* 13; EA Wilson and MJ Brodie, 'Severe persistent visual field constriction associated with vigabatrin' (1997) 314 *British Medical Journal* 1693; ICK Wong, GE Mawer, JWAS Sander, 'Reaction might be dose dependent' (1997) 314 *British Medical Journal* 1693; N Blackwell, J Hayllar and G Kelly, 'Patients taking vigabatrin should have regular visual field testing' (1997) 314 *British Medical Journal* 1693.

[356] MC Lawden et al, 'Visual Field Defects associated with vigabatrin therapy' (1999) 67(6) *Journal of Neurology, Neurosurgery and Psychiatry* 716.

[357] See Opinion of the Committee for Proprietary Medicinal Products Pursuant to Article 12 Of Council Directive 75/319/EEC as amended, for Vigabatrin (CPMP/1357/99-EN), App II, section 4.3, available at www.ema.europa.eu/docs/en_GB/document_library/Referrals_document/Vigabatrin_31/WC500014088.pdf.

[358] For example, see L Frisén and K Malmgren 'Characterization of vigabatrin-associated optic atrophy' (2003) 81(5) *Acta Ophthalmologica Scandinavica* 466, doi:10.1034/j.1600-0420.2003.00125.x; JR Buncic et al, 'Characteristic retinal atrophy with secondary "inverse" optic atrophy identifies vigabatrin toxitiy in children' (2004) 111(10) *Ophthalmology* 1935, doi:10.1016/j.ophtha.2004.03.036.

[359] Opinion of the Committee, n 358.

[360] Art 12 of Council Directive 75/319/EEC (as amended).

[361] CSM 'Vigabatrin (Sabril) and visual field defects' (March 1998) 24 *Current Problems in Pharmacovigilance* 1 (updated in CSM, 'Vigabatrin (Sabril): visual field defects' (November 1999) 25 *Current Problems in*

European Commission approved the continued marketing of Sabril in the EU, provided Aventis undertook a number of commitments relating to animal and clinical studies on Sabril,[362] which it did.

A technical appraisal by NICE in 2004[363] concluded that Sabril failed to demonstrate superior seizure control compared to other alternative therapies, either for partial seizures or for West syndrome. The risk of visual field constriction associated with Sabril use must be balanced against both the risks of adverse events associated with other therapies and the risks of adverse events due to uncontrolled seizures. The conclusion was that Sabril remained an important treatment option for these groups of patients, subject to an appropriate risk–benefit analysis. The use of Sabril as an antiepileptic drug appears to be declining.[364]

iv. Litigation

Litigation began in the UK in December 2000, but not in earnest as a group action until March 2003. The Sabril Group action started life with a letter before action in December 2000, seeking 'kitchen sink' disclosure from the manufacturer, which was refused. For three years thereafter, relatively little happened whilst the claimants' lawyers collected together a cohort of legally-aided claimants. At its height, the group was some 270 strong, but it finally settled at 164 claimants. This was from a maximum patient database in the UK of approximately 14,000 patients. The first claim form was served in July 2004 and the case settled in July 2008, three months before trial.

v. Conclusion

Visual field constriction was identified by medics in 1997, and warnings were introduced. Litigation began in the UK in December 2000.

Pharmacovigilance 13, available at webarchive.nationalarchives.gov.uk/20141206195217/http://www.mhra.gov.uk/home/groups/pl-p/documents/websiteresources/con2023713.pdf.

[362] November 1999 (new restrictions on prescribing and monitoring requirements).

[363] National Institute for Clinical Excellence, Final Appraisal Determination, 'Newer drugs for epilepsy in children' (March 2004), available at www.nice.org.uk/guidance/ta79/documents/final-appraisal-determination-newer-drugs-for-epilepsy-in-children2.

[364] R Ackers et al, 'Prioritizing children's medicines for research: a pharmacoepidemiological study of antiepileptic drugs' (2007) 63(6) *British Journal of Clinical Pharmacology* 689.

E. Mirapexin/Sifrol/Daquiran (pramipexole)

i. Description

Pramipexole is a non-ergoline dopamine agonist binding at the D_2 family of receptors, with relatively high selectivity for the D_3 Dopamine receptor. It is indicated for treating early-stage Parkinson's disease (PD) and restless legs syndrome (RLS). It has also been prescribed off label as a treatment for cluster headaches and to counteract the problems with sexual dysfunction experienced by some users of the SSRI class of antidepressants.[365] Pramipexole has shown robust effects on pilot studies in a placebo-controlled proof of concept study in bipolar disorder.[366] It has also been investigated for the treatment of clinical depression and fibromyalgia.[367]

ii. Safety Issue

From July 1997, there were 20 reports of sudden onset of falling asleep, described as 'sleep attacks', recorded in the US in patients taking pramipexole. In many of these cases, the episode of sleep was reported to have occurred without warning signs. It was found that the incidence of somnolence increased at doses higher than 1.5mg daily. This resulted in the updating of prescriber and patient product information for pramipexole, with stronger warnings about the risks of driving.[368]

Various lawsuits have alleged that there were reports of compulsive behaviours within the original clinical trial cohort. Published reports from 2003 onwards indicate an association between pramipexole and compulsive gambling.[369] Post-marketing ADR reports indicate several adverse effects of pramipexole on impulse control, including compulsive gambling, hypersexuality and over-eating,[370] in patients without any prior

[365] C DeBattista et al, 'Pramipexole augmentation of a selective serotonin reuptake inhibitor in the treatment of depression' (2000) 20(2) *Journal of Clinical Psychopharmacology* 274.

[366] CA Zarate, Jr et al, 'Pramipexole for bipolar II depression: a placebo-controlled proof of concept study' (2004) 56(1) *Biology Psychiatry* 54.

[367] P Cassano et al, 'Pramipexole in treatment-resistant depression: an extended follow-up' (2004) 20(3) *Depression Anxiety* 131; AJ Holman and RR Myers, 'A randomized, double-blind, placebo-controlled trial of pramipexole, a dopamine agonist, in patients with fibromyalgia receiving concomitant medications' (2005) 52(8) *Arthritis & Rheumatology* 2495.

[368] See EMA's 'Public Statement on Sifrol, Daquiran, Mirapexin (Pramipexole) – Sudden Onset of Sleep' (EMEA/20642/99), available at www.ema.europa.eu/docs/en_GB/document_library/Public_statement/2010/08/WC500095434.pdf; and CSM 'Pramipexole and the Sudden Onset of Sleep' (November 1999) 25 *Current Problems in Pharmacovigilance* 17, available at webarchive.nationalarchives.gov.uk/20141206195217/http://www.mhra.gov.uk/home/groups/pl-p/documents/websiteresources/con2023713.pdf.

[369] E Driver-Dunckley, MD, J Samanta, MD, M Stacy, MD, 'Pathological Gambling Associated With Dopamine Agonist Therapy in Parkinson's Disease' (2003) 61 *Neurology* 422.

[370] For example, see M Dodd et al, 'Pathological gambling caused by drugs used to treat Parkinson's disease' (2005) 62 *Archives of Neurology* 1377; Driver-Dunckley et al, n 370; KJ Klos et al, 'Pathological hypersexuality predominantly linked to adjuvant dopamine agonist therapy in Parkinson's disease and multiple system atrophy' (2005) 11 *Parkinsonism Related Disorders* 381; R Kurlan, 'Disabling repetitive behaviours in Parkinson's disease' (2004) 19(4): *Movement Disorders* 433. For a review, see EC Wolters et al, 'Parkinson's disease-related disorders in the impulsive-compulsive spectrum' (2008) 255(5) *Journal of Neurology* 48.

history of these behaviours.[371] These behaviours have been reported to manifest in almost 14% of patients on dopamine agonist therapies.[372]

More recently evidence has come to light that there may be a link between pramipexole and heart failure,[373] which will not be addressed in this case study.

iii. Marketing and Regulatory History

a. In the EU

Product authorisations were granted to Pfizer and Boehringer by the EMA through the centralised procedure. Products included Sifrol on 14 October 1997, Daquiran on 27 October 1997 and Mirapexin on 23 February 1998.

From August 2005 the increased risk of compulsive disorders was known to the European regulators;[374] it was clearly highlighted in a Netherlands Pharmacovigilance Centre article entitled 'Pergolide and pathologic gambling' In 2005, during the Sifrol (pramipexole) variation procedure to add warnings about pathological gambling, France proposed that the need to add pathological gambling as an adverse reaction to all dopamine agonists should be considered. Sweden also communicated this issue on its website in October 2005. In July 2006, label changes for special warnings and precautions for use were recommended by the European Union's Pharmacovigilance Working Party for all dopamine agonists, and applied to products containing dopamine agonists for all indications, including RLS, endocrine disorders and PD.[375]

Since the controversy arose, newer formulations of pramipexole have been authorised in the EU.[376]

Daquiran was withdrawn at the request of the marketing authorisation holder on 23 May 2006, as it had never actually been marketed within the EU.[377] Sifrol and Mirapexin remain licensed.[378]

b. In the USA

The FDA approved an application for Mirapex on 1 July 1997.[379] In February 2006, Boehringer applied to include new wording in the information for patients in the

[371] JM Bostwick, 'Frequency of new-onset pathologic compulsive gambling or hypersexuality after drug treatment of idiopathic Parkinson disease' (2009) 84(4) *Mayo Clinic Proceedings* 310.

[372] V Voon et al, 'Prevalence of repetitive and reward-seeking behaviors in Parkinson disease' (2006) 67(7) *Neurology* 1254, doi:10.1212/01.wnl.0000238503.20816.13.

[373] See at www.fda.gov/Drugs/DrugSafety/ucm319779.htm.

[374] For background, see at webarchive.nationalarchives.gov.uk/20141206130325/http://www.mhra.gov.uk/home/groups/pl-p/documents/websiteresources/con2025150.pdf.

[375] ibid.

[376] Pramipexole Accord on 19 October 2011 and Pramipexole Teva on 10 March 2009; see www.ema.europa.eu for further details.

[377] See the EMA's Public Statement on Daquiran: Withdrawal of the marketing authorization in the European Union (23/05/2006), available at www.ema.europa.eu/docs/en_GB/document_library/Public_statement/2009/11/WC500014725.pdf.

[378] Statement on EMA website at www.ema.europa.eu.

[379] See at www.accessdata.fda.gov/scripts/cder/daf/index.cfm?event=overview.process&ApplNo=020667#collapseTE.

'Precautions' section of the label, to include information on compulsive gambling, hypersexuality and impulse control issues. This was amended again in February 2007, and by August 2008 the wording was as follows:[380]

> There have been reports of patients experiencing intense urges to gamble, increased sexual urges, and other intense urges and the inability to control these urges while taking one or more of the medications that increase central dopaminergic tone, that are generally used for the treatment of Parkinson's disease, including Mirapex. Although it is not proven that the medications caused these events, these urges were reported to have stopped in some cases when the dose was reduced or the medication was stopped. Prescribers should ask patients about the development of new or increased gambling urges, sexual urges or other urges while being treated with Mirapex. Patients should inform their physician if they experience new or increased gambling urges, increased sexual urges or other intense urges while taking Mirapex. Physicians should consider dose reduction or stopping the medication if a patient develops such urges while taking Mirapex.

Prescribing information was strengthened in 2013 to encourage prescribers to engage with next-of-kin over impulse control issues, as the patients often did not recognise their own behaviour as aberrant.[381]

c. In Canada

Mirapex was first licensed in Canada in February 1998. The label was updated in 2004 to include warnings of 'increased or decreased libido'. Pathological gambling was added to the label in 2005. The current product monograph, dated January 2018, warns of a range of compulsive behaviours, including gambling and hypersexuality.[382] Health Canada records post-marketing adverse event reports, and there are a considerable number of adverse event reports listed for compulsive behaviours.[383]

Generic versions of pramipexole are also available in Canada.

iv. Litigation

a. In the EU and UK

In England and Wales, solicitors Leigh Day considered commencing a class action in 2006.[384] However, the difficulties of litigating this action under English law meant that this matter fizzled out and a class action was never undertaken. There were a handful of successful claims[385] brought against prescribers for lack of warning, but neither Boehringer nor Pfizer paid any compensation.

A similar litigation pattern is seen in mainland Europe, and the few cases launched have tended to list prescribers rather than manufacturers as defendants.

[380] FPL for approved supplement NDA 20-667/S-014, S-017 and S-018, available at www.accessdata.fda.gov/drugsatfda_docs/appletter/2008/020667s014,020667s017,020667s018ltr.pdf.

[381] See at www.accessdata.fda.gov/drugsatfda_docs/label/2013/020667s029lbl.pdf.

[382] See at pdf.hres.ca/dpd_pm/00043483.PDF.

[383] See at cvp-pcv.hc-sc.gc.ca/arq-rei/index-eng.jsp.

[384] See at www.leighday.co.uk/LeighDay/media/LeighDay/documents/Complex-Claims-Brochure-06-06-07.pdf.

[385] For example, see www.kiteleys.co.uk/news/2015/06/pramipexole-induced-gambling/.

b. In the USA

The first successful case was brought in the District Court of Minnesota by Gary Charbonneau[386] for recovery of moneys ($260,000) lost due to compulsive gambling. The case, which commenced in 2002, alleged that pramipexole caused the plaintiff's gambling problem and, furthermore, that Boehringer Ingelheim and Pfizer (the marketing authorisation holders in the US) knew about its potential to cause compulsive behaviour and failed to issue appropriate warnings or take steps to investigate the scope of the problem. In August 2008 the jury returned a verdict for the plaintiff and awarded $8.3 million (the majority of this sum, $7.8 million, was punitive damages). A class action followed,[387] and settlement was achieved for the plaintiffs.

c. In Canada

The case of *Schick v Boehringer Ingelheim (Canada) Ltd* was brought by the firm Thomson Rogers.[388] It commenced in May 2005[389] and was certified as a class action on 27 July 2012 by the Ontario Superior Court of Justice.[390] This opt-out class action alleged that Mirapex caused impulse control orders, including pathological gambling, hypersexuality, binge eating and compulsive shopping. It was claimed that the defendants knew about, or ought to have known about, ADR reports of excessive gambling and similar behaviour, which were first seen during clinical trials in 1993 and confirmed through medical studies, but warnings about which were not added to the product label until 2005, eight years after the drug was introduced. This class action applied to anyone prescribed Mirapex in Canada (except for Quebec) prior to 27 July 2012. Settlement was reached late in 2014 and was approved by the Court Settlement Agreement by Order of Mr Justice Belobaba of the Ontario Superior Court of Justice on 18 February 2015. A separate class action was launched in Quebec in February 2009 and was also certified as a class action in November 2011.[391] The Quebec case was founded in product liability law and applied to residents of Quebec prescribed Mirapex up to 13 July 2011. Again, a settlement was reached.[392] Cases concerning generic versions of pramipexole are ongoing in Canada.[393]

v. Conclusion

Mirapexin remains marketed with strong warnings. Newer formulations or pramipexole have been added to the retinue of available drugs since these side-effects came to light, and are marketed with warnings.

[386] *Gary E Charbonneau, et al v Boehringer Ingelheim, et al*, Case no 06-CV-1215(JMR/FLN).
[387] *In Re Mirapex Products Liability Litigation*, MDL 07-1836, details and document available at www.gpo.gov/fdsys/granule/USCOURTS-mnd-0_07-md-01836/USCOURTS-mnd-0_07-md-01836-8.
[388] See at www.thomsonrogers.com/practice-areas/class-action/mirapex/.
[389] See at cbaapp.org/ClassAction/PDF.aspx?id=6451.
[390] Action #05-CV-288851CP (*Schick v Boehringer Ingelheim (Canada) Ltd*).
[391] Case 500-06-000463-097 (*France Lépine against Boehringer Ingelheim (Canada) Ltd*).
[392] See at cbaapp.org/ClassAction/PDF.aspx?id=5978.
[393] See at www.merchantlaw.com/class-actions/current-class-actions/pramipexole-dihydrochloride-generic-mirapex-class-action.

V. Non-Steroidal Anti-Inflammatories

A. Opren (benoxaprofen)

i. Description

Benoxaprofen is a non-steroidal anti-inflammatory drug indicated for the treatment of arthritis.

ii. Safety Issue

Safety issues regarding Opren were first reported on 8 May 1982, when a short piece in the *British Medical Journal* reported that six elderly patients who had been on Opren had died of a rare hepato-renal complication.[394] However, in later reports to the US courts it transpired that there had been 11 roughly contemporaneous reports to the FDA of deaths in the US.

iii. Marketing and Regulatory History

Opren had a novel mechanism of action, and the results of clinical trials indicated that it appeared to impede the progress of painful arthritic disease. Benoxaprofen was marketed by Eli Lilly and Company under the brand name Oraflex in the US and as Opren in Europe in 1980. In the UK, the first marketing authorisation was granted on 15 May 1980 for a 300mg suppository, followed on 16 March 1982 by authorisation for a 300mg oral dispersible tablet. While the 600mg formulation was never authorised, it remained the initial recommended dose. The adverse effects noted in the product information included transient photosensitivity (redness and rash on skin when exposed to sunlight) and onycholysis (lifting of nail from the nailbed) in some patients. Caution was advised when prescribing the product to patients with impaired liver or kidney function.

The FDA licensed Oraflex tablets on 19 April 1982. Nineteen days later the first published reports of liver toxicity by Taggart & Allerdice were reported in the *British Medical Journal.*

In response to the safety signals, in June 1982 Opren's manufacturer, Eli Lilly, distributed a letter to all doctors recommending that the daily dose be reduced to 300mg (half the standard previously recommended dose) for elderly patients, due to possible decreased renal function. In July 1982, additional reports emerged in the *British Medical Journal* letters regarding side-effects, including deaths, associated with Opren.[395] On 3 August 1982, the UK Licensing Authority imposed a three-month suspension on the promotion and supply of Opren,[396] and on 4 August 1982 Eli Lilly voluntarily ceased marketing of Opren worldwide.

[394] H Taggart and JM Alderdice, 'Fatal cholestatic jaundice in elderly patients taking benoxaprofen' (1982) 284 *British Medical Journal* 1372.

[395] A Duthie et al, 'Fatal cholestatic jaundice in elderly patients taking benoxaprofen' (1982) 285 *British Medical Journal* (Clinical Research Edition) 62.

[396] CSM, 'Dear Doctor' letter, 'Opren: Suspension of product licenses' (3 August 1982).

iv. Litigation

a. In the USA

Several cases were brought in the US concerning deaths and other less severe side-effects. Eli Lilly successfully defended some of these cases, but there were several high-profile civil actions, and a criminal prosecution.[397] The cases that attracted the most attention were the wrongful death cases, particularly *Borom v Eli Lilly*,[398] in which an award of $6 million was made (composed entirely of punitive damages). This was the largest ever product liability award for a wrongful death caused by a medicine, and Eli Lilly launched an appeal, but entered into a voluntary settlement before the appeal was heard. Around 100 cases were brought, including an application to have 27 cases centralised into an MDL and transferred to Ohio, but this was denied.[399] The majority of cases were settled out of court and for far more modest sums than the *Borom* case.

In addition to the civil cases for compensation, a criminal action was launched for failing to comply with FDA regulations on reporting adverse events and failing to label the drug with information on potential side-effects. Twenty-five charges were laid against the company and 15 against Dr William Shedden, the Vice President and Chief Medical Officer at the time that Oraflex was licensed. While Eli Lilly were charged with failing to inform the FDA of adverse incidence reports (including deaths), there was no allegation of any intentional withholding of information to impact on the licensing decision, nor of any fraud. Neither the company nor Shedden contested the fines that were levied, of $25,000 against the company and $15,000 against Shedden.

b. In England and Wales

In England and Wales,[400] the regulatory events in 1982 were followed by a media campaign focusing attention on the side-effects of the product reported to the CSM. The most common complaints were related to conditions detailed in existing products warnings, photosensivity and onycholysis. The media publicised the intention of 'victims' to sue Eli Lilly. This media campaign lasted until the settlement of the original litigation in 1988.

The Opren Action Group was formed in August 1982, and commenced legal proceedings in the US, in Indiana where Eli Lilly was based, rather than in the UK. On 5 June 1984, the Indiana District Court declined to hear the claims in the US on the ground that the proper forum for English litigants was in England. On 11 February 1985, a writ was served in England brought by Joseph Owen Davies, which subsequently became the nominal 'lead action'. Landmark decisions were subsequently handed down by the High Court, which set out guidelines for conducting multi-party litigation in England and Wales. A total of 2,000 plaintiffs came forward between 1983 and 1993. The plaintiffs alleged a number of different

[397] For more detail see R Patterson, *Drugs in Litigation: Damage Awards involving prescription and non-prescription* (LexisNexis, 2017).

[398] *Clarence Borom v Eli Lilly & Company*, Middle District of Georgia, Court of Appeal no 83-0038-COL was tried in November, 1983.

[399] *In Re Eli Lilly & Co Oraflex Products Liability*, 578 F Supp 422 (JPML 1984).

[400] See A Ware, 'Opren Litigation' in Hodges (ed), n 191, ch 18.

side-effects, with a substantial number alleging long-term and/or permanent opren-induced light and heat sensitivity. The proceedings were managed so that the short-form statement of claim had to contain certain core details, including the dates of ingestion of Opren, other medications prescribed and allegations of the injuries suffered.

These cases did not go to trial and were settled out of court in 1987, without an admission of causation or liability, for relatively low-value sums – around £1,800 per plaintiff on average. The settlement was confidential, but it was known from statements by Hidden J, the judge in the case, that over 1,300 cases were settled in this way. The total compensation awarded by the settlement was reported to be £2,275,000, with an additional £4 million in costs.[401]

Subsequently a further group of 587 cases applied to join. The vast majority of these were time barred, and were struck out by the court in 1992 under the law on limitation of actions.

The side-effects that were claimed were many and varied, and included a substantial number of claims where it was alleged that the plaintiff had suffered long-term and/or permanent Opren-induced light and heat sensitivity. Because of the settlement and the striking out of the remaining cases, the question of whether these effects were attributable to Opren was never tested in court.

v. Conclusion

The safety signal came from a short medical report in May 1982, which was followed by swift regulatory action and a voluntary withdrawal in August 1982, with litigation then ensuing. There were considerable differences in the outcomes of successful litigation in the US and compensation via the settlement fund in England and Wales, despite there being little difference in the nature of the claims. The settlement fund reflected (with a discount for early settlement) the approximate value of a successful court claim; a small part of this discrepancy is due to the relative differences in compensation quantum, but it is predominantly due to the inclusion of punitive damages under the US system.

[401] C Dyer, 'Settlement of the benoxaprofen case' (1988) 296(6615) *British Medical Journal (Clinical Research Edition)* 109.

B. Vioxx (rofecoxib)

i. Description

Vioxx (rofecoxib) was a non-steroidal, anti-inflammatory drug (NSAID) functioning as a COX-2 inhibitor, indicated to treat a number of painful conditions including osteoarthritis, acute pain and dysmenorrhoea.

ii. Safety Issue

The post-marketing VIGOR (Vioxx GI Outcomes Research) study compared Vioxx, a selective COX-2 inhibitor, and another older, non-selective NSAID, naproxen, in patients with rheumatoid arthritis. The study examined whether Vioxx significantly reduced the risk of gastrointestinal perforations, ulcers and bleeds when compared to naproxen. In the study, patients in the Vioxx arm experienced significantly fewer serious gastrointestinal events than those in the naproxen arm. However, patients in the Vioxx arm experienced significantly more serious thrombotic events over the 12-month study period than those in the naproxen arm.[402] Results of the VIGOR study, which Merck scientists believed were explained by the cardioprotective antiplatelet activity of naproxen, were studied and promptly submitted to the FDA in March 2000. In May 2000, a paper discussing the VIGOR results was submitted to the *New England Journal of Medicine*, which published it in November 2000. Merck continued to analyse the data throughout this period, sent a report to the FDA at the end of June 2000 and, in October 2000, provided FDA with a Safety Update Report. The data that had been submitted to the FDA in March 2000 and described in the *Journal* paper of May 2000, had been the data as at February 2000. Subsequently, after the report sent to the FDA in June 2000, additional adjudications confirmed three additional myocardial infarctions in the Vioxx arm of the study. These three cases were included in Merck's October 2000, Safety Update Report to the FDA. In April 2002 the FDA approved changes to the labelling, which reflected the data on gastrointestinal and cardiovascular events and included a direction to use caution in prescribing rofecoxib for patients with ischemic heart disease.

During 2005, five years after publication of the VIGOR study in the *New England Journal of Medicine*, it came to the attention of the editors that the three additional adjudicated cases had not been included in the article. The article was based on data as at February 2000, and these three cases had come to light after the article was submitted to the *Journal* in May 2000 but before it was published in November 2000. In December 2005, coinciding with the starting of jury deliberations in the first federal Vioxx trial, various press releases and news articles were issued reporting that the editors of the *New England Journal of Medicine* had published an 'Expression of Concern', accusing the VIGOR authors of purposely withholding data on the three additional cases from the public.[403] The allegations raised in the

[402] C Bombardier et al, 'Comparison of Upper Gastrointestinal Toxicity of Rofecoxib and Naproxen in Patients with Rheumatoid Arthritis' (2000) 343 *New England Journal of Medicine* 1520.

[403] GD Curfman et al, 'Expression of Concern: Bombardier et al., Comparison of Upper Gastrointestinal Toxicity of Rofecoxib and Naproxen in Patients with Rheumatoid Arthritis' (2005) 353 *New England Journal of Medicine* 2813, doi:10.1056/NEJMe058314.

Expression of Concern were firmly denied in letters to the *Journal* by both the non-Merck authors of the paper and by Merck,[404] but they became part of the plaintiffs' lawyers' presentations to jurors in the US litigation.

In 2001 Merck had commenced the APPROVe (Adenomatous Polyp PRevention On Vioxx) study, a placebo-controlled trial with the primary aim of evaluating the efficacy of Vioxx in patients with a history of colorectal adenomas. The study was terminated early in September 2004 when Merck was advised that preliminary data indicated an increased relative risk of adverse thrombotic cardiovascular events, beginning after 18 months of Vioxx therapy. This study suggested that in participants, long-term use of Vioxx resulted in nearly twice the risk of suffering from a heart attack as compared to patients receiving a placebo. Shortly after receiving the interim results of this study, Merck voluntarily withdraw the drug from the market worldwide on 30 September 2004. Thousands of lawsuits followed. It was alleged in litigation that during the five years that Vioxx was on the market, it caused tens of thousands of heart attacks, many of which were likely to be fatal.[405] The allegation was denied.

iii. Marketing and Regulatory History

Merck's painkiller was approved by the US FDA on 20 May 1999, and by regulatory agencies in many other countries around the world at different times. The UK licence was granted on 4 June 1999. It has been estimated that approximately 20 million people used Vioxx in the US,[406] and with over 80 million prescriptions globally.

Simultaneously with approval of Vioxx, Merck began an intense and successful multi-million dollar direct-to-consumer advertising campaign in the US, which permits direct-to-consumer marketing. It described Vioxx as providing anti-inflammatory relief comparable to traditional NSAIDs,[407] but with a reduced risk of the serious gastrointestinal problems – including potentially fatal bleeding ulcers – that NSAIDs can cause.

Shortly after receiving the interim APPROVe study results, which indicated a statistically significant increase in the incidence of confirmed cardiovascular thrombotic events from long-term use, Merck voluntarily withdrew the product globally on 30 September 2004.[408]

After the withdrawal, thousands of US court cases were filed against Merck, with the associated litigation-driven media reports. Against this backdrop the integrity and effectiveness of regulators across the globe came under attack, for not withdrawing the product sooner.[409] The FDA was accused of purposefully withholding recall of the blockbuster drug

[404] See at www.nejm.org/doi/full/10.1056/NEJMe058314#article_letters.

[405] J Karha and EJ Topol, 'The sad story of Vioxx, and what we should learn from it' (2004) 71(12) *Cleveland Clinic Journal of Medicine* 933.

[406] H Won Tesoriero et al, 'Merck's Tactics Largely Vindicated As It Reaches Big Vioxx Settlement' *Wall Street Journal* (10 November 2007) at A1.

[407] A non-steroidal anti-inflammatory drug.

[408] Press Release, Merck & Co, Inc, 'Merck Announces Voluntary Worldwide Withdrawal of VIOXX®' (30 September 2004) (announcing the voluntary withdrawal of Vioxx); PS Kim, 'Vioxx: Setting the Record Straight' (2005) 83(1) *Chemical & Engineering News* 5 (asserting that the increased risk observed in the trial did not become statistically significant until after approximately 30 months). The product's UK licence was cancelled on 4 October 2004.

[409] K Abbasi, 'Is drug regulation failing?' (2004) 329 *British Medical Journal* 865.

as a favour to Merck,[410] and of being too corrupt to place patients' best interests first.[411] The UK MHRA was criticised as lagging behind the FDA in requiring sponsored studies of the drug that would have provided the independent evidence necessary for an earlier recall.[412] In 2004 and 2005 the FDA and the US Department of Health and Human Services (HHS) announced the creation of the Drug Safety Oversight Board and asked the Institute of Medicine (IOM) to convene a committee to assess the US pharmaceutical safety system and to make recommendations to improve risk assessment, surveillance and the safe use of pharmaceuticals. The FDA also began its own ongoing assessment of its drug safety program. The 2006 IOM report specifically cited the lack of clear regulatory authority, chronic under-funding, organisational problems, and a scarcity of post-approval data about drug risks and benefits as the reasons behind what the Report saw as the FDA's weakening aptitude to evaluate and address the safety of prescription drugs after they had reached the market.[413] The FDA responded by referring to its long-standing commitment to strengthening drug safety, largely agreeing with most of the recommendations of the IOM report directed at the FDA.[414]

iv. Litigation

Litigation followed the medical and regulatory events in 2004. While there was some litigation relating to Vioxx prior to the voluntary withdrawal, numerous claims were brought in the US, Canada and many other countries from 2004.[415] The plaintiffs' primary allegation in the litigation was that the company withheld information about Vioxx's cardiovascular safety. Merck defended individual cases by presenting evidence that the company had carefully studied Vioxx both before and after approval, and had responsibly disclosed the results of those studies to the medical community and regulatory agencies.

Merck also presented evidence in individual cases that it was the plaintiffs' pre-existing risk factors, not Vioxx, that caused the alleged injuries.[416] After a series of jury trials in the US, of which the plaintiffs won five (two of which were subsequently overturned) and Merck won 12, a settlement was negotiated with the US claimants' lawyers totalling $4.85 billion, in which eligible claimants would be allocated payments based on an individualised evaluation of their claims.[417] The company made no admission of wrongdoing or causation.[418]

[410] R Horton, 'Vioxx, the implosion of Merck, and aftershocks at the FDA' (2005) 364(9450) *The Lancet* 1995.

[411] J Avorn, 'Paying for Drug Approvals – Who's Using Whom?' (2007) 356 *New England Journal of Medicine* 1697.

[412] ASD Spiers, 'Save the FDA' (2005) 330 *British Medical Journal* 308.

[413] Institute of Medicine, *The Future of Drug Safety: Promoting and protecting the health of the public* (National Academy of Sciences, 2006).

[414] R Lofstedt, 'The Impact of the Cox-2 Inhibitor Issue on Perceptions of the Pharmaceutical Industry: Content Analysis and Communication Implications' (2007) 12(5) *Journal of Health Communication* 417.

[415] Over 60,000 potential individual claims were made in the US: see Press Release, Merck & Co, Inc, Merck Progress Report on Enrolment in Program to Resolve US VIOXX® Product Liability Lawsuits (3 March, 2008).

[416] See, eg, Press Release, Merck & Co, Inc, 'Merck Wins Product Liability Case in Florida Circuit Court' (5 October 2007), (explaining that the evidence showed that the plaintiff's longstanding cardiovascular disease caused his heart attack); Press Release, Merck & Co, Inc, 'Merck Wins Product Liability Case in Madison County, Ill' (27 March 2007), (explaining that the evidence showed that the plaintiff's multiple risk factors put her at increased risk for sudden cardiac death, having nothing to do with Vioxx).

[417] See Settlement Agreement Between Merck & Co, Inc and The Counsel Listed on the Signature Pages Hereto (9 November 2007) (amended 17 January 2008).

[418] ibid, at §13.1.

Outside the US, several hundred individual cases were litigated and dismissed, many of them in Europe.[419]

Merck faced a class action in Australia during 2009, the *Peterson* class action.[420] In 2010, the Federal Court of Australia dismissed it in its entirety as to:

(a) Merck & Co Inc ('Merck had done everything that might reasonably be expected of it in the discharge of its duty of care');
(b) all claims for alleged injuries other than myocardial infarction; and
(c) the product defect claim under section 75AD of the Trade Practices Act (liability for defective products).

The Court dismissed the applicant's claims against Merck Sharp & Dohme Australia, except for those under:

(a) section 74B of the Trade Practices Act (goods to be fit for purpose); and
(b) section 74D of the Trade Practices Act (goods to be of mechantable quality).

Peterson was awarded AUD$330,476.35. Merck Sharp & Dohme Australia appealed, and the Full Court of the Federal Court of Australia upheld the company's appeal against the first instance judgment and dismissed the cross-appeals of Mr Peterson and the other group members, with full costs to the company.[421] In 2012 the High Court denied the applicant's and other group members' request for special leave to appeal.

Subsequently, the parties negotiated, and the Court approved, an Australia-wide resolution of the remaining claims of the other 1,660 registered group members in the *Peterson* action, according to which the sum of AUD$497,500 would be distributed to those group members satisfying certain criteria, adjusted by a points system discounting for the individual circumstances of each group member.[422]

v. Conclusion

The safety issue was identified in a medical placebo controlled post-marketing study, APPROVe. Upon receiving the interim study results the manufacturer voluntarily withdrew the product, notifying the regulators of the interim results of the study and of its voluntary withdrawal of the drug. Litigation followed. Interestingly, some studies conducted after Vioxx's market withdrawal have indicated that Vioxx has a similar cardiovascular safety profile to some traditional NSAIDs that remain on the market[423] (including some over-the-counter drugs).

[419] BBC Transcript, *Face the Facts*, 27 December 2007, available at bbc.co.uk/radio4/facethefacts/transcript_20071227.shtml; Press Release, Merck & Co, Inc, trifft Vereinbarung über US-amerikanische VIOXX®Klagen (9 November 2007).

[420] *Peterson v Merck Sharp & Dohme (Australia) Pty Ltd* (VID 451 of 2006) (the *Petersen* class action).

[421] *Merck Sharp & Dohme (Australia) Pty Ltd v Peterson* [2011] FCAFC 128.

[422] *Peterson v Merck Sharp & Dohme (Aust) Pty Ltd (No 7)* [2015] FCA 123.

[423] For example, see EL Fosbol et al, 'Cardiovascular safety of non-steroidal anti-inflammatory drugs among healthy individuals' (2010) 9(6) *Expert Opinion on Drug Safety* 893, doi:10.1517/14740338.2010.501331.

VI. Pancreatic Function (Endocrine and Exocrine) and Obesity Treatments

A. Adifax/Isomeride/Redux (dexfenfluramine) and Ponderax (fenfluramine)

i. Description

Dexfenfluramine and fenfluramine (fenfluramine consists of a racemix – a mixture containing equal parts of each of the stereoisomers, dexfenfluramine and levofenfluramine) were appetite suppressants indicated for the possible long-term treatment of particularly severe refractory cases of obesity.[424] They were thought to function by increasing levels of the neurotransmitter serotonin by disrupting vesicular serotonergic storage.

In the USA, fenfluramine was prescribed off label by doctors in parallel with phentermine to form the Fen-Phen anti-obesity combination.

ii. Safety Issue

An association between fenfluramine and primary pulmonary hypertension (PPH) was reported as early as 1981.[425] Reports continued, both through the pharmacovigilance system and in published case reports.[426] In response to the European experience, the Medical Research Council of Canada sponsored the International Primary Pulmonary Hypertension Study (IPPHS), with the funding for the study provided by Sevier. The aim of the IPPHS was to ascertain the role of several potential risk factors, including fenfluramine and dexfenfluramine, in causing PPH. The IPPHS was international in scope, with eminent specialists including Dr Lucien Abenhaim of McGill University in Montreal, Canada; Dr Francois Brenot of Antoine Beclere Hospital in Paris, France; and Dr Stuart Rich of the Rush Heart-Lung Institute in Chicago, Illinois. It was a case-controlled epidemiological study with patients selected from across Europe, which analysed 95 diagnosed PPH cases, each PPH case being compared to four physician-based control cases (a total of 335 controls).[427] The full IPPHS findings were reported in the *New England Journal of Medicine* in 1996: it found an increase in PPH – a 23.1-fold increase in patients taking the drugs for >3 months, rising to a 42-fold increase in patients who had been prescribed them for more than one year. This confirmed the causative association between fenfluramine and dexfenfluramine and PPH.

[424] JP Louvet, 'Isomeride and treatment of overweight' (1989) 140(1) *Annales de Medecine Interne (Paris)* 17 (in French).

[425] JG Douglas et al, 'Pulmonary hypertension and fenfluramine' (1981) 283 *British Medical Journal* 881.

[426] PG Antanasoff et al, 'Pulmonary hypertension and dexfenfluramine' (1992) 339 *The Lancet* 436; N Roche et al, 'Pulmonary hypertension and dexfenfluramine' (1992) 339 *The Lancet* 436; F Brenot et al, 'Primary pulmonary hypertension and fenfluramine use' (1993) 70 *British Heart Journal* 537; P Cacoub et al, 'Pulmonary hypertension and dexfenfluramine' (1995) 48 *European Journal of Clinical Pharmacology* 81; SHL Thomas et al. 'Appetite suppressants and primary pulmonary hypertension in the United Kingdom' (1995) 74 *British Heart Journal* 660.

[427] L Abenhaim et al, 'Appetite-suppressant drugs and the risk of primary pulmonary hypertension' (1996) 335 *New England Journal of Medicine* 609.

In 1997, the Mayo Clinic also reported a link to abnormal heart valves.[428] This link was subsequently confirmed by other reports.[429]

iii. Marketing and Regulatory History

Fenfluramine was developed by the French company Laboratoires Servier and approved for marketing in France in 1966. American Home Products (AHP, subsequently known as Wyeth) introduced the drug to the US market in 1973. Ponderax was licensed in the UK by Servier in the early 1970s (originally as a product licence of right) and was granted a full reviewed licence on 14 May 1984.

Dexfenfluramine was launched in France in 1985 by Laboratoires Servier under the brand name Isomeride. It was licensed in the UK as Adifax on 20 March 1990.[430] By the mid-1990s, concerns had been raised about PPH and both drugs. Early indications of the findings of the IPHHS were made available to regulators, and were publicly reported by Dr Abenhaim in 1995:[431] these results underlined the significant risk of the condition associated with fenfluramine and dexfenfluramine use. The findings led to significant worldwide concerns.[432] Servier had licensed dexfenfluramine to AHP for the US market: it received FDA approval in April 1996 and was marketed as Redux. This approval occurred after the association with PPH had been raised.

Concern in Europe over the association between the use of fenfluramine and dexfenfluramine and PPH triggered a risk–benefit analysis by the CPMP, carried out in 1995–96.[433] The report recommended the these drugs should only be prescribed for refractory obesity, and only when prescribed by a specialist in obesity with appropriate warnings given to the patient and careful consideration given to the duration of treatment. In response, the French regulatory authorities further limited the availability of prescription fenfluramine to prescriptions of short duration (less than three months) for treatment of refractory obesity by specialists.[434] The CSM in the UK similarly revised recommendations for both

[428] HM Connolly et al, 'Valvular heart disease associated with fenfluraminephentermine' (1997) 337 *New England Journal of Medicine* 581.

[429] DJ Graham and L Green, 'Further cases of valvular heart disease associated with fenfluramine-phentermine' (1997) 337 *New England Journal of Medicine* 635; LB Cannistra, SM Davis and AG Bauman, 'Valvular heart disease associated with dexfenfluramine' (1997) 337 *New England Journal of Medicine* 636; MA Khan et al, 'The prevalence of cardiac valvular insufficiency assessed by transthoracic echocardiography in obese patients treated with appetite-suppressant drugs' (1998) 339 *New England Journal of Medicine* 713; H Jick, et al, 'A population-based study of appetite-suppressant drugs and the risk of cardiac-valve regurgitation' (1998) 339 *New England Journal of Medicine* 719; CDC, 'Cardiac Valvulopathy Associated with Exposure to Fenfluramine or Dexfenfluramine: US Department of Health and Human Services Interim Public Health Recommendations, November 1997' (1997) 46(45) *Morbidity and Mortality Weekly Reporter* 1061, available at www.cdc.gov/mmwr/preview/mmwrhtml/00049815.htm.

[430] Licensing of Adifax in the UK was revoked on 1 May 2001.

[431] For example, see Dr Abenhaim's report to the FDA at Official transcript, FDA Endocrinologic and Metabolic Drug Advisory Committee, Open Session 28 September 1995, available at wayback.archive-it.org/7993/20170403223111/https://www.fda.gov/ohrms/dockets/ac/95/3107t1a.pdf; also see L Abenhaim et al, 'Pharmacoepidemiology of primary pulmonary hypertension' (1995) 4 (Suppl 1) *Pharmacoepidemiology and Drug Safety* 86.

[432] See the World Health Organization's (1996) 10(4) *World Drug Information*, available at apps.who.int/medicinedocs/index/assoc/s14161e/s14161e.pdf.

[433] CPMP Assessment Report for Anorectic Agents, CPMP/127/96 Rev 6, 18 July 1996.

[434] 'Appetite suppressants limited in France' (1995) 559 *Reaction Weekly* 2, available at doi.org/10.2165/00128415-199505590-00001.

drugs following the publication of the full IPHHS in 1996 in the *New England Journal of Medicine*.[435]

In the USA the label was updated and letters were sent to 300,000 healthcare providers, informing them of the higher risk of PPH and recommending that the drug should be reserved for the treatment of obese patients.[436]

In Canada, a 'Dear Doctor' letter was sent out, warning that these drugs were for short-term use in obese patients.[437]

The association with cardiac valvular abnormalities was raised raised at the end of August 1997; and following discussions with various national regulators, the drug manufacturers voluntarily withdrew both fenfluramine and dexfenfluramine worldwide on 1 October 1997.[438] Doctors and pharmacists were made aware of this through an Epinet message and by a letter from the companies.

Following the suspension of marketing authorisation in several Member States, an Article 15a referral[439] was made to the EMA in October 1997 by the affected Member States.[440] The CPMP[441] reviewed the evidence, and in an opinion of April 1999 considered the benefit–risk balance of dexfenfluramine and fenfluramine medications to be unfavourable and that the drugs' marketing authorisations should be withdrawn. This was appealed by the marketing authorisation holders, but the appeal did not alter the CPMP position, and the Committee's opinion of 31 August 1999[442] again concluded that the marketing authorisation for fenfluramine products should be withdrawn.

Formal withdrawal of marketing authorisation varied: in France, the marketing authorisation was withdrawn in October 1999;[443] in the UK, the licence was not formally revoked until 1 May 2001.[444] In practice, the date of the formal withdrawal of marketing authorisation had no impact, as the products were not available.

iv. Litigation

Around 1,000 cases were brought in the US in 1997, which were handled by AHP. The fenfluramine, dexfenfluramine and Fen-Phen cases were centralised into a single class action,[445] which was heard in Pennsylvania. A settlement was reached in November 1999,[446] when AHP paid approximately $20 million in compensation.

[435] Abenhaim et al, n 432.

[436] FDA Talk Paper, T96-58, 22 August 1996.

[437] 'Dear Doctor' letter from Health Protection Branch, Canada, dated 21 October 1996.

[438] CDC, n 430.

[439] Art 15a of Directive 75/319/EEC, as amended.

[440] See at www.ema.europa.eu/en/medicines/human/referrals/benfluorex, specifically at ec.europa.eu/health/documents/community-register/2000/200003093427/anx_3427_en.pdf.

[441] This later became the Committee for Medicinal Products for Human Use (CHMP).

[442] CPMP/2164/99.

[443] *La Revue Prescrire*, vol 19, no 199, October 1999.

[444] See CSM, 'Fenfluramine (Ponderax Pacaps), Dexfenfluramine (Adifax) and Pulmonary Hypertension' (June 1992) 34 *Current Problems in Pharmacovigilance* 1; CSM, 'The risks and benefits of anorectic agents (fenfluramine, dexfenfluramine and phentermine' (Feb 1997) 23, *Current Problems in Pharmacovigilance* 1; CSM, 'Fenfluramine and dexfenfluramine withdrawn' (Dec 1997) 23 *Current Problems in Pharmacovigilance* 13.

[445] *In Re Diet Drugs*, MDL Docket no 1203 American Home Products Corporation, Civ no 99-20593.

[446] See at www.settlementdietdrugs.com/index.asp.

In Europe, only a few cases were brought against EU licence holder, Servier. The discrepancy between Europe and the US is likely to reflect both the differences in the litigation systems and the differences in prescribing practices, partly a reflection of the fact that regulatory warnings were stricter in the EU. In the US, co-prescription with phentermine (as Fen-Phen) was common, whereas the single prescription was standard in EU medical practice and the combination with phentermine was rare.

In 2010, AFSSAPS stated that 11 cases of valve damage in patients taking Isomeride were reported to drug safety authorities in France between 1997 and 2006. Despite significant publicity, only a handful of French cases were brought against Servier regarding isomeride (dexfenfluramine), all which were dealt with through the normal legal mechanisms as there was no class action in France. There were some very high-profile cases, in particular those of Anna Paulos, who was awarded 2.5 million French Francs in 2000 (upheld by the Court of Cassation in 2006), and Nicole Goudman (deceased), whose case was finally settled for €145,500 by the Court of Appeal in Versailles in 2011.[447] An association for the victims of Isomeride (dexfenfluramine) and mediator (benfluorex) was set up, which supports affected individuals, including campaigning for compensation.[448]

v. Conclusion

The safety issues were identified through the pharmacovigilance system and medical scrutiny. Litigation occurred subsequently.

Both PPH and valvular abnormalities are rare and would not be detected by routine medical examinations. Detecting these kinds of signals is therefore difficult, but questions have been raised over the similarities between other serotonergic anorectics and PPH, which meant that this adverse event was, to some extent, predictable.[449]

[447] 'Isoméride: Servier condamné' *Le Figaro* (22 January 2011), available at www.lefigaro.fr/flash-actu/2011/01/22/97001-20110122FILWWW00470-isomeride-servier-condamne.php.

[448] See at www.victimes-isomeride.asso.fr.

[449] D Langleben, 'Relearning the Lessons of History: Anorexigens and Pulmonary Hypertension' (1998) 114 *CHEST* 55S–57S, available at journal.chestnet.org/article/S0012-3692(15)48032-8/pdf.

B. Mediator (benfluorex)

i. Description

Mediator was indicated as an adjunct therapy for the treatment of diabetes, and was also used off label for the treatment of obesity. It is structurally related to fenfluramine. It is a hyperlipidemia that acts as an appetite suppressant and increases the potency of insulin signalling.

ii. Safety Issue

The drug was widely prescribed off label by the medical profession as an appetite suppressant. Benfluorex is structurally related to the amphetamines, and, like fenfluramine, is partially metabolised to norfenfluramine.[450] From 2003, reports confirmed that benfluorex caused heart valve damage similar to that caused by fenfluramine.[451]

iii. Marketing and Regulatory History

The compound was used from the 1960s, although Mediator was licensed in France by Laboratoires Servier in 1976. Some 145 million packets were sold up to 2009.

Mediator was available in France, Greece, Italy, Spain and Portugal (under various brand names, including Mediator, Benfluorex Mylan and Benfluorex Qualimed), and was licensed, but not sold, in Cyprus and Luxembourg.[452] Mediator was never licensed in the UK or the US.

There were early concerns about benfluorex, both nationally and at a European level. In September 1998, three eminent professors wrote to the French regulators, warning that the drug was being widely used outside the scope of the marketing authorisation; approximately one-third of prescriptions were off-label as an appetite suppressant, rather than for the licensed use as an adjunct diabetes therapy.[453] They also noted that Mediator was chemically similar to amphetamines, which had much heavier regulatory restrictions on their use. The letter recommended a reconsideration of the uses of Mediator. The letter concerned the off-label usage of Mediator, but did not link Mediator use with any specific adverse events.

In 1998, the Italian member of the CPMP[454] sent a letter to the EMA asking whether benfluorex could be considered a fenfluramine-containing product due to its related chemical structure. At that point in time there were three on-going Article 15a referrals[455]

[450] M Andrejak and C Tribouilloy, 'Drug-induced valvular heart disease: An update' (2013) 106(5) *Archives of Cardiovascular Diseases* 333.

[451] JR Ribera et al, 'Valvular heart disease associated with benfluorex' (2003) 56 *Revista Española de Cardiología* [English edn] 215; P Noize et al, 'Valvular heart disease in a patient taking benfluorex' (2006) 20 *Fundamental and Clinical Pharmacology* 577; K Boutet et al, 'Fenfluramine-like cardiovascular side-effects of benfluorex' (2009) 33 *European Respiratory Journal* 684; JP Gueffet, N Piriou and JN Trochu, 'Valvular heart disease associated with benfluorex' (2010) 103 *Archives of Cardiovascular Diseases* 342.

[452] See at www.ema.europa.eu/medicines/human/referrals/benfluorex.

[453] The letter is at www.lefigaro.fr/assets/pdf/secu_mediator.pdf.

[454] This later became the Committee for Medicinal Products for Human Use (CHMP).

[455] Art 15a of Directive 75/319/EEC.

triggered by Member States for anorectic agents. This letter was circulated and discussed at the October 1998 CPMP meeting. The CPMP considered that benfluorex should not be included in the scope of the referral on anorectics. It was agreed that the PhVWP would investigate if there was a safety issue with this compound.[456]

In response, at the November 1999 meeting of the Pharmacovigilance Working Party (PhVWP), an Assessment Report was presented, prepared by the Italian delegate in collaboration with his French colleagues. This Assessment Report included a List of Questions to be sent to the marketing authorisation holder by France. The minutes of the meeting state that together, France and Italy had agreed upon a List of Questions regarding efficacy and safety in drug use longer than six months. If the data requested in the questions were not available, it was specified that 'the [marketing authorisation holder] should carry out a long-term study (more than one year) with periodic echocardiographic, glycaemic, serum lipid levels level controls and measurement of pharmacokinetic parameters'. It was noted that in France, a pharmacovigiliance efficacy review by the national advisory board was pending. It was decided that the response from the marketing authorisation holder and the national efficacy review would be assessed by Italy and France, with an oral update in January 2000 and a discussion in May 2000. Additional changes to the SmPC were also proposed.[457]

In 2003 the first report of an association between Mediator and heart-valve disorders was received by regulators in Spain.[458] The same year, Servier voluntarily withdrew benfluorex from the Spanish and the Italian markets by not applying to renew the marketing authorisation. This was ostensibly on the grounds that there were low volumes of sales in these countries. Subsequently it has been suggested that these actions were taken to avoid the possibility of a forced withdrawal, which could have impacted marketing authorisations in other EU countries.[459]

There were case reports in France (with two cases being reported to the regulator in 1999): a single patient was reported to have developed heart valve complications while taking benfluorex in 2006;[460] and in March 2009 a cluster of six cases of benfluorex complications (five of severe pulmonary arterial hypertension and one case of valvular heart disease) were published in the *European Respiratory Journal*.[461] One of the authors of the *Journal* article was Irène Frachon, a pneumonologist from Brittany, who later publicly highlighted the adverse events associated with benfluorex. Despite these case reports, the French regulator, AFSSAPS, only commenced an investigation in 2009. In November 2009, AFSSAPS withdrew the marketing authorisation for benfluorex after 33 years on the market. This was based on safety concerns arising from the pre-publication results from cohort studies,[462] where analysis of over 1 million diabetic patients found that the relative

[456] Benfluorex: Summary background on discussions at CPMP (1998), PhVWP (1998–2003) and CHMP (2009), 18 May 2011, EMA/394445/2011 available at www.ema.europa.eu/docs/en_GB/document_library/Report/2011/05/WC500106457.pdf.

[457] ibid.

[458] Ribera et al, n 452 (article in Spanish).

[459] A Mullard, 'Mediator scandal rocks French medical community' (2011) 377(9769) *The Lancet* 890, doi.org/10.1016/S0140-6736(11)60334-6.

[460] Noize et al, n 452.

[461] Boutet et al, n 452.

[462] A Weill et al, 'Benfluorex and valvular heart disease: A cohort study of a million people with diabetes mellitus' (2010) 19 *Pharmacoepidemiology and Drug Safety* 1256.

risk of hospitalisation due to specific cardiovascular complications was about three times higher in patients treated with benfluorex than it was in those who had not been given the drug, case control studies showing linkage,[463] and a head-to-head comparison of benfluorex and the antidiabetic pioglitazone, carried out by Servier at AFSSAPS's request, which showed that benfluorex treatment was associated with valvular anomalies. Interestingly, the withdrawal from the market passed relatively unnoticed in France.

In 2009, the reports from AFSSAPS on the withdrawal of benfluorex from the French market meant that the EMA was required to conduct a review[464] of the safety and effectiveness of benfluorex. The review concluded that the benefits of benfluorex no longer outweighed its risks, and that all marketing authorisations for medicines containing benfluorex should be revoked throughout the EU. In June 2010, the European Commission formally withdrew the marketing authorisation for benfluorex across the EU.[465]

In 2010, two case control studies,[466] a randomised trial (unpublished) and a cohort study,[467] confirmed the link between benfluorex and valvular heart disease. Initial estimates that 500 French deaths could have been caused by the drug were soon raised to 1,300,[468] and that number was later raised to 2,000 possible deaths. In France an enormous public storm arose,[469] driven partly by the publication of Irène Frachon's 2010 book, *Mediator 150 mg: Combien de morts?* Questions were raised about the activities of researchers, payments by the company to the Government,[470] what the company and all others involved actually knew about the drug, and the level of scrutiny by AFSSAPS.

By 2011, Servier had acknowledged there was a 'real risk' that the product was linked to heart-valve damage. Investigators alleged that the company deliberately concealed the risks.[471] In September 2011 the company was placed under investigation for criminal offences. A 2011 report by the public welfare inspectorate, Inspection Générale des Affaires Sociales (IGAS),[472] raised serious issues about the activities of everyone involved and concluded that benfluorex should have been withdrawn in 1999, following reports to the French regulators of two cases of cardiovascular complications from benfluorex use. Servier was accused of relentlessly marketing the drug 'at odds with its medical properties', and of applying undue lobbying pressure to regulators and to the medical community to ensure the successful commercialisation of its product. The report concluded that there were too

[463] I Frachon et al, 'Benfluorex and unexplained valvular heart disease: a case-control study' (2010) 5(4) *Public Library of Science One* e10128.

[464] Art 107 of Directive 2001/83/EC, as amended.

[465] Commission Decision c(2010)4127, available at ec.europa.eu/health/documents/community-register/2010/2010061474148/dec_74148_en.pdf.

[466] Frachon et al, n 464; C Tribouilloy et al, 'Restrictive organic mitral regurgitation associated with benfluorex therapy' (2010) 11(7) *European Journal of Echocardiography* 614.

[467] Weill et al, n 463.

[468] A Fournier and M Zureik, 'Estimate of deaths due to valvular insufficiency attributable to the use of benfluorex in France' (2012) 21(4) *Pharmacoepidemiology and Drug Safety* 343.

[469] See at www.thelancet.com:80/journals/lancet/article/PIIS0140-6736(11)60334-6/fulltext.

[470] *Le Monde* (5 June 1022), available at translate.google.com/translate?hl=en&sl=fr&tl=en&u=http%3A%2F%2Fwww.lemonde.fr%2Fweb%2Frecherche_breve%2F1%2C13-0%2C37-1156194%2C0.html.

[471] Scott Sayare, 'Scandal over Mediator, a French Weight-Loss Drug, Prompts Calls for Wide Changes' *New York Times* (11 December 2011), available at http://www.nytimes.com/2011/12/12/health/scandal-widens-over-french-weight-loss-drug-mediator.html?pagewanted=all&module=inline.

[472] A Morelle, AC Bensadon and E Marie France, *Enquête sur le Mediator* (Inspection Générale des affaires sociales, 2011), available at www.igas.gouv.fr/spip.php?article162.

many authorities involved, which diluted responsibilities and made the system dysfunctional, slow and unresponsive. AFSSAPS was criticised as being 'inexplicably tolerant of a drug with no real therapeutic value'. It was also described as an 'overworked' bureaucracy, 'entangled in cumbersome and complex legal procedures', 'restrained by fear of litigation' and 'desensitized to risk'. The broader medical and scientific communities were also attacked for irresponsible behaviour. The report noted:[473]

> Pharmacovigilance has failed in its purpose, which is to identify and to investigate, within a reasonable period of time, and in order to guide decisions by health authorities, cases of severe adverse effects linked to the use of medicines. The principal reason for this collective failure should be sought in a poor public health culture, and most particularly in a precautionary principle functioning in reverse …

The head of AFSSAPS, Jean Marimbert, resigned shortly after the publication of the report. Criminal prosecutions followed and are ongoing.

iv. Litigation

Extensive litigation commenced in France following the wide publicity in 2009. Investigations continued for many years: in September 2017 fresh criminal charges were announced.[474] The criminal prosecutions will take place against Servier for 'aggravated deception, fraud, injuries and unintentional homicides, and trading in influence', while ANSM (formerly AFSSAPS) is charged only with 'injuries and unintentional homicides'. There are known to be over 4,100 civil claimants who have joined the criminal prosecution as *parties civile* (see chapter 1, section I.E). A date has not been set for trial, which was expected to be in 2018 but may be delayed into 2019. As such, the claims are currently unresolved.

v. Conclusion

The safety signal should have been apparent from the earlier fenfluramine and isomeride cases, yet was not publicly identified by the regulators, the company or the medical profession. The specific identification of problems with Mediator should have been identified by the regulator and resolved by removing it from the market in 1998, but action was taken only in 2009. The system failed, particularly the French system, and the resulting scandal has ensured that the French authorities have reorganised and restructured with the aim of preventing any similar future events. The extent to which deception and criminality were responsible for the systematic failure to remove benfluorex from the market in a timely manner has yet to be ascertained. It is clear that litigation had no role in removing the drug for the market, and is proving very slow in providing redress to those affected.

[473] Translation from *Prescrire* (21 January 2011) at english.prescrire.org/en/81/168/46752/0/NewsDetails.aspx.

[474] O Dyer, 'France to prosecute its drug regulator and Servier in scandal over diabetes drug' (2017) 358 *British Medical Journal* j4231, doi.org/10.1136/bmj.j4231.

C. Human Insulin

i. Description

Insulin is used to treat diabetes, a metabolic disorder occurring from a fundamental defect in insulin secretion or action. Insulin is normally synthesised naturally in the pancreas and lowers blood sugar. If the body does not produce enough insulin, blood sugar rises, and this can lead to various symptoms and ultimately to coma and death. It is believed that approximately 2% of the population is diabetic, one-third of whom are insulin-dependent.

Three forms of insulin are available in the UK:[475] animal insulin, human insulin, and human analogue insulin (also known as analogue insulin). Animal insulin is collected from the pancreases of animals killed for meat, usually either pigs or cattle, then purified to decrease immunoreactivity.[476] The majority of human insulin is produced either by modified *Escherichia coli* (E. coli) bacteria,[477] or by modified yeast,[478] but other expression systems can also be used. The first synthetic human insulin was made in E. coli that had been modified to contain a plasmid (a circle of DNA) that contains the DNA code for the human insulin protein. Due to the plasmid insert, the E. coli produce the human insulin protein, which is then extracted and purified. Production in yeast follows a similar process. Analogue (or analog) human insulin is produced in the same way as human insulin, but the plasmid DNA code that produces the human insulin protein is changed by genetic engineering to alter the resulting insulin protein. The aim of this is to produce an insulin that has slightly different properties from standard human insulin and that is processed differently by the recipient's body. Dependent upon the initial changes made the plasmid DNA, it is possible to create analogue insulins that act either more slowly or more quickly. The majority of analogue insulins are long-lasting formulations.

The case study detailed here relates to human insulin and does not relate to analogue human insulin.

ii. Alleged Safety Issue

Before the early 1980s, diabetic patients relied on beef or porcine insulin. From that time, human insulin began to be produced from cell cultures, and many patients switched. Bovine and porcine insulins differ slightly from human insulin in chemical constitution: consequently, the human body recognises them as foreign proteins and forms antibodies. It was thought that human insulin would offer advantages to diabetics, even compared to highly purified animal insulin. The expected advantages of human insulin included less likelihood of producing insulin antibodies, better control of diabetes and a reduced risk of long-term complications associated with conventional diabetic therapy. However,

[475] Correct at August 2018.

[476] Animal insulin has been phased out in a lot of countries. Wockhardt still produce animal insulin for the UK market, though they are discontinuing their bovine insulin and aim to continue producing porcine insulin. See at http://www.wockhardt.co.uk.

[477] First created by Eli Lilly in 1982.

[478] Novo Nordisk began producing insulin in this way in 1987.

no major significant differences were found between animal and human insulin in clinical practice.

The aim of insulin treatment is to control blood sugar within the normal range, and ultimately to prevent the long-term complications of diabetes. Acute hyperglycaemia (too much blood sugar) can be lethal. Non-acute long-term exposure to elevated blood sugar levels (combined with insulin resistance and insulin deficiency) can cause long-term conditions associated with diabetes, such as retinopathy, peripheral vascular problems, atherosclerosis, cataracts, peripheral and autonomic neuropathy. Equally, hypoglycaemia (too little blood sugar) is damaging, and some diabetics may also develop autonomic neuropathy as a long-term complication of their disease, which can contribute to hypoglycaemic unawareness.

In order to keep blood sugars within a normal range, insulin dosage must be carefully titrated against the food intake and activity of the individual. Maintaining blood sugars within the normal range requires that the individual regularly tests blood sugar and is aware when he or she is entering hypoglycaemia. Hypoglycaemia has two major clinical manifestations: neuroglycopenia and autonomic symptoms.[479] Neuroglycopenia (depriving the brain of blood glucose) causes cognitive impairment. Autonomic symptoms include sweating, increased heart rate and palpitations, and tremors. The persistent inability to detect hypoglycaemia is referred to as hypoglycaemic unawareness. It was alleged that a shift from porcine and bovine insulins to human insulin caused increased hypoglycaemic unawareness.

Medical literature worldwide from 1987 to 1991 portrayed a difference of scientific opinion as to whether loss of warning symptoms of hypoglycemia could be attributable to human insulin itself, to a change from animal insulin to synthetic human insulin, or to other factors including tighter glycaemic control.[480] A group of Swiss investigators published research that they believed raised a suspicion of the hazard,[481] but their results were never replicated, and at the time the vast majority of diabetologists thought that the type or species of insulin was irrelevant to this safety issue.

Since 1991 the issue has been studied by a number of leading medical experts in diabetes in specially designed studies. The findings from their research indicate that increased risk of hypoglaecemic unawareness is not connected with any species of insulin but is probably associated with the regime of treatment that has increasingly been pursued in the 1980s, namely, tighter glycaemic control.[482] Intensive therapy is associated with a deterioration in glycaemic control when compared with conventional insulin therapy, but tighter glycaemic

[479] For more detail see BM Frier, 'Impaired awareness of hypoglycaemia' in BM Frier, S Heller and R McCrimmon (eds), *Hypoglycaemia in Clinical Diabetes*, 3rd edn (Willey & Sons, 2013) 114.

[480] For example, see A Teuscher and WG Berger, 'Hypoglycaemia unawareness in diabetics transferred to human insulin' (1987) 2(8555) *The Lancet* 382; W Berger et al, 'Warning symptoms of hypoglycaemia during treatment with human and porcine insulin in diabetes mellitus' (1989) 1(8646) *The Lancet* 1041; DG Altman and CJ Dore, 'Randomisation and baseline comparisons in clinical trials' (1990) 335(8682) *The Lancet* 149.

[481] M Egger et al, 'Influence of human insulin on symptoms and awareness of hypoglycaemia: a randomised double blind crossover trial' (1991) 303 *British Medical Journal* 622.

[482] For example, see A Maran et al, 'Human insulin does not affect hypoglycaemia in diabetes mellitus: a clinical and laboratory study' (1992) 41 (Suppl 1) *Diabetes* 57A; and SP Wolff, 'Trying times for human insulin' (1992) 356 *Nature* 375. Also see SA Amiel, 'Risks of intensive therapy' in Frier et al (eds), n 480, 145.

control has the benefit of decreasing retinopathy,[483] and reducing macrovascular disease and mortality,[484] cardiovascular disease and death.[485]

Empirical research has consistently found that patients who are treated intensively to control blood sugar (most of those patients transferred to human insulin) have a three-fold higher rate of severe hypocglycaemia than that of patients on conventional insulin therapy.[486] The consensus is that in any one year, 10% of insulin-dependent diabetics on conventional therapy will suffer hypoglycaemia severe enough to require medical treatment, usually in hospital. This figure is trebled by intensive (tight glycaemic control) therapy. Therefore, allegations of increased hypoglycaemic unawareness attributed to human insulin may be explained by its introduction to the market coinciding with trends towards tighter control of blood sugar levels, as opposed to a unique feature of the substance itself.

The British Diabetic Association released a statement in October 1991 saying that the link between human insulin and hypoglycaemia was unfounded, and 'no other country has reported possible concern regarding human insulin, even where a large percentage of human insulin is used (USA, Canada), or totally used (as in Denmark)'. However, despite strong evidence that no relevant difference existed between animal and human insulin, the British Diabetic Association stuck to its recommendation that patients should be allowed to go back to animal insulin if they so desired.

iii. Marketing and Regulatory History

Human insulin was introduced to UK by Novo Nordisk and Eli Lilly and Co in 1982. The UK marketing authorisation for Novo's Actrapid was granted on 9 June 1982, and marketing authorisation for Lilly's Humulin was granted a few months later in September 1982. Approval in the US quickly followed, with Humulin approved at the end of October 1982[487] and Novo's Novolin R (the US brand name) approved on 30 August 1983.[488]

In 1986, Novo Laboratories Ltd sent out letters explaining the discontinuation of two types of animal insulin, Actrapid MC and Monotard MC, which were replaced by human actrapid and monotard. As described, from 1987 medical articles from around the world

[483] The Diabetes Control and Complications Research Group, 'The Effect of Intensive Treatment of Diabetes on the Development and Progression of Long-Term Complications in Insulin-Dependent Diabetes Mellitus' (1993) 329 *New England Journal of Medicine* 977.

[484] DM Nathan et al for the Diabetes Control and Complications Trial/Epidemiology of Diabetes Interventions and Complications (DCCT/EDIC) Study Research Group, 'Intensive diabetes treatment and cardiovascular disease in patients with type 1 diabetes' (2005) 353(25) *New England Journal of Medicine* 2643; DM Nathan et al, 'Intensive diabetes therapy and carotid intima-media thickness in type 1 diabetes mellitus' (2003) 348 *New England Journal of Medicine* 2294.

[485] RR Holman et al, '10-Year Follow-up of Intensive Glucose Control in Type 2 Diabetes' (2008) 359 *New England Journal of Medicine* 1577.

[486] The Diabetes Control and Complications Trial Research Group, 'Epidemiology of severe hypoglycemia in the Diabetes Control and Complications Trial' (1991) 90 *American Journal of Medicine* 450; The Diabetes Control and Complications Research Group, n 484; The Diabetes Control and Complications Trial Research Group, 'Hypoglycemia in the Diabetes Control and Complications Trial' (1997) 46 *Diabetes* 271.

[487] New Drug Application no 018780, approved 28 October 1982: see at www.accessdata.fda.gov/scripts/cder/daf/index.cfm?event=overview.process&ApplNo=018780.

[488] New Drug Application no 018778, approved 30 August 1983.

contributed to the debate on the benefits of human insulin as compared to animal insulins.[489] Regulatory and marketing action was taken regularly in response to the developing medical information.

More specifically, in 1990, it was agreed to amend the warning and precautions sections of the data sheets, the package inserts and patient information leaflets of all insulin products, following a review of the issue of hypoglycaemic unawareness by the Medicines Control Agency. A statement indicating that there was no link between the species of insulin and hypoglycaemic unawareness was added: this was class-wide; exactly the same information was added to data sheets for all companies for both animal and human insulins. This position was further reinforced in the CSM's statement in *Current Problems* (number 29), circulated to prescribers in August 1990.[490]

iv. Litigation

From mid-1991 there were press reports of steps being taken in preparation for proposed litigation by certain diabetics, alleging injuries caused by being transferred from animal insulin to synthetic human insulin. The basic allegations were that the warning symptoms associated with an impending attack of hypoglycaemia, which were experienced by patients when taking animal insulin, disappeared when the patients took human insulin. It was alleged that the main producers of human insulin had been negligent in the supply of human insulin to the market. The main focus was on Novo Nordisk, because it had removed two of its animal insulins (Actrapid MC and Monotard MC) from the market in the mid-1980s, effectively 'replacing' them with human insulins Actrapid and Monotard. In contrast, Eli Lily had provided an additional human insulin, Humulin, without removing an animal insulin.

A coordination meeting of 31 solicitors representing over 400 potential complainants in England and Wales took place on 29 August 1991 at The Law Society.[491] It was reported that legal aid certificates had been granted to 'a number' of individuals, and that a legal aid certificate had been issued to cover the investigation by a steering committee into the detailed medical and legal aspects of the matter. Mr Peter Scott, Chairman of the coordinating committee, stated, 'it will be years rather than months before the research is completed and we have obtained sufficient medical and legal advice to know if our case is well founded'. A 'cautious' estimate of two years was put on the length of the contemplated investigation, and Novo Nordisk was identified as one of the potential defendants.

In early January 1993, the initial grant of legal aid for investigation purposes was not continued, and legal aid was refused to take the claims further. A comprehensive review of medical literature did not support the existence of a causal link between human insulin and hypoglycaemic unawareness.[492] For this reason, it was thought that the plaintiffs

[489] For example, see Teuscher and Berger, n 481; Berger et al, n 481; Altman et al, n 481.

[490] Available at webarchive.nationalarchives.gov.uk/20141206135907/http://www.mhra.gov.uk/home/groups/pl-p/documents/websiteresources/con2024447.pdf.

[491] Robert Rice, 'Group to Co-ordinate Insulin Litigation' *Financial Times* (30 August 1991) 8; *Financial Times* Web (30 April 2018); Nick Nuttall, Technology Correspondent, 'Diabetics launch legal fight' *The Times* (30 August 1991) 2; *The Times Digital Archive* Web (30 April 2018).

[492] LN Jorgensen, A Dejgaard and SK Pramming, 'Human insulin and hypoglycaemia: A literature survey' (1994) 11 *Diabetic Medicine* 925.

were unlikely to be able to prove individual causation and so funding was not granted to commence litigation. The cases did not proceed.

v. Conclusion

The safety issue was identified by medical research, and medical understanding grew as a corpus of individual studies became available, following which a sentence was added in the warning section, that a few patients had reported less pronounced warning symptoms after transferring from animal to human insulin. Legal claims were investigated, but ceased when review by the legal aid authorities concluded that there was no legal basis for establishing causation. No regulatory changes resulted from litigation.

D. Pancreatic Enzymes

i. Description

Approximately 90% of patients with cystic fibrosis develop symptoms of exocrine pancreatic insufficiency – the inability to properly digest food due to a lack of digestive enzymes usually produced by the pancreas. This can be relieved by taking pancreatic enzyme supplements.[493] Pancreatic enzyme supplements can take a variety of forms, including powders, tablets and capsules, and were initially made from porcine pancreatic extracts containing lipases, amylase and proteases. High-strength pancreatic enzymes were introduced from 1991 onwards in the USA, and from 1992 onwards in the UK.

ii. Safety Issue

In November 1994 it was reported that between October 1993 and November 1994, 13 children with cystic fibrosis who were receiving high-strength pancreatic enzyme supplements in the UK were reported to have developed large bowel strictures, or fibrosing colonopathy.[494] A case-control study in the UK on the cystic fibrosis population was performed to investigate this novel drug reaction.[495] A further case was later discovered. It was found that the introduction of high-strength pancreatic enzymes in the UK was strongly associated with the development of the adverse condition. It was also found that patients developing large bowel strictures were taking almost twice as many capsules as the controls.[496]

In the US these British reports led a retrospective survey to ascertain the prevalence of this condition in the US, conducted collaboratively between the Cystic Fibrosis Foundation and the FDA. In 1996 the survey results were published: 15 patients were found to have developed fibrosing colonopathy between 1990 and 1993.[497] This led to a case-control study to investigate the potential role of pancreatic enzyme supplements in fibrosing colonopathy in the US.[498] Fitzsimmons et al found a dose-response relationship between pancreatic enzymes and fibrosing colonopathy, which included all pancreatic enzyme preparations and was not limited to high-strength formulations.

iii. Marketing and Regulatory History

Porcine pancreatic extracts have been used to treat exocrine pancreatic insufficiency since the 1930s. These were originally dried total pancreatic extracts and were not very efficient,

[493] SC FitzSimmons, 'The changing epidemiology of cystic fibrosis' (1993) 122(1) *Journal of Pediatrics* 1.

[494] (1994) 20 *Current Problems in Pharmacovigilance* 13, available at webarchive.nationalarchives.gov.uk/20090218113337/http://www.mhra.gov.uk/home/groups/pl-p/documents/publication/con2023216.pdf.

[495] RL Smyth et al, 'Fibrosing colonopathy in cystic fibrosis: results of a case-control study' (1995) 346(8985) *The Lancet* 1247.

[496] CSM, (1995) 21 *Current Problems in Pharmacovigilance* 11, available at webarchive.nationalarchives.gov.uk/20090218113301/http://www.mhra.gov.uk/home/groups/pl-p/documents/publication/con2023217.pdf.

[497] JP Freiman and SC FitzSimmons, 'Colonic strictures in patients with cystic fibrosis: results of a survey of 114 cystic fibrosis care centers in the United States' (1996) 22 *Journal of Pediatric Gastroenterology and Nutrition* 153.

[498] SC Fitzsimmons et al, 'High-Dose Pancreatic-Enzyme Supplements and Fibrosing Colonopathy in Children with Cystic Fibrosis' (1997) 336 *New England Journal of Medicine* 1283.

as the majority of the enzymes in these preparations did not survive the acidic conditions in the stomach. Pancreatic enzyme supplements formulated as microspheres and microtablets, coated with an acid-resistant film to prevent inactivation of the enzymes by gastric acid, were introduced in the 1970s. Standard-strength pancreatic enzymes included Nutrizym GR. High-strength microencapsulated pancreatic enzyme supplements were usually defined as >20,000 units of lipase.

High-strength pancreatic enzymes available in the UK included Creon 25,000, launched in April 1992; Pancrease HL, launched July 1992; Nutrizym 22, launched September 1992; and Panzytrat 25,000, launched July 1993. The first UK case of fibrosing colonopathy was identified in 1993, the year after the high-strength formulations were introduced there.

In the US, the introduction of high-strength enzymes passed without the need for formal approval, as the original enzymes pre-dated the introduction of the modern regulatory system. The first high-strength formulations became available there in 1991, the same year that the first US case was (retrospectively) identified as having occurred.

By November 1994 the UK advice given in *Current Problems*[499] was as follows:

> We currently recommend that, **unless special reasons exist, patients with cystic fibrosis should not use high-potency pancreatins.** We also advise that all patients treated with these products should be monitored carefully, and that the possibility of a large bowel stricture should be considered if symptoms suggestive or gastro-intestinal obstruction occur.

The 1995 UK study[500] found fibrosing colonopathy linked to the use of high-strength pancreatic enzymes Pancrease HL and Nutrizym 22. (There was only minimal use of Panzytrat 25,000 in the UK at the time, but patients treated with an identical preparation in Denmark were said to have developed colitis and extensive colonic damage.)[501]

From the mid-1990s onwards, reports emerged of fibrosing colonopathy in patients treated with the standard-strength pancreatic enzyme preparation Nutrizym GR. To investigate this new evidence of the link between pancreatic enzymes and fibrosing colonopathy,[502] the CSM established a Working Party. Based on its findings in May 1995,[503] the CSM produced series of guidelines for drug dosing, published in November 1995.[504]

Interestingly, the US response to this issue was more extensive: by the end of 1995 manufacturers had voluntarily withdrawn the high-strength pancreatic enzymes formulations from the market.

The finding of a dose-response relationship between pancreatic enzymes and fibrosing colonopathy was repeated by Fitzsimmons et al in 1997, indicating that any formulation of pancreatic enzymes had the potential to be problematic if the dosage given was high

[499] (1994) 20 *Current Problems in Pharmacovigilance* 13, available at webarchive.nationalarchives.gov.uk/20090218113337/http://www.mhra.gov.uk/home/groups/pl-p/documents/publication/con2023216.pdf (original emphasis).

[500] Smyth et al, n 496.

[501] N Knabe et al, 'Extensive pathologic changes of the colon in cystic fibrosis and high-strength pancreatic enzymes' (1994) 343 *The Lancet* 1230.

[502] R Jones et al, 'Colonic strictures in children with cystic fibrosis on low-strength pancreatic enzymes [letter]' (1995) 346 *The Lancet* 499; and D van Velzen, 'Colonic strictures in children with cystic fibrosis on low-strength pancreatic enzymes [comment upon the letter]' (1995) 346 *The Lancet* 499.

[503] Committee on Safety of Medicines, *Report of the Pancreatic Enzymes Working Party* (Stationery Office, 1995).

[504] (1995) 21 *Current Problems in Pharmacovigilance* 11, available at http://webarchive.nationalarchives.gov.uk/20090218113301/http://www.mhra.gov.uk/home/groups/pl-p/documents/publication/con2023217.pdf

enough. However, this view remained contentious, with others claiming that the dosage was not the relevant factor, and that fibrosing colonopathy was due to the methacrylate acid copolymer coating used on some brands of enzymes.[505]

iv. Litigation

A change in warnings triggered the threat of a group action in the UK in 1995. Cases did not proceed after the LSC heard representations, including from the defendant companies, and determined that public funding was not justified based on the strength of evidence.

v. Conclusion

Pancreatic enzyme supplements were in use in the US before the 1938 Food, Drug and Cosmetic Act required studies on the safety of all new drugs; data on the safety of pancreatic-enzyme supplements prior to 1994 were therefore scarce.[506] Adverse drug reaction reports and medical literature resulted in the withdrawal of high-strength pancreatic enzyme supplements in the US and stricter warnings in the UK from 1995. Litigation was threatened but did not proceed in the UK.

[505] For example, see Correspondence, 'Pancreatic enzymes and fibrosing colonopathy' (1999) 354 *The Lancet* 249, available at www.thelancet.com/pdfs/journals/lancet/PIIS0140-6736(99)90126-5.pdf?code=lancet-site.

[506] E Lebenthal, 'High strength pancreatic exocrine enzyme capsules associated with colonic strictures in patients with cystic fibrosis: "more is not necessarily better"' (1994) 18 *Journal of Pediatric Gastroenterology and Nutrition* 423.

VII. Contaminated Human-Tissue-Derived Products

A. Blood Products

i. Description

A blood product is any component of the blood that is collected from a donor for use in the treatment of adverse conditions. Donated blood can be used either as whole blood or as blood products.[507] Whole blood is it transplanted without further processing: whole blood is seldom used nowadays, but historically it was more widely utilised. Blood products fall into two categories: blood components and plasma derivatives. Blood components are prepared in the blood transfusion centre and include red cells, platelets, fresh frozen plasma and cryoprecipitate. Plasma derivatives are manufactured from pooled plasma donations at plasma fractionation centres, and include albumin, coagulation factors and immunoglobulins. The differences in the manufacture of these had a significant impact on their iatrogenic potential. Whole blood and blood components will generally only be used to treat a few individuals, therefore a donation from an infected donor can only infect a handful of recipients. In contrast, plasma derivatives are manufactured from pooled donations, which are then used to treat a large number of individuals, so a donation from a single infected donor has the potential to infect many recipients. Among the plasma derivatives, Factor VIII and Factor IX were the key blood-clotting agents collected from blood donors for the treatment of haemophilia.[508]

ii. Safety Issue

On 16 July 1982, the US CDC reported that three hemophiliacs had acquired HIV. Epidemiologists started to believe that the disease was being spread through blood-based therapies, with grave implications for haemophiliacs who had routinely injected themselves with concentrate made from giant pools of donated plasma. Without an AIDS test, health officials had no idea how many plasma donors or recipients carried the disease.[509]

In January 1983, the manager of plasma procurement for Bayer's Cutter Biological division acknowledged in a letter that '[t]here is strong evidence to suggest that AIDS is passed on to other people through … plasma products'.[510] In March 1983, the CDC warned that blood products 'appear responsible for AIDS among hemophilia patients'.[511]

In many countries, such as Britain, France, West Germany and Australia, the number of haemophiliacs infected with HIV before precautions had been taken had risen to well over

[507] For further detail, see Joint United Kingdom (UK) Blood Transfusion and Tissue Transplantation Services Professional Advisory Committee, *Transfusion Handbook*, 5th edn (2014), available at www.transfusionguidelines.org/transfusion-handbook.

[508] S Connor and S Kingman, *The Search for the Virus* (Penguin Books, 1989).

[509] Walt Bogdanich and Eric Koli, '2 Paths of Bayer Drug in 80's: Riskier One Steered Overseas' *New York Times* (22 May 2003), available at www.nytimes.com/2003/05/22/business/2-paths-of-bayer-drug-in-80-s-riskier-one-steered-overseas.html.

[510] ibid.

[511] ibid.

50% by 1987. The situation was far worse in the US, where the proportion was close to 100%, and all the evidence suggested that Factor VIII imported into European countries from the US was much more likely to be contaminated with HIV than Factor VIII made in Europe.[512]

iii. Marketing and Regulatory History

Factor VIII was developed and widely used from the 1970s. Commercial manufacturers (notably Bayer, Baxter, Armour, Immuno) and public bodies (such as the National Blood Laboratory in UK) supplied blood-based therapies.

The first reports of haemophiliacs with what became identified as HIV were seen in July 1982 in the US and in November 1983 in the UK. These cases suggested a possible transmissible agent in blood products. In 1984 the AIDS virus was isolated. The first (not wholly reliable) test for antibodies became available in 1985.

Heat treatment of Factor VIII was implemented in 1984/85 for the purpose of killing any viruses in the products. There was no unified international standard applied to heat treatment; responses varied both by manufacturer[513] and by country.[514] For example, in England in July 1984 the CSM rejected Armour's application for a licence for its dry heat-treated Factor VIII.[515] It took until January 1987 for the FDA to revoke Armour's licence to market concentrates in the US. In Canada, the Bureau of Biologics did not revoke Armour's licence until December 1987.

By 1986, doubts around the effectiveness of the various heat-treatment protocols were in the public domain.[516] In December 1987, a cluster of Canadian patients who had been treated with Armour's T. Factorate Anti-Hemophilic (Human) clotting factor tested HIV positive.[517] This product was derived from donor-screened blood that had been heat treated. In response Armour recalled 208 lots of T. Factorate Anti-Hemophilic (Human) clotting factor and Armour's Canadian licence was withdrawn.

Similar problems subsequently occurred with Hepatitis C contamination from blood donations from the USA and the UK, and in the 1990s with 'new variant Creutzfeldt-Jacob Disease (vCJD)' (see section VII.B on 'Human Growth Hormones').

iv. Litigation

In several European states, special compensation schemes were established by governments and/or manufacturers. Some individual cases may have been settled in some EU states.

512 ibid.

513 See Committee to Study HIV Transmission Through Blood and Blood Products, Division of Health Promotion and Disease Prevention, Institute of Medicine, *HIV and the Blood Supply: An Analysis of Crisis Decision Making*, eds B Lauren et al (National Academy Press Washington, 1995) ch 4.

514 For a detailed description of historical context of heat inactivation of viruses in blood products, see chs 23 and 24 of *The Penrose Inquiry Final Report*, March 2015 SG/2015/15 ISBN: 978-0-85759-022-0, available at www.penroseinquiry.org.uk/finalreport/index.html.

515 Connor and Kingman, n 508; *The Penrose Inquiry Final Report*, n 514.

516 Connor and Kingman, n 508.

517 Remis et al, 'HIV transmission to patients with haemophilia by heat-treated, donor-screened factor concentrate' (1990) 142(11) *Canadian Medical Association Journal* 1247.

An ex gratia fund had been set up in 1987 for haemophilia sufferers who contracted HIV from Factor VIII and Factor IX, but the sums available to claimants were modest.[518] Group litigation was commenced from 1997 in the UK and Ireland against regulatory authorities (on contamination of the blood supply) and manufacturers. The UK litigation involving 560 claimants was funded by legal aid, and the complex trial was scheduled to last for 26 weeks. In the face of mounting political and media pressure, the Government increased the funds available to the *ex gratia* scheme and made provision for the claimants' costs, which resulted in the discontinuation of the group litigation.[519] Some individual cases for clinical negligence were continued, but all of these were settled before trial. The terms of and reforms of the *ex gratia* schemes have been a source of ongoing challenges.[520]

Litigation against manufacturers was commenced, but it could not identify which product was defective and which manufacturer had produced it. A group of cases continued against the UK Government but was settled with the establishment of a national *ex gratia* set of trust funds and charities to compensate claimants.

Subsequent litigation in the US, which added Hepatitis C to the previous HIV issues, involved non-US plaintiffs, mainly from Latin America, Asia and Europe, including about 270 British patients, most of who were represented by two US law firms that instructed them on a contingency fee basis. After the claims of the British patients (amongst others) had been dismissed in the US on the grounds of *forum non conveniens*, the claimants instituted proceedings in the UK. Almost all the claims have been resolved after the parties reached a settlement to bring decades of litigation to an end.

In February 2007 a non-statutory public inquiry was announced, to be held into the supply of contaminated NHS blood to haemophiliacs in the UK. Former Solicitor General, Labour peer Lord Archer of Sandwell, was to conduct the inquiry after a campaign by Lord Morris of Manchester, the ex-Minister for the Disabled, who said that 1,757 haemophilia patients, who were exposed to HIV- and/or Hepatitis C-contaminated NHS blood and blood products, had died since being infected. The inquiry ended with a report issued by Lord Archer in February 2009, followed by a judgment of the High Court of London regarding the implementation of Lord Archer's recommendations in April 2010.

A public inquiry, the Penrose Inquiry, was undertaken in Scotland from 2008.[521] It was a statutory national public inquiry into Hepatitis C- and HIV-acquired infections from NHS treatment in Scotland from blood and blood products. It was chaired by Lord Penrose. The final report was published on 25 March 2015: it did not apportion blame and made only one recommendation – that a blood test for Hepatitis C should be offered to anyone in Scotland who received a blood transfusion prior to 1991. There has been considerable criticism of the Penrose Inquiry.

The renewed interest in the contaminated blood scandal has also led to a resurrection of litigation in England and Wales. A GLO, the Contaminated Blood Products Group

[518] For the remits and historical contexts of the five ex gratia compensation schemes for HIV/HepC compensation, see the *Inquiry into the Current Support for those affected by the Contaminated Blood Scandal in the UK*, All-Party Parliamentary Group (APPG) on Haemophilia and Contaminated Blood (January 2015), available at www.haemophilia.org.uk/what_we_do/influencing_advocacy/appg_hcb_fr.pdf.

[519] See S Pearl, 'HIV Haemophilia Litigation' in Hodges (ed), n 191, ch 19.

[520] *R (Smith) v Secretary of State for Health* [2016] CO/5208/2016.

[521] See at www.penroseinquiry.org.uk/.

Litigation (CBPGL), was sought on 4 July 2017 by Collins Solicitors.[522] The GLO was entered on 27 October 2017. Collins Solicitors have stated that they feel that compelling new evidence has been uncovered, and so they are now acting for over 400 claimants against the Secretary of State for Health on the grounds of negligence and/or misfeasance in a public office, comprising failure to notify the claimants in a timely manner of information and/or knowledge that the Department of Health had relating to their infection. This action has been initiated, but it is likely to face substantial difficulties due to limitation. Until the facts are clearer, the impact of limitation is difficult to gauge.[523]

On 11 July 2017, the Prime Minister Theresa May announced a public inquiry into the tainted blood scandal; this was one week after the GLO was lodged and followed considerable campaigning, notably from Andy Burnham MP.[524] There was considerable dissatisfaction with the involvement of the Department of Health in the drafting of the terms of reference of the inquiry.[525] In November 2017 it was confirmed that the inquiry would be overseen by the Cabinet Office, rather than the Department of Health, to avoid any potential conflicts of interest. The inquiry commenced in 2018,[526] chaired by Mr Justice Langstaff: it has yet to report.

v. Conclusion

Litigation followed medical and regulatory developments. No regulatory action arose out of the litigation.

[522] See at www.gov.uk/guidance/group-litigation-orders#contaminated-blood-products-group-litigation.
[523] See at www.collinslaw.co.uk/contaminated-blood.
[524] See at www.gov.uk/government/news/pm-statement-on-contaminated-blood-inquiry-11-july-2017.
[525] See at haemophilia.org.uk/2017/10/09/clear-conflict-interest-dh-involvement-contaminated-blood-inquiry/.
[526] See at www.infectedbloodinquiry.org.uk/.

B. Human Growth Hormone

i. Description

Human Growth Hormone (HGH) is a protein-based peptide hormone extracted from the pituitaries of cadavers. It stimulates growth, cell reproduction and regeneration in humans and other animals.

ii. Safety Issue

In 1985, three cases of CJD were established at post-mortems on American recipients of HGH, and one British case of CJD was established. The UK program of harvesting and administration was terminated on 9 May 1985 on the basis of the US evidence, by which time more than 1,800 children had been treated.[527]

iii. Marketing and Regulatory History

Human Growth Hormone manufactured using the Wilhelmi method was supplied to 2,000 children between 1959 and 1985. The product was on the UK market before licensing began in the early 1970s. The Medical Research Council and later the Department of Health were responsible for production of the product. The first full marketing authorisation was granted on 16 May 1978. No records of adverse reaction reports are held at MHRA.

All licences were cancelled by 1989. Synthetic hormones began to be licensed in the 1990s.

iv. Litigation

Claims were identified from 1989, and a group action was commenced in England and Wales in 1994 alleging negligence against the Medical Research Council and the Department of Health, which resulted in 1998 in a judgment against the Department of Health.[528] By the time of the generic trial in 1996, 16 UK recipients had died: the number had risen to 34 by 1999. Those awarded compensation included some who had no damage and were unlikely to suffer damage, but who were compensated for the emotional strain attending the uncertainty as to whether they would develop CJD.

A no-blame compensation scheme for those diagnosed with iatrogenic vCJD was established in 2001,[529] removing the need for further litigation.

v. Conclusion

The safety issue was identified by medical post-mortems in the US. Litigation in the UK followed some years later.

[527] See D Body, 'Creutzfeldt-Jakob Disease (Human Growth Hormone) Litigation' in Hodges (ed), n 191, ch 26.
[528] ibid.
[529] See at http://www.vcjdtrust.co.uk.

VIII. Cardiovascular Pharmaceuticals

A. Eraldin (practolol)

i. Description

Practolol was a cardio-selective beta-blocker, a drug that blocks the beta-adrenergic receptors in the heart and the action of hormones like adrenalin. Beta-blockers are indicated for a variety of cardiac disorders, including angina, heart failure, atrial fibrillation, heart attack and hypertension.

ii. Safety Issue

The most common adverse reactions consisted of widespread fibrosing and scleorosing of the mucus membranes (causing symptoms ranging from dryness of the eye to blindness). The term 'Oculomucocutaneous syndrome' (OC), was used to describe this damage. The majority of OC cases improved once the patient ceased taking the medication, but some patients were left with irreversible permanent damage.

Severe psoriasis-like skin rashes and potentially fatal sclerosing of the serous membrane surrounding the abdomen, lungs and/or heart were also observed. There were cases of sclerosing peritonitis, a where the visceral and parietal surfaces of the abdominal cavity become inflamed, leading to abdominal pain, vomiting, severe constipation, pleurisy and in some cases death. Incidents of sclerosing peritonitis could occur some months after treatment with practolol had been discontinued.

Forty deaths had been reported to the CSM by 1 February 1981.[530] Other serious potential ADRs were also reported by November 1978, including sclerosing peritonitis (197 cases), eye conditions (around 1,130 reported cases), skin rashes (1,256 reported), deafness (309 reports) and 589 other ADRs.[531] It must be remembered that these adverse event numbers are not definitive; in some cases the drug use may have been coincidental rather than causal, and some other ADRs may not have been reported. As a single patient could report more than one adverse event, these numbers must be treated with caution. It has been said that ICI's Senior Safety Officer, who oversaw the compensation scheme, estimated that over 8,000 people had been affected.[532]

iii. Marketing and Regulatory History

Imperial Chemical Industries (ICI) Plc synthesised and developed the new chemical, practolol, known as IC 50,172 in 1964.[533] This compound was found to be more cardio-selective

[530] Hansard HC Deb 18 March 1981 vol 1 col 24W, available at hansard.millbanksystems.com/written_answers/1981/mar/18/eraldin-compensation#S6CV0001P0_19810318_CWA_166.

[531] Hansard HC Deb 13 December 1978 vol 960 cols 231–232W available at hansard.millbanksystems.com/written_answers/1978/dec/13/eraldin#S5CV0960P0_19781213_CWA_205.

[532] J Abraham and D Courtney, 'Testing Times: The Emergence of the Practolol Disaster and its Challenge to British Drug Regulation in the Modern Period' (2006) 19(1) *Social History of Medicine* 127.

[533] For a detailed description, see V Quirke, 'Thalidomide, Drug Safety Regulation and the British Pharmaceutical Industry: The Case of Imperial Chemical Industries' in J-P Gaudilliere and V Hess (eds), *Ways of Regulating Drugs in the 19th and 20th Centuries* (Palgrave Macmillan, 2013) 151.

than other available beta-blockers and had little depressant activity on the heart, and it had fewer bronchoconstriction effects than other beta-blockers. This profile meant that it was viewed as a good option for the treatment of heart conditions in asthmatics. Human trials began in 1968, including double blind trials for angina and hypertension.

On 26 June 1970 the CSD approved the sale of practolol for angina pectoris and cardiac dysrhythmias. This approval was on the basis of animal toxicity tests and clinical trials demonstrating the drug's safety. There is no evidence that ICI was non-compliant with the regulatory requirements of the day.

By 1973 there were research reports indicating that practolol altered intraocular pressure.[534] This raised the possibility of its use as a treatment for glaucoma (increased intraocular pressure). However, the cardiovascular research team was unaware of the OC caused by practolol, as no indication of this was detected from either pre-marketing or post-marketing testing of practolol. Interestingly, skin reactions were also noted at this time, and early in 1974 ICI changed the label to advise of skin rashes. There have been suggestions that there were indications of the adverse drug events associated with OC syndrome in the pre-marketing and post-marketing testing, but that these were disregarded as both eye conditions and skin reactions were relatively common; and as it was a rare condition, no association was made between sclerosing peritonitis and the drug.[535]

Practolol was hugely successful and was widely used in the UK. However, between 1970 and 1975 the CSM received reports of adverse events via the yellow card reporting system. There were also case reports in the medical literature.[536] Later this would be recognized as practolol-induced OC syndrome. In July 1975, ICI voluntarily withdrew the oral form of the drug from the UK market in response to the adverse drug events data that had accumulated. Practolol remained available for use in hospitals for a short while.

There is no suggestion that ICI failed to comply with its legal responsibilities to test its drugs, but it has been suggested that the regulatory regime was reluctant to act proactively to restrict access to the market or to remove products from the market.[537]

iv. Litigation

Liability was never tested in court. In a pre-emptive move, ICI set up a voluntary compensation scheme in 1975, which was at least as generous as court assessed compensation would

[534] J Vale and CI Phillips, 'Practolol (Eraldin) eye drops as an ocular hypotensive agent' (1973) 57(3) *British Journal of Opthalmology* 210.

[535] WHW Inman, *Don't Tell the Patient: Behind the Drug Safety Net* (Highland Park Productions, 1999).

[536] RA Wiseman, 'Practolol – Accumulated Data on Unwanted Effects' (1971) 47(Suppl 2) *Postgraduate Medical Journal* 68; P Brown et al, 'Sclerosing Peritonisis, An Unusual Reaction to a β-Adrenergic-Blocking Drug (Practolol)' (1974) 304(7895) *The Lancet* 1477; WO Windsor, F Kurrein and NH Dyer, 'Fibrinous peritonitis: a complication of practolol therapy' (1975) 2 *British Medical Journal* 68; P Wright, 'Untoward Effects Associated with Practolol Administration: Occulomucocutaneous Syndrome' (1975) 1 *British Medical Journal* 595. Letters to the Editor including MGM Rowland and CJ Stevenson, 'Exfoliative dermatitis and practolol' (1972) 299(7760) *The Lancet* 1130; R Felix and A Ive, 'Letter: Skin Reactions to practolol' (1974) 2(5914) *British Medical Journal* 333; P Wright, 'Letter: Skin Reactions to practolol' (1974) 2(5918) *British Medical Journal* 560; A Henson et al, 'Sclerosing peritonitis and practolol' (1975) 305(7901) *The Lancet* 275; RBH Meyboom, 'Sclerosing peritonitis and practolol' (1975) 305(7902) *The Lancet* 334; K Bendtzen et al, 'Sclerosing peritonitis and Practolol' (1975) 305(7907) *The Lancet* 629; K Kristensen, JS Kristensen and JV Thorburg, 'Sclerosing peritonitis and practolol' (1975) 305(7909) *The Lancet* 741; W Halley and JD Goodman, 'Letter: Practolol and sclerosing peritonitis' (1975) 2 *British Medical Journal* 337; 'Editorial: Side Effects of Practolol' (1975) 2 *British Medical Journal* 577; S Soimakallio, K Vallinmaki and H Lehmus, 'Sclerosing peritonitis and practolol' (1975) 306(7939) *The Lancet* 812.

[537] Abraham and Courtney, n 533.

have been, if not more so.[538] Therefore, there was no major litigation in England and Wales. The scheme was an administrative tariff-based mechanism for awarding compensation. Eligibility for compensation was based on presenting with permanent injury due to taking practolol. The quantum of compensation was determined by the severity of the injury.

v. Conclusion

Despite causing a large number of people serious injuries, the practolol story has largely been forgotten. In part that is likely to be because there was a voluntary withdrawal, followed by attempts to correct any perceived regulatory deficits to prevent a similar problem in the future and the voluntary provision of generous compensation for the individuals affected. The withdrawal of practolol from the market, the resulting regulatory changes and the compensation were driven by observations of the adverse effects by doctors: litigation played no part in any of these changes.

[538] Interestingly, the payment without proof of liability raised concerns, there were suggestions that it would have been useful for the case to have been tested in court to establish if pharmaceutical manufacturers were liable in such situations. See Anon, 'Compensation for Unforeseen Adverse Drug Reactions' (1977) 309(8015) *The Lancet* 788.

B. Manoplax (flosequinan)

i. Description

Manoplax is a quinolone vasodilator indicated for preventative use against chronic congestive heart failure (CHF).

ii. Safety Issue

Studies on flosequinan at doses ranging from 50–150 mgs were conducted throughout the 1980s.[539] Deaths were evident at the higher doses, but these deaths were attributed to the nature of the disease in the patients being treated. The mortality statistics of those treated were consistent with natural mortality rates of those suffering from CHF.

The mortality statistics resulted in indications for flosequinan as a quinolone vasodilator only for patients found intolerant of first-line therapies. More specifically, Professor David Barnett published in *The Lancet* that flosequinan might be useful for two clinical indications: as additional therapy in patients who remained symptomatic on combined treatment with diuretics and angiotensin-converting enzyme (ACE) inhibitors, and as an alternative therapy in patients intolerant of or who faced contraindications to ACE inhibitors.[540]

In response to Professor Barnett's article,[541] it was agreed that Manoplax was a potentially useful and important addition to therapies treating heart failure. However, the respondents also said that Manoplax had not shown any reduction of mortality in connection with heart failure, and so should only be used following ACE inhibitor therapy and combination therapies.

iii. Marketing and Regulatory History

Boots Co Plc researched and developed the new chemical entity flosequinan through the 1980s, and a product licence was granted for 50 and 100mg doses on 10 August 1992. The normal dose recommended for treatment was 100mg per day. The product was launched on the UK market on 21 September 1992 under the name Manoplax in 50 and 100mg doses. Boots Pharmaceuticals Inc, a US subsidiary of Boots, also sought a licence in the US, which was granted in December 1992.

Promotion in the UK was restricted to key cardiology clinicians in the 84 largest hospitals. Larger-scale promotion to practitioners did not take place. Nevertheless, the

[539] For examples, see PD Kessler and M Packer, 'Hemodynamic effects of BTS 49465, a new long acting systemic vasodilator drug, in patients with severe congestive heart failure' (1987) 113 *American Heart Journal* 137; and JS Elborn et al, 'Effect of flosequinan on exercise capacity and symptoms in severe heart failure' (1989) 61 *British Heart Journal* 33; AJ Cowley, RD Wynne and JR Hampton, 'The effects of BTS 49465 on blood pressure and peripheral arteriolar and venous tone in normal volunteers' (1984) Suppl 2(3) *Journal of Hypertension* S547; AJ Cowley et al, 'Flosequinan in heart failure: acute haemodynamic and longer term symptomatic effects' (1988) 297 *British Medical Journal* 169.

[540] DB Barnett, 'Flosequinan' (1993) 341(8847) *The Lancet* 733.

[541] WG Haynes and DJ Webb, 'Flosequinan in Heart Failure' (1993) 341(8852) *The Lancet* 1100.

product was taken up quickly, as offering great potential in the life-threatening conditions where available treatments were limited.[542]

At the time Manoplax was launched, emphasis on the development of specific post-marketing surveillance data was becoming more commonplace in drug regulation practice. Manoplax was an example of a drug in widespread use in clinical practice that could be monitored during its post-marketing experience for additional data on safety and efficacy. Regulatory authorities increasingly made the performance of such post-marketing studies a *de facto* condition of a licence grant, particularly if grant applications had specific limitations in studies submitted at the time.

The UK Licensing Authority did not request the performance of any post-marketing study on Manoplax. However, Boots itself chose to explore the product's safety and efficacy profile further, and funded a large long-term multi-centre placebo-controlled study to measure the effect of Manoplax on survival and mortality in CHF patients. The study, called PROFILE,[543] was managed by a US subsidiary and conducted in North America, Norway and Sweden. It sought to assess outcomes when the product was prescribed as an additional treatment on top of conventional therapies for CHF that included diuretics, digoxin and ACE inhibitors. The study followed a double blind method and utilised the 75 and 100mg doses.

In April 1993, the independent Data Safety Monitoring Committee of the PROFILE study disclosed to Boots the preliminary results involving 3,000 patients. These showed a statistically significant increase in mortality in patients treated with 100mg of Manoplax as compared with patients not receiving additional treatment with Manoplax. The study suggested that the benefits of Manoplax in terms of reduced symptoms and increased quality of life were being gained by a cost of reduced life expectancy.

On 24 April 1993 the company circulated a 'Dear Doctor' letter, advising doctors to inform patients enrolled in the PROFILE study of the findings. On 26 April 1993 another 'Dear Doctor' letter informed all doctors about the increased mortality linked to Manoplax at a dose of 100mg. Boots terminated the 100mg clinical trials, and the 100mg dose was withdrawn from US and UK markets.[544] In addition, warnings in relation to the 50mg dose were introduced.

In May 1993 the UK Licensing Authority set in motion procedures to revoke the product licences for both the 50 and 100mg doses, which were appealed by Boots through the procedure in the medicines legislation. A hearing before the CSM was planned for the Autumn of 1993. The Licensing Authority did not consider it necessary to suspend the licences on grounds of safety while the appeals procedure took it course. In July 1993, Boots decided that the continued use of Manoplax could no longer be recommended after the PROFILE

[542] The product was swiftly included in 43 prescribing formularies of major teaching and large hospitals. By February 1993, prescriptions were running at close to 2,500 per month. Sales exceeded expectations by a factor of four.

[543] Prospective Randomised FlosequInan Longevity Evaluation. The trial finally reported primary results in 2017 after 24 years: see M Packer et al, 'Long-Term Effects of Flosequinan on the Morbidity and Mortality of Patients with Severe Chronic Heart Failure: Primary Results of the PROFILE Trial After 24 Years' (2017) 5(6) *Journal of the American College of Cardiology: Heart Failure*, available at heartfailure.onlinejacc.org/content/5/6/399.full.

[544] Similar actions were taken in parallel in the US: the FDA sent two 'Dear Doctor' letters to physicians, noting revised labelLing, and included information about continued consultations with the FDA.

trial revealed potential adverse consequences for patients on the 75mg dose; the 75mg arm of PROFILE trial was then closed. The 75 mg product was voluntarily withdrawn from the market by the company before the revocation procedures could progress, leaving the 50mg as the sole formation. While the product licences remained valid, Boots decided against action towards maintaining them.[545]

iv. Litigation

Litigation was threatened in England after the regulatory changes were announced, but it was not pursued.

v. Conclusion

The safety issue was identified shortly after launch of the product in a voluntary post-marketing study sponsored by the company, and notified to the authorities and doctors. Claims were threatened as a result of the regulatory action and the decision of the company that flowed from it, but were not pursued.

[545] McKenna and Co, *Report for the Boots Co, PLC on the Product Liability Implications of the Research and Marketing of Manoplex* (1993).

C. Lipobay (cerivastatin)

i. Description

Lipobay is an HMG CoA reductase inhibitor,[546] which belongs to a therapeutic class of drugs known as statins. Statins are indicated for inhibiting the enzyme involved in cholesterol synthesis, especially in the liver. Cholesterol occurs in two main forms, LDL (low density lipoprotein) and HDL (high density lipoprotein): LDL cholesterol is often referred to as 'bad cholesterol', because too much can contribute to the progression of coronary atherosclerosis, and more generally to cardiovascular disease; HDL is often considered to be 'good cholesterol', because it has cardio-protective properties. Statins have been found to be very effective in specifically lowering LDL cholesterol levels.

ii. Safety Issue

Controversy around cerivastatin concerns a relatively narrow area of adverse reactions, namely effects on the muscle (which is a class effect of all statins) and in particular the condition rhabdomyolysis, in which rapid skeletal muscle deterioration occurs causing the release of myoglobin into the bloodstream. Excess circulating myoglobin can lead to kidney damage and, if left untreated, even death. Rhabdomyolysis, although serious, is rare across all statins, including Lipobay. However, in 1999, pharmacovigilance reports arising from outside the UK suggested to the manufacturer Bayer that rhabdomyolysis appeared to be reported at a higher rate with Lipobay than with other drugs in the statin class, particularly when co-prescribed with gemfibrozil (a cholesterol-lowering agent outside the statin class).

The issue was most acute in the US because of the higher level of co-prescription with gemfibrozil. This practice continued, despite the evidence of contraindication of co-prescription with gemfibrozil and diligent efforts taken to change physicians' prescribing behaviour. Reports of ADRs associated with co-prescriptions did also occur outside the US, though they were generally at much lower levels in the EU and specifically in the UK. This is likely to be due to national differences in the rates of co-prescription. The rate of co-prescription in the US was 1.5%, while in the UK it was 0.1%. In the UK there where very few cases of rhabdomyolysis reported, and none appears to have been fatal.

Although co-prescription was heavily implicated as a cause of rhabdomyolysis, a 2002 study by Staffa et al indicated that while the risk of rhabdomyolysis was substantially elevated by co-prescription, even monotherapy with cerivastatin carried a higher risk of rhabdomyolysis than monotherapy with other commonly used statins.[547] In the US this was contested by Bayer, which commissioned an epidemiological study that found an elevated risk of rhabdomyolysis compared to other statins when cerivastatin was co-prescribed with

[546] 3-hydroxy-3-methylglutaryl coenzyme A reductase inhibitors, also known as statins, block HMG-CoA reductase (3-hydroxy-3-methylglutaryl coenzyme A reductase), an enzyme that is involved in the synthesis of mevalonate. The body converts mevalonate into sterols, including cholesterol.

[547] JA Staffa, J Chang and L Green, 'Cerivastatin and Reports of Fatal Rhabdomyolysis' (2002) 346 *New England Journal of Medicine* 539.

gemfibrozil, but not for when it was used as a monotherapy.[548] Interestingly, in Europe, the CHMP Opinion[549] summarised an analysis of published studies conducted by Bayer, which indicated a higher rate of confirmed rhabdomyolysis cases relative to other statins at both 400 mcg and 800 mcg doses. No major difference was seen between cerivastin and other statins for unconfirmed rhabdomyolysis cases.[550] Other studies have indicated that cerivastatin as a monotherapy carries a higher risk of rhabdomyolysis than other statins, though with a lower overall death rate from the condition.[551] These discrepancies may, at least in part, be due to the studies' using different datasets, methodologies and definitions.

iii. Marketing and Regulatory History

Cerivastatin was approved in the US[552] and the UK at the same time in 1997.[553] The UK was the Reference Member State for EU approval for 100–400mcg doses of cerivastatin, which was obtained via the mutual recognition procedure.[554]

Tablets containing 100, 200, and 300mcg of cerivastatin were first approved for marketing in the UK under the trade name Lipobay on 13 February 1997, and the product was first launched in the UK on 14 April 1997. On 8 December 1999 a marketing authorisation was granted in the UK for the higher dose of 400mcg, and on 1 March 2001 Bayer obtained approval in the UK for tablet strength of 800mcg, which was the highest strength approved. Approved prescribing information recommended titration of the dose from the lower end of the dosage range to the higher doses, depending upon the patient's response in terms of lowering serum cholesterol to optimal levels.

In the US, tablets containing 50, 100, 200 and 300mcg of cerivastatin were first approved for marketing on 26 June 1997.[555] On 24 May 1999[556] a marketing authorisation was granted for the higher dose of 400mcg, and on 21 July 2000 Bayer obtained approval in the US for a tablet strength of 800mcg,[557] which was the highest strength approved.

From the outset, the US warning under the 'Skeletal Muscle' subsection included the following:[558]

> Rare cases of rhabdomyolysis with acute renal failure secondary to myoglobinuria have been reported with other HMG CoA reductase inhibitors.

[548] JD Piorkowski Jr, 'Bayer's response to "potential for conflict of interest in the evaluation of suspected adverse drug reactions: use of cerivastatin and risk of rhabdomyolysis"' (2004) 292(21) *Journal of the American Medical Association* 2655, particularly the discussion at 2658–59, specifically Reference 38 Bayer Exhibit 131, *Hollis N Haltom v Bayer Corporation, et al*, Trial Court Cause No 02-60165-2, Nueces County, Texas ['The Risk of Myopathy Subsequent to HMG Use in a Managed Care Organization'; 14 February 2002].

[549] Committee for Proprietary Medicinal Products Opinion following an Article 36 Referral: Cerivastatin CPMP/3962/02, September 2002, available at www.ema.europa.eu/ema/index.jsp?curl=pages/medicines/human/referrals/Cerivastatin/human_referral_000108.jsp.

[550] See ibid, Annex I, tables 5 and 6.

[551] A Ardati et al, 'Letter: Statin-associated rhabdomyolyis' (2005) 14 *Pharmacoepidemiology and Drug Safety* 287.

[552] New Drug Application (NDA) 020740, approved 26 June 1997, available at www.accessdata.fda.gov/scripts/cder/daf/index.cfm?event=overview.process&applno=020740.

[553] BM Psaty et al, 'Potential for Conflict of Interest in the Evaluation of Suspected Adverse Drug Reactions Use of Cerivastatin and Risk of Rhabdomyolysis' (2004) 292(21) *Journal of the American Medical Association* 2622.

[554] Committee for Proprietary Medicinal Products Opinion, n 550.

[555] New Drug Application (NDA) 020740, n 552.

[556] See at www.accessdata.fda.gov/drugsatfda_docs/nda/99/20-740S002_Baycol_Approv.pdf.

[557] See at www.accessdata.fda.gov/drugsatfda_docs/appletter/2000/20740S8,13LTR.PDF.

[558] See at www.accessdata.fda.gov/drugsatfda_docs/nda/99/20-740S003_Baycol.pdf.

On 4 January 1999 this was changed to:[559]

> Rare cases of rhabdomyolysis (some with acute renal failure secondary to myoglobinuria) have been reported with cervastatin and other drugs in this class.

At this point a specific warning on co-prescribing with gemfibrozil was also included. The label had previously read:

> The use of fibrates alone occasionally may be associated with myopathy. The combined use to HMG-CoA inhibitors and fibrates generally should be avoided.

This was updated to read:

> The combined use to HMG-CoA inhibitors and fibrates generally should be avoided. The use of fibrates alone occasionally may be associated with myopathy including rhabdomyolysis and associated renal failure. **The combined use of cerivastatin and gemfibrozil is contraindicated due to a risk for rhabdomylosis.**

In the EU, adverse event reports, including deaths, were recorded, and by Spring 2001 the Spanish compentent authority (where several deaths had occurred) was sufficiently concerned to commission a study. Bayer also commissioned an independent investigation into the issue.[560] These studies both reported back in early Summer 2001, and both confirmed the higher incidence of rhabdomyolysis associated with co-prescription of Lipobay and gemfibrozil as compared with other statins. In response to this, on 21 June 2001 Bayer voluntarily suspended UK sales of the 800mcg formulation in the UK. A week later, on 26 June 2001, an EU-wide Urgent Safety Restriction was issued to update prescribing information to contraindicate co-prescription of cerivastatin and gemfibrozil, and to recommend a maximum dose of 400mcg.

On 7 August 2001, increased frequency of adverse event reports resulted in Bayer's decision to voluntarily withdraw Lipobay worldwide, while further analysis of the available data took place.[561] It was initially thought that this would allow time to explore the possibility of accessing other databases that would provide useful comparative data for other statins.

On 19 September 2001, Portugal notified the EMA of an Article 15a referral[562] for cervistatin, requesting a full assessment of the risk–benefit of the product be carried out because of concerns over the putative elevated risk of rhabdomyolysis. This process commenced in September 2001. In January 2002, following further dialogue with the relevant EU regulatory authorities, Bayer decided to surrender the authorisations for all Lipobay products in EU Member States. The decision was taken to surrender authorisations in Europe when it became apparent that any attempt to reintroduce Lipobay was precluded by practical commercial considerations deriving from the difficulties of preventing co-administration of cerivastatin and gemfibrozil, the adverse publicity surrounding

[559] See at www.accessdata.fda.gov/drugsatfda_docs/nda/99/20-740S003_Baycol.pdf.

[560] Including an independent review of the General Practice Research Database commissioned by Bayer.

[561] The withdrawal letter to healthcare professionals was dated 8 August 2001. See also CSM, 'Cerivastatin (Lipobay) Withdrawn' (2001) 27 *Current Problems in Pharmacovigilance* 9, available at webarchive.nationalarchives.gov.uk/20141206195208/http://www.mhra.gov.uk/home/groups/pl-p/documents/websiteresources/con007456.pdf.

[562] Art 15a of Directive 75/319/EEC (now Art 36 of Directive 2001/83/EC).

Lipobay, and the availability of other medications for the treatment of high cholesterol. Regulators in the EU were surprised at the short notice given by Bayer of its voluntary suspension of marketing and withdrawal of the product; they were effectively informed only when Bayer made a public announcement.

Despite the surrender of the marketing authorisations, a decision was taken that it would be in the public interest to continue with the Article 15a referral, with the opinion being published in September 2002.[563]

iv. Litigation

After the decision by Bayer to withdraw Cerivastatin from the worldwide market voluntarily, around 15,000 cases were brought in the US, including class actions.[564] The company won all six jury trials brought by plaintiffs. The company settled about 3,000 cases where plaintiffs had suffered rhabdomyolysis;[565] the remaining cases (except a few that are still pending) were dismissed.

Outside the US about 130 cases were filed against Bayer, mainly in South America, Canada and Europe. As regards the litigation in Europe, about 20 cases were brought in Germany, all of which the company won. A few patients attempted unsuccessfully to obtain legal aid funding in UK, and no litigation ensued. Some cases were brought in Italy, the vast majority of which ended in the company's favour; a few remain enmeshed in the court system. About 25 cases were brought in France, of which two are still pending: of the others, either the company won or the cases did not proceed after the expert analysis was completed. Isolated cases were brought in Spain and Greece. Criminal investigations were instituted in Germany, France, Switzerland, Greece and Italy, which were all closed with no further action taken by the authorities.

v. Conclusion

The safety issue was identified by the pharmacovigilance system. Litigation followed after the voluntary withdrawal of the product from the worldwide market by Bayer.

[563] Committee for Proprietary Medicinal Products Opinion, n 550.

[564] Including *Slaughter v Bayer Corporation,et al*, Civil Cause no 2002-41-CV8, Jones County, Mississippi; *Hollis N Haltom v Bayer Corporation et al*, Trial Court Cause no 02-60165-2, Nueces County, Texas; *In re Baycol Products Litigation*, MDL no 1431, United States District Court, D Minnesota. See at www.mnd.uscourts.gov/MDL-Baycol/index.shtml for further details of the MDL.

[565] For a detailed analysis of the settlement, see J Anderson, 'Understanding Mass Tort Defendant Incentives for Confidential Settlements: Lessons from Bayer's Cerivastatin Litigation Strategy' in JW Doherty, RT Reville and L Zakaras (eds), *Confidentiality, Transparency, and the US Civil Justice System* (Oxford University Press, 2012) 100.

IX. Anti-Protozoan Medications

A. Emaform, Entero-Form or Chinoform (clioquinol)

i. Description

Clioquinol (5-chloro-7-iodo-8-quinolinol) has anti-bacterial, anti-protozoan and anti-fungal properties, and works by preventing microbial growth. It is used as a topical preparation (3% cream or ointment or powder) for the treatment of bacterial and fungal skin infections and external ear infections.[566]

Historically, in the 1920s to 1970s, clioquinol was widely used as a gastrointestinal disinfectant, and it is still used in some cases for the treatment of certain protozoan gastro-intestinal infections.[567]

ii. Safety Issue

From the mid-1950s, patients began to appear with what became known as subacute myelo-optico neuropathy (SMON).[568] The first cases were sporadic, but by 1957 there were epidemics affecting a large number of people in various Japanese regions. In total approximately 11,000 people were affected with SMON. Initially it was thought that a contagious virus was responsible, and significant efforts were made to try to identify the virus that caused SMON. Many years later, in the 1970s, causation would be attributed to Clioquinol.

The initial symptoms of SMON were gastrointestinal symptoms, including severe abdominal pain and/or distention and constipation. Neurological symptoms followed, including numbness, tingling or a tight feeling, starting in the toes and spreading upwards to the thorax. Both superficial and deep sensation were impaired. Half of the patients suffered motility disturbances, with weakened lower limb muscles and ataxia (disturbances in balance, proprioception and coordination, leading to increased incidence of falls). Visual impairments were observed in 20–30% of patients, with blindness reported in 5%. Autonomic nervous system impairment was noted, with symptoms including cold feet, urinary disturbances (incontinence in severe cases) and bowel symptoms, including diarrhoea, constipation and alternating bouts of diarrhoea and constipation.

A green hairy tongue and greenish urine and stools were associated with SMON, and were key to discovering the link between SMON and Clioquinol.

More women than men were affected with SMON, with the ratio of male to female SMON patients being 1:3. Children were seldom affected – but when they were, they had higher levels of visual deficits and spastic paralysis.

The epidemic seen in Japan has not been repeated anywhere else in the world, where only occasional cases are seen. This is in part due to the dosing schedule and also the

[566] National Institute of Health Toxicology Data Network record for Cliquinol (NIH Toxnet), available at toxnet.nlm.nih.gov/.

[567] F van Hunsel et al, 'Clioquinol use for Dientamoeba fragilis infections is questionable' (2017) 161 *Nederlands tijdschrift voor geneeskunde* D1477 (in Dutch).

[568] Information taken from the Research Committee on SMON website, at www.hosp.go.jp/~suzukaww/smon/en/index.html.

prescribing tradition, which meant that individuals received far larger doses over a longer time period than would have happened elsewhere. The time taken to discover the causal nature of clioquinol was a major contributor to the numbers affected. Once the putative link between clioquinol and SMON was raised, the change in the status of clioquinol to prevent further use provided epidemiological confirmation.

Interestingly, orally administered clioquinol is potentially being repurposed as an anti-Alzheimer's Disease medication and as an anti-cancer therapeutic. Caution is being applied to the use of oral clioquinol, and SMON is now recognised as a possible side-effect, so care is being taken to balance the benefits of the medication and the potential risks associated with it.

iii. Marketing and Regulatory History

Clioquinol was developed as a bactericidal topical medicine in Switzerland in 1898. It was originally developed as a powder to disinfect wounds. It was reformulated into an oral intestinal disinfectant in the 1920s, and was thought to pass through the intestines without being absorbed. In 1935, following a case of suspected SMON in Argentina, the Swiss and Japanese Governments determined that Clioquinol was harmful. However, the advent of war and the need for disinfectants for troops led to a reversal of this determination and an increase in the production of clioquinol for use by the Japanese Army.

After World War II, several uses were added to the clioquinol label, and an increased dosage schedule was agreed as part of the reforms under the National Healthcare Act of 1958. The 1958 Act included provisions for a public health insurance system and came into force in 1961. This dosing schedule permitted far higher levels of drug ingestion than were recommended anywhere else in the world. Clioquinol was available both over the counter and on prescription, in almost 200 different formulations. The way in which drugs were prescribed in Japan is also likely to have contributed to the SMON epidemic. Under the 1958 Act, a prescription could only be issued for two weeks, after which a patient had to return and obtain a new prescription, even if this was a repeat prescription for the same medication. This applied to all conditions, including chronic conditions such as asthma and diabetes. Doctors were paid for each prescription, therefore the duration of the treatment, and cumulative dosage, directly correlates to the income the doctor received.

The first cases of SMON were considered to be caused by a virus: SMON had first been observed at a time when polio was rife in Japan, and presented with polio-like symptoms. In 1964 the Government formed a SMON commission to research the disease. The SMON Commission had a board that included eminent virologists. The presumption that SMON was caused by a virus was the primary focus for the majority of SMON researchers for many years. Considerable expertise and resources were put into efforts to identify and isolate the putative virus. Despite some seemingly promising leads, no substantive progress was made. In 1967 the SMON Commission dissolved, without having identified the cause of the epidemic. After further outbreaks, a new official investigating body was created by the Ministry of Health and Welfare in 1969, the SMON Research Committee. This was far better resourced and became the largest research program into a single disease in Japan. A highly respected virologist, Reisaku Kono, was appointed chair of the SMON Research Committee. However, evidence that SMON was not viral had begun to be recognised, and by 1970 the green tongue and then green urine of SMON patients was noted and analysed. This analysis led to the discovery that the greenish colour was a chelate form of clioquinol and ferric (III) iron. As the initial symptoms of SMON were gastrointestinal, it had been assumed that the clioquinol was given in response to SMON, rather than being causative. The findings of chelated clioquinol on the tongues of patients, and in their stools and urine, proved that clioquinol did not pass through intestines but could be absorbed. Epidemiological studies confirmed that SMON patients had taken clioquinol. This evidence was enough for the Japanese Government to suspend the use of clioquinol from September 1970.[569] Initially the suspension was temporary, but as the clioquinol ban started, new SMON cases did not arise. It seemed that the causative agent had been found, a result that was further confirmed by animal studies, and that SMON was not caused by a virus but by a pharmaceutical. Despite this, the debate on the causes of SMON was not finalised, with some researchers still claiming that they had isolated the virus that led to SMON after the ban.

The SMON epidemic led to regulatory changes. On 7 September 1979 the Diet passed two laws: the Law to Establish a Relief Fund for the Side-effect Damage due to Pharmaceutical Products, and the Law for the Partial Revision of the Drugs, Cosmetics and Medical Instruments Act. These Acts set in place the current pharmaceutical damage scheme[570] run by the Pharmaceutical and Medicines Devices Agency (PMDA), and allowed the Government to underwrite the debts a pharmaceutical company accrues when paying compensation for ADRs.

iv. Litigation

The first action was listed in the Tokyo District Court in May 1971, against the Japanese Government, and listing three other defendants, Ciba-Geigy, Tanabé and Takeda,[571] with multiple actions in other regions. According to Shigeto Tsuru, a total of almost 6,000 plaintiffs launched over 30 law suits.[572] Causation was contested for many years. In 1976 the defendants decided to offer an out-of-court settlement. This included three key points;

(a) an admission of a causal relationship between clioquinol and SMON in Japan;
(b) an agreement to take responsibility for the social implications of the SMON disaster in Japan; and
(c) an agreement to pay compensation to the SMON victims.

There was hesitation about accepting this out-of-court settlement from both the plaintiffs and the Japanese Government, but the presiding District Court Judge, Judge Tsuneo Kabé, recommended its acceptance in September 1976. Despite this, in late October 1976 Tanabé reneged on this offer, denied any causal link between clioquinol and SMON, claimed that

[569] For reviews in English, see A Igata, 'Subacute myelo-optic neuropathy, beriberi, and HTLV-I-associated myelopathy: elucidation of some neurological diseases in Japan' (2012) 122(Suppl 1) *Polskie Archiwum Medycyny Wewnetrznej* 32; and K Sonoda, 'SMON and other socially induced diseases in Japan' (1978) 2A *Social Science & Medicine* 497.

[570] Summarised in Macleod and Hodges, n 261.

[571] *SMON patients v The State; Ciba-Geigy (Japan) Limited; Takeda Chemical Industries, Ltd; Tanabe Seiyaku Co Ltd, et al* (1978). This case was filed in May 1971, but a formal Decision of the Tokyo District Court was not reached until 3 August 1978. English edition, Kicadis, Tokyo.

[572] S Tsuru, *The Political Economy of the Environment: The Case of Japan* (Bloomsbury, 2012).

the disaster could not have been foreseen and tried to call new expert witnesses for the defence. District Judge Kabé continued with his efforts to secure an 'amicable' settlement' between the plaintiffs and Ciba-Geigy and Takeda. Tanabé would not accept an amicable settlement, and eventually the proceedings were completed in the Tokyo District Court on 3 August 1978, with Judge Kabé finding for the plantiffs. His judgment was categorical: clioquinol caused SMON and the dangers could have been foreseen from 1955 onwards. The judge ordered compensation be set aside for the plaintiffs and for an apology to be issued to them. An apology was subsequently issued by Ciba-Geigy.

Numerous cases in other areas[573] also found for the plaintiffs, and Tanabé agreed to accept an amicable settlement in May 1979. A document detailing compensation quantum was agreed by the parties and signed on 15 September 1979. This served as the template for all pending court settlements. The last case to settle was the Hiroshima District litigation, which ended with a victory for the plaintiffs in 1987.

The litigation over Clioquinol and SMON had lasted 16 years. The final result was a combination of an agreed amicable settlement and litigation victories for the plaintiffs.

v. Conclusion

Pressure was bought by the SMON patients group to ensure that litigation provided compensation and that there were regulatory changes to ensure that further adverse drug events would be compensated without the need for litigation.

[573] Including District Court Decisions in Kanazawa (1 March 1978), Fukuoka (14 November 1978), Hiroshima (22 February 1979) and Sapporo (10 May 1979).

B. Lariam (mefloquine)

i. Description

Lariam is an orally administered 4-quinolinemethanol synthetic quinoline that has been used in the prevention and treatment of malaria, including chloroquine resistant *P. falciparum* malaria. Mefloquine occurs as a racemix of (+) and (−) enantioners.

ii. Safety Issue

Large observational studies from 1993 suggest that severe neuropsychiatric reactions to prophylactic doses of mefloquine occur at a frequency of about 1 in 10,000 to 20,000 patients.[574] These neuropsychiatric effects can be severe and protracted, but it is not confirmed if this is a causal relationship.[575] Observed effects include depression and suicidal ideation, anxiety, panic, confusion, hallucinations, paranoid delusions and convulsions. Minor effects include dizziness, headache, insomnia and vivid dreams.[576]

As with other chiral molecules, most (in)famously thalidomide, only one of the isomers is implicated in the neuropsychiatric adverse drug events. It is thought that the (+) isomer provides the anti-malarial benefits, while the (-) isomer causes the negative side-effects by binding to adenosine receptors in the brain.[577] Superficially, it would appear that efficient cost-effective manufacturing of just the (+) isomer could potentially resolve these issues.[578] However, clinical trials comparing (+) mefloquine and the racemix indicate that (+) mefloquine is not superior.[579]

iii. Marketing and Regulatory History

Substantial numbers of US combat troops contracted malaria during the Vietnam War, which prompted the US Army to search for new anti-malarial drugs. From the early 1960s the Walter Reed Army Institute of Research (WRAIR) developed and screened over a quarter of a million potential anti-malarial pharmaceuticals. Mefloquine[580] was one of the

[574] R Steffen et al 'Mefloquine compared with other malaria chemoprophylactic regimens in tourists visiting east Africa' (1993) 341(8856) *The Lancet* 1299, doi.org/10.1016/0140-6736(93)90814-W; GA Luzzi and TEA Peto, 'Adverse Effects of Antimalarials: An Update' (1993) 8(4) *Drug Safety* 295.

[575] P Schlagenhauf et al, 'The position of mefloquine as a 21st century malaria chemoprophylaxis' (2010) 9 *Malaria Journal* 357.

[576] HO Alkadi, 'Antimalarial drug toxicity: a review' (2007) 53(6) *Chemotherapy* 385.

[577] M Schmidt et al, 'Determining the Absolute Configuration of (+)-Mefloquine HCl, the Side-Effect-Reducing Enantiomer of the Antimalaria Drug Lariam' (2012) 134(6) *Journal of the American Chemical Society* 3080, doi:10.1021/ja209050k.

[578] WRAIR has focused some attention on producing solely the (+) isomer: for a review of chirality and the importance of the different isomers, see SW Smith, 'Chiral Toxicology: It's the Same Thing … Only Different' (2009) 110(1) *Toxicological Sciences* 4, doi.org/10.1093/toxsci/kfp097.

[579] R Tansley et al, 'A randomized, double-blind, placebo-controlled study to investigate the safety, tolerability, and pharmacokinetics of single enantiomer (+)-mefloquine compared with racemic mefloquine in healthy persons' (2010) 83(6) *American Journal of Tropical Medicine and Hygiene* 1195, doi:10.4269/ajtmh.2010.10-0228.

[580] Originally known as compound WR 142 490.

anti-malarial compounds screened during the study and was developed shortly after the end of the war.[581] However, the US military was, and still is, forbidden by Congress from operating in the commercial sector. To avoid this, the marketing of mefloquine was the first Public Private Venture (PPV) between the US Department of Defense and a pharmaceutical company. The exact nature of the agreement is not public, but it has been reported that WRAIR transferred all of its phase I and phase II clinical trial data to Hoffman-La Roche and Smith Kline.

Mefloquine was approved by the FDA for prophylactic use on 2 May 1989.[582] This approval did not draw on any phase III safety and tolerability trials on healthy volunteer travellers, and has been deemed inadequate.[583] Because of the drug's very long half-life, the CDC initially recommended a mefloquine dosage of 250mg every two weeks. However, Peace Corps volunteers on this dose developed malaria at an unacceptably high rate, so the drug regimen was switched to 250mg weekly.[584]

Approval was granted in the UK on 5 October 1989.

Although the majority of early adverse event reports for mefloquine were related to gastrointestinal symptoms,[585] there were reports from 1989 onwards of neurological and psychiatric adverse events.[586] This prompted a *Review of central nervous system adverse events related to the antimalarial drug Mefloquine (1985–1990)*,[587] jointly undertaken by the World Health Organization and Hoffman-La Roche. The Review was published in 1991 and notes that a meeting with the CDC had been held in May 1991 to identify future research issues regarding mefloquine and that further monitoring was needed. Hoffman-La Roche published a retrospective analysis of spontaneous reports of psychiatric adverse events in 1991.[588] When combined with other available data it was estimated that the risk of serious neuropsychiatric adverse effects during prophylaxis was 1 in 10,600 for mefloquine, compared to 1 in 13,600 for chloroquine.

During the early 1990s in the UK, public awareness of the neuropsychiatric side effects of mefloquine increased: in particular, a BBC 'Watchdog' programme, shown on 6 November 1995, highlighted the issue on adverse events and led to declining sales of Lariam to travellers.[589]

[581] AM Croft, 'A lesson learnt: the rise and fall of Lariam and Halfan' (2007) 4(4) *Journal of the Royal Society of Medicine* 170.

[582] New Drug Approval 019591, granted on 2 May 1989.

[583] AM Croft, 'Developing safe antimalaria drugs: Key lessons from mefloquine and halofantrine' (2007) 19(3) *International Journal of Risk and Safety in Medicine* 153; Croft, n 582.

[584] P Schlagenhauf, 'Mefloquine for malaria chemoprophylaxis 1992–1998' (1999) 6(2) *Journal of Travel Medicine* 122.

[585] AM Rønn et al,; Neuropsychiatric manifestations after mefloquine therapy for Plasmodium falciparum malaria: comparing a retrospective and a prospective study' (1998) 3(2) *Tropical Medicine & International Health* 83.

[586] J Bernard et al, 'Encephalopathie toxique à la méfloquine'(1987) 16 *Presse Médicale* 1654; PC Stuiver, RJ Ligthelm and ThJLM Goud, 'Acute Psychosis after Mefloquine' (1989) 334(8657) *The Lancet* 282, doi.org/10.1016/S0140-6736(89)90474-1; B Rouveix et al, 'Mefloquine and an Accute Brain Syndrome' (1989) 110(7) *Annals of Internal Medicine* 577, doi: 10.7326/0003-4819-110-7-577.

[587] World Health Organization, Malaria Control Unit, *Review of central nervous system adverse events related to the antimalarial drug, Mefloquine (1985–1990)* (World Health Organization, 1991), available at www.who.int/iris/handle/10665/61327.

[588] JL Bern, L Kerr and D Stuerchler, 'Mefloquine prophylaxix: an overview of spontaneous reports of severe psychiatric reactions and convulsions' (1992) 95 *Journal of Tropical Medicine & Hygiene* 167.

[589] S Clift and P Grabowski, 'Malaria prophylaxis and the media' (1996) 348(9023) *The Lancet* 344, doi.org/10.1016/S0140-6736(05)64522-9.

In 1996, the MHRA produced a *Current Problems* article describing the frequency of neuropsychiatric reactions.[590] Despite this risk, the CSM maintained that risks associated with prophylactic anti-malarials were far outweighed by their benefit of protection against malaria. Mefloquine was described as effective against all forms of malaria, including *P. falciparum*, which is resistant to other anti-malarials.[591] The publication offered guidelines to protect against the adverse events associated with premature discontinuation of the anti-malarial prophylaxis.

A 1997 review[592] of studies on mefloquine toxicity was critical of the way mefloquine was originally licensed without representative field trials, noted the controversy over mefloquine in the UK, Canada and the Netherlands, and concluded:

> [B]ased on the best evidence to date … the usefulness of mefloquine in prophylaxis is limited to fit, highly motivated occupational subgroups or individual travellers at high risk of infection with chloroquine resistant *Plasmodium falciparum*. Even for these travellers, mefloquine should be prescribed only when the travel destination is one where reliable diagnostic and treatment facilities are not readily available.

In 2001 the first field study on travellers[593] confirmed higher neuropsychiatric adverse events with mefloquine that with atovaquone-profuanil. Further studies[594] have verified mefloquine's neurotoxicity and the significant potential for neuropsychiatric side-effects.

In July 2003, the FDA required further labelling on Lariam and that dispensing pharmacists included a medication guide, detailing potential side-effects, along with the medication.[595]

A 2004 study[596] said that mefloquine produces psychosis in 1 out of 10,000 people who take it; although it is twice as high as the rates in patients taking proguanil and/or chloroquine, or doxycycline, the difference between the drugs is not statistically significant. A 2006 study[597] out of WRAIR suggested that the drug could lead to permanent damage to the central nervous system in rats, providing a biological basis for some of the clinical neurological effects associated with mefloquine.

On 2 February 2009, the US military dropped mefloquine as its primary anti-malarial and replaced it with doxycycline, a generic antibiotic. Army Surgeon Lt Gen Eric

[590] MHRA/CSM, 'Mefloquine (Lariam) and neuropsychiatric reactions' (1996) 22 *Current Problems in Pharmacovigilance* 6.

[591] KJ Palmer et al, 'Mefloquine. A review of its antimalarial activity, pharmacokinetic properties and therapeutic efficacy' (1993) 45(3) *Drugs* 430.

[592] A Croft and P Garner, 'Mefloquine to prevent malaria: a systematic review of trials' (1997) 315 *British Medical Journal* 1412.

[593] D Overbosch et al, 'Atovaquone-proguanil versus mefloquine for malaria prophylaxis in nonimmune travelers: results from a randomized double-blind study' (2001) 33 *Clinical Infectious Diseases* 1015.

[594] I Potasman et al, 'Does mefloquine prophylaxis affect electroencephalographic patterns?' (2002) 112 *American Journal of Medicine* 147; P Schlagenhauf et al, 'Tolerability of malaria chemoprophylaxis in non-immune travellers to sub-Saharan Africa: multicentre, randomised, double blind, four arm study' (2003) 327 *British Medical Journal* 1078.

[595] NDA 19-591/S-019, available at www.accessdata.fda.gov/drugsatfda_docs/appletter/2003/19591slr019ltr.pdf.

[596] CR Meier, K Wilcock and SS Jick, 'The risk of severe depression, psychosis or panic attacks with prophylactic antimalarials' (2004) 27 *Drug Safety* 203.

[597] G Dow et al, 'Mefloquine Induces Dose-Related Neurological Effects in a Rat Model' (2006) 50(3) *Antimicrobial Agents and Chemotherapy* 1045, doi:10.1128/AAC.50.3.1045-1053.2006.

Schoomaker said, 'In areas where doxycycline and mefloquine are equally efficacious in preventing malaria, doxycycline is the drug of choice.'[598]

In August 2009, Hoffman-La Roche stopped marketing Lariam in the US, but Lariam is still licensed in the UK, with guidelines on the prevention of malaria in UK travellers,[599] detailed advice on the risks of malaria for different destinations, and the risks of adverse reactions from the available anti-malarials.

In 2013 the FDA put a black-box warning on the label and issued a safety alert for mefloquine.[600] Following the black-box warning the US Army strengthened its position, stating that mefloquine should only be used as a drug of last resort.[601]

The British Army continued to use mefloquine routinely until 2016, despite considerable public pressure for it to stop.

iv. Litigation

a. Civilian Litigation

The touch paper was lit for litigation in England and Wales in 1995, by a BBC TV 'Watchdog' programme.[602] After this aired, almost 1,000 potential litigants contacted Lawrence Tucketts, Solicitors, of Bristol, stating they felt they had a claim for lariam-induced damage. The Legal Aid Board awarded Lawrence Tucketts the contract to investigate the strength of the case.[603] The majority of the cases fell away, due to evidential inadequacies, but almost 200 remained, and legal aid was awarded in 70 of them. Writs were issued, but in 1998 legal aid was withdrawn on the basis that the prospects of success were slim.[604] The claimants' own barrister acknowledged that to succeed, they would have had to prove that the side-effects were more severe than those claimed by Hoffman-La Roche, to have demonstrated that Hoffman-La Roche had not revealed information it had about the drug's safety and, crucially, that patients would not have taken the drug had they known the risk of side-effects.

In the US a handful of cases were launched against Hoffman-La Roche for failure to warn. The majority were successfully defended, with a small number settled out of court. There were attempts to gather together class actions in the US and in Canada, but these attempts stalled.

b. Military Claims

In the UK, a further tranche of lariam litigation was initiated from 2016 onwards following the claims by MPs on the Defence Select Committee that the drug was used outside the

[598] US Army Office of the Surgeon General. *Memorandum. Subject: Updated Guidance on the Use of Mefloquine for Malaria Prophylaxis* (US Army Office of the Surgeon General, 2009).

[599] DJ Bradley and DC Warhuist 'Guidelines for the prevention of malaria in travellers from the United Kingdom' (1997) 7(10) Communicable Disease Report R137.

[600] See at www.fda.gov/drugs/drugsafety/ucm362227.htm.

[601] See at archive.defense.gov/news/newsarticle.aspx?id=120857.

[602] Shown on 6 November 1995.

[603] C Dyer, 'Legal Aid won for malaria drug case' (1996) 313 *British Medical Journal* 643.

[604] Lynn Eaton, 'Consumer report: Larium' *Telegraph* (30 October 1999).

manufacturer's guidelines, namely that prescribers did not have 'face to face' consultations with recipients.[605] This litigation differs substantially from the first tranche in that it has not been directed against manufacturers but against the Ministry of Defence for breach of duty of care. This litigation is still live, with various UK firms seeking to recruit claimants[606] and with the first settlement having been reached.[607]

In the US, veterans are able to claim compensation for mefloquine injuries from the Department for Veterans Affairs.[608]

v. Conclusion

Regulators in the UK determined that the risks associated with mefloquine were outweighed by the benefits of its effectiveness in the prevention of malaria. Warnings about the risks associated with the drug reflected study data and were deemed adequate by the Legal Aid Commission, and so funding for claims was withdrawn. Strict guidelines exist in the UK for drug dosing, but in the US the drug was dropped as the military's primary anti-malarial.

[605] Defence Committee, Oral evidence: An acceptable risk? Use of Lariam for military personnel, HC 567 (12 January 2016), available at data.parliament.uk/writtenevidence/committeeevidence.svc/evidencedocument/defence-committee/an-acceptable-risk-the-use-of-lariam-for-military-personnel/oral/26789.html.

[606] See at hmsolicitors.co.uk/military-accidents/lariam-anti-malaria-drug-compensation-claim/; www.irwinmitchell.com/personal/personal-injury-compensation/military-injury-claims/lariam-mefloquine-compensation-claims; www.groupactionlawyers.co.uk/lariam-compensation-claims-british-soldiers.

[607] Mark Hookham, 'MoD cash for soldier hit by malaria drug siezures' *Sunday Times* (14 January 2018).

[608] See at http://www.publichealth.va.gov/exposures/mefloquine-lariam.asp.

X. Breast and Other Cosmetic Implants

A. Dow-Corning Silicone Implants

i. Description

Dow Corning began to manufacture and market silicone breast implants in 1964.[609] Until 1992, Dow Corning silicone implants were sold in the US for both augmentation and reconstruction. In 1992 the FDA put in place a moratorium on the use of silicone breast implants for augmentation within the US. After 1992, Dow Corning silicone implants were available for reconstruction in the US, but could be used for augmentation in other countries in accordance with national laws. Although around half of Dow Corning's breast implant sales occurred outside the US,[610] this study will focus on the US, as this is where the major litigation took place and where the settlement fund was established. The settlement fund provided was open to US residents and others from specified countries outside the US.

In addition to producing silicone-filled silicone breast implants, Dow Corning also produced a number of other implant types, including: chin; small joint; testicular and penile; large hip joint; large knee joint; and different forms of temporomandibular joints (TMJs). The regulatory and litigation history of these joints will not be covered, as the number of implants is relatively small compared to the breast implants. The recipients of these implants were also eligible for awards from the settlement fund.

ii. Safety Issue

From the mid- to late 1970s, silicone breast implant safety began to be questioned. The safety issues raised tended to be localised in the breast area, concerning ruptures, capsular contractions, infections and scarring, etc.

During the 1990s the potential for silicone breast implants to cause systemic symptoms was being widely reported in the media; in particular, a 1990 TV programme, 'Face to Face with Connie Chung',[611] led to a rapid increase in concern and litigation. There have been claims of an association and/or causal relationship between silicone implants and systemic body diseases such as scleroderma, systemic lupus, erythymatosis and other symptoms, including chronic fatigue, joint pain and muscle pain. This is despite a lack of evidence of a causal association. And the current consensus of opinion does not support a causal link between connective tissue disorders and silicone breast implants.[612]

[609] *In Re Dow Corning Corp*, 211 BR 550 (Bankr ED Mich 1997).

[610] *In Re Silicone Gel Breast Implant Product Liability Litigation*, MDL, no 926, Case no CV 92-P-10000-S.

[611] CBS, originally shown on 10 December 1990.

[612] See at http://www.fda.gov/downloads/MedicalDevices/ProductsandMedicalProcedures/ImplantsandProsthetics/BreastImplants/UCM260090.pdf.

iii. Marketing and Regulatory History

In 1976 the powers of the FDA were extended to include reviewing and approving the safety and effectiveness of medical devices.[613] At this point in time, with over a decade of marketing behind them, silicone breast implants were classified as class II devices, which entailed a moderate risk. Implants that were already on the market (including Dow Corning's silicone implants) were 'grandfathered in'. Any new-to-the-market implants went through the pre-market notification or 501(k) process.[614]

In 1988 silicone breast implants were reclassified as class III devices. Thereafter, all new-to-market implants had to undergo pre-market approval (PMA). The FDA did not require PMA for implants that were already on the market[615] until April 1991, from which point the FDA required a PMA application for all silicone breast implants. In the PMA application manufacturers had to demonstrate that their implants were safe and effective.

The requirements for proof-of-safety information in the PMA proved difficult for various manufacturers, including Dow Corning. The FDA's General and Plastic Surgery Devices Panel made two key recommendations in November 1991:

(a) it determined that there was insufficient information in the PMA to find that Dow Corning's silicone implants were safe;
(b) the Panel's members unanimously advised the FDA not to take silicone implants off the market while the manufacturers collected further data, as implants fulfilled a public health need.

Despite the Panel's advice to leave the devices on the market, a voluntary 45-day moratorium on the use of silicone implants was implemented starting on 6 January 1992. Dow Corning left the breast implant market early in January 1992 when the voluntary moratorium commenced; the following information is general background.[616]

On 20 February 1992, a second Panel meeting recommended restrictions on the marketing of silicone implants until the data required in the PMA had been supplied, but did not seek their total removal from the market on public health grounds.

On 16 April 1992, the FDA ruled that silicone implants would only be available

> under controlled clinical studies for reconstruction after mastectomy, correction of congenital deformities, or replacement for ruptured silicone-gel filled implants for augmentation; silicone breast implants would no longer be available for augmentation patients.

This was in effect a total ban on all silicone implants, not just Dow Corning's. At this point the only silicone implants on the US market were those that had been 'grandfathered in', and the FDA determined that none of the silicone implant PMAs submitted for these implants contained sufficient information for them to be approved. The moratorium on silicone breast implants for augmentation was reversed in 2006.

[613] Congress amended the federal Food, Drug and Cosmetic Act.

[614] For a more detailed timeline, see US FDA, 'Regulatory History of Breast Implants in the US', at www.fda.gov/MedicalDevices/ProductsandMedicalProcedures/ImplantsandProsthetics/BreastImplants/ucm064461.htm.

[615] Implants that were on the market before the reclassification were reviewed under the 501(k) process between the reclassification and April 1991.

[616] For a detailed timeline, see O Mascarenhas, *Responsible Marketing: Concepts, Theories, Models, Strategies and Cases* (Roval Publishing, 2007) ch 11, 'Dow Corning Corporation's Silicone Gel-Filled Breast Implants: An Ethical Analysis'.

iv. Litigation

In 1977, the first known successful case resulted in a jury awarding the claimant $170,000 for the rupture of one of her implants, which award was upheld on appeal.[617] Between this case and 1989 there were only a handful of trials, and Dow Corning only lost a single case, that of Maria Stern in 1984, who was awarded $211,000 in compensatory damages and $1.5 million in punitive damages.[618]

In the 1990s, litigation case numbers and their complexity soared, as did the value of the compensation sought. Claims were made for systemic diseases such as scleroderma, systemic lupus, erythymatosis and other symptoms, including chronic fatigue, joint pain and muscle pain. Causation was usually the core issue in these cases, which were characterised by complex, often conflicting, expert testimony. Claimants usually opted for trial by jury in these cases, with some States perceived as being more sympathetic. Juries made several multimillion dollar awards: in 1991, $7.34 million was awarded to a claimant;[619] awards tended towards an upward trajectory, and in 1992, $25 million was awarded against Bristol-Myers Squibb.[620]

In 1992, an MDL suit was filed against Dow Corning in Cincinnati, Ohio.[621] The MDL included both US and foreign claimants, and by the end of it over 400,000 claims had been filed. The potential scale and defence cost of the litigation were enormous. On 1 September 1994, the MDL was settled,[622] and the Dow Corning Settlement Trust (DCST) was created. At the time of creation of the DCST, the liabilities due to the entire settlement were assessed at $4,225,070,000.[623] However, due to increasing liabilities, on 15 May 1995 Dow Corning voluntarily filed for Chapter 11 bankruptcy protection, as it was unable to meet the liabilities arising from the DCST.[624] The bankruptcy halted all litigation against Dow Corning, and gave the company protection from further law suits.

In 1998 Dow Corning filed for bankruptcy reorganisation. The Amended Joint Plan of Reorganisation[625] (the Plan) was confirmed by the Bankruptcy Court on 30 November 1999. The Plan was delayed by the considerable number of appeals and other litigation; it finally took effect on 1 June 2004.[626] Under the Plan claimants could either accept the settlement, or opt out of it and pursue litigation.[627]

[617] *V Mueller & Co v Corley*, 570 SW2d 140 (1978) Court of Civil Appeals of Texas, Houston (1st Dist) 27 July 1978.

[618] The only successful claim against Dow Corning between 1977 and 1989 was that of Maria Stern in 1984, who was awarded $211,000 in compensatory damages and $1.5 million in punitive damages: *Stern v Dow-Corning Corp*, no C83-2348 MHP (MD Cal 15 November 1984).

[619] *Hopkins v Dow-Corning Corp*, no 92-16132, 1992 WL 176560.

[620] *Johnson v Bristol-Myers Squibb Corp et al*, CN 91-21770 (TX Dist Ct, 125 Jud Dist 1992).

[621] *MDL 926 Breast Implant Litigation*.

[622] See the Settlement Notice and Orders 15–20 of *In re Silicone Gel Breast Implant Products Liability Litigation*, MDL 926, Civil Action no CV 94-P-11558-S, available at www.tortcomm.org/mdl_orders/1994-09-01%20OPINION%20GLOBAL%20SETTLEMENT%20CORRECTED.pdf.

[623] Thought had clearly been given to the ability of Dow Corning and others to meet their liabilities arising from the DCST. See fn 2 of Opinion (Corrected) (Approval of Settlement) from *In re Silicone Gel Breast Implant*, ibid.

[624] Filed at the Eastern District of Michigan, Case no 95-20512; further information available at www.mied.uscourts.gov/ under 'Cases of Interest'.

[625] Available at www.sfdct.com/_sfdct/resources/Final%20Plan1.pdf.

[626] Available at www.sfdct.com/_sfdct/resources/Final%20SFA1.pdf.

[627] For a more detailed description of the DCST and the Plan, see Macleod and Hodges, n 261, ch 30.

Various other types of silicone implants were produced by Dow Corning; recipients of these devices were also covered by the DCST as class 9 claimants.

v. Conclusion

The safety issues around systemic disorders caused by silicone implants are disputed, highlighting the difficulty when experts provide differing testimony. Regulators maintain that there is a lack of sufficient evidence to prove a causal link between silicone implants and connective tissue diseases. However, this did not prevent successful litigation on these grounds. The scale of the litigation was such that Dow Corning filed for Chapter 11 bankruptcy and subsequent bankruptcy reorganisation. The DCST has provided financial awards for claimants, without requiring them to prove that their silicone implants caused their disease/symptoms.

B. Trilucent Breast Implants

i. Description

Trilucent breast implants were round implants with a textured silicone shell, filled with a triglyceride filling (Trilipid Z^{6} ™), available in volumes of 120cc to 510cc. They were marketed between 1995 and 1999.

Lipomatrix Inc developed Trilucent implants, and marketing in Europe started in 1995. The triglyceride filler was an alternative to silicone-filled implants; it was derived from soya bean oil and was perceived as more natural, both in implant texture and in having a plant-derived filling. The intention was to produce a radiolucent breast implant that enabled better detection of early cancers in women who had had breast implants.

ii. Safety Issue

Early indications showed an increased rate of capsular contractions with these implants. Capsular contraction consists of a tight capsule of scar tissue around the implant, which can result in hard and/or misshapen breasts. All breast implants carry a risk of capsular contraction. Initially there was uncertainty as to whether the capsular contraction was intrinsic to the implant or was associated with the transaxillary implantation technique, which was often used to minimise scarring.

Subsequent analysis of the shells by the Rubber and Plastics Research Association (RAPRA) and the oil filler by the Department of Chemistry, London University, indicated that the filler was genotoxic. The oxidation of the filling material and the way this interacted with the shell were found to be the causes of the adverse events.[628]

iii. Marketing and Regulatory History

Clinical testing began in Europe in 1993; in the US the FDA approved a clinical trial of Trilucent implants that commenced in December 1994.

The European approach to breast implants was governed by the Medical Devices Directive 92/42/EEC. In 1994, implantable breast implants were classified as class IIb devices. As such, Lipomatrix had responsibility for assessing and declaring the conformity of Trilucent breast implants with the Directive. As part of this conformity assessment, Lipomatrix had to commission a notified body for medical devices to certify its quality assurance system; the notified body used was TüV Munich. In 1994 Trilucent implants were CE marked, and marketing began in the EU in 1995. By 1997 Trilucent implants held 7% of the EU market share of breast implants. Sales predominantly occurred in nine countries, with relatively high volumes of sales in the UK and Germany, and smaller sales volumes in Spain, Portugal, Switzerland, Benelux, Scandinavia and Italy.[629] It is thought that

[628] For more detailed analysis, see WN Kirkpatrick and BM Jones, 'The History of Trilucent Implants, and a Chemical Analysis of the Triglyceride Filler in 51 Consecutively Removed Trilucent Breast Prostheses' (2002) 55 *British Journal of Plastic Surgery* 479; and S Monstrey et al, 'What Exactly Was Wrong with the Trilucent Breast Implants? A Unifying Hypothesis' (2004) 113 *Plastic and Reconstructive Surgery* 847.

[629] 'Trilucent Breast Implants', *Sales Training Manual* (LipoMatrix Inc).

around 9,000 women were implanted with Trilucent implants, with approximately half of all Trilucent breast implants carried out in the UK. Consequently, this case study will focus on the UK.

Due to their low relatively low opacity, enabling clearer imaging of the breast, Trilucent implants were marketed as safer than other available breast implants. Trilucent implants contained a passive transponder, providing a unique Vigilance Identification Device System^{TM}. Each implant had an individual alphanumeric code, which could be read by a handheld reader that activated the transponder. This individual alphanumeric code provided total traceability for that implant. This system also had the advantage that a woman could be certain whether or not her implant was a Trilucent implant, without the need for surgical inspection, even if her medical records had been lost.

In March 1999, in response to adverse event reports indicating high capsular contraction rates, the Medical Devices Agency (MDA) requested a voluntary withdrawal of Trilucent implants from the market in the UK[630] in order to investigate.

Further testing revealed that the adverse events were being caused by oxidation of the filling material and the way this interacted with the shell. On 6 June 2000, once the test results were known, the MDA issued a Hazard Notice, which recommended removal of Trilucent implants.[631] The Hazard Notice also recommended that women should not become pregnant or breastfeed while Trilucent implants were still place.

In response to the Hazard Notice, an expert panel was convened, and AIE Inc sponsored a multi-centre study on Trilucent safety. The study concluded that there was no evidence of local or systemic disease risk once the implants has been explanted.[632]

A final alert was issued by the MDA in December 2004, to notify women of the study findings and of the closure of the Trilucent Care Centre.[633]

iv. Litigation

In England and Wales, in the time period between the voluntary withdrawal and the issuing of the Hazard Notice, court proceedings were issued by several women who had had Trilucent implants removed after complications occurred.[634]

Concurrent with the Hazard Notice,[635] an announcement was made that AEI Inc[636] would bear the cost of removal and replacement of Trilucent implants from this point

[630] Available at webarchive.nationalarchives.gov.uk/20141206071200/http://www.mhra.gov.uk/Safetyinformation/Safetywarningsalertsandrecalls/MedicalDeviceAlerts/Advicenotices/CON2025118.

[631] Available at webarchive.nationalarchives.gov.uk/20141206070832/http://www.mhra.gov.uk/Safetyinformation/Safetywarningsalertsandrecalls/MedicalDeviceAlerts/Hazardnotices/CON008727.

[632] GM Williams et al, 'Multicenter study to assess potential hazards from exposure to lipid peroxidation products in soya bean oil from Trilucent™ breast implants' (2009) 53(2) *Regulatory Toxicology and Pharmacology* 107, doi.org/10.1016/j.yrtph.2008.10.009.

[633] MDA/2004/047, available at www.gov.uk/drug-device-alerts/medical-device-alert-trilucent-soya-bean-oil-filled-breast-implants-update-on-actions-from-previous-risks.

[634] Personal communication, Paul Balen, consultant at Freeths LLP (www.freeths.co.uk), who represented many of the claimants.

[635] Negotiations had previously been undertaken with Paul Balen, ibid.

[636] In January 1996, Collagen Corporation purchased LipoMatrix Inc. In November 1998, LipoMatrix Inc was sold to Sierra Medical Technologies Inc. Collagen Corporation became Collagen Aesthetics (with a subsidiary AEI Inc), and in November 1999 Collagen was purchased by Inamed. Allergan acquired Inamed in 2006.

forward. The Trilucent Care Centre was established to care for patients with these implants, including a two-tier compensation scheme.[637] Although some cases were started in the courts, no trials were litigated in England and Wales.

v. Conclusion

The safety signal was detected due to adverse event reporting to the regulators. The launch of the Trilucent Care Centre meant that while proceedings were commenced, not one case proceeded to judgment in the UK. Litigation played no part in the detection of the safety signal, the ensuing regulatory action or in compensating affected individuals.

See US Securities and Exchange Commission, Washington, DC, Inamed Corporation (IRS Employer Identification No 59-0920629) Form 10-K Annual Report pursuant to s 13 or 15(d) of the Securities Exchange Act of 1934 for the fiscal year ended 31 December 2001, available at www.sec.gov/Archives/edgar/data/109831/000091205702012689/a2073866z10-k.htm.

[637] For a more detailed description of the Trilucent Care Scheme and the compensation available, see Macleod and Hodges, n 261, ch 31.

C. Poly Implant Prothese (PIP) Hydrogel Breast Implants

i. Description

Hydrogel breast implants consist of a silicone elastomer shell filled with a hydrogel filler. Hydrogels are polymeric molecules containing hydrophilic structures that are able to hold water within their three-dimensional networks without dissolving. There are many different types of hydrogel. The Poly Implant Prothese (PIP) breast implants should have contained 92% of physiological saline gelled with 8% of a polysaccharide hydroxypropyl cellulose. In later models the physiological saline was replaced with a buffer solution.

The women opting for these products often perceived them to be a safer option than silicone breast implants, which had been associated with a number of health scares.

ii. Safety Issue

These products were voluntarily withdrawn from the market in December 2000.[638] Prior to the withdrawal, a single adverse event – a report of filler leak – had been reported for PIP hydrogel breast implants. However, a review of all of the breast implant fillers available in the UK by the MDA in 2000 concluded that the manufacturer's biological safety assessment of the implants was inadequate. The Committee on Toxicity[639] (COT) considered that the available data[640] were deficient and that some of the changes seen were of concern.

The following issues were raised:

- there were insufficient long-term toxicity data;
- there was insufficient long-term clinical follow up;
- there were methodological flaws in some of the pre-clinical tests.

Specific concerns were:

- uncertainty over the metabolic fate of the hydrogel filler; and
- implantation of the filing material into rats resulted in pathological changes that suggested a systemic effect. No long-term toxicity data existed to allow an assessment of the significance or reversibility of these effects.

In September 2000 a COT Statement was issued. It concluded that there was no direct evidence that the product was unsafe; rather, there was a lack of evidence to demonstrate that it was safe and further testing was required.[641]

[638] DA 2000/07 – Breast Implants: PIP Hydrogel, available at webarchive.nationalarchives.gov.uk/20080609170156/http://www.mhra.gov.uk/Publications/Safetywarnings/MedicalDeviceAlerts/Devicealerts/CON008915.

[639] The Committee on Toxicity of Chemicals in Food, Consumer Products and the Environment (COT) is an independent scientific committee that provides advice to the Department of Health and other government departments and agencies on matters concerning the toxicity of chemicals.

[640] A short-term study had been used, ie FC Picard and M Therin, 'Subacute toxicity in the rat on a gel (Hydrogel AQT 10-15) used in the filling of mammary prosthesis', unpublished study no 121E4041 carried out by BIOMATECH, Chasse sur Rhone, France (1996). Submitted to the Medical Devices Agency by Poly Implant Prosthesis, ZAC les Playes Jean Monnet, 83500 La Seyne sur Mer, France.

[641] COT Statement COT/00/09 (September 2000), available at webarchive.nationalarchives.gov.uk/20080609152125/http://www.advisorybodies.doh.gov.uk/cotnonfood/pip2000.htm.

Further testing was carried out, and a COT Statement of 2002[642] reached similar conclusions to the 2000 Statement, that is that there was no direct evidence that the product was harmful but that testing was insufficient to determine that it was safe. A two-year study was undertaken, and in 2006 a third COT Statement was issued,[643] which was more reassuring that the previous two as the liver, kidney and lymph node issues seen in previous studies did not occur in the properly designed studies, so could be discounted as indicative of a toxic effect. A marginal effect on the kidneys was still seen in the more extensive studies. Overall, the conclusion was that subcutaneous exposure to hydrogel would not lead to toxic effects in women with these implants.

iii. Marketing and Regulatory History

In 1994 implantable breast implants were classified as class IIb devices. As such, PIP had responsibility for assessing and declaring the conformity of Trilucent breast implants with the Medical Devices Directive.[644] As part of this conformity assessment, PIP had to commission a notified body for medical devices to undertake the certification of its quality assurance system. PIP hydrogel breast implants were placed on the European market in 1994. They were manufactured in France by PIP and supplied to the UK market by Clover Leaf Products Ltd. Between 1994 and December approximately 4,000 women in the UK had PIP hydrogel implants. In 2000 a voluntary product withdrawal was undertaken while further evidence was gathered. This was not because there was evidence of harm from these implants, but because there was not enough evidence of a lack of harm. The CE mark was removed in 2002.

Routine explantation of PIP hydrogel implants was never recommended; removal was only recommended upon implant rupture. In 2006 the analysis of more comprehensive studies into safety proved reassuring.

iv. Litigation

Around 4,000 women in the UK had had PIP hydrogel implants fitted.[645] Litigation was launched by women in 2004.[646] The cases in England and Wales were handled by Paul Balen of Freeths LLP.[647] Several cases[648] were conceded early in the litigation in November 2004 and were paid by PIP's insurer MMA; at this stage PIP indicated that it would seek to settle the outstanding cases.

In June 2006 evidence came to light that PIP's textured saline implants had a statistically significantly higher rupture rate than Mentor's (a competitor) saline implants

[642] COT/02/1 (March 2002), available at webarchive.nationalarchives.gov.uk/20080609152113/http://www.advisorybodies.doh.gov.uk/cotnonfood/pip2002.htm.

[643] COT Statement COT/06/3 (January 2006), available at webarchive.nationalarchives.gov.uk/20080609152117/http://www.advisorybodies.doh.gov.uk/cotnonfood/hydrogel.htm.

[644] 93/42/EEC.

[645] See at publications.parliament.uk/pa/cm200001/cmselect/cmhealth/308/1032204.htm.

[646] *Clare Martignette and others v Poly Implant Prothèse* (unreported).

[647] See at www.freeths.co.uk.

[648] Order of 5 November 2004 that judgment was entered for Doreen Jones (damages to be assessed); Vanessa Riper (£18,000 plus costs); Lisa Popely (£11,500 with costs to be assessed).

at two-, three- and four-year follow ups.[649] These implants were not filled with hydrogel or silicone, but it is interesting to note that there was some evidence that the silicone shells used by PIP were 3.5 times more prone to rupture over a four-year period than those of competitors. As part of the hydrogel litigation the claimants commissioned an expert to examine the shells, and the report indicated that the hydrogel shells were considered by the expert to be of poor and inconsistent quality. The claimants' expert also reported that the hydrogel filler was not a natural product, as had been claimed, and had the potential to swell through water absorption and to cause undesirable immune responses in some women. The swelling by fluid absorption by hydrogels had previously been documented in the scientific literature.[650]

At the end of 2006 PIP instructed DLA Piper, and a change of approach ensued. PIP obtained its own expert reports, which sought to blame the use of incorrect or inappropriate techniques by implanting surgeons, and the remaining cases were litigated and not settled. In October 2007, DLA Piper withdrew from acting for PIP.

In December 2007 judgment was obtained in the UK courts for the claimants: this was effectively in default, as PIP (who was acting in person at this stage) had failed to comply with court orders. In March 2008 damages were assessed by a judge. Despite their earlier assurances that they were looking to settle, MMA (PIP's insurers) walked away from the hydrogel litigation and refused to pay the judgments. It later transpired that on 16 October 2006 MMA had written to PIP revoking its insurance cover. This was because PIP had been withholding information about adverse events from MMA and from the regulator. These adverse events reports covered all PIP products, not just hydrogel implants. Given the scale of the deception (up to 2002 PIP had received over 2,000 complaints, but had only notified its insurer and the regulator of four), MMA withdrew cover in October 2006 and refused to pay the subsequent hydrogel awards. The withdrawal of cover was subject to litigation following the discovery of non-conformity of the IMGHC silicone implants (see section X.D).

After judgments were entered in England they remained unpaid. Therefore, the claims against PIP were registered in France. PIP appealed this, but the appeal was dismissed in November 2008. On 4 May 2009, PIP opened a voluntary safeguarding position[651] and appointed an administrator.[652] A subsequent appeal to the Court of Appeal was also dismissed on 22 September 2009. Execution proceedings commenced; but before the French judgment could be executed, PIP voluntarily converted the safeguarding position to liquidation on 30 March 2010[653] and was then wound up in that year. This in effect ended the hydrogel litigation. This was not particularly satisfactory for the women involved.

[649] GW Stevens et al, 'A Comparison of 500 Prefilled Textured Saline Breast Implants versus 500 Standard Textured Saline Breast Implants: Is There a Difference in Deflation Rates?' (2006) 117(7) *Plastic and Reconstructive Surgery* 2175, available at 10.1097/01.prs.0000218199.28082.9d.

[650] JV Berthe and JP Van Geertruyden, 'Osmotic instability of hydrogel-filled breast implants' (2001) 54 *British Journal of Plastic Surgery* 465.

[651] *Procédure de sauvegarde* – akin to a US Chapter 11, the French safeguard proceedings enable solvent debtors facing difficulties that they cannot overcome to restructure under the protection of the court.

[652] *Bodacc* [*Bulletin officiel des annonce civiles et commerciales*] *A n° 20090097*, published on 22 May 2009, available at www.bodacc.fr/annonce/detail-annonce/A/20090097/1404.

[653] *Bodacc A n° 20100074*, published on 16 April 2010, available at www.bodacc.fr/annonce/detail-annonce/A/20100074/2699.

PIP wound up because the IMGHC silicone breast implant scandal had hit the news headlines. The PIP IMGHC silicone implants affected far more women and caused a huge public outcry, and meant that there was effectively no chance of compensation for women with hydrogel implants.

v. Conclusion

There was no proven safety issue with hydrogel breast implants, but a voluntary withdrawal was undertaken after regulators questioned the adequacy of the information supplied with the conformity assessment. Litigation played no part in the detection of the safety signal, nor in the withdrawal from the market. Questions about the adequacy of the pre-marketing conformity assessment are raised by this case.

Questions are also raised about the roles of the insurer and regulator. The insurer removed cover because PIP had seriously and systematically failed to report adverse events about all types of PIP implants, potentially putting the safety of patients at risk. The regulator was also being deceived. The regulator has no remit to consider the insurance arrangements of a manufacturer (some manufacturers self-insure, so there are no insurance policies to consider). However, the regulator is obliged to act on safety issues. It appears that a potential safety signal can fall into a gap between the different remits of the different parties, and can therefore be lost. Had the regulator acted upon the discrepancy between the numbers of ADRs being reported to PIP and the numbers being reported by PIP back in 2006, it is possible that the IMGHC silicone implants may have been removed from the market four years earlier than they were (see section X.D).

D. Poly Implant Prothese (PIP) IMGHC Silicone Breast Implants

i. Description

Poly Implant Prothese (PIP) manufactured various implants in their factory in La Seyne-sur-Mer in France, amongst which were IMGHC silicone filled breast implants[654] that were made between 1997 and April 2010.[655] The main approved constituents of a PIP IMGHC silicone implant were a NUSIL (MED 3 6400) shell and a NUSIL (MED 3 6300) gel filler. This gel filler is specifically formulated for medical applications.

ii. Safety Issue

a. The Manufacturing Process

In April 2010, French agency AFSSAPS found that PIP was substituting the silicone gel used in the manufacturing process for part of their IMGHC silicone implants; instead of using medical grade NUSIL gel (as per their CE marking documentation), PIP was using non-medical grade silicone. Regarding the constituent parts of the implants:

(a) *Shells*. French AFSSAPS inspectors were told when they inspected in March 2010 that PIP shells were made from several layers of NUSIL (MED 3 6400), according to the required technical specifications. *Post hoc* testing could not establish the shell ingredients.

(b) *Filler*. The filling silicone gel of the IMGHC breast implants was supposed to be NUSIL (MED 3 6300). In 2010 it was discovered that PIP had been substituting the filler gel for part of their IMGHC silicone breast implants. Prior to 2008 a gel called 'PIP1' had been used; after 2008, 'PIP2' had been used. These two in-house gel formulations were made from the same raw materials used in different proportions. It appears that there were no written protocols for the production of either PIP1 or PIP2 gels. The formulation was thought to be as shown in Table 3.4,[656] but was subject to batch variation.

Table 3.4 Composition of PIP1 and PIP2

Raw Material	PIP1	PIP2
trimethylated silicone oil: Silop (W10000) or Rhodorsil (H47V1000)	29kg	29kg
SILOP (U165) vinyl terminated silicone oil	1.35kg	2.68kg
Rhodorsil RTV 141 Part A	350g	140g
Rhodorsil RTV 141 Part B	65g	140g

[654] IMGHC products were high cohesive silicone gel breast implants (Implant mammaire texture pré-rempli de gel haute cohésivité).

[655] The IMGHC silicone gel breast implants were CE-marked under the then newly applicable European Medical Device Directive 93/42/EEC.

[656] Taken from section 1.2.2 of *Situation Update on checking procedures performed by the Health Authorities on Poly Implant Prostheses company*, available at ansm.sante.fr/var/ansm_site/storage/original/application/e044aa9eb-27fc2eca49b93165c9020ae.pdf.

The design dossier for PIP IMGHC silicone implants specified that NUSIL raw materials would be used to create the gel filling the implants. The use of non-medical grade silicone and less stringent controls on the cross-linking process appears to have led to a more variable product, where some samples had a higher level of low molecular weight components. Lower molecular weight silicone is associated with higher levels of migration and leakage into tissues.[657]

Once the fraud had been discovered, several studies were carried out by health authorities concerning the non-compliant implants. Notably by AFSSAPS in France, the MHRA in the UK and the Therapeutic Goods Administration (TGA) in Australia. The results from these studies were variable, with different countries reporting different rupture rates. Once the scandal was known, there was increased media attention. The majority of authorities and other institutions recommended intense screening and, in some cases, preventive explantations. Given that PIP silicone implants were, understandably, subject to greater scrutiny than other types of implants, the detection of ruptures was more likely, and often happened earlier than it might otherwise have done. This potentially adds an artefact to the debate on the relative rupture rates of PIP implants compared to other silicone implants.

Briefly, in August 2010 the MHRA received test results that were negative for mutagenicity and genotoxicity. AFSSAPS results were released late in September 2010 and show no genotoxicity or chemical toxicity, but mechanical testing revealed that there might be an increased risk of rupture. One of the tests for genotoxicity was inconclusive, and AFSSAPS stated that further testing was to be conducted by early 2011. The Agency also reported that '[t]he results of the intradermal irritation test show an irritant behaviour of PIP gel'. On this basis it recommended ultrasound of all PIP implanted patients within six months, and removal of any implants subsequently found to rupture.

On 29 September 2010 the Australian regulator, TGA, reported its own test results to the MHRA. These were not consistent with the French results and showed negative cytotoxicity results on both the shell and the gel; also, the TGA's mechanical testing revealed adequate tensile strength in the shell.

On 14 April 2011, AFSSAPS obtained final test results and updated their website to say that there were no genotoxic effects of the filler.

At this point in time, none of the competent authorities had any information that there was a direct health risk posed by PIP implants.

b. Cancer Risk

On 5 November 2008, an article was published in the *Journal of the American Medical Association*, reporting on cases of Anaplastic Large Cell Lymphoma (ALCL) in women with silicone breast implants. This was not the first case study, but it provided the first epidemiological evidence. This article reported a study of a population of women in the Netherlands and suggested a mildly elevated risk of ALCL in women with silicone prosthesis, irrespective of the brand of the prosthesis. The report's authors were clear that their findings were preliminary and would require further studies to confirm,[658] and there remains some

[657] RR LeVier et al, 'What is silicone?' (1993) 92 *Plastic and Reconstructive Surgery* 163.

[658] D de Jong et al, 'Anaplastic Large-Cell Lymphoma in Women With Breast Implants' (2008) 300(17) *Journal of the American Medical Association* 2030, doi:10.1001/jama.2008.585.

controversy over whether this is a true reflection or an artefact.[659] There have been studies indicating that women with silicone breast implants have a lower risk of cancer than the general population.[660] These studies were for silicone breast implants generally, not specifically for PIP silicone implants.

In late November 2011, AFSSAPS informed all other competent authorities of the press reports regarding the death of a French PIP breast implant patient who developed lymphoma. The MHRA immediately began internal consideration of the implications of this case. There were no reported incidents where lymphoma was confirmed to be in association with a UK PIP breast implant. The MHRA's conclusion was that there was no established linked between PIP implants and any form of cancer, including ALCL.

iii. Marketing and Regulatory History

The European approach to breast implants was governed by the Medical Devices Directive 92/42/EEC. Prior to the entry into force of Directive 2003/12/EC on 3 February 2003, implantable breast implants were classified as class IIb devices, after this time they became class III devices.

Within the EU, based on the New Approach, manufacturers are responsible for assessing and declaring that their medical devices conform with the requirements of the Directive. Pursuant to Annex II of Medical Device Directive 93/42/EEC, PIP, as the manufacturer, had responsibility for assessing and declaring conformity of its breast implants with the requirements of the Directive. As part of this conformity assessment, PIP had to commission a notified body for medical devices for two specific tasks:

(a) the certification of its quality assurance system; and
(b) (from 2004) the certification of its design dossier.

Since 1997, TÜV Rheinland LGA Products GmbH had audited and certified the quality assurance system of PIP. From 2004 onwards, TÜV Rheinland LGA Products GmbH also examined and certified the design dossier of PIP's IMGHC silicone gel breast implants.

Throughout these years, PIP, as manufacturer, remained solely responsible for issuing the CE declaration of conformity and affixing the CE marking on its implants.

a. Recapitulation Studies by AFSSAPS

In April 2003, AFSSAPS produced two recapitulation summaries, presumably in response to the reclassification, which included analysis of the breast implant fillers. These appeared to show that the PIP implants were compliant, and that there were no differences between the PIP implants tested and those of other manufacturers. This is hardly surprising, as the recapitulation studies tested samples that PIP had sent to AFSSAPS. This information was available to AFSSAPS but the MHRA did not have it, and it is not known if other

[659] S Li and AK Lee, 'Silicone implant and primary breast ALK1-negative anaplastic large cell lymphoma, fact or fiction?' (2010) 3(1) *International Journal of Clinical and Experimental Pathology* 117.

[660] L Lipworth, RE Tarone and JK McLaughlin, 'Breast implants and lymphoma risk: a review of the epidemiologic evidence through 2008' (2009) 123(3) *Plastic and Reconstructive Surgery* 790.

EU notified bodies and competent authorities did. Interestingly, had this information been shared it would have provided reassurance, which might potentially have slowed any investigations into PIP.

b. Adverse Events and Concerns about PIP Silicone Implants

The PIP adverse events listed in Table 3.5 were reported to the MHRA between 2001 and 2009.[661] Until 2009, figures broadly accorded with what would be expected for a silicone breast implant.

Table 3.5 Sales, adverse incident reports and rupture reports and rates 2000–09

Year	Sales	Adverse incident reports	Adverse incidences as % of sales	Reports of ruptures	Ruptures as % of Adverse Incidents	Ruptures as % of sales
2001	4575	1	0.02	0	0.00	0.00
2002	4461	6	0.13	5	83.33	0.11
2003	6168	3	0.05	2	66.67	0.03
2004	16639	13	0.08	10	76.92	0.06
2005	12844	11	0.09	8	72.73	0.06
2006	9030	10	0.11	10	100.00	0.11
2007	9042	50	0.55	46	92.00	0.51
2008	12875	73	0.57	68	93.15	0.53
2009	8678	102	1.18	91	89.22	1.05

Throughout this time period AFSSAPS had also been monitoring. The Agency calculated an incident rate based on the number of incidents reported in a year divided by the number of sales for that year. This showed the 'incident rate' was 5 times higher in 2009 than 2007 (0.56% vs. 0.11%). PIP's 'incident rate' was also higher than that of two competitor brands. This triggered an inspection of PIP's factory. This inspection took place on 16–18 March 2010. On 17 March, thanks in part to an anonymous tip off showing photographs of non-NUSIL filler raw material with PIP's address on it, the inspectors discovered the use of inappropriate filler material in implants.

On 29 March 2010, AFSSAPS recalled PIP silicone implants and halted their distribution on the basis of non-conformity; this decision was made public on 30 March 2010.[662] On 31 March 2010, the MHRA issue a medical device alert, instructing that implantation should cease and stock should be quarantined.[663]

[661] App 1, 'Chronology of key events of Poly Implant Prosthèse (PIP) silicone breast implants', Reviews of the actions of the Medicines and Healthcare Products Regulatory Agency (MHRA) and Department of Health, available at www.gov.uk/government/news/review-into-pip-implants-published.

[662] See at ansm.sante.fr/content/download/25265/334617/version/2/file/dpsImplantMamairePIP.pdf.

[663] MDA/2010/025.

iv. Litigation

Various cases have been brought in relation to the PIP scandal, both criminal and civil and in many jurisdictions.

In December 2013, the Marseilles Criminal Court (*Tribunal Correctionnel de Marseille*) found company founder Jean-Claude Mas[664] guilty of 'aggravated deceit' and fraud, and sentenced him to four years' imprisonment and a €75,000 fine.[665] Four of his former co-directors and managers were also found guilty and were sentenced to between 18 months' and three years' imprisonment (one of which was suspended). Jean-Claude Mas was banned from managing a company and being involved in a medically-related business. He appealed, but the conviction was upheld.[666] A further appeal on a point of law relating to Mas and three others is pending in the French Criminal Supreme Court.

In the criminal proceedings, 7,445 women joined as *parties civiles* (see chapter 1), about one-third of whom are not French nationals, and were eventually awarded compensation.[667] However, the accused claimed not to have sufficient funds to meet the judgment (valued at over €40 million). However, French law provides that if *parties civiles* are found to be victims of a criminal act they are entitled to compensation from the French statutory fund SARVI. As the appellate judgment is now finalised against one of the accused, compensation by SARVI is now possible.

a. Product Liability Claims

Many women in England are being represented by Hugh James Solicitors, Cardiff. On 9 March 2010, a GLO was made by the High Court, Cardiff. This includes approximately 1,000 women, with various clinics as defendants. The UK distributor and clinic insurers are joined under part 20 of the Civil Procedure Rules 2010. The claims under this GLO are predominantly against clinics that carried out the implantations, and are contractual claims under the Sale of Goods Act 1979 and the Supply of Goods and Services Act 1982. The trial was listed for October 2016 but has been adjourned; the majority of claims were resolved, with judgments entered against various defendants.

This route is only available where the implanting clinic still exists. Harley Street Medical carried out approximately one-third of the PIP implant surgeries, but it went into financial restructuring in November 2012, leaving women operated on by the clinic without a defendant to sue.

b. Consumer Credit Claims

Where the implants were purchased on a credit card, many UK women pursued claims under the section 75 of the Consumer Credit Act 1974.

[664] In parallel, a judicial investigation is under way against Jean-Claude Mas and former co-directors, managers and employees at PIP on the basis of involuntary harm and manslaughter.

[665] Tribunal correctionnel Marseille, 10 Dec 2013 (Numero minute: 7206/13), (Numero parquet: 12048000148).

[666] Judgment given at Cour d'appel d'Aix-en-Provence on 2 May 2016, available at news.europawire.eu/tuv-rheinland-jean-claude-mas-and-four-other-individuals-involved-at-pip-with-confirmed-conviction-in-france-7654321234567890/eu-press-release/2016/05/05.

[667] *Le Monde*, Blogs Chroniques judiciaires, 27 April 2013, available at prdchroniques.blog.lemonde.fr/2013/04/27/laffaire-pip-et-le-prejudice-de-la-perte-de-confiance/.

c. Insurer Claims

Various claims have been brought against the insurer (Allianz MMA) with which PIP held a civil liability insurance contract covering, inter alia, loss and damage sustained by third parties arising out of its activities.[668] Several judgments awarding compensation to victims have been handed down,[669] although the insurer has appealed them.[670]

Allianz asked the French courts to cancel the policy on the grounds of dishonesty, but this was not allowed as a matter of public policy.[671] The practical benefit of this insurance cover was limited, as the policy was capped at €3 million and it was only applicable in France, so compensation is only available to claimants who had the surgery in France. Allianz have compensated French claimants as ordered to do so by French courts up to the €3 million cap, as determined by the Aix en Provence Court of Appeal.

d. TÜV Rheinland LGA Products GmbH and TÜV Rheinland France SAS Claims

In Germany, several different district courts (inter alia Frankenthal, Nurenberg-Fürth and Munich) found that TÜV Rheinland LGA Products GmbH had complied with the requirements of the Directive.[672] Overall, around 100 cases have been dismissed by about 25 different courts of first and second instance in Germany. The European Court of Justice confirmed[673] that there was no obligation for notified bodies under Directive 93/42/EEC to carry out unannounced inspections, to generally perform product tests on the medical devices or to review the manufacturer's business records. In June 2017, the German Federal Court of Justice, the *Bundesgerichtshof*, confirmed that TÜV Rheinland LGA Products GmbH was not liable.[674]

In France, the picture is similar. Professional judges deciding on the merits of the PIP case, have dismissed the damages claims against the notified body TÜV Rheinland LGA Products GmbH. Only the Toulon Commercial Court (*Tribunal de Commerce de Toulon)*, composed of lay judges, decided otherwise. On 14 November 2013, the Commercial Court found the defendant TÜV Rheinland companies liable towards around 1,700 individuals alleging they have or have had PIP implants, and to six former distributors of the implants (in Bulgaria, Brazil, Italy, Syria, Mexico and Romania). The Court ordered the defendants

[668] Such insurance is compulsory under Art L 1142-2 of the *Code de la santé publique* (Public Health Code).

[669] A decision of the Cour d'appel in Nîmes, on 9 October 2010, awarded €1000 in compensation to one victim, while a decision of the Tribunal de grande instance in Lyon, on 18 June 2012 awarded €19,650 in compensation to another.

[670] Tribunal de commerce de Toulon, 14 June 2012 (3ème Ch no RG 2010F00318); Tribunal de grande instance de Lyon, 18 June 2012 (4ème Ch no RG 11/01149).

[671] First Instance – Tribunal de commerce de Toulon, 14 June 2012, no 2010F00479. This was appealed by Allianz (Cour d'appel d'Aix-en-Provence, 22 January 2015, no RG 12/11337), but the original decision was upheld.

[672] District Court in Frankenthal (Judgment dated 14 March 2013, Az 6 O 304/12). The claimants' appeal against this decision was also rejected by the higher court, OLG Zweibrücken (Judgment dated 30 January 2014, 4 U 66/13). The District Court of Nürnberg-Fürth (Judgment dated 25 September 2013, Az 11 O 3900/13) dismissed the action. In a similar case, the District Court in Munich confirmed the decision in the Nürnberg-Fürth case, and returned a verdict that TÜV Rheinland LGA Products GmbH could not be held liable.

[673] Judgment of the Court (First Chamber) of 16 February, Schmitt, Case C-219/15 ECLI:EU:C:2017:128; see curia.europa.eu/juris/liste.jsf?num=C-219/15.

[674] BGH, 22.06.2017 – VII ZR 36/14.

to make immediate interim payments pending expert assessments of the damage alleged by the claimants. These were set at €3,000, plus €400 legal costs, for each of the 1,700 claimants. The defendants challenged the preliminary enforcement of the interim payments. This request was dismissed on 21 January 2014. In parallel, the defendants lodged an appeal against the merits of the first instance judgment. On 2 July 2015, the Aix-en-Provence Court of Appeal excluded all liability of the defendant TÜV Rheinland companies in the PIP case. The Court held that TÜV Rheinland LGA Products GmbH committed no fault in its mission as notified body for PIP. The District Court of Paris (*Tribunal de Grande Instance de Paris*) had already reached the same conclusion in a judgment of 29 September 2014 that has since become final.

In spite of all the findings of all other courts, the Toulon Commercial Court again found the defendant TÜV Rheinland companies liable in two judgments of 20 January 2017. The defendants appealed against these judgments. The appellate proceedings are currently ongoing before the Aix-en-Provence Court of Appeal.

v. Conclusion

The fraud perpetrated by PIP was not detected for many years, and the discovery was made possible by a whistleblower.

Litigation has followed, but has not proved particularly satisfactory for a substantial number of claimants.

Regulatory changes have followed the PIP scandal, with the adoption in September 2013 of Commission Regulation No 920/2013[675] on the designation and the supervision of notified bodies, and the Commission Recommendation of 24 September 2013[676] on the audits and assessments performed by notified bodies in the field of medical devices. These measures imposed higher obligations on scrutiny of notified bodies and more in-depth controls on manufacturers, including systematic unannounced audits, in order to restore patient and professional trust in medical devices. In 2017, after extensive political debate over the PIP case, considerably extended EU regulatory requirements were passed, in Regulation (EU) 2017/745.

[675] Commission Regulation No 920/2013, available at eur-lex.europa.eu/LexUriServ/LexUriServ.do?uri=OJ:L:2013:253:0008:0019:EN:PDF.

[676] Commission Recommendation (2013/473/EU), available at eur-lex.europa.eu/LexUriServ/LexUriServ.do?uri=OJ:L:2013:253:0027:0035:EN:PDF.

XI. Urinary Incontinence and Pelvic Prolapse Treatments

A. Micturin (terodiline)

i. Description

Micturin is an urological antispasmodic, indicated for the treatment of urinary incontinence.

ii. Safety Issue

The drug was initially described as effective.[677] After two years on the market, spontaneous reports from the UK ADR scheme arose about a prolonged QT interval,[678] or the measure of the duration of ventricular repolarisation (the time between the start of the Q wave and the end of the T wave in the heart's electrical cycle), associated with the drug. Prolongation of QT can degenerate into a potentially fatal form of tachyarrhythmia called Torsades de Pointes (TdP). In 1991, the *British Medical Journal* published an article that described the possible benefit of terodiline as 'likely to be small'.[679]

iii. Marketing and Regulatory History

Micturin was approved for marketing in the UK by Kabi Pharmacia-Pfizer on 21 May 1986. Micturin was also available in various EU countries, but the major markets were Sweden, the UK and Japan.[680] It was not marketed in the US.

The only place where adverse events were reported was the UK. This may have been because the routinely recommended dose in the UK was higher than that used in Sweden and Japan.[681] After the ADR reports, a 'Dear Doctor' letter was issued by the CSM on 25 July 1991, warning doctors about severe cardiac adverse reactions (ventricular tachycardia), which may be fatal. Following the warning even more reports were received, resulting in a total of 69 reports of cardiac arrhythmias, including 14 cases of sudden or unexpected deaths possibly associated with terodiline.[682]

[677] HD Langtry and D McTavish, 'Terodiline. A review of its pharmacological properties, and therapeutic use in the treatment of urinary incontinence' (1990) 40(5) *Drugs* 748.

[678] McLeod and MacConnell each reported a single case; Connolly reported on five cases, three of which had been notified to the manufacturer previously: AA McLeod et al, 'Torsades de pointes complicating treatment with terodiline' (1991) 302(6790) *British Medical Journal* 1469; TJ MacConnell et al, 'Torsades de pointes complicating treatment with terodiline' (1991) 302(6790) *British Medical Journal* 1469; MJ Connolly et al, 'Torsades de pointes ventricular tachycardia and terodiline' (1991) 338(8763) *The Lancet*, 344.

[679] PA Wiseman et al, 'Terodiline with bladder retraining for treating detrusor instability in elderly people' (1991) 302(6783) *British Medical Journal* 994.

[680] See JR Turner and TA Durham, *Integrated Cardiac Safety: Assessment Methodologies for Noncardiac Drugs in Discovery, Development and Post-Marketing Surveillance* (Wiley, 2008), 'Case Study 1 Terodiline and UK Regulatory Activities' at 11.3.1.

[681] ibid.

[682] See at webarchive.nationalarchives.gov.uk/20141206135829/http://www.mhra.gov.uk/home/groups/pl-p/documents/websiteresources/con2024450.pdf.

The drug was withdrawn worldwide by the company in 13 September 1991,[683] because of the increasing number of reports of drug-related cardiac arrhythmias. This was initially to assess the situation, but later it became clear that this would be a permanent withdrawal.

iv. Litigation

Claims were threatened in 1992 after withdrawal from market of Micturin in 1991. However, there was no large-scale litigation.

v. Conclusion

The safety issue was identified the ADR reports in the UK. Litigation was threatened after the product was withdrawn.

[683] 'Withdrawal of Micturin' (1991) 321(8769) *The Lancet* 752. Notice of the product withdrawal with details of the safety issue was published by the CSM, (October 1991) 32 *Current Problems in Pharmacovigilance* 1, available at webarchive.nationalarchives.gov.uk/20141206135829/http://www.mhra.gov.uk/home/groups/pl-p/documents/websiteresources/con2024450.pdf.

B. Urogynaecological Mesh

i. Description

Mesh is intended to strengthen/reinforce weak areas by providing a scaffold for the body. Initially the support comes from the mesh itself, and later the tissues to grow into the 'holes' in the mesh. It has been used in surgery for a variety of purposes, predominantly hernia repair and urogynaecological reconstruction surgery, with other less common uses such as breast augmentation and vascular repair.

Mesh may be used to treat stress urinary incontinence (SUI) and/or pelvic organ prolapse (POP). Stress urinary incontinence is involuntary urinary leakage upon exertion or effort, straining or coughing. It can be caused when the pelvic tissues, ligaments and muscles, which support the bladder and urethra, become weak and allow the urethral closure mechanism to fail.[684] This form of SUI can be resolved by surgically supporting the mid-urethra. During surgical repair of prolapse of the bladder, rectum, uterus or vaginal vault, the surgeon may opt to insert an implant[685] to reinforce the patient's own tissues. Implants can be either synthetic or biological (usually made from cow or pig tissue). Synthetic implants can be either absorbable, where they are broken down by the body over time, or permanent, where they are intended to remain in the body. Permanent synthetic implants come in many forms, which are not always self-explanatory: for example, 'tape' can describe a strip that has a mesh-like structure, or can describe a more 'solid' strip without large holes. Permanent implants have traditionally been made of polypropylene, though other materials have been considered.[686]

In urogynaecological surgery, polypropylene mesh can be used in two main forms: either flat mesh is cut to the required size and shape by the surgeon (commonly called mesh-inlay), or a pre-shaped mesh product is used (which can be further cut by the surgeon as desired). Pre-shaped mesh products are often part of a mesh kit, which contains the pre-shaped mesh product along with insertion tools, and may include fixings for the product as well, such as the barbs for SUI tapes. In the case of sacrocolpopexy,[687] flat mesh has been cut and utilised, and more recently 'Y shaped' mesh devices have been developed. Mesh-inlay is placed using a single incision, usually inside the vagina. Mesh products and mesh kits can be placed using a single incision through the full thickness of the vaginal wall and/or can require multiple skin incisions and placement using introduction needles and/or trocars, depending upon the product/kit design.

[684] PE Petros and UI Ulmsten, 'An integral theory and its method for the diagnosis and management of female urinary incontinence' (1993) 153 *Scandinavian Journal of Urology and Nephrology Supplement* 1.

[685] For the International Urogynecological Association (IUGA)/International Continence Society (ICS) jointly agreed terminology, see BT Haylen et al, 'An International Urogynecological Association (IUGA)/International Continence Society (ICS) joint terminology and classification of the complications related directly to the insertion of prostheses (meshes, implants, tapes) & grafts in female pelvic floor surgery' (2011) 22 *International Urogynecology Journal* 3, doi.org/10.1007/s00192-010-1324-9.

[686] S Shafaat et al, 'Demonstration of improved tissue integration and angiogenesis with an elastic, estradiol releasing polyurethane material designed for use in pelvic floor repair' (2018) 37 *Neurourology and Urodynamics* 716, doi.org/10.1002/nau.23510.

[687] Sacrocolpopexy is a repair carried out on women who have had a hysterectomy and who are suffering from a vaginal vault prolapse. The vaginal vault is lifted and secured in place using a strip of mesh; one end of the mesh is stitched to the apex of the vagina and the other end is sutured to the sacrum.

This case study will primarily focus on mesh products and kits, as the associated regulatory background for these is more easily identified. As such this is not a complete description of the products, regulation or adverse event issues associated with urogynaecological mesh use.

ii. Safety Issue

Polypropylene mesh has been used to reinforce weak tissues for many decades.[688] While there have been reports of adverse events with many different surgery types, this case study will focus on the use of mesh in urogynaecological surgery for SUI and POP.

There have been various adverse events reported after the insertion of mesh to treat SUI and POP. Pain, impaired mobility, recurrent infections, incontinence/urinary frequency, prolapse, fistula formation, sexual and relationship difficulties, depression, social withdrawal or exclusion/loneliness and lethargy have all been reported. Additionally, one of the difficulties with establishing a causal relationship between the insertion of mesh and these adverse events is that these adverse events can all occur after conventional pelvic surgery that has not involved the insertion of mesh.

There is one complication, mesh exposure, which can be squarely attributed to the presence of inserted mesh. Mesh exposure occurs when the mesh becomes visible through tissue and exposed, usually in the vaginal walls. This can lead to pain. A 2017 *Cochrane Review* of mid-urethral synthetic slings mesh for SUI found the exposure rate was 2%.[689] Mesh exposure after vaginal POP surgery ranges from 4% to 19%.[690] Crosby et al reported[691] that 95% of mesh exposures were treated successfully, but only 51% of pelvic pain apparently associated with mesh was successfully treated by surgical removal of the mesh. Shrinkage has also been implicated in the adverse events.

The death of Chrissy Brajcic, a Canadian mesh recipient and subsequent advocate against mesh, had been widely reported by some sections of the media as being due to infection caused by her mesh.[692] There has, however, been no official declaration on the cause of her death. Reportedly, the coroner is currently investigating,[693] and once the investigation is

[688] FC Usher, 'Further observations on the use of marlex mesh: a new technique for the repair of inguinal hernias' (1959) 25 *The American Surgeon* 792; JE Morgan, 'A sling operation, using Marlex polypropylene mesh, for treatment of recurrent stress incontinence' (1970) 106(3) *American Journal of Obstetrics and Gynecology* 369; HP Drutz and LS Cha, 'Massive genital and vaginal vault prolapse treated by abdominal-vaginal sacropexy with use of Marlex mesh: review of the literature' (1987) 156(2) *American Journal of Obstetrics and Gynecology* 387; KR Baker, JM Beresford and C Campbell, 'Colposacropexy with Prolene mesh' (1990) 171(1) *Surgery, Gynecology and Obstetrics* 51; TM Julian, 'The efficacy of Marlex mesh in the repair of severe, recurrent vaginal prolapse of the anterior midvaginal wall' (1996) 175(6) *American Journal of Obstetrics and Gynecology* 1472; R Migliari et al, 'Tension-free vaginal mesh repair for anterior vaginal wall prolapse' (2000) 38(2) *European Urology* 151.

[689] AA Ford et al, 'Mid-urethral sling operations for stress urinary incontinence in women' (2017) 7 *Cochrane Database Systematic Reviews* CD006375, doi:10.1002/14651858.CD006375.pub4.

[690] AL Milani et al, 'The use of mesh in vaginal prolapse' (2013) 157(31) *Nederlands Tijdschrift voor Geneeskunde* A6324 (in Dutch, translated for the author by a colleague.)

[691] EC Crosby et al, 'Symptom Resolution After Operative Management of Complications from Transvaginal Mesh' (2014) 123(1) *Obstetrics & Gynecology* 134, doi:10.1097/AOG.0000000000000042.

[692] Harriet Marsden, 'The vaginal mesh scandal has claimed its first victim – and she probably won't be the last' *Independent* (5 December 2017); Joanne McCarthy, 'Canadian woman Christina Lynn Brajcic dies after receiving pelvic mesh implant' *Sydney Morning Herald* (3 December 2017).

[693] Personal communication from the Office of the Chief Coroner & Ontario Forensic Pathology Service 6/6/18.

concluded, a decision will be made as to whether to open an inquest. If an inquest is opened and it is determined that it is in the public interest, information on Ms Brajcic's death will be made publicly available. It will be interesting to note the impact on litigation rates, if any, of the as yet unsubstantiated media reports of her cause of death.

iii. Marketing and Regulatory History

a. In the USA

During the 1960s and 1970s, gynaecologists began using mesh for the repair of POP carried out through an abdominal incision (sacrocolpopexy).[694] At the time, the available meshes were flat meshes that had been cleared by the FDA for hernia repair. Surgical techniques evolved, and starting in the 1990s the same mesh was being used for the surgical treatment of SUI via the mid-urethral sling,[695] and was being inserted through transvaginal incisions for the repair of POP.[696] There appeared to be a gap in the market and demand from surgeons, which led manufacturers to develop pre-shaped mesh products and kits specifically designed for SUI and POP surgery. Late in 1996, Boston Scientific's protogen sling, the first pre-shaped surgical mesh product specifically designed for SUI surgery, was cleared by the FDA. From this point on, many other mesh products and kits were developed by various manufacturers.

When the initial vaginal meshes (whether inlay, pre-shaped product or a kit) were launched they were classed as class II devices.[697] As such, clearance is usually through the 510K process,[698] which involves notifying the FDA at least 90 days before the product is marketed, detailing how the new product is substantially equivalent to a product that has already been cleared. In 2017 Henegan et al provided an interesting overview of the marketing authorisation process for mesh products, which process has been criticised for clearing products based on insufficient evidence.[699]

Table 3.6 has been generated from the 501K database and shows many (but not all) of the widely used vaginal meshes. Some of the products included here are flat meshes that may be used to reinforce other areas of the body. This table is arranged in manufacturer blocks,

[694] FE Lane, 'Repair of posthysterectomy vaginal-vault prolapse' (1962) 20 *Obstetrics and Gynecology* 72; TJ Williams and RW Telinde, 'The sling operation for urinary incontinence using mersilene ribbon' (1962) 19 *Obstetrics and Gynecology* 241; JE Morgan, 'A sling operation, using Marlex polypropylene mesh, for treatment of recurrent stress incontinence' (1970) 106(3) *American Journal of Obstetrics & Gynecology* 369; DH Nichols, 'The Mersilene mesh gauze-hammock for severe urinary stress incontinence' (1973) 41(1) *Obstetrics and Gynecology* 88; GB Feldman and SJ Birnbaum, 'Sacral colpopexy for vaginal vault prolapse' (1979) 53(3) *Obstetrics and Gynecology* 399.

[695] U Ulmsten et al, 'An ambulatory surgical procedure under local anesthesia for treatment of female urinary incontinence' (1996) 7(2) *International Urogynecology Journal – Pelvic Floor Dysfunction* 81.

[696] Julian, n 689; Migliari et al, n 689.

[697] Section 513(a)(1) of the Food, Drugs and Cosmetic Act (21 USC § 360c(a)(1)) and also at www.fda.gov/MedicalDevices/DeviceRegulationandGuidance/Overview/ClassifyYourDevice/default.htm.

[698] See at www.fda.gov/downloads/MedicalDevices/DeviceRegulationandGuidance/GuidanceDocuments/UCM284443.pdf.

[699] CJ Heneghan et al, 'Trials of transvaginal mesh devices for pelvic organ prolapse: a systematic database review of the US FDA approval process' (2017) 7(12) *British Medical Journal Open* e017125, doi: 10.1136/bmjopen-2017-017125

with products in alphabetical order and with variations of a product listed with the most recent product uppermost. This demonstrates the way in which medical devices evolve in an iterative way.

Table 3.6 510K approvals for selected mesh products

Product	Manufacturer	510(K) number	Date (dd/mm/yyyy)
Avaulta solo synthetic support system Avaulta plus biosynthetic support system	CR Bard,Inc	K083839	15/01/2009
Avaulta support system	CR Bard,Inc	K082571	30/09/2008
Avaulta support system Avaulta plus biosynthetic support system	CR Bard,Inc	K063712	12/03/2007
Bard pelvisoft acellular collagen biomesh	CR Bard, Inc	K031332	15/05/2003
Pelvilace to system	CR Bard, Inc	K042949	09/11/2004
Ajust helical adjustable single-incision sling	CR Bard, Inc	K123179	02/11/2012
Ajust adjustable single-incision sling	CR Bard, Inc	K092607	20/11/2009
Collament FM implant	CR Bard, Inc	K082687	17/10/2008
Bard Collament implant models 1175102, 1175103, 1175104, 1175105, 1175106	CR Bard, Inc	K063178	21/11/2006
Bard Collament implant models 1175101, 1175102, 1175103, 1175104, 1175105	CR Bard, Inc	K052322	10/04/2006
Pelvicol	CR Bard, Inc	K992556	17/02/2000
parietene ds composite mesh	Sofradim Production	K163212	29/06/2017
parietene macroporous mesh	Sofradim Production	K142091	17/10/2014
Parietene self-gripping polypropylene mesh	Sofradim Production	K140941	07/05/2014
parietene duo and quadra polypropyl-ene mesh	Sofradim Production	K072951	19/12/2007
parietene polypropylene mesh	Sofradim Production	K991400	12/07/1999
Uretex to trans-obturator urethral support	Sofradim Production	K041176	17/05/2004
Uretex Sup Pubourethral sling	Sofradim Production	K012949	04/10/2001

(continued)

Table 3.6 *(Continued)*

Product	Manufacturer	510(K) number	Date (dd/mm/yyyy)
Ugytex dual knit mesh	Sofradim Production	K051503	05/08/2005
Ugytex mesh	Sofradim Production	K033376	15/01/2004
AMS Elevate PC	American Medical Systems Inc	K112842	25/10/2011
AMS Elevate PC apical and posterior (and anterior and apical) prolapse repair system with Intepro lite	American Medical Systems Inc	K111118	01/07/2011
Elevate prolapse repair system with pc coated Intepro lite – apical and posterior prolapse repair system, anterior and apical.	American Medical Systems Inc	K090713	02/04/2009
AMS Elevate anterior and apical prolapse repair system with Intepro lite	American Medical Systems Inc	K082677	23/12/2008
AMS Elevate apical and posterior prolapse repair system with Intepro lite AMS Elevate apical and posterior prolapse	American Medical Systems Inc	K082730	26/11/2008
AMS Elevate with Intepro lite prolapse repair system AMS Elevate with Intexin LP prolapse repair system	American Medical Systems Inc	K080185	10/04/2008
Apogee and Perigee systems with intepro and intexin, part of the AMS; Pelvic floor repair system	American Medical Systems Inc	K082387	04/12/2008
Apogee and Perigee systems with pc coated intepro lite	American Medical Systems Inc	K081710	15/10/2008
AMS perigee system	American Medical Systems Inc	K040623	17/05/2004
SPARC system and MONARC, MONARC and MONARC C systems	American Medical Systems Inc	K131339	05/12/2013
SPARC/ MONARC, MONARC, MONARC C and MONARC + systems	American Medical Systems Inc	K081613	17/09/2008

(continued)

Table 3.6 *(Continued)*

Product	Manufacturer	510(K) number	Date (dd/mm/yyyy)
SPARC, MONARC, BIOACR SP and BIOARC To sling systems	American Medical Systems Inc	K041948	11/08/2004
Modification to SPARC sling system	American Medical Systems Inc	K0211263	15/05/2002
Modification to SPARC sling system	American Medical Systems Inc	K020663	28/03/2002
SPARC sling system	American Medical Systems Inc	K013355	26/10/2001
SPARC sling system	American Medical Systems Inc	K011251	01/08/2001
Bioarc SP sling kit and Bioarc To sling	American Medical Systems Inc	K040538	17/03/2004
Bioarc SP sling kit	American Medical Systems Inc	K030123	06/02/2003
AMS Large pore polypropylene mesh	American Medical Systems Inc	K121805	16/10/2012
Modification to AMS large pore polypropylene mesh	American Medical Systems Inc	K040521	24/03/2004
AMS large pore polypropylene mesh	American Medical Systems Inc	K033636	31/12/2003
MiniARC pro single-incision sling system	American Medical Systems Inc	K121641	07/09/2012
MiniARC precise single-incision sling system	American Medical Systems Inc	K100807	07/06/2010
AMS MiniARC sling system	American Medical Systems Inc	K073703	30/01/2008
AMS MiniARC sling system	American Medical Systems Inc	K071902	24/08/2007

(continued)

Table 3.6 *(Continued)*

Product	Manufacturer	510(K) number	Date (dd/mm/yyyy)
Blue Sui sling (Obtryx II system)	Boston Scientific products	K121754	10/10/2012
Obtryx System (Halo or curved) and Prefyx PPS system	Boston Scientific products	K040787	04/14/2004
Advantage, Advantage Fit and Lynx System	Boston Scientific products	K020110	03/04/2002
Pinnacle Lite pelvic floor repair kit, posterior uphold light vaginal support system	Boston Scientific products	K122459	13/12/2012
Pinnacle pelvic floor repair kit II	Boston Scientific products	K081048	22/08/2008
Pinnacle pelvic floor repair kits	Boston Scientific products	K071957	08/11/2007
Polyform synthetic mesh	Boston Scientific products	K171271	15/12/2017
Protogen sling collagen impregnated material	Boston Scientific products	K963226	15/11/1996
Prolene™ soft polypropylene mesh	Ethicon Inc	K172089	05/10/2017
Prolene™ soft polypropylene mesh	Ethicon Inc	K163152	11/03/2017
Gynecare Prolene™ fastener system	Ethicon Inc	K042603	22/12/2004
Gynemesh Prolene™ soft (polypropylene) non absorbable synthetic surgical mesh for pelvic floor repair	Ethicon Inc	K013718	08/01/2002
Prolene™ (polypropylene) 3D patch non absorbable synthetic surgical mesh	Ethicon Inc	K010722	27/04/2001
Vypro mesh vicryl Prolene™ partially absorbable synthetic surgical mesh	Ethicon Inc	K002672	22/11/2000
Prolene™ soft (polypropylene) nonabsorbable synthetic surgical mesh	Ethicon Inc	K001122	23/05/2000
Modification of Prolene™ (polypropylene)	Ethicon Inc	K984220	23/02/1999
Prolene™ polypropylene mesh nonabsorbable	Ethicon Inc	K962530	09/08/1996

(continued)

Table 3.6 *(Continued)*

Product	Manufacturer	510(K) number	Date (dd/mm/yyyy)
Prolene™ polypropylene mesh nonabsorbable w/onlay patch	Ethicon Inc	K915774	02/03/1992
Gynecare prolift +M* Pelvic floor repair systems	Ethicon Inc	K071512	15/05/2008
Gynecare prosima pelvic floor repair system	Ethicon Inc	K063562	26/02/2007
Gynecare TVT exact continence system	Ethicon Inc	K132054	23/08/2013
Gynecare TVT abbrevo continence system	Ethicon Inc	K100936	01/07/2010
Gynecare TVT exact continence system	Ethicon Inc	K100485	16/03/2010
Gynecare TVT secur system	Ethicon Inc	K052401	28/11/2005
Gynecare TVT obturator system	Ethicon Inc	K033568	08/12/2003
TVT system	Ethicon Inc	K974098	28/01/1998
Ultrapro Mesh	Ethicon Inc	K033337	01/04/2004
Mentor ObTape trans-obturator surgical kit	Mentor Corp	K042851	09/11/2004
Mentor ObTape trans-obturator tape	Mentor Corp	K031767	17/07/2003
Mentor Novasilk mesh	Mentor Corp	K053414	27/12/2005
Mentor Aris Trans-obturator tape and surgical kit	Mentor Corp	K050418	09/03/2005
T-Sling	Caldera	K050516	03/02/2006
IVS Tunneller	Tyco	K010035	04/04/2001
Coated Surgipro™ polypropylene surgical mesh	Tyco	K915526	29/05/1992

Another potential layer of confusion arises from reports that some mesh products were placed on the market without any regulatory 'approval'; while further communications with the FDA indicated that it provides a guidance document to manufacturers for determining when to file a specific 510k clearance submission for a device, and companies can rely on the FDA guidance and determine in good faith that a specific 510k submission is not necessary for a device.[700] While this has been noted, it will not be explored further.

[700] David Voreacos and Alex Nussbaum, 'J&J Marketed Vaginal Mesh Implant without US Approval' *Bloomberg Business* (21 March 2012), available at www.bloomberg.com/news/articles/2012-03-21/j-j-sold-vaginal-mesh-implant-without-u-s-regulatory-approval.

In October 2008, the FDA issued a Public Health Notification[701] following adverse event reports with transvaginal urogynecologic mesh. This stated that there were

> risks of erosion through vaginal epithelium, infection, pain, urinary problems, and recurrence of prolapse and/or incontinence. There were also reports of bowel, bladder, and blood vessel perforation during insertion. In some cases, vaginal scarring and mesh erosion led to a significant decrease in patient quality of life due to discomfort and pain, including dyspareunia.

But these events were 'rare'. The FDA advised clinicians to obtain specialist training, monitor for and report adverse events, and to ensure that patients were fully informed of the risks prior to surgery. This 2008 Notification did not distinguish between SUI and POP.

Following this Notification, the number of adverse event reports increased dramatically. In response, the FDA conducted an internal review, including a systematic literature review, and then issued a second safety update in July 2011, which focused on transvaginal prolapse mesh for POP.[702] The message in this update was different from the message in 2008, with the 2011 update stating that 'serious adverse events are NOT rare, contrary to what was stated in the 2008 PHN' and 'transvaginally-placed mesh in POP repair does NOT conclusively improve clinical outcomes over traditional non-mesh repair'. Further:

> There does appear to be an anatomic benefit to anterior repair with mesh augmentation. This anatomic benefit may not result in superior symptomatic outcomes or lower rates of repeat surgery for recurrent prolapse compared to traditional POP repair without mesh.

The FDA announced that it was considering whether transvaginal mesh products for POP repair would be reclassified as the higher-risk class III.

On 3 January 2012 the FDA used its power under section 522 of the Food, Drug and Cosmetic Act[703] to order that manufacturers carry out post-marketing safety and efficacy studies. Table 3.7 shows the studies undertaken on a section 522 order dated 3 January 2012, taken from the 522 database.

Table 3.7 Section 522 studies on mesh ordered by the FDA on 3 January 2012

522 number	Manufacturer	Device Name	Medical Specialty	Study Name	Study Status
PS120001	Acell, Inc	Acell matristem pelvic floor matrix	General & Plastic Surgery	POP AE & Effectiveness rates registry	Progress Inadequate
PS120002	American Medical Systems, Inc	Ams large pore polypropylene mesh	Obstetrics/ Gynecology	AE & Effectiveness rates	Other

(continued)

[701] Public Health Notification: Serious Complications Associated with Transvaginal Placement of Surgical Mesh in Repair of Pelvic Organ Prolapse and Stress Urinary Incontinence (20 October 2008), available at wayback.archive-it.org/7993/20170111190506/http://www.fda.gov/MedicalDevices/Safety/AlertsandNotices/PublicHealthNotifications/ucm061976.htm.

[702] Urogynecologic Surgical Mesh: Update on the Safety and Effectiveness of Transvaginal Placement for Pelvic Organ Prolapse (13 July 2011), available at http://www.fda.gov/downloads/MedicalDevices/Safety/AlertsandNotices/UCM262760.pdf.

[703] Section 522 of the Food, Drug and Cosmetic Act, 21 USC § 360l.

Table 3.7 *(Continued)*

522 number	Manufacturer	Device Name	Medical Specialty	Study Name	Study Status
PS120003	American Medical Systems, Inc	Ams large pore polypropylene mesh	General & Plastic Surgery	AE & Effectiveness rates	Other
PS120005	American Medical Systems, Inc	Ams elevate anterior & apical prolapse repair system with intepro lite	Obstetrics/ Gynecology	AE & Effectiveness rates	Other
PS120007	American Medical Systems, Inc	Ams elevate apical and posterior prolapse repair system with intepro lite or intexen lp	General & Plastic Surgery	AE & Effectiveness rates	Other
PS120008	American Medical Systems, Inc	Ams elevate apical and posterior prolapse repair system with intepro lite or intexen lp	Obstetrics/ Gynecology	AE & Effectiveness rates	Other
PS120009	American Medical Systems, Inc	Apogee and perigee systems with intepro lite and intexen lp part of the ams pelvic floor repair system; Ams collagen dermal matrix, ams apogee system with pre-connected collagen dermal matrix, ams perigee system with pre-connected collagen dermal matrix	General & Plastic Surgery	Apogee & Perigee System w/ IntePro Lite	Other
PS120010	American Medical Systems, Inc	Apogee and perigee systems with intepro lite and intexen lp part of the ams pelvic floor repair system; Ams collagen dermal matrix, ams apogee system with pre-connected collagen dermal matrix, ams perigee system with pre-connected collagen dermal matrix	General & Plastic Surgery	Apogee AE & Eff Rates	Other
				Perigee AE & Eff Rates	Other

(continued)

Table 3.7 *(Continued)*

522 number	Manufacturer	Device Name	Medical Specialty	Study Name	Study Status
PS120011	American Medical Systems, Inc	Apogee and perigee systems with intepro lite and intexen lp part of the ams pelvic floor repair system; Ams collagen dermal matrix, ams apogee system with pre-connected collagen dermal matrix, ams perigee system with pre-connected collagen dermal matrix	General & Plastic Surgery	AE & Effectiveness rates	Other
PS120012	American Medical Systems, Inc	Apogee and perigee systems with intepro lite and intexen lp part of the ams pelvic floor repair system; Ams collagen dermal matrix, ams apogee system with pre-connected collagen dermal matrix, ams perigee system with pre-connected collagen dermal matrix	General & Plastic Surgery	AE & Effectiveness rates	Other
PS120013	American Medical Systems, Inc	Apogee and perigee systems with pc coated intepro lite	General & Plastic Surgery	AE & Effectiveness rates	Other
PS120014	American Medical Systems, Inc	Elevate prolapse repair system with pc coated intepro lite- apical and posterior prolapse repair system anterior and ap	General & Plastic Surgery	AE & Effectiveness rates	Other
PS120015	American Medical Systems, Inc	Ams collagen dermal matrix, ams apogee system with pre-connected collagen dermal matrix, ams perigee system with pre-connected collagen dermal matrix	Obstetrics/ Gynecology	AE & Effectiveness rates	Other

(continued)

Table 3.7 *(Continued)*

522 number	Manufacturer	Device Name	Medical Specialty	Study Name	Study Status
PS120090	American Medical Systems, Inc	Miniarc precise single-incision sling system	General & Plastic Surgery	AE & Effectiveness rates	Other
PS120091	American Medical Systems, Inc	Miniarc precise single-incision sling system	General & Plastic Surgery	SUI AE & Effectiveness rates	Consolidated
PS120092	American Medical Systems, Inc	Miniarc precise single-incision sling system	General & Plastic Surgery	SUI AE & Effectiveness rates	Consolidated
PS120004	Astora Womens Health	Ams elevate anterior & apical prolapse repair system with intepro llite	General & Plastic Surgery	POP AE & effectiveness rates, registry	Other
PS120006	Astora Womens Health	Ams elevate apical and posterior prolapse repair system with intepro lite	General & Plastic Surgery	POP AE & Effectiveness rates, registry	Other
				Elevate System w/ InteXen LP	Other
PS120089	Astora Womens Health	Miniarc precise single-incision sling system	General & Plastic Surgery	SUI AE & Effectiveness rates	Other
PS120081	Boston Scientific	Xenform soft tissue repair matrix	General & Plastic Surgery	POP AE & Effectiveness rates registry	Progress Adequate
PS120021	Boston Scientific Corporation	Lite pelvic floor repair kits	Obstetrics/ Gynecology	AE & Effectiveness rates for Uphold LITE	Other
				DUET Lite	Other
				Posterior LITE	Other
				Anterior LITE	Other
PS120022	Boston Scientific Corporation	Pelvic floor repair system (pinnacle duet)	General & Plastic Surgery	AE & Effectiveness rates – Duet	Other

(continued)

Table 3.7 *(Continued)*

522 number	Manufacturer	Device Name	Medical Specialty	Study Name	Study Status
PS120023	Boston Scientific Corporation	Pinnacle pelvic floor repair kit ii (uphold)	General & Plastic Surgery	AE & Effectiveness rates – Uphold	Other
PS120024	Boston Scientific Corporation	Pinnacle pelvic floor repair kits (pinnacle)	General & Plastic Surgery	AE & Effectiveness rates – Anterior	Other
				AE & Effectiveness rates-Posterior	Other
PS120093	Boston Scientific Corporation	Solyx Single Incision Sling System	General & Plastic Surgery	SUI AE & Effectiveness rates	Progress Adequate
PS120027	CR Bard Inc	Avaulta solo synthetic support system avaulta plus biosynthetic support system; Avaulta support system	General & Plastic Surgery	AE & Effectiveness rates	Other
PS120028	CR Bard Inc	Avaulta solo synthetic support system avaulta plus biosynthetic support system; Avaulta support system	General & Plastic Surgery	AE & Effectiveness rates	Other
PS120029	CR Bard Inc	Avaulta solo synthetic support system avaulta plus biosynthetic support system; Avaulta support system	General & Plastic Surgery	AE & Effectiveness rates	Other
PS120030	CR Bard Inc	Bard prolapse repair system	Obstetrics/ Gynecology	AE & Effectiveness rates	Terminated
PS120031	CR Bard Inc	Bard pelvisoft acellular collagen biomesh	General & Plastic Surgery	AE & Effectiveness rates	Other

(continued)

Table 3.7 *(Continued)*

522 number	Manufacturer	Device Name	Medical Specialty	Study Name	Study Status
PS120094	CR Bard Inc	Ajust adjustable single incision sling	General & Plastic Surgery	AE & Effectiveness rates	Other
PS120032	Caldera Medical Inc	Popmesh	General & Plastic Surgery	AE & Effectiveness rates – PoP Mesh	Other
PS120033	Caldera Medical Inc	Ascend blue ac mesh; Ascend blue pc mesh	General & Plastic Surgery	AE & Effectiveness rates	Other
PS120034	Caldera Medical Inc	Ascend blue ac mesh; Ascend blue pc mesh	General & Plastic Surgery	AE & Effectiveness rates	Other
PS120035	Coloplast Corp	Exair anterior and posterior prolapse repair systems	General & Plastic Surgery	POP AE & Effectiveness rates, registry	Other
PS120036	Coloplast Corp	Exair anterior and posterior prolapse repair systems	Obstetrics/ Gynecology	POP AE & Effectiveness rates, registry	Consolidated
PS120037	Coloplast Corp	Mentor novasilk mesh	General & Plastic Surgery	AE & Effectiveness rates	Other
PS120038	Coloplast Corp	Restorelle polypropyl-ene mesh; Restorelle polypropylene mesh	Obstetrics/ Gynecology	AE & Effectiveness rates	Other
				Restorelle P, EZA, EZP, and L models	Other
PS120055	Coloplast Corp	Minimesh polypropyl-ene mesh	General & Plastic Surgery	AE & Effectiveness rates	Other
				Restorelle P, EZA and L model	Other
PS120056	Coloplast Corp	Minimesh polypropyl-ene mesh	General & Plastic Surgery	AE & Effectiveness rates	Other
				Restorelle P, EZA and L models	Other

(continued)

Table 3.7 *(Continued)*

522 number	Manufacturer	Device Name	Medical Specialty	Study Name	Study Status
PS120096	Coloplast Corp	Gyne ideas minitape rp device	General & Plastic Surgery	AE & Effectiveness rates	Other
PS120097	Coloplast Corp	Minitape urethral sling	General & Plastic Surgery	AE & Effectiveness rates	Other
PS120098	Coloplast Corp	Minitape urethral sling	General & Plastic Surgery	AE & Effectiveness rates	Other
PS120040	Cousin Biotech SARL	Biotech SAS for Biomesh® Pl and Biomesh® Plug and Patch	General & Plastic Surgery	AE & Effectiveness rates	Terminated
PS120071	Covidien	Parietene duo and quadra polypropylene meshes	General & Plastic Surgery	AE & Effectiveness rates	Other
PS120072	Covidien	Ugytex dual knit mesh	General & Plastic Surgery	AE & Effectiveness rates	Other
PS120075	Covidien	Permacol surgical implant t-piece permacol surgical implant rectocele-piece models 5928-150 5645-150	General & Plastic Surgery	AE & Effectiveness rates	Other
PS120076	Covidien	Permacol surgical implant t-piece permacol surgical implant rectocele-piece models 5928-150 5645-150; Permacol surgical implant	General & Plastic Surgery	AE & Effectiveness rates	Other
PS120041	CryoLife, Inc	Propatch soft tissue repair matrix	General & Plastic Surgery	AE & Effectiveness rates	Terminated
PS120042	CryoLife, Inc	Propatch soft tissue repair matrix	General & Plastic Surgery	AE & Effectiveness rates	Terminated
PS120052	Cytori Therapeutics, Inc	Macropore surgiwrap (ts)	General & Plastic Surgery	AE & Effectiveness rates	Other

(continued)

Table 3.7 *(Continued)*

522 number	Manufacturer	Device Name	Medical Specialty	Study Name	Study Status
PS120048	DSM Biomedical	Bioblanket surgical mesh	General & Plastic Surgery	AE & Effectiveness rates	Other
PS120049	DSM Biomedical	Bioblanket surgical mesh	General & Plastic Surgery	AE & Effectiveness rates	Other
PS120050	DSM Biomedical	Medeor matrix models 30010-xx (hydrated); 30020-xx (dry)	General & Plastic Surgery	AE & Effectiveness rates	Terminated
PS120051	DSM Biomedical	Kensey nash ecm surgical patch	General & Plastic Surgery	AE & Effectiveness rates	Terminated
PS120043	Ethicon, Inc	Gynecare prolift +m* pelvic floor repair systems	General & Plastic Surgery	AE & Effectiveness rates	Other
PS120044	Ethicon, Inc	Gynecare prosima pelvic floor repair systems	General & Plastic Surgery	AE & Effectiveness rates	Other
PS120045	Ethicon, Inc	Tbd ethicon mesh (gynecare gynemesh m)	General & Plastic Surgery	AE & Effectiveness rates	Other
PS120046	Ethicon, Inc	Gynemesh Prolene™ soft (polypropyl-ene) nonabsorbable synthetic surgical mesh for pelvic floor repair	Obstetrics/ Gynecology	AE & Effectiveness rates	Other
PS120095	Ethicon, Inc	Gynecare tvt secur system	General & Plastic Surgery	AE & Effectiveness rates	Other
PS120057	Neomedic International	SURELIFT PROLAPSE SYSTEM	Obstetrics/ Gynecology	AE & Effectiveness rates	Other
PS120058	Organogenesis, Inc	FORTAFLEX SURGICAL MESH	General & Plastic Surgery	AE & Effectiveness rates	Other
PS120059	Organogenesis, Inc	FORTAFLEX SURGICAL MESH	General & Plastic Surgery	AE & Effectiveness rates	Other

(continued)

Table 3.7 *(Continued)*

522 number	Manufacturer	Device Name	Medical Specialty	Study Name	Study Status
PS120060	Organogenesis, Inc	FORTAFLEX SURGICAL MESH	General & Plastic Surgery	AE & Effectiveness rates	Other
PS120047	PFM Medical	Timesh also known as timesh-tc models 6000001 & 6000004	Obstetrics/ Gynecology	AE & Effectiveness rates	Terminated
PS120066	Promethean Surgical Devices, Inc	Hydrocoat mesh	General & Plastic Surgery	AE & Effectiveness rates	Other
PS120099	Prosurg, Inc	Minisling adjust-able polymer sling & surgical mesh with self-anchoring system (easy lift prolapse repair & minisling)	General & Plastic Surgery	AE & Effectiveness rates	Other
PS120067	Proxy Biomedical Ltd.	Polyform synthetic mesh	Obstetrics/ Gynecology	AE & Effectiveness rates	Terminated
PS120068	RTI Biologics, Inc	Tutopatch tutomesh	General & Plastic Surgery	AE & Effectiveness rates	Other
PS120069	Shelhigh, Inc	Shelhigh porcine peri-cardial patch	General & Plastic Surgery	AE & Effectiveness rates	Terminated
PS120070	Shelhigh, Inc	SHELHIGH NO-REACT TISSUE REPAIR PATCH/ UROPATCH.	General & Plastic Surgery	AE & Effectiveness rates	Terminated
PS120062	Smith & Nephew	Immix thin film models: Pss-004-s pss-004-sp pss-004-m pss-004-mp pss-004-l pss-004-lp	General & Plastic Surgery	AE & Effectiveness rates	Other
PS120061	Smith & Nephew, Inc	Immix plastifilm	General & Plastic Surgery	AE & Effectiveness rates	Other
PS120073	Sofradim Production	Ugytex mesh	General & Plastic Surgery	AE & Effectiveness rates	Other

(continued)

Table 3.7 *(Continued)*

522 number	Manufacturer	Device Name	Medical Specialty	Study Name	Study Status
PS120074	Sofradim Production	Parietex	General & Plastic Surgery	AE & Effectiveness rates	Terminated
PS120025	Stellen Medical	Brennen medical surgical mesh glucamesh/glucatex	General & Plastic Surgery	AE & Effectiveness rates	Other
PS120026	Stellen Medical	Dermmatrix surgical mesh	General & Plastic Surgery	AE & Effectiveness rates	Other
PS120063	Synovis Surgical Innovation	Orthadapt pr; Orthadapt bioimplant; Pegasus biologics orthadapt surgical mesh	General & Plastic Surgery	AE & Effectiveness rates	Terminated
PS120064	Synovis Surgical Innovation	Orthadapt pr; Orthadapt bioimplant; Pegasus biologics orthadapt surgical mesh	General & Plastic Surgery	AE & Effectiveness rates	Terminated
PS120017	Synovis Surgical Innovations	Peri-strips	Obstetrics/ Gynecology	AE & Effectiveness rates	Other
PS120065	Synovis Surgical Innovations	Orthadapt pr; Orthadapt bioimplant; Pegasus biologics orthadapt surgical mesh	General & Plastic Surgery	AE & Effectiveness rates	Terminated
PS120077	Synovis Surgical Innovations	Veritas collagen matrix	General & Plastic Surgery	AE & Effectiveness rates	Terminated
PS120078	Synovis Surgical Innovations	Veritas collagen matrix	General & Plastic Surgery	AE & Effectiveness rates	Terminated
PS120016	Synovis Surgical Innovations/ Baxter	Peri-guard cv peri-guard ocu-guard supple peri-guard peri-strips – sleeve peri-strips-strips peri-strips dry vasc	General & Plastic Surgery	AE & Effectiveness rates	Terminated

(continued)

Table 3.7 *(Continued)*

522 number	Manufacturer	Device Name	Medical Specialty	Study Name	Study Status
PS120018	Synovis Surgical Innovations/ Baxter	Supple peri-guard pericardium	General & Plastic Surgery	AE & Effectiveness rates	Terminated
PS120019	Synovis Surgical Innovations/ Baxter	Peri-guard pericardium	General & Plastic Surgery	AE & Effectiveness rates	Terminated
PS120020	Synovis Surgical Innovations/ Baxter	Supple peri-guard pericardium	General & Plastic Surgery	AE & Effectiveness rates	Terminated
PS120080	Tei Biosciences Inc	Tissuemend soft tissue repair matrix	General & Plastic Surgery	AE & Effectiveness rates	Other
PS120082	Tei Biosciences Inc	Xenform soft tissue repair matrix	General & Plastic Surgery	AE & Effectiveness rates	Other
PS120079	Tepha, Inc	Tephaflex surgical mesh	Obstetrics/ Gynecology	AE & Effectiveness rates	Terminated
PS120083	WL Gore & Associates, Inc	Seamguard staple line reinforcement material	General & Plastic Surgery	AE & Effectiveness rates	Terminated
PS120084	WL Gore & Associates, Inc	Modification to seamguard staple line reinforcement material	General & Plastic Surgery	AE & Effectiveness rates	Terminated
PS120085	WL Gore & Associates, Inc	Gore bioabsorbable mesh	General & Plastic Surgery	AE & Effectiveness rates	Terminated
PS120086	WL Gore & Associates, Inc	Seamguard staple line reinforcement material	General & Plastic Surgery	AE & Effectiveness rates	Terminated
PS120087	Xylos Corporation	Xylos porous surgical mesh	General & Plastic Surgery	AE & Effectiveness rates	Other
PS120088	Xylos Corporation	Xylos porous surgical mesh	General & Plastic Surgery	AE & Effectiveness rates	Other

Several things are immediately obvious from Table 3.7:

(a) Not all mesh products are classified under the 'Obstetrics/Gynecology' specialty. It may be that some products are for other uses. For example, the Shelhig porcine pericardial patch is self-evidently not an 'Obstetrics/Gynecology' device. However, some urogynaecological devices, for example the CR Bard Avaulta products, are classified under 'General & Plastic Surgery', and the AMS Elevate apical and posterior prolapse repair system has two classifications – 'Obstetrics/Gynecology' and 'General & Plastic Surgery'. This lack of consistency is interesting, and probably reflects the aetiology of how these devices arose from more general surgical mesh.

(b) Few of the studies are completed. Section 522 post-marketing studies are not available for products such as Ethicon's TVT Secur, Prosima, Prolift and Prolift + M, which were (globally) withdrawn before the post-marketing surveillance studies were undertaken. These studies are listed as 'Other', although the products have not been marketed for years.

(c) The sheer number of different products and manufacturers is remarkable: in the 15 years since the first urogynaecological mesh was approved, the market had developed at a considerable pace. While not all of the devices in Table 3.7 are urogynaecological devices, the majority are. Section 522 studies were intended to provide additional evidence about the performance and safety of these products.

As a result of the safety notices and widespread media attention and litigation advertising, transvaginal mesh in urogynaecological POP surgery in the US dropped by 60% from 2010 to 2014.

In January 2016, transvaginal mesh for POP repair was reclassified as a class III device,[704] which required pre-market authorisation[705] and had a higher evidential threshold, including information from human studies.[706] All new products required a PMA, and the manufacturers of products already on the market had 30 months from the notice date to submit a PMA. This reclassification did not include mesh products used for transabdominal POP repair, or those, such as polypropylene products used in mid-urethral slings and abdominal apical support procedures, used for SUI treatment, which all remained unchanged as class II.

b. In the EU

Mesh is a class IIb medical device, so once a product has been CE marked, it can be sold throughout the EU. Pelvic mesh will move to class III in 2020.[707] Most mesh products would have been subject to PMA on the basis of 'equivalence' to a device that was already on the market.

[704] Federal Register 21 CFR 884, effective date 5 January 2016, available at www.federalregister.gov/documents/2016/01/05/2015-33163/effective-date-of-requirement-for-premarket-approval-for-surgical-mesh-for-transvaginal-pelvic-organ.

[705] Federal Register 81 FR 363, effective date 5 January 2016, available at www.federalregister.gov/documents/2016/01/05/2015-33163/effective-date-of-requirement-for-premarket-approval-for-surgical-mesh-for-transvaginal-pelvic-organ.

[706] See at www.fda.gov/NewsEvents/Newsroom/PressAnnouncements/ucm479732.htm.

[707] Regulation (EU) 2017/745.

It is difficult to obtain information on how the specific devices within a class obtained marketing authorisation in the EU, as each one is considered individually and confidentially. There is no centralised database or publically available resource on regulatory approval decisions. Given that the market for such devices is, in effect, global in nature, it is unlikely that the manufacturers and/or products will differ substantially between the US and the EU, but there may be some variations.

The first major cause for concern in the EU occurred when the 2011 FDA safety update was issued. In response, the MHRA commissioned a *Summary of the Evidence* by the York Economics Consortium, which was published in 2012.[708] This was followed in 2014 by the MHRA's *Summary of the Evidence of the Benefits and Risks of Vaginal Mesh Implants*.[709] This report concluded that pelvic mesh is safe when used for the treatment of SUI, but that more caution was needed when using mesh for treating POP. In 2015, NHS England set up the Mesh Oversight Group to address concerns about the safety and efficacy of pelvic mesh use for SUI and POP.

In 2015, the Scientific Committee on Emerging and Newly Identified Health Risks (SCENIHR) (EU) Opinion[710] was published. It included several recommendations:

- Synthetic sling surgery for SUI is an acceptable procedure for most patients with moderate to severe SUI.
- Transvaginal mesh treatment of POP should be only considered in complex cases after failed primary repair surgery.
- Surgeons should attempt to limit the amount of mesh used during procedures.
- To ensure competence, a certification system for surgeons should be introduced.
- More appropriate patient selection and counselling should be undertaken to improve efficacy and ensure that informed consent is received.

In 2016, the PROSPECT (PROlapse Surgery: Pragmatic Evaluation and randomised Controlled Trials) results were published.[711] At first sight these appeared quite damning, the conclusion being that the use of transvaginal prolapse mesh or graft material did not improve women's outcomes in terms of effectiveness, quality of life, adverse effects or any other outcome in the two-year follow up. In addition, 12% of the patients had a mesh complication (not all of which were serious). The vast majority of POP mesh usage was of hand-cut POP mesh; mesh kits made up < 1% of the mesh used. Serious adverse events, such as intraoperative complications, thrombosis, infection, urinary retention, bowel obstruction, blood loss, dyspareunia or other pain, or death, excluding mesh complications,

[708] See at http://www.mhra.gov.uk/home/groups/comms-ic/documents/websiteresources/con205383.pdf.

[709] See at assets.publishing.service.gov.uk/government/uploads/system/uploads/attachment_data/file/402162/Summary_of_the_evidence_on_the_benefits_and_risks_of_vaginal_mesh_implants.pdf.

[710] Scientific Committee on Emerging and Newly Identified Health Risks, Opinion on the safety of surgical meshes used in urogynecological surgery (December 2015), available at ec.europa.eu/health/scientific_committees/emerging/docs/scenihr_o_049.pdf.

[711] PROlapse Surgery: Pragmatic Evaluation and randomised Controlled Trials. CMA Glazener et al (on behalf of the PROSPECT Group). 'Mesh, graft, or standard repair for women having primary transvaginal anterior or posterior compartment prolapse surgery: two parallel-group, multicentre, randomised, controlled trials (PROSPECT)' (2017) 389(10067) *The Lancet* 381, doi: 10.1016/S0140-6736(16)31596-3.

occurred with similar frequency in the groups over one year. When the PROSPECT data were added to the Cochrane Review results on 6 July 2016,[712] the summary statistics still favoured mesh, in terms both of awareness of prolapse and anatomical recurrence. This was with the caveat that the PROSPECT trial utilised a homogeneous study population, making it more consistent, whereas the Cochrane Review used a heterogeneous study population from different trials.

In the light of the PROSPECT results and other findings, the 2017 Scottish *Transvaginal Mesh Implants Independent Review Final Report*[713] recommended that transvaginal mesh should not be offered for POP, but that for SUI all options should be offered, including mesh where appropriate. Later that year the Mesh Oversight Group Report[714] concluded that pelvic mesh is safe and effective for SUI and POP, but should not be first-line surgery for POP and that NICE Guidelines should be followed. It recommended that more information and support should be available, and that a registry should be developed.

The NICE guidelines[715] were changed shortly afterwards to recommend that mesh can only be used for research purposes in transvaginal POP surgery, not as a standard treatment. The 2017 NICE guidelines[716] concerning abdominal sacrocolpopexy using mesh to repair vaginal vault prolapse, found that evidence on efficacy was adequate in quantity and quality. The evidence showed that sacrocolpopexy using mesh to repair vaginal vault prolapse has serious but well-recognised safety issues, and so the 2017 NICE guidelines recommended that that procedure could be used, but only subject to specified arrangements for clinical governance, consent and audit being in place.

In 2018, the Report of the Welsh Task and Finish Group[717] made recommendations following NICE guidelines on mesh use. Additionally, the Group advocated for creating a new pathway for women's pelvic health, with the aim of improved decision making and of providing women in Wales with access to specialist services.

In February 2018 the Secretary of State for Health and Social Care announced an Independent Medicines and Medical Devices Safety Review (IMMDS Review).[718] One of the interventions the Review was tasked with considering was the use of mesh in pelvic surgery. The Chair of the IMMDS Review, Baroness Julia Cumberlege, called for a pause on the use of vaginally-inserted mesh for SUI in July 2018, which was implemented by NHS England.[719] This has not banned mesh in this type of surgery, but has made it a last resort, overseen by a high-vigilance framework.

[712] C Maher et al 'Transvaginal mesh or grafts compared with native tissue repair for vaginal prolapse' (2016) 2 *Cochrane Database Systematic Review*, CD01207.

[713] The Scottish Independent Review of the use, safety and efficacy of transvaginal mesh implants in the treatment of Stress Urinary Incontinence and Pelvic Organ Prolapse in women, Final Report (March 2017), available at www.gov.scot/Resource/0051/00515856.pdf.

[714] Mesh Oversight Group Report (July 2017), available at www.england.nhs.uk/wp-content/uploads/2017/07/mesh-oversight-group-report.pdf.

[715] 2017 NICE (UK) Guidance IPG59913.

[716] 2017 NICE (UK) Guidance IPG583, available at www.nice.org.uk/guidance/ipg583/chapter/1-Recommendations).

[717] Report of the Welsh Task and Finish Group to Review the Use of Vaginal Synthetic Mesh Tape and Sheets for Stress Urinary Incontinence and Pelvic Organ Prolapse (May 2018), available at https://gov.wales/docs/dhss/publications/180504reporten.pdf.

[718] See at www.immdsreview.org.uk.

[719] See at www.gov.uk/government/news/government-announces-strict-rules-for-the-use-of-vaginal-mesh.

NICE is currently revising its guidelines for the management of SUI and POP, and draft guidelines were issued for consultation in October 2018.

The IMMDS Review has yet to report, so further regulatory action may follow.

iv. Litigation

The claims concerning vaginal mesh have involved many thousand claimants seeking billions of dollars. The scale of the litigation means that it would be impossible to cover it in its entirety here, so this will be a brief summary rather than a comprehensive description.

Litigation has been on several bases, with manufacturers variously being accused of having failed to test/research mesh products adequately, failed to warn of the potential complications and injuries (including in some instances accusations of intentional misleading), and failed to devise safe and effective techniques for mesh removal.

a. Multi-District Litigation

1. ObTape MDL

The first MDL was the ObTape MDL, a relatively small mesh MDL with 862 litigants, created in 2008 and listed in the Middle District of Georgia, heard by Judge Clay D Land.[720] Despite the relatively low number of cases, the judge was critical of plaintiff lawyers for lodging unfounded or time-barred cases.[721]

The first bellwether trial of six plaintiffs for the first wave was listed for June 2010, but a settlement was reached. Further cases were settled or withdrawn with only a few cases going all the way to trial. The most notable trial was the first bellwether trial, Irene Morey's case,[722] which was won by the defence. In contrast was the case of Teresa Taylor,[723] who was awarded \$4.4 million, \$4 million of which was in punitive damages, in February 2016. Judge Land pushed hard for the defendants to settle, and by 2018 the litigation was over and there were no open cases. A substantial number of claims had been struck out or had been withdrawn, reflecting the judge's complaints about claims that lacked merit being initiated.

2. West Virginia MDL

In February 2012, the US Judicial Panel on Multidistrict Litigation agreed to assign cases against three companies into a separate MDL in the Southern District of West Virginia, where an existing pelvic-mesh MDL was pending. Further manufacturers were added, and finally the following instances of MDL ended up being assigned to the US District Court for the Southern District of West Virginia by Judge Joseph R Goodwin:

- CR Bard, MDL No 2187[724]
- American Medical Systems, MDL No 2325[725]

[720] *In re Mentor Corp Obtape Transobturator Sling Products Liability Litigation*, MDL Docket no 2004 4:08-MD-2004 (CDL), available at www.gamd.uscourts.gov/mdl-cases.

[721] ibid, Order Document 1039, Order Filed 9 July 2016, available at ecf.gamd.uscourts.gov/cgi-bin/show_public_doc?2008-02004-1039-4-md.

[722] *Irene Morey v Mentor Worldwide, LLC*, Case no 4:11-CV-5065 (CDL).

[723] *Teresa Taylor v Mentor Worldwide, LLC*, Case no 4:12-CV-176 (CDL).

[724] www.wvsd.uscourts.gov/MDL/2187/index.html.

[725] www.wvsd.uscourts.gov/MDL/amsinc/index.html.

- Boston Scientific, MDL No 2326[726]
- Johnson & Johnson, Ethicon, MDL No 2327[727]
- Coloplast Corp, MDL No 2387[728]
- Cook Medical, MDL No 2440[729]
- Neomedic Pelvic Repair System, MDL No 2511.

At its peak this litigation dealt with 105,743 plaintiffs. The scale of this is startling: to try all of these cases individually would have taken decades and cost billions of dollars. However, the majority of cases have now settled, gone to trial or been dismissed (see Table 3.8).[730] Given the scale of the litigation, it is impressive that the majority of cases have been resolved, largely affected by the way in which Judge Goodwin has actively driven the litigation and firmly encouraged settlement.

Table 3.8 Pending actions in the West Virginia pelvic-mesh MDL as at 15 May 2018

MDL Number	MDL Name	Pending Actions	Total Actions
MDL -2187	In re CR Bard, Inc, Pelvic Repair System Products Liability Litigation	2,180	15,683
MDL -2325	In re American Medical Systems, Inc, Pelvic Repair System Products Liability Litigation	2,331	21,224
MDL -2326	In re Boston Scientific Corp Pelvic Repair System Products Liability Litigation	4,068	25,562
MDL -2327	In re Ethicon, Inc, Pelvic Repair System Products Liability Litigation	13,002	39,980
MDL -2387	In re Coloplast Corp Pelvic Support Systems Products Liability Litigation	75	2,652
MDL -2440	In re Cook Medical, Inc, Pelvic Repair System Products Liability Litigation	73	642
Total		**21,729**	**105,743**

Given the scale of the litigation, it is not possible to detail an exhaustive list of outcomes, therefore only key cases and settlements will be outlined here:

(a) *CR Bard*.[731] The first trial in the West Virginia MDL, *Donna and Dan Cissons v CR Bard Inc*, commenced in July 2013 and resulted in a judgment against the

[726] www.wvsd.uscourts.gov/MDL/boston/index.html.
[727] www.wvsd.uscourts.gov/MDL/ethicon/index.html.
[728] www.wvsd.uscourts.gov/MDL/2387/index.html.
[729] www.wvsd.uscourts.gov/MDL/2440/index.html.
[730] Data taken from the Judicial Panel on Multi-District Litigation website at www.jpml.uscourts.gov/sites/jpml/files/Pending_MDL_Dockets_By_District-May-15-2018.pdf.
[731] Information taken from the 2017 10-K filing for CR Bard Inc, available at www.sec.gov/Archives/edgar/data/9892/000119312517040742/d298442d10k.htm.

company of approximately $2 million,[732] which was upheld by the Fourth Circuit in 2016.[733] In 2014 the District Court ordered that the company prepare 200,[734] and then another almost 300, individual cases[735] for trial. Substantially all of the 500 individual cases have settled or are part of agreements in principle to settle. As of 31 December 2016, CR Bard Inc had reached agreements or agreements in principle with various plaintiffs' law firms to settle their respective inventories of cases totalling approximately 11,000 Women's Health Product Claims, including approximately: 560 during 2014; 6,285 during 2015; and 4,155 during 2016. Each agreement is subject to certain conditions, including requirements for participation in the proposed settlements by a certain minimum number of plaintiffs. CR Bard Inc continues to engage in discussions with other plaintiffs' law firms regarding potential resolution of unsettled Women's Health Product Claims. It has been reported that the company spent almost a quarter of a billion dollars on West Virginia MDL settlements between 2013–15.

In addition to the West Virginia MDL, CR Bard Inc also defended the first Avaulta® products trial in California in July 2012, which resulted in a judgment against the company of approximately $3.6 million.[736] CR Bard Inc appealed the judgment on the grounds that the jury instructions had been incorrect; the original judgment was upheld in November 2014.[737] CR Bard Inc's subsequent petition to the California Supreme Court for review was denied in February 2015.

(b) *AMS/Endo.* In 2011, AMS was taken over by Endo Pharmaceutical Holdings (subsequently becoming Endo Health Solutions, then Endo International PLC). AMS/Endo Health Solutions Inc was an early adopter of settlements. In July 2013 AMS entered into a Master Settlement Agreement (MSA) to pay $54.5 million for an unspecified number of certain mesh claims without admissions of liability or fault.[738] Over the next few years further MSAs were entered into, and in 2017 Endo International PLC set aside $775.5 million, which is expected to cover the remaining 22,000 known US mesh claims.[739] By the end of 2017 the total of liability payments made was approximately $2.9 billion.[740]

(c) *Boston Scientific.* In 2015, Boston Scientific entered into their first major settlement, when $119 million was set aside for 2,970 pending cases and claims. This figure is very high because it included provision for the case of Marth Salazar and Felix Salazar,

[732] *Cisson et al v CR Bard, Inc*, Civil Action no 2:11-cv-00195 (SDW Va, 20 January 2015).

[733] *Cisson v CR Bard, Inc*, no 15-1102 (4th Cir 2016), available at law.justia.com/cases/federal/appellate-courts/ca4/15-1102/15-1102-2016-01-14.html.

[734] MDL 2187 Pre-trial order 102, available at www.wvsd.uscourts.gov/MDL/2187/pdfs/PTO_102.pdf.

[735] MDL 2187 Pre-trial order 131, available at www.wvsd.uscourts.gov/MDL/2187/pdfs/PTO_131.pdf.

[736] *Christine Scott v CR Bard*, Case no S-1500-CV-266034 (Cal, Kern Co, Super 24 July 2012).

[737] *Christine Scott et al v CR Bard, Inc*, F066039 (Super Ct no CV-266034), available at www.courts.ca.gov/opinions/archive/F066039.PDF.

[738] Information taken from the 2014 10-K filing for Endo Health Solutions, available at www.sec.gov/Archives/edgar/data/1100962/000144530514000793/endp-12312013x10k.htm.

[739] Information taken from the 2018 10-K filing for Endo International PLC, available at www.sec.gov/Archives/edgar/data/1593034/000159303418000010/endp-12312017x10k.htm.

[740] ibid.

who had been awarded $34.64 million[741] by a jury in the District Court of Dallas County. Boston Scientific launched an appeal against this verdict, but settled the case for an undisclosed sum before the appeal.[742] In total, by 31 January 2018 around 49,000 transvaginal surgical mesh product liability claims had been brought against Boston Scientific. The vast majority of these claimants, approximately 44,000 cases, either had already entered into MSAs or were in the final stages of entering one. At this point 20,000 cases were already finally settled. These MSAs provide that the settlement and distribution of settlement funds to participating claimants are conditional upon, amongst other things, achieving minimum required claimant participation thresholds. All settlement agreements were entered into solely by way of compromise and without any admission of any liability or concession of wrongdoing.

The 2018 10-K filing for Boston Scientific does not exactly specify the transvaginal mesh cases and claims spend, but indicates that it is likely to have been around $1 billion in 2016–17.

(d) *Johnson & Johnson.* Johnson & Johnson was the defendant with the largest number of claims against it in the West Virginia MDL and has only entered into relatively modest-scale settlements. Aside from the ObTape settlement (see section XI.B.iv.a.1), Johnson & Johnson has tended towards litigation rather than settlement. Johnson & Johnson has won some cases and lost others. Some individual cases have resulted in very substantial awards: for example, in 2017 the $57.1 million awarded to Ella Ebaugh;[743] and in 2018 the *Kaiser* case, which resulted in a jury awarding $35 million to the plaintiffs[744] ($25 million of which was punitive damages, subsequently reduced to $10 million).

When settlement talks commenced in October 2013, Johnson & Johnson was the only one of the six defendants in the West Virginia MDL that did not join the talks. However, in January 2016 an agreement was made to pay just over $120 million to settle up to 3,000 claims. It is potentially unsurprising that Johnson & Johnson has the highest proportion of unresolved claims. In mid-May 2018, 32.5% of Johnson & Johnson's cases in MDL 2327 were still pending.

(e) *Coloplast.* A settlement in principle was agreed in January 2014, which was reported to be $16 million for around 400 claimants, including the claimant in what was due to be the first bellwether Coloplast trial. This agreement materialised over the next few years when the company went on to agree to settlements with nearly a score of plaintiff law firms.[745] In November 2015, Coloplast announced that another $448 million had been set aside for pelvic-mesh cases.[746] By mid-May 2018, Coloplast only had 75 outstanding cases in the MDL, less than 3% of their total cases.

[741] Originally on 8 September 2014 the jury returned compensation of $73.46 million to the Salazars – see *Martha and Felix Salazar v Jorge Francisco Lopez and Boston Scientific Corporation*, DC-12-14349, (Dallas, Dist Co, 95 Div, 8 September 2014) – which was capped at $34.64 by Judge Molberg a few weeks later on 2 October 2014 by the application of the Texas Civil Practice and Remedies Code, § 41.008.

[742] Order of 26 October 2015, *Boston Scientific Corporation v Martha Salazar & Felix Salazar* 05-14-01617-CV, Fifth Court of Appeal Dallas, Texas, available at www.search.txcourts.gov/Case.aspx?cn=05-14-01617-CV&coa=coa05.

[743] *Ella Cederberg-Ebaugh, et al v Ethicon, Inc, et al*, no 1307000866, Pa Comm Pls, Philadelphia Co. Ethicon stated that it would appeal the verdict.

[744] *Barbara Kaiser & Anton Kaiser et al, v Johnson & Johnson, et al*, no 17-114, ND (Ind, Hammond Div 8 March 2018).

[745] MDL 2387 pre-trial orders, available at www.wvsd.uscourts.gov/MDL/2387/orders.html.

[746] See at www.reuters.com/article/2015/09/23/us-coloplast-charge-idUSKCN0RN0LQ20150923.

(f) *Cook.* With just under 650 cases, Cook had the smallest MDL. Initially, in 2014, during the discovery phase of the litigation, Cook was accused of stonewalling and refusing to produce documents.[747] The first four bellwether cases were dismissed by the defendants. By 2015 Cook was actively pursuing settlement, as can be seen from the Order of 23 October 2015,[748] which sought to stay the discovery phase to allow time to reach a global settlement of all cases. By the middle of June 2017 an Order had been made requiring all remaining plaintiffs to attend a Settlement Conference.[749] As at mid-May 2018, all but 73 of the cases against Cook had settled, been dismissed or been tried. A substantial number of the Cook cases were dismissed.

b. Multi-County Litigation

1. Bard & Gynecare MCL in Bergen

Almost 9,000 claims have been centralised to MCL for pelvic-mesh products manufactured by Ethicon, Inc, Ethicon Women's Health and Urology, Gynecare, and/or Johnson & Johnson and CR Bard, Inc.[750] It was originally assigned to Atlantic in 2010, but in 2014 was reassigned to be heard at Bergen County Superior Court, overseen by Judge Rachelle L Harz.

Johnson & Johnson was the defendant in the first MCL vaginal mesh trial, the case of Linda and Jeffrey Gross.[751] A jury awarded $3.35 million to the claimants for Johnson & Johnson's failure to warn of the risks with the Gynecare Prolift, which was upheld on appeal.

CR Bard's first bellwether trial, *Mary McGinnis v CR Bard*,[752] in April 2018 resulted in an $85 million award to the plaintiff, which CR Bard had said it will appeal.

These bellwether trials did not auger well for the defendants, and it has been reported that CR Bard at least is pushing to achieve settlements in the MCL.

2. England and Wales

Mesh litigation in England and Wales has tended to start a few years later than in the US. It is currently underway, with around 1,000 claimants represented by various law firms. As at June 2018 there is no GLO. Claimants are suing either the manufacturer on the grounds of defective devices, or the NHS/implanting doctor for lack of warning/ informed consent. Clearly, this is nothing like the scale of the US litigation, and as there are no punitive damages, it is unlikely that pay-outs (assuming there are any) will reach anything like the sums seen in America. As the litigation is ongoing, no further comment will be made here.

[747] MDL 2440 Pre-trial Order #34 – 5 April 2014 (Plaintiffs' Motion to Compel Production of Documents), available at www.wvsd.uscourts.gov/MDL/2440/orders.html.

[748] MDL 2440 Pre-trial Order #67 – 23 October 2015 (Fifth Amended Docket Control Order for Remaining Cook MDL Cases (Cool Wave 1)), available at www.wvsd.uscourts.gov/MDL/2440/orders.html.

[749] MDL 2440 Pre-trial Order #80 – 12 June 2017 (Order: Mandatory Settlement Conference for Cook Plaintiffs), available at www.wvsd.uscourts.gov/MDL/2440/orders.html.

[750] See at www.judiciary.state.nj.us/attorneys/mcl/bergen/pelvicmesh.html.

[751] *Gross v Gynecare Inc*, Superior Court of Atlantic County, New Jersey, Atl-L-6966-10; *Linda Gross, et al v Gynecare, et al*, no A-0011-14T2 (NJ Super App Div, 29 March 2016).

[752] *Mary McGinnis v CR Bard*, Docket no BER-L-17717-14, NJ Super Ct.

v. Conclusion

The safety issue with primarily transvaginal POP mesh became apparent from adverse events reports: post-marketing safety assessments were initiated to investigate the adverse events. The reports of adverse events prompted regulators to review the way in which mesh was being used. Litigation did not inform the regulatory decisions, but the costs associated with litigation may have caused manufacturers to cease marketing products and withdraw products from the market for commercial reasons.

4

Conclusions

This chapter will draw together some of the key findings and themes that have been highlighted by the case studies, and then discuss the wider implications that these findings have for the regulatory and legal systems. The following factors specific to medicinal product litigation are noted in passing:

- *Litigation failure rates.* Medicine and medical device litigation involves significant obstacles for claimants. The following UK case studies illustrate that there is a high rate of attrition and/or failure rate of medical product litigation: Primodos (1982), DTP vaccine (1988), insulin (1993), Benzodiazepines (1994), Gravigard (1996), HRT (1997), Lariam (1998), Norplant (1999), MMR vaccine (2003), oral contraceptives (2003), and Valproate (2010) and Seroxat (2010). This appears to apply less in the US: several cases studies have succeeded in the US but not in other jurisdictions – HRT for example. This may be to do with the jury system. While this may make the American system seem attractive to claimants, the case studies seem to indicate that the jury system tends to result in numerous appeals and overturned first instance decisions. This is such a small sample that further confirmation would be necessary.
- *Difficulty establishing prospects of success.* The legal aid spend in the UK is indicative of the difficulty in establishing whether a case is likely to succeed. Several of the case studies, for example Benzodiazepines (1994, £30–35 million spent in legal aid), MMR vaccine (2003, £15 million spent in legal aid) and Valproate (2010, after £4 million spent on legal aid), have cost millions from the public purse to establish that there is little chance of success.
- *High transactional costs of litigation.* Litigation is expensive. There are several examples of manufacturers stating that they will settle rather than litigate, as the cost and risks associated with the litigation are so high – such as Gravigard and many of the pelvic-mesh MDL settlements that were entered into without any admission of liability.
- *Adverse effects of publicity of mass litigation.* Mass litigation attracts publicity. This can have an effect on lawyers, patients and occasionally doctors. For example, the MMR scandal was triggered by one rogue doctor, Andrew Wakefield, and the resulting publicity drove the litigation, resulting in further publicity and leading to a drop in vaccination rates, which adversely affected public health.
- *Difficulties in attributing liability and market share.* The DES litigation demonstrates the problems (and potential solutions) to attributing market share liability. None of these solutions is entirely satisfactory.
- *Limited remit and resolution.* It is interesting to note that in the UK there is an ongoing review into the way regulators and the NHS responded to concerns raised about

three of the products included in the case studies: hormonal pregnancy tests, valproate-containing medicines and pelvic mesh.[1] Two of these – hormonal pregnancy tests and valproate – resulted in litigation being commenced against manufacturers, but the cases could not continue due to difficulties in establishing causation. Clearly, litigation has not provided answers or resolved issues for these cohorts. There is ongoing litigation over pelvic mesh. The desire for a review highlights that for some of those affected, product liability litigation is unsatisfactory, as it either provides no answers at all or the answers are on a narrower remit than the claimants would want.

I. Prevention is Better than a Cure

It is fitting that the first case study is thalidomide, a drug that has done more to shape regulatory policy than any other pharmaceutical. The debate over whether the effects of exposure to thalidomide *in utero* could have been predicted is a well-trodden path, but it is worth briefly re-examining certain key facts. Thalidomide damage was seen extensively in Germany, where the drug was manufactured. In neighbouring France thalidomide was not licensed. This created a geographical boundary, with affected children on one side but not the other. This arbitrary boundary confirmed that there could not be a natural mechanism at work: pathogens do not politely respect national lines. The same was seen on the border between Canada, where thalidomide was widely available, and the US, where it was not. Interestingly the USA had had a centralised drug regulatory system for some years. Following the Stalinon disaster in 1959,[2] France had tightened up the already strict regulatory requirements for marketing a medicine. Both of these systems required evidence of the safety of a medicine before it was placed on the market. Thalidomide was not sold in the US and was only licensed in France for a few months from December 1961. Both the US and France were largely spared the thalidomide tragedy.[3] More stringent centralised systems protected these two countries. Since the mid-twentieth century, when thalidomide and products covered by the earliest of the case studies were on the market, the regulation of the marketing of medicinal products has changed beyond recognition. One of the legacies of thalidomide is that centralised pharmaceutical regulatory systems are now the norm. Although the current regulatory frameworks are huge improvements on what went before, they remain a work in progress. Every regulatory failing should be analysed to see what could be learnt.

II. Adverse Event Reporting

You cannot take steps to remedy a problem if you do not know it exists. Equally, you cannot test for all eventualities in the clinical testing stages: rare side-effects, drug interactions,

[1] See at www.immdsreview.org.uk.

[2] Between 1954 and 1957, Stalinon, a medication to treat staphylococcal infections, killed over 100 people. It was found that the marketed product contained over 5 times more of the active ingredient than had been tested in the clinical trials. '"Stalinon": a Therapeutic Disaster' (1958) 1 *British Medical Journal* 515.

[3] Clinical trials of thalidomide were undertaken in the US, so there were some cases there. There were a handful of cases in France from the short time it was available in that country.

etc cannot be predicted from clinical trials. Follow-up studies and adverse event reporting remain the backbone of post-marketing safety surveillance. Adverse event reporting is now open to a far wider group of individuals than it used to be: clinicians, patients and carers, and, in the US, even claimant lawyers.

Figure 4.1 shows the number and type of reports made each year to the FDA in the 50 years from 1968 to 2017. The number of reports is many times greater than what it once was. Despite this increase, it is widely acknowledged that adverse events are woefully under-reported. In its 2000 Guidelines, the World Health Organization estimated that only 10% of ADRs were reported.[4] Efforts have been made to improve reporting by making it easier, for example with smartphone apps and expanding the pool of people who are eligible to report. Numbers of reported incidents have increased, as shown in Figure 4.1, but so has use of medicinal products, and for all the efforts made to increase adverse event reporting, the reporting rates remain stubbornly low. This can be partially remedied by sharing and pooling of adverse events data: Hodges describes pooling between EU member states as follows:[5]

> The legislation … recognizes that use of medicinal products under normal conditions will always involve adverse reactions. The purpose of the pharmacovigilance system is to monitor and evaluate all adverse reactions systematically so as constantly to review the recorded information on the level of safety of products and to review decisions as to the continuation of marketing authorizations or conditions attaching to them. The advantage of a pharmacovigilance system which covers the whole of the EU Member States lies in the statistical power of a system of this size.

Under-reporting carries clear risks that a safety signal could be missed, and pooling will only work effectively if all the parties submitting data work to the same adverse events reporting criteria. However, signal detection is not simply a numbers game. The FDA is very clear that the data in FAERS are not a panacea, for the following reasons:

- Some reports appear in the database more than once: for example, if a doctor and a patient both report the same side-effect, there will be two reports relating to the same incident.
- Some reports are incomplete and do not contain enough information to allow any meaningful conclusion to be drawn.
- There is no verification of the veracity of reports.
- Causation has not been established: the reported adverse event may be entirely coincidental with the product use, rather than caused by it.

For these reasons, the rates of occurrence cannot be established using the data on this system, or other post-marketing adverse events data. This type of data provides an early warning system, a sign that a product should be examined in more detail, not proof of causation. The obvious limitations of this type of data have not stopped enterprising claimant lawyers from attempting to use FAERS data to establish that a drug is 'unsafe' on the basis it has a high level of adverse events associated with its use. The US Accutane litigation

[4] *Safety Monitoring of Medicinal Products: Guidelines for Setting Up and Running a Pharmacovigilance Centre* (WHO, 2000) available at http://apps.who.int/medicinedocs/en/d/Jh2934e/6.3.html#Jh2934e.6.3

[5] C Hodges, 'The Regulation of Medicinal Products and Medical Devices' in J Laing and J McHale (eds), *Principles of Medical Law*, 4th edn (Oxford University Press, 2017) para 17.112.

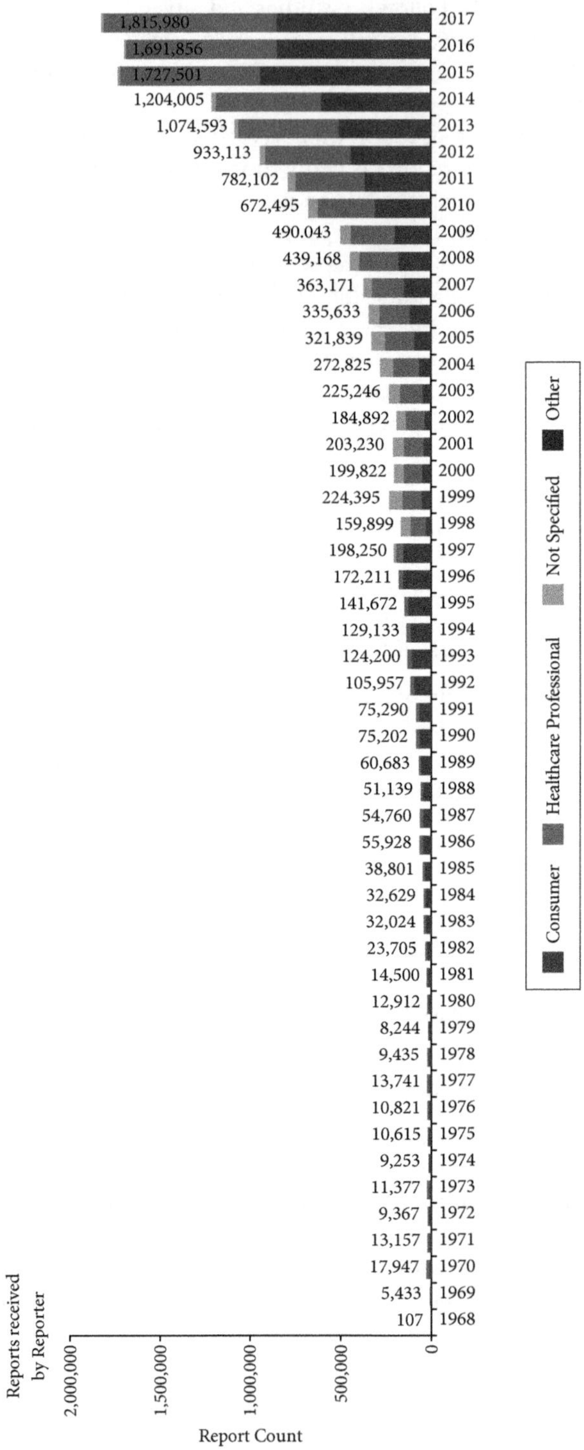

Figure 4.1 Adverse event reports to the FDA 1968–2017

is a particularly strong example, in which claimant lawyers have sought to use FAERS data to demonstrate high levels of side-effects. However, 88% of the adverse event reports of IBS/UC associated with Accutane were made by claimant lawyers themselves.[6] This behaviour is clearly self-serving and unscientific, and demonstrates the driver of a potential financial incentive to reporting adverse events that distorts the safety position.

This story raises questions over how best to balance the advantages of a wider reporting pool against these potential disadvantages. A pharmacovigilance or device vigilance system should capture data without having its data captured. Separation of the vigilance and liability systems seems the most straightforward and obvious solution.

III. Correlation or Causation?

Adverse event detection for medical products usually falls into a recognised pattern: initial case single reports (either from practitioners or from the affected individual), case series, then observational studies, such as cohort studies (either retrospective or prospective), case control studies, and wider population and epidemiological studies. As knowledge accumulates then secondary research in the form of reviews (narrative and/or systematic) and meta-analysis can be undertaken. Although the quality of scientific studies has generally improved since the 1940s, this core ADR reporting pattern has not changed because there is little scope for change.

In the initial stages, the question is whether the observed event is due to a correlation between the medical product and the adverse event, or if the medicinal product is causative. While ascertaining this sounds straightforward, it is not always so. Negative publicity about a medicinal product can generate significant adverse events reports. For example, the claimed MMR vaccine link to autism was unfounded,[7] but large numbers of individuals reported autism as an adverse reaction. Figure 4.2 demonstrates the difficulty in separating a true signal from the 'noise' associated with negative publicity. Adverse event reports are only useful in context, which includes the veracity and interests of those making the negative claims. Distinguishing between noise and signal is increasingly difficult as social media amplifies the impact of negative publicity and reporting is both simple and unverified.

IV. Thresholds

The existence of a correlation does not equate to causation.[8] The hormonal pregnancy test case study is particularly interesting on this point. There were various studies that found a correlation between use of hormonal pregnancy tests and foetal malformations; but equally,

[6] S Tenner, 'Editorial: Isotretinoin and Inflammatory Bowel Disease: Trial Lawyer Misuse of Science and FDA Warnings' (2014) 109 *The American Journal of Gastroenterology* 570, doi:10.1038/ajg.2014.34.

[7] Dr Andrew Wakefield, who triggered the MMR scare, was struck off for acting dishonestly and irresponsibly, including not disclosing conflicts of interests and financial gains from the scandal see *BMJ* 2011;342:c7452.

[8] See at www.tylervigen.com/spurious-correlations.

Figure 4.2 Claims filed with the Vaccine Injury Compensation Program 1989–2007[9]

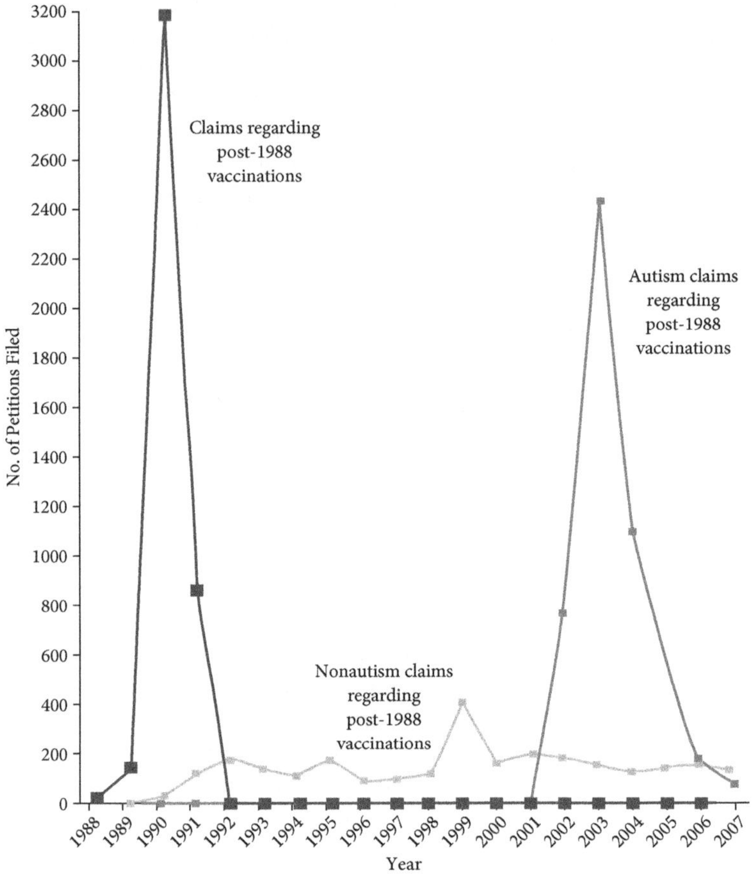

other studies did not. The UK litigation collapsed due to lack of sufficient proof of causation. However, the regulatory decision, taken a few years earlier, was to remove the indication for pregnancy testing based on an efficacy and risk–benefit assessment. Although there was no confirmed evidence of a causal link, the potential risk that the correlations had suggested was sufficient for the manufacturer to agree to remove that indication. The claimants in the litigation on hormonal pregnancy tests felt that the removal of the pregnancy testing indication signified an acceptance of the causal nature of the risk by the regulator and manufacturers.

This highlights the divergence between the functions of the regulatory and the liability systems. The primary function of a regulatory system is to protect the public from harm. The primary function of litigation is recognition of a legal wrong and provision of associated

[9] Post-1988 vaccinations are those that occurred on or after 1 October 1988; pre-1988 vaccinations are those that occurred before that date. Source: Health Resources and Services Administration. Reproduced from S Macleod and C Hodges, *Redress Schemes for Personal Injuries* (Hart Publishing, 2017).

compensation. The evidential thresholds for these differ. Evidence of correlation may be sufficient for the former, but proof of causation is required for the latter. The rationale behind these differences is self-evident. No drug is entirely safe, so regulators are constantly undertaking risk–benefit analyses; regulators are required to respond promptly to prevent harm to the public, rather than waiting for the harm to occur and then acting. Liability requires proof of a legal wrong and proof of causation.

It is interesting to note that the thresholds required to demonstrate legal causation are different in different jurisdictions. This applies even between the UK and the US, despite both being common law jurisdictions historically derived from a shared heritage. The US Norplant litigation lasted years and cost multimillions, but the UK litigation did not get off the ground, and no compensation was awarded. Without further research it is difficult to say exactly where this difference has its roots, but any or all of the following seem likely:

(a) slightly different thresholds being applied;
(b) the use of private enforcement as deterrence in the US, such as the awarding of punitive damages;
(c) procedural issues, such as the way in which such cases are tried (jury trials in the US, judge-led trials in the UK); and
(d) other socio-cultural factors.

Clearly the quantum of compensation will be affected by the costs associated with living in a particular location, but the more fundamental decision as to whether to compensate at all is also regional. Regardless of their cause, these discrepancies between jurisdictions raise issues about access to justice in the broadest sense. Manufacturers work in a global market, but an identical injury may be deemed worthy of compensation in one location and not in another. This has a potential impact for both manufacturers and consumers. If legal thresholds are so high that genuine injuries are not compensated in one jurisdiction, this is detrimental to the consumer. Equally, if thresholds are too low, the manufacturers are required to pay compensation where they ought not to be held liable, and this impacts on them. The variability between international jurisdictions is long-standing and is clearly factored into commercial practices. Manufacturers can choose whether to operate within a given jurisdiction, but claimants are usually restricted to litigating in the jurisdiction in which they live.

While national litigation is the standard mechanism for providing compensation, one potential solution is to look for alternative transnational mechanisms to achieve the same result. The Dow Corning settlement fund was open to international applicants and was not limited to American women alone. Recently there have been other examples of manufacturers responding to a product issue by creating transnational schemes to provide redress and rectify the issues. The ASR scheme created by DePuy, for example, was an option for ASR hip recipients in many jurisdictions.[10] Access to justice should not be conflated with access to litigation; it is a far broader concept. Such transnational schemes remove the need for (and time and cost associated with) national litigation, and provide access to redress for claimants based on their injuries, not on the jurisdiction in which they happen to live.

[10] See Macleod and Hodges, n 8, ch 32.

V. Product Withdrawals

It has been suggested that litigation acts to protect claimants by ensuring that 'unsafe' products are removed from the market. Figure 4.3 illustrates the time on the market and the time spent in litigation for the 35 case study products. It provides an interesting oversight into the case studies, in particular on the potential role played by litigation in the decision to carry on marketing a product.

Figure 4.3 Marketing and litigation for the cases study products from 1940–2018

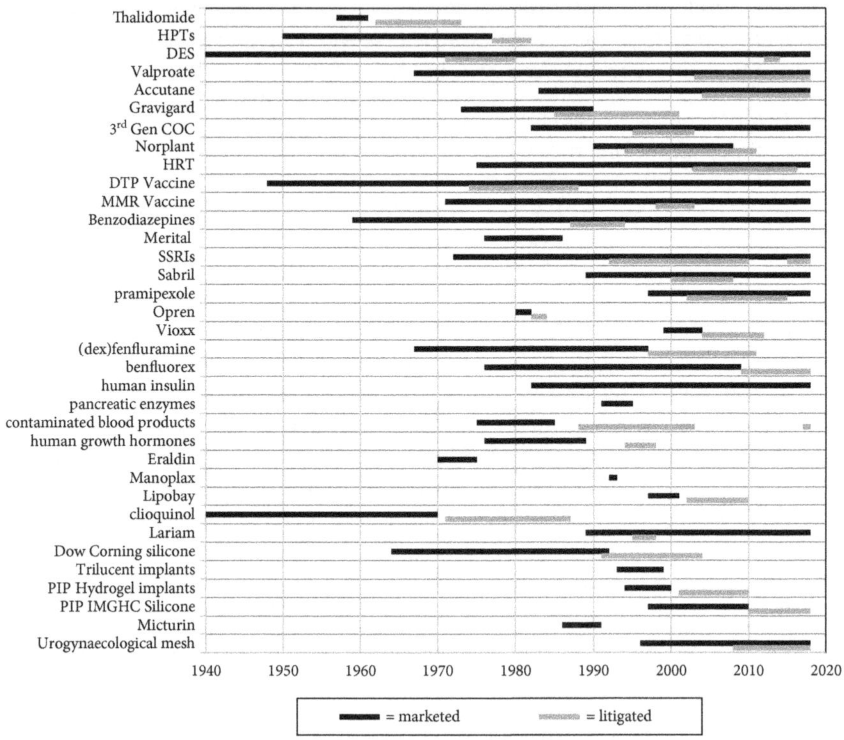

Litigation does not automatically cause a product to be withdrawn from the market: 13 of the case study products remained on the market as at August 2018. The majority of these products have had additional warnings added to the packaging and/or have been the subject of further safety studies. For example, medicines containing sodium valproate remain on the market as it is a useful addition to the therapeutic arsenal for treating seizures, but the risk–benefit assessment has changed as more knowledge has become available. Over the years more detailed warnings have been added and more onerous restrictions have been put on prescribing it to women of childbearing age. The majority of the increased warnings in the UK were added before the litigation commenced, and the litigation collapsed as legal aid was withdrawn, after it was found that the defendant was unlikely to be found liable.

There are three case studies where the product was removed from the market after litigation commenced: Gravigard/Copper 7, Dow Corning Silicone implants and DES.

Neither of the two devices was removed from the market because they were known to be unsafe. The overlap between litigation starting and product withdrawal was short in both cases. Dow Corning implants were voluntarily withdrawn in the US (the major market) in January 1992 as part of the voluntary moratorium on silicone breast implants. At this point in time the FDA was considering taking regulatory action to restrict the marketing of silicone breast implants. Silicone implants were not considered unsafe per se, but they were felt not to have adequately proved their safety. Dow Corning faced some claims at the point the silicone breast implants were removed from the market, but the litigation really stepped up in June 1992, when the MDL was consolidated. Gravigard retained the confidence of the regulatory authorities throughout: the withdrawal of Gravigard was a commercial decision. Subsequent evidence established that the underlying issue was sexual lifestyle and chlamydia rather than the product. Unsurprisingly, these are both cases where the issue of causation was highly contentious, with a lack of clear, undisputed evidence. Litigation over both products proved extremely lengthy, contentious and costly (Dow Corning was bankrupted by the liabilities).

DES was slightly anomalous: it was eventually withdrawn voluntarily, but this was not due to adverse events. The teratogenicity (which took some years to become apparent) did not cause a market withdrawal but a significant change in indications, including the addition of contraindications and restrictions on prescribing. By the time DES was eventually withdrawn in 1997, all the indications that risked teratogenic exposure had long been deleted. The market withdrawal was due to its having been replaced by more effective treatments for its remaining indications.

In all the other cases studies, litigation has no immediate impact on protecting the public from a 'dangerous product' because it takes place after the product is no longer available. In most, though not all, cases litigation follows fairly shortly after the removal of the product following the detection of a safety signal. Thalidomide, the first case study and the earliest litigation, followed this pattern. The withdrawal of thalidomide was a voluntary decision, not a regulatory one; in most of the countries where it was marketed there was no formal drug regulation or mechanism to enforce market withdrawal, so it could not have been removed by regulators. The expansion in regulation and post-marketing vigilance have meant that, in the more recent cases, withdrawal decisions have tended to involve discussions with the regulator beforehand, though the vast majority were still voluntary rather than forced withdrawals.

In several of the case studies there was no litigation after the withdrawal. The reasons for this vary. For example, Eraldin was not litigated, as a compensation scheme was set up that was just as generous as a court award would have been, but without the difficulties and delays inherent in litigation. It is hardly surprising that there were no litigated cases. A similar resolution was achieved for Trilucent breast implants. Other case studies may have avoided litigation because of the potential claimant profile. Micturin was used for urinary incontinence, which tends to be prescribed in older patients who are less likely to bring a complaint/claim. Similarly, Merital was an antidepressant, which was often used effectively in patients who were refractory to other medications. Given this usage profile, it is not entirely surprising that claimants who had recently stopped taking Merital did not proceed to litigation.

One of the quieter revolutions in medicinal product regulation is the increase in reporting requirements on marketing authorisation holders following a product withdrawal.

This allows the regulator to identify and communicate potential safety issues quickly. For example, in the EU a marketing authorisation holder making a change to marketing that may raise a public health concern must notify the EMA by emailing a designated email address in a specified format, and must notify the Member State(s) concerned. Regulators also now have the power to enquire about the reasons for product withdrawals.

VI. Compensation or Redress?

Litigation provides a mechanism for claimants to obtain compensation. To do so, claimants must prove that a legal right has been breached, the breach caused the damage and that there is subsequent loss. This is not a straightforward process. Table 4.1 shows the litigation outcomes for each of the case studies (some of the litigation is still ongoing, so elements of this table should be checked before relying upon them).

Table 4.1 Litigation outcomes for the case studies

	Product	Litigation outcome
1.	Thalidomide (alpha-phthalimido-glutarimide)	England – group action, £12 million compensation fund for *c* 350 claimants, further funds added. Germany – litigation stopped, compensation fund, 100 million DM paid by Grunenthal, 100 million DM paid by German Government for those affected in Germany and certain other countries.
2.	Primodos (hormone combination)	England – group action discontinued before trial as no prospect of success.
3.	DES (diethylstilbestrol)	US – group action. *Sindell v Abbott* established a new principle of market share responsibility between the manufacturers. In the Netherlands – joint and several liability akin to 'alternative causation'; €37 million compensation fund. France – 'joint and several liability' of two manufacturers with unequal shares. UK – no significant litigation
4.	Epilim/Depakote/ Depakene (sodium valproate, valproic acid, magnesium valproate, valproate semisodium or valpromide)	England – litigation withdrawn before trial; £4 million legal aid cost. France – litigation ongoing, national compensation scheme established, initial €10 million paid in by French Government. US litigation – MDL in settlement talks after failure of bellwether approach and global settlement process.
5.	Accutane/Roaccutane (isotretinoin)	US – 7,000 claims: MDL in Florida, ended in summary judgment for the defendant; MCL in New Jersey, so far all claimant victories overturned on appeal, litigation finalised after appeal on the evidential standards required.

(continued)

Table 4.1 *(Continued)*

	Product	Litigation outcome
6.	Gravigard/Copper 7	US – *c* 800 claims, one major claimant victory, $8.15 million in the *Kociemba* case, prompted settlement of all other claims generally for low sums.
		England – group action started then stalled when legal aid was withdrawn. Australia – *c* 300 claimants, 14 years of litigation ended in a confidential voluntary settlement.
7.	Third-generation COCs	England – group action judgment for defendants
8.	Norplant	US litigation – MDL in Texas, defendant won 5 bellwether trials, summary judgment on 12,000 claims, settled the remaining claims for $54 million; Louisiana class action, *c* 3,500–4,000 defendants, 17 years of litigation ended in $29.5 million voluntary settlement. England – threatened litigation not pursued.
9.	HRT	England – claims not pursued. US – multiple claims taking over a decade, mixed litigation outcome with verdicts for both claimants and defendants, settlement achieved. Defendants spent over $1 billion/
10.	DTP vaccine	Scotland – claim dismissed. England – group action resulted in judgment for company after £2 million spend in legal aid. Ireland – single claim succeeded. US – several cases succeeded, led to the introduction of Vaccine Compensation and the Vaccine Courts.
11.	MMR vaccine	England – group action discontinued when legal aid removed; over £15 million had been spent in legal aid.
12.	Benzodiazepines	England – group action (*c* 5,000 claims) discontinued when legal aid removed; £30–35 million had been spent in legal aid.
13.	Merital (nomifensine)	No litigation.
14.	SSRIs	US – litigation substantial, multimillion dollar cases following the *Tobin* case in 2001. England – group action re Seroxat, legal aid withdrawn in 2010, disposing of most of the cases; *c* 100 cases resumed in 2015 under alternative funding, which are ongoing.
15.	Sabril (vigabatrin)	England – group action settled.

(continued)

Table 4.1 *(Continued)*

	Product	**Litigation outcome**
16.	Mirapexin/ Sifrol/ Daquiran (pramipexole)	UK – group litigation threatened, did not appear. Europe – a handful of cases for lack of warning. US – Minnesota class action resulted in multimillion-dollar settlement for claimants. Canada – class actions in Ontario and Quebec resulted in settlements for the defendants.
17.	Opren (benoxaprofen)	England – group litigation, £2.2 million compensation fund (costs £4 million).
18.	Vioxx (rofecoxib)	US – claims settled, $4.85 billion fund. England – group failed to get funding. Australia – judgment overturned on appeal.
19.	Adifax/ Isomeride/Redux (dexfenfluramine) and Ponderax (fenfluramine)	US – Fen-Phen litigation 1,000 claimants settled for $20 million. France – handful of individual cases found for the claimant.
20.	Mediator (benfluorex)	France – claims started in 2010, ongoing.
21.	Human insulin	England – group action failed when legal aid removed.
22.	Pancreatic enzymes	England – group action did not proceed after public funding not granted.
23.	Blood products: Factor VIII and IX	Many EU states established compensation funds. England and Ireland – group litigation discontinued against manufacturers; UK Government established trust fund.
24.	Human growth hormone	England – group action, judgment against Department of Health followed by compensation fund.
25.	Eraldin (Practolol)	UK – C 8,000 affected, no claims brought, compensation fund established.
26.	Manoplax (flosequinan)	No claims brought.
27.	Lipobay (cerivastatin)	US litigation – 15,000 cases including class actions. Defendant won all six trials, settled 3,000 rhabdomyolysis claims, remaining claims dismissed. Germany – 20 cases all won by company. England – attempt to get legal aid funding was rejected. France – cases ongoing.
28.	Emaform, Entero-Form or Chinoform (Clioquinol)	Japan – *c* 6,000 claimants, litigation in many districts, all settled and a compensation scheme established.

(continued)

Table 4.1 *(Continued)*

	Product	Litigation outcome
29.	Lariam (mefloquine)	England – group action dropped after legal aid withdrawn as warnings were adequate.
30.	Dow Corning Silicone Implants	US litigation – Ohio MDL, 400,000 claimants. Settlement reached for $4,225,070,000 then Dow Corning went into chapter 11 bankruptcy, settlement rearranged during bankruptcy proceedings.
31.	Trilucent breast implants	Claims commenced, but settlement was reached prior to trial.
32.	PIP Hydrogel breast implants	Claims won in England, enforcement sought in France, but PIP went into administration before this could be executed.
33.	PIP IMHGC silicone breast implants	Multiple strands of litigation against various defendants, as PIP went into voluntary bankruptcy.
34.	Micturin (terodiline)	No claims brought.
35.	Mesh for urogynaecological surgery	US – several multimillion-dollar MDLs and MCLs involving hundreds of thousands of claimants; some defendants have settled, some litigation is still ongoing. England – *c* 1,000 claimants, litigation ongoing.

One of the striking things about compensation is that it is binary: either a financial settlement is awarded, or it is not. The objective of tort law is to put the claimant in the position that he or she would have been in were it not for the defective product. The proxy used to achieve this for the claimant is financial compensation, but, as has long been acknowledged, that is a fiction in a large number of cases. As the cases studies amply demonstrate, there is often no way in which a claimant can be restored to the position he or she was in, particularly where a product has caused death or irreversible injury.[11]

Compensation is only available under specific heads of damage. Once awarded, financial compensation can be used by the claimant in whatever way he or she sees fit.[12] Some of the compensation personal injury claimants receive is used in ways that bear little relationship to the 'purpose' for which it was awarded under the specified heads of damage.[13] There is no head of damage for providing gifts or treats for family and friends, but this is a commonly occurring theme when claimants are retrospectively asked how they had spent their damages.[14] This disparity suggests that the rigid criteria imposed by the legal system do not reflect claimants' priorities.

[11] This concurs with the findings of the Law Commission Report, which found that for some claimants no amount of money could ever be enough: HG Genn, 'Personal Injury Compensation: How Much Is Enough?' (1994) Law Com 225, at 202, available at assets.publishing.service.gov.uk/government/uploads/system/uploads/attachment_data/file/235636/0666.pdf; T Relis, 'It's not about the Money, a Theory on Misconception of Plaintiffs' Litigation Aims' (2007) 68(3) *Pittsburgh Law Review* 701; AJ Akkermans, 'Reforming Personal Injury Claims Settlement: Paying More Attention to Emotional Dimension Promotes Victim Recovery' *Torts & Products Liability*, eJournal, 2009, http://dx.doi.org/10.2139/ssrn.1333214; C Vincent, M Young and A Phillips, 'Why do people sue doctors? A study of patients and relatives taking legal action' (1994) 1609(343) *The Lancet* 13.

[12] With provisos when the claimant does not have the capacity to manage his or her own affairs.

[13] Genn, n 11, ch 10.

[14] ibid.

Obvious though it may sound, it is worth remembering that compensation is only available where there is a solvent defendant. The PIP cases, first hydrogel and then the IMGHC silicone implants, highlight this point. There is no redress for these women. The hydrogel implants litigation successfully obtained judgment for the claimants, but they were unable to enforce it due to the bankruptcy of PIP. Had PIP been solvent enough to pay compensation, it seems unlikely that the raft of litigation against multiple defendants described in the case study would have occurred. The role of insurance is also raised by this case. Insurance seems an obvious solution and, for the majority of cases that do not involve fraud, is a workable means of ensuring that appropriate compensation is available. Understandably, though, insurers will only insure *uberrimae fides*. This is a perfectly logical business model, but it is entirely unhelpful for those unfortunate enough to be victims of fraud or deception. The French Government's decision to force Allianz to honour PIP's insurance provision for the IMGHC implants in French women is unusual, and had a fairly limited impact on the issue as a whole, as a large number of the recipients were not domiciled in France. Alternative models exist, such as the risk-pooling arrangements for pharmaceutical insurance seen in the Nordic states, coordinated by national trade associations. Risk pooling has the advantage for claimants that they have a degree of protection from the rogue actions of an individual manufacturer.

VII. Public Regulation v Private Regulation

The examples discussed so far in this chapter highlight the similarities and differences between public and private regulation of drug and medical device safety. The case studies indicate that the usual pattern is that a safety signal is detected by medical practitioners, examined by regulators and that regulatory action then follows, via either increased labelling or product withdrawal. This is all public regulation, and there is little in the findings of this book to suggest that private regulation in the form of litigation has any impact on public safety in relation to the product being litigated. There remains a role for private enforcement in providing compensation (a compensatory function) and, potentially, in preventing future occurrences (a deterrence function).

A. Compensation – Redress

There is a plethora of studies dating back years that suggest that claimants' rationale for litigation is more complex than a desire for financial compensation.[15] In general claimants want:

(a) to know that what happened to them will not happen to someone else in the future;
(b) an explanation of what happened and why;

[15] S Lloyd-Bostock and L Mulcahy, 'The Social Psychology of Making and Responding to Hospital Complaints: An Account Model of Complaint Processes' (1994) 16 *Law and Policy* 123; Vincent et al, n 11; A Simanowitz, 'The patient's perspective' in MM Rosenthal, L Mulcahy and S Lloyd-Bostock (eds), *Medical Mishaps. Pieces of the*

(c) compensation that reflects their suffering and which will provide for future care; and
(d) for those responsible to be held to account.[16]

What is strikingly obvious is that litigation struggles to address some of these goals. Given the reasons that claimants give for litigating, it is not entirely surprising that money is not enough for some claimants. Moreover, the newly emerging interdisciplinary research field of Compensation Health Research (CHR) assesses the unintended anti-therapeutic effects of legal proceedings on claimants. It has long been recognised that claimants find no-blame compensation schemes less burdensome, and that no-blame schemes are less detrimental to claimant health than litigation.[17] The cohort of claimants undertaking litigation for personal injury has, by definition, suffered in some way. It is not difficult to see why a drawn-out, adversarial process, which cannot provide some of the outcomes they seek, is not ideally suited.

Redress can incorporate a far greater range of remedies than just financial compensation, including apologies, non-financial redress, care packages and many other variations. Extensive study has revealed that, as well as being preferred by claimants, redress schemes are almost invariably quicker and less expensive in resolving claims.[18] There is an additional advantage that redress schemes have far more flexibility than can usually be achieved in litigation. Damages can be more appropriately tailored to the needs of the individuals, and claimants can be drawn from as wide or as narrow a pool as is desired.

For a claimant, successful litigation results in compensation. The case studies highlight that a number of claims have been started but then stopped, due to low prospects of success. For example, the hormonal pregnancy tests and sodium valproate litigation in the UK. Claimants have begun an adversarial process, gathered all their evidence on how they have been harmed by the defendant, only to be told that they will not receive any answers in court, nor any compensation, because they cannot prove legal harm. Given that they are no longer able to pay their lawyers, they may also have to deal with the added issue that a pillar of support has been removed. It is hard to imagine a less satisfactory process for attempting to resolve an issue. It is interesting to note these issues have never been resolved to the satisfaction of the claimants. There is currently an independent review into the way the healthcare system responded to patient concerns about these products, as well as calls for a full-scale public inquiry.[19]

Puzzle (Open University Press, 1999) 228; L Mulcahy, *Mediating medical negligence claims: an option for the future* (The Stationery Office, 2000); National Audit Office, *Handling Clinical Negligence Claims in England: Report by the Comptroller and Auditor General*, Session 2000–2001, HC 403, 3 May 2001; J Mellor, *Report on selected summaries of investigations by the Parliamentary and Health Service Ombudsman. October to November 2014* (Parliamentary and Health Service Ombudsman, 17 June 2015); *RESOLVE News from the Ombudsman Service* (Parliamentary and Health Service Ombudsman, December 2015).

[16] Relis, n 11; Akkermans, n 11; Vincent et al, n 11.

[17] K. Lippel, 'Therapeutic and anti-therapeutic consequences of workers' compensation.' (1999) 22(5-6) *International Journal of Law and Psychiatry* 521, doi.org/10.1016/S0160-2527(99)00024-2; NA Elbers et al, 'Differences in perceived fairness and health outcomes in two injury compensation systems' (2016) 16(658) *BioMed Central Public Health* 1, doi:10.1186/s12889-016-3331-3.

[18] Macleod and Hodges, n 8.

[19] See at www.immdsreview.org.uk/.

B. Deterrence

It has long been argued, particularly in the US, that litigation and high levels of damages can be used to enforce compliance with safety regulation by deterring manufacturers from engaging in non-compliant behaviour. If this is the case then it would be logical to assume that countries that use deterrence would be safer for patients, as manufacturers would be less likely to be non-complaint, and would be likely to remove products from the market more quickly upon evidence of a safety issue. Eight of the case study products were withdrawn from the US market. Table 4.2 details the withdrawal dates for the US and other jurisdictions for these eight products. This is a very small sample, but it does not indicate any particular differentiation between different jurisdictions. The majority of products were withdrawn at the same time in different jurisdictions.

Table 4.2 Timing of product withdrawals from the US and other markets

Product	Withdrawn in US	Withdrawn elsewhere
DES	2000	Still available in UK
Gravigard/Copper 7	1986	1990
Norplant	2002	1999 in UK
Opren	Worldwide withdrawal	Worldwide withdrawal
Vioxx	Worldwide withdrawal	Worldwide withdrawal
Manoplax	Withdrawal at the same time in USA and UK	Withdrawal at the same time in US and UK
Lipobay	Worldwide withdrawal	Worldwide withdrawal
Dow Corning silicone implants	1992 – voluntary	1995 bankruptcy

There are considerable gaps in both the theoretical and empirical evidence as to what mechanisms influence the decisions being taken within manufacturers on drug and device safety. These case studies do not provide the data required to answer these questions, neither do we have sufficient evidence of the impact of insurance on such decisions. It is an area where further research is needed, but the lack of evidence has to raise questions about the reliability of these theories. The transactional costs of the US litigation system are sky high, in large part due to punitive damages awarded as a form of deterrence. If such measures do not make patients safer then a substantial part of their validity becomes questionable.

VIII. Conclusions

The first definition of 'public' in the *Cambridge English Dictionary* is 'relating to or involving people in general, rather than being limited to a particular group of people'. This definition fits the current public regulatory arrangements. Medicines and devices are marketed globally, and while each regulator makes its own decision, regulators now discuss potential risks internationally. No medicine or medical device will ever be risk-free, but the increased availability of data that international cooperation affords, particularly when combined with powerful analysis tools, should aid in early signal detection. Public regulation can, when necessary, remove a product from the market to protect the public.

In contrast 'private' is defined, inter alia, as 'only for one person or group and not for everyone'. Litigation remains firmly focused on retrospectively compensating a defined cohort, usually restricted on a national basis. Private regulation simply does not have the capacity to detect early-warning signals, nor the ability to mandate the removal of a product from the market. To describe litigation on medicines and medical devices as private regulation is something of a misnomer.

The public regulatory framework is equipped to protect the public in a way that private enforcement simply cannot. There have been enormous improvements in medicine and medical device regulation from the time of the earliest cases studies, but there is clear scope to improve further. However, the focus should be on improving public regulation and providing redress mechanisms that meet the needs of claimants.

INDEX

Bold page references indicate references within a table.
Italic page references indicate references within figure.

Abbreviated New Drug applications (ANDA) (USA), 59
Accutane, *see* **isotretonoin**
Active Implantable Medical Devices Directive (AIMDD) (EU), 43
  clinical investigations, 45–46
Adifax, *see* **obesity treatments**
advanced therapy medicinal products (ATMPs) (EU):
  EU regulation, **30**, 39
adverse drug reactions (ADR):
  EU reporting requirements, 40–42
  mandatory reporting:
    advanced therapy medicinal products, 39
    human cells, tissues and tissue-based products, 70
    investigational new drug reporting, 65–67
    post-marketing reporting of biological products, 69–70
    post-marketing reporting of drug, 68
    prescription drug without approved new drug application, 67–68
  USA, 65–70
  yellow-card reporting system, 24, 40, 85, 87
  see also pharmacovigilance; reporting requirements; and *individual case studies*
after-the-event insurance, 12
  Seroxat litigation in England and Wales, 162–63
Agence Française de sécurité sanitaire des produits de santé (AFSSAPS) (F):
  benufluorex complications, 182–84
  breast implants, 228–29
    product recall, 231
    recapitulation studies, 230–31
  isomeride and cardiac concerns, 180
  sodium valproate regulation, 103
Agence nationale de sécurité du medicament et des produits de santé (ANSM) (F):
  benufluorex complications, 182–84
  sodium valproate regulation, 103
AIDS, *see* **HIV/AIDS**
alerts:
  medical devices, 81
  medicinal products, 72
alpha-phthalimido-glutarimide, *see* **thalidomide**
anti-malarials, *see* **mefloquine**
anti-protozoan medications, *see* **clioquinol; mefloquine**
arbitration:
  United States, 13–14
Australia:
  breast implants, 229
  contaminated blood products, 193–94
  DTP vaccine, 142
  IUDs, 121
    litigation, 123–24, **275**
  Seroxat, 162
  thalidomide tragedy, 84
  Vioxx, 176, **276**

before-the-event insurance, 12
behaviour modification:
  aggression, 111–12, 157–59, 162
  autism, 147
  compulsive behaviours:
    pramipexole, 166–69
  depression/suicidal thoughts:
    isotretinoin, 110–12, 115–16
    mefloquine, 212–15
    SSRIs, 157–59, 160–61, 162
  psychosis:
    mefloquine, 212–15
bellwether trials, 13
  contraceptive implants, 130, **275**
  sodium valproate, 106–7, **274**
  urogynaecological mesh, 259, 262–63
benfluorex, *see* **Mediator**
benoxaprofen, *see* **Opren**
benzodiazepines, 4, 153
  description, 150
  litigation, 151–52
  marketing and regulatory history, 150–51
  safety concerns, 150
bioequivalence:
  abbreviated new drug applications, 59
  exceptions to pre-clinical tests and clinical trials, 35

biologicals, regulation of:
EU,
UK, historic, 21
centralised approval, 33
USA, 52
approval processes, 63
biologic device product, 64
legislation, 63
licensing, 63–64
reporting requirements, 69–70, **69**
therapeutic biologics applications, 63–64
biologics license application (BLA), 61, 63
post-market safety evaluations, 71
biosimilars:
abbreviated pathway for biosimilar approval, 64
black-box warnings:
isotretinoin, 109
mefloquine, 215
sodium valproate, 104
SSRIs, 160
blood products, 7
description, 193
inquiries:
Scotland, 195
UK, 195
litigation:
EU, 194–95
group litigation order, 195–96
UK, 195–96
USA, 195
marketing and regulatory history, 194
safety issue, 193–94
breast implants, *see* **Dow Corning silicone implants; poly implant protheses (PIP) hydrogel breast implants; poly implant protheses (PIP) IMGHC silicone breast implants; trilucent implants**
oral contraception, 126

Canada:
anti-malarials, 214, 215
contaminated blood products, 194
human insulin, 187
Lipobay, 207
obesity treatments, 177, 179
pramipexole, 168
litigation, 169, **276**
thalidomide, 266
Vioxx, 175
cardiovascular pharmaceuticals, *see* **Eraldin; Lipobay; Manoplax**
case studies summary, 2–9
causation, 10, 265–66, 267
adverse drug events, 269
alternative causation, 98, **274**
breast implants, 219
clioquinol, 208–10
correlation compared, 269
DES, 98
evidential thresholds, 269–71
hormonal pregnancy tests, 91, 269–71
human insulin, 188–89
Investigational New Drug applications, 66–67
isotretinoin, 117, 118
IUDs, 123
oral contraception, 128
rofecoxib, 172, 175
vaccines:
DTP vaccine, 140, 142–44
MMR vaccine, 149
Center for Biologics Evaluation and Research (CBER) (USA), 63
experimental biologics, 64
humanitarian device exemptions, 78
monitoring of FAERS reports, 71
post-market safety evaluations, 72, **72**
reporting adverse events, 70
therapeutic biologics applications, 63–64
Center for Devices and Radiological Health (CDRH) (USA):
classification of devices, 73–74
approved medical devices, 74
cleared medical devices, 74
post-marketing requirements, 78–81
pre-market approval procedures, 77–78
pre-market notification 510(k) procedures, 74–77
MAUDE database, 80
alerts, 81
healthcare provider letters, 81
recall, 81
reclassification of devices, 81
section 522 studies, 80–81
post-marketing requirements, 78–79
mandatory reporting, 79–80
spontaneous reporting, 80
pre-market approval procedures, 77–78
humanitarian device exemption, 78
pre-market notification 510(k) procedures, 74
abbreviated 510(k) notification, 76
special 510(k) notification, 76
third party 510(k) review procedures, 77
traditional 510(k) notification, 75–76
Center for Drug Evaluation and Research (CDER) (USA):
CDER Small Business and Industry Assistance, 62
humanitarian device exemptions, 78
monitoring of FAERS reports, 71
post-market safety evaluations, 72, **72**
pre-market evaluations, 58

reviewing over-the-counter drugs, 59
role, 56, 58
standardisation of application review processes, 61
Centers for Disease Control and Preventions (CDC) (USA):
contaminated blood products, 193
DTP vaccine, 141
mefloquine, 213
Monitoring System for Illness following Immunization, 141
centralised regulation, 32–33
advanced therapy medicinal products, 39
advantages of, 266
EU law, **27**, 32–33
European Medicines Agency, *31*, *32*, 32–33, 167
Medicines Act, 24–25, 84
Medicines and Healthcare Products Regulatory Agency, 33
pharmacovigilance, 41
post-authorisation studies, 42
USA, 51, 83, 266
cerivastatin, *see* **Lipobay**
Chinoform, *see* **clioquinol**
class actions:
Australia, 176
Canada, 169
England and Wales, 15, 168
EU, 168
reluctance to adopt collective action mechanisms, 14
France, 15, 105–6, 180
litigation outcomes, **274–77**
Netherlands class action settlement procedure, 14, 98
Nordic States, 14
Scotland, 16
USA, 12–13, 98, 106–7, 161–62, 163, 169, 179, 207, 215
see also group litigation orders; multi-county litigation; multi-district litigation
clinical investigations:
EU regulation (devices) 45–46
clinical investigation plans, 46
general requirements, 46
FDA regulation (medicinal products), 54, 60–61
clinical trials:
Dunlop Committee, 23–24
EU, **29**, 34–35
USA, 60–61
IND applications, 58–59
clioquinol, 8, 211
description, 208
litigation, 210–11
marketing and regulatory history, 209–10
safety concerns, 208–9
collective redress, *see* **class actions**
combined oral contraceptives (COCs), 3
thromboembolisms, 125–28
Committee for Medicinal Products for Human Use (CHMP) (EU), *31*
combined oral contraceptives, 127–28
creation, **29**, 29–30, *32*, 127–28
isotretinoin, 115–16
role, 32
Committee for Proprietary Medicinal Products of the EU (CPMP) (EU):
combined oral contraceptives, 127
creation, **27**, 28, **28**, **29**, *32*
isotretinoin, 114
obesity treatments, 178–79, 181–82
Committee for the Safety of Drugs (CSD), *see* **Dunlop Committee**
Committee for the Safety of Medicines (CSM) (UK):
anti-malarials, 214
benzodiazepines, 150–51, 153
combined oral contraceptives, 125, 126
contaminated blood products, 194
DES, 95
Eraldin, 198, 199
hormonal pregnancy tests, 90, 91
hormone replacement therapy, 134–35
human insulin, 188
isotretinoin, 118
Manoplax, 202–3
MMR, 147
nomifensine, 155
obesity treatments, 178–79
Opren, 171
pancreatic enzymes, 191
pre-marketing applications, 25, 84–85
sodium valproate, 102
SSRIs, 159
urinary incontinence, 235
yellow-card reporting system, 24, 40, 85
Committee on Review of Medicines (CRM) (UK), 25
benzodiazepines, 151
compensation claims, 274–78
alternative causation approach, 98, **274**
compensation orders, 15
EU, 14–15
heads of damage, 277
insolvent defendants, 278
IUDs, 122
litigation outcomes, **274–77**
market share liability, 10, 97–98, 265, **274**
Netherlands, 14
outcomes, **274–77**
piggy-back option, 15

regional and national differences, 271
sodium valproate, 106
strict liability, 10
thalidomide:
Germany, 85
UK, 15
compensation schemes, 10
breast implants:
PIP IMGHC silicone implants, 232
Trilucent Care Centre, 222–23, 273
contaminated blood products:
EU, 194
human growth hormone, 197
UK, 195
Eraldin, 198, 199–200, 273
evidential thresholds, 270–71
France:
civil procedure for victims of criminal acts, 15
PIP IMGHC silicone breast implants, 232
sodium valproate, 106
Japan:
subacute myelo-optico neuropathy, 208–11
UK:
vaccine damaged children, 142
USA:
anti-malarial treatments, 216
non-steroidal anti-inflammatories, 171–72
obesity treatments, 179
Vaccine Courts, 144
vaccine damaged children, 144
vaccine injury, 142–144, *270*
voluntary compensation schemes, 16
Eraldin, 198, 199–200, 273
Trilucent Care Centre, 222–23, 273
conditional fee agreements, 12
Consumer Protection Act (1987) (UK):
defective products, 162
general product safety, 50
strict liability, 10
MMR claims, 148–49
contingency fee basis, 11, 195
contraceptive implants, *see* **levonorgestrel**
contraceptives, *see* **Copper 7 Intrauterine Device; third-generation oral contraceptives**
Copper 7 Intrauterine Device, 3, 124
description, 119
litigation:
Australia, 123–24
England and Wales, 122–23
USA, 121–22
marketing and regulatory history, 120
Australia, 121
UK, 120–21
USA, 120
safety concerns
pelvic inflammatory disease, 119–20
correlation:
adverse events, 269
causation distinguished, 269
cost-shifting, 12
qualified one-way cost shifting rules, 12
Creutzfeldt-Jakob disease (CJD), 7, 197

Daquiran, *see* **pramipexole**
death:
EU reporting requirements, 48, **49**
FDA reporting requirements, 67–70, **79, 80**
decentralised regulation, 31–32
reporting requirements, 41–42
deep vein thrombosis (DVT), 125, 132
Depakene, *see* **sodium valproate**
Depakote, *see* **sodium valproate**
DES, 2
description, 92
litigation:
EU, 98
UK, 98–99
USA, 97–98
marketing and regulatory history:
EU, 93, **93–94,** 95
UK, 93, 95
USA, 92–93, 94–95
safety concerns, 92, 99
carcinogenic concerns, 95–96
teratogen concerns, 96–97
deterrence, regulation through, 13, 271, 280
dexfenfluramine, *see* **obesity treatments**
diabetes:
Mediator, *see* Mediator
human insulin, *see* human insulin
diethylsilboestrol, *see* **DES**
diphtheria, pertussis and tetanus (DTP), *see* **DTP vaccine**
diptheria, *see* **DTP vaccine**
discontinuation symptoms, *see* **withdrawal symptoms**
donation of human tissues and cells:
EU regulation, 38–39
infected donors:
blood donors, 194
plasma donors, 193
Dow-Corning silicone implants, 8, 220
description, 217
litigation, 219–20
marketing and regulatory history, 218
safety concerns, 217
DTP vaccine, 4, 144
description, 138

litigation:
England and Wales, 142–44
Ireland, 144
Scotland, 144
USA, 144
marketing and regulatory history:
Japan, 141
other countries, 141–42
UK, 139–40
USA, 141
safety concerns, 138–39
Dunlop Committee (Committee for the Safety of Drugs) (UK):
composition, 23
origins, 23
product registration, 23–24
subcommittees, 24
terms of reference, 23
voluntary nature, 23–24
duty of care, 10, 176, 215–16

Emaform, *see* **clioquinol**
England and Wales:
compensation orders, 15
group litigation orders, 15
Law Commission:
strict liability, 10
legal system, 1
litigation:
cost-shifting rule, 12
insurance policies, 12
legal aid, 12
qualified one-way cost shifting, 12
multi-party personal injury cases, 15
regulation systems (medicinal products), 17–18
legislative provisions, **20–21**
NHS, 21–22
origins, 18–21
statutory regulation, 24–25
thalidomide tragedy, 22–23, 87
voluntary self-regulation, 23–24
strict liability, 10
see also individual case studies
Entero-Form, *see* **clioquinol**
Epilim, *see* **sodium valproate**
Eraldin, 7, 200
description, 198
litigation, 199–200
marketing and regulatory history, 198–99
safety concerns, 198
Eudra-vigilance database, 40
European Agency for the Evaluation of Medicinal Products (EMEA) (EU), 28
European Medicines Agency (EMA) (EU), 28–29
clinical trials, 34
collaboration with WHO, 40
combined oral contraceptives, 127–28
creation, **29**, 30
evolution, *32*
expert committees, *31*
isotretinoin, 114
marketing authorisation applications, 34, 274
notification, 274
obesity treatments, 179, 181, 182, 183
pharmacovigilance, 40, 42
pramipexole, 167
role, 30
sodium valproate, 102–3
statins, 206
structure, 30–31
European Union:
collective action mechanisms, 15
development controls of medicinal products, 33
advanced therapy medicinal products, 39
clinical trials, 34
human tissues and cells, 38–39
marketing authorisation applications, 34–39
pharmacovigilance, 40–42
product development, 34
general product safety, 50
regulation of medical devices:
Active Implantable Medical Devices Directive, 43
conformity assessment, 46, 47
essential requirements, 44–46
harmonised standards, 46
In Vitro Diagnostics Directive, 43
Medical Devices Directive, 43
national competent authorities, 43–44
New Legislative Framework, 42–43
origins, 42
reporting requirements, 47–50
regulation of medicinal products:
background, 25–26
Brexit, impact of, 26
centralised regulation, 32–33
Committee for Proprietary Medicinal Products, 28
decentralised regulation, 31–32
development controls, 33–42
European Agency for the Evaluation of Medical Products, 28
European Medicines Agency, 28–29, 30–33, *31*, *32*
increased harmonisation, 28
legislation, **27–28**, **28–29**, **30**
mutual recognition, regulation, 31–32
origins, 26–28
Review 2001, 29–30

strict liability, 10
see also individual case studies
evidential thresholds, 269–70
insufficient proof of causation, 91, 270–71

FAERS, *see* **Food and Drug Administration Adverse Event Reporting System**
fenfluramine, *see* **obesity treatments**
flosequinan, *see* **Manoplax**
Food and Drug Administration (FDA) (USA):
biologics licences, 63–64
biosimilars, 64
Center for Drug Evaluation and Research, 56–58
clinical trials, 60–61
drug approval pathways, 55–56, *57*, 62–63
fees, 55
labelling, 53
marketing authorisations, 61–62
abbreviated new drug applications, 59
investigational new drug applications, 58–59
new drug applications, 59
over-the-counter drugs, 59
new drug application pathway, 55–56, *57*
organisation, 56
origins, 51–53
patient information leaflets, 54
pharmacovigilance, 65
alerts, 72
FAERS, 71
healthcare provider letters, 72
mandatory reporting, 65–70
post-market safety evaluations, 71–72
recall, 73
voluntary reporting, 71
post-market safety evaluations, 71–72
prescription only medicines, 53–54
product development, 60
remit, 51–52
Risk Evaluation and Mitigation Strategy, 62
thalidomide tragedy, impact of, 54
food and drug administration adverse event reporting system (FAERS) (USA), 65, 71, 267–69
isotretonoin and irritable bowel syndrome, 113, 118
Food, Drug and Cosmetic Act 1938 (USA), 53, 63
safety of medical devices, 80–81
section 522 studies, 80–81, 245, **245–46**
France:
breast implants, 225, 226, 228–29, 233–34, 278
compensation schemes, 15, 16
contaminated blood products, 193–94
DES litigation, 98, **274**
litigation outcomes, **274–77**
Mediator, 181–84
litigation, 184
regulatory requirements, 266
sodium valproate concerns and litigation, 103, 105–6
thalidomide tragedy, impact of, 266
fraud, 9, 51–52, 184, 229, 232, 234, 278

gene therapy medicinal products, *see* **advanced therapy medicinal products**
general product safety (GPS), 50
generic medicines, 22
Germany:
poly implant protheses (PIP) IMGHC silicone breast implants, 233–34
thalidomide tragedy, 83–84
litigation, 85
third-generation oral contraceptives, 126
good laboratory practice (GLP),
EU standards, **27**, 34
US standards, 60
Gravigard, *see* **Copper 7 Intrauterine Device**
group litigation orders (GLO) (UK):
contaminated blood products, 195–96
Part 19 Civil Procedure Rules 1999, 15, 148
PIP IMGHC breast implants, 232
Seroxat, 162
urogynaecological mesh, 263

haemophilia:
contaminated blood scandal, 193–96
healthcare provider letters:
medical devices, 81
medicinal products, 72
HIV/AIDS crises:
centralised regulation of drugs, 33
contaminated blood scandal, **7**, 193–96
experimental biologics, 64
impact on drug approval processes, 55
hormonal pregnancy tests
available products, **89**
description, 88
litigation, 91
collapse of litigation, 91
marketing and regulatory history, 89–90
early concerns, 90
warning notices, 90
safety issues, 88–89
hormone replacement therapy (HRT), 4, 136
description, 132
litigation, 136
multi-county litigation, 136
multi-district litigation, 136
settlements, 136
UK, 136
USA, 136

marketing and regulatory history, 132
UK, 134–36
USA, 132–34
safety concerns, 132
human growth hormone, 7
Creutzfeldt-Jakob disease, 197
description, 197
litigation, 197
marketing and regulatory history, 197
safety concerns, 197
human insulin, 6, 189
description, 185
litigation, 188–89
marketing and regulatory history, 187–88
safety concerns, 185–87
humanitarian device (HUD), 78
humanitarian device exemption (HDE), 74, 78
human-tissue-derived products
EU regulation, 38–39
USA regulation, 65
reporting requirements, 70
see also blood products; human growth hormone; human insulin

implants, *see* **Dow Corning silicone implants; poly implant protheses (PIP) hydrogel breast implants; poly implant protheses (PIP) IMGHC silicone breast implants; trilucent implants**
In Vitro Diagnostics Directive (IVDD), 43
Inspection générale des affaires sociales (IGAS) (F):
Mediator, 183
sodium valproate, 103
insurance policies, 12, 233
see also after-the-event insurance; before-the-event insurance
intrauterine devices (IUDs), *see* **Copper 7 Intrauterine Device**
Investigational New Drug (IND) applications (USA):
accelerated approval mechanisms, 55
applicable pharmaceuticals, 58
emergency use INDs, 58
format, 59
functions, 58
investigator INDs, 58
parallel track investigations, 55
reporting of adverse drug events:
causation, 66–67
other factors, 67
reporting requirements, **65**
serious adverse event, 66
serious suspected adverse reaction, 66
suspected adverse reaction, 66
unexpected adverse event, 66
unexpected suspected adverse reaction, 66
required information, 59
treatment INDs, 58
Isomeride, *see* **obesity treatments**
isotretonoin, 3
description, 108
litigation:
UK, 118
USA, 116–17
marketing and regulatory history, 108–9
depressions/suicide, 110–12, 115–16
Europe, 114–16
irritable bowel syndrome/ulcerative colitis, 112–14
teratogenicity, 109–10, 114–15
USA, 109–14
safety concerns, 108

joint and several liability, 98, **274**
Joint Standing Committee on the Classification of Proprietary Preparations (UK), 22
hormone pregnancy tests, 89–90
new terms of reference, 24

labelling, 53, 278
active ingredients, 19
benzodiazepines, 151, 153
clioquinol, 209,
compulsive gambling, 168, 169
designated responsible persons, 39
Eraldin, 199
EU regulation, **28**, 36, 39, 48
standards, 46
FAERS, 71
FDA, 52, 53, 55–56, *57*, 61–62
over-the-counter drugs, 59
hormone replacement therapy, 134
IUDs, 120
marketing authorisation requirement, 36
mefloquine, 214–15
New Legislative Framework, 44
nomifensine, 155, 156
obesity treatments, 179
Opren, 171
oral contraceptives, 126
Paxil, 161,
pharmacovigilance, 67–69
Pharmacy and Medicines Act 1941, **21**
pramipexole, 167–69
sodium valproate, 104
SSRIs, 159–61, 163
substantial equivalence, 75
Vioxx, 173
see also black-box warnings

Lariam, *see* **mefloquine**
Law Commission of England and Wales:
strict product liability, 10
legal aid, 12, 15–16, 265, 272
benzodiazepines, 152, 153, 265
contaminated blood products, 195
Copper 7 IUD litigation, 122–23
DTP vaccines, 142–43
hormone pregnancy test, 91
human insulin, 188–89
litigation outcomes, 265, **274–77**
mefloquine, 215, 216
MMR vaccines, 148, 265
Norplant contraceptive implants, 131
Seroxat litigation, 162
sodium valproate, 105, 265, 272
legal liability:
causation, 10
duty of care, 10
negligence, 10
no fault regimes, 10–11
reasonableness, 10
strict liability, 10
Legal Services Commission (LSC) (UK), 12, 105, 148
see also legal aid
legal systems, 1
levonorgestrel, *see* **Norplant**
liability, attribution of, 265
Licensing Authority (UK), 33
combined oral contraceptives, 127
legal powers, 25, 84
Manoplax, 202–3
Opren, 170
Lipobay, 7, 207
description, 204
litigation, 207
marketing and regulatory history, 205–7
safety concerns, 204–5
litigation, 11, 280–81
adverse effects of litigation, 265
benzodiazepines, 151–52
case studies, **274–77**
chances of success, 265
claimants' rationale, 278–79
clioquinol, 210–11
contaminated blood products:
EU, 194–95
group litigation order, 195–96
UK, 195–96
USA, 195
Copper 7 Intrauterine Device:
Australia, 123–24
England and Wales, 122–23
USA, 121–22
DES:
Europe, 98
UK, 98–99
USA, 97–98
Dow-Corning silicone implants, 219–20
DTP vaccine:
England and Wales, 142–44
Ireland, 144
Scotland, 144
USA, 144
England and Wales:
cost-shifting rule, 12
insurance policies, 12
legal aid, 12
qualified one-way cost shifting, 12
Eraldin, 199–200
failure rates, 265
France:
DES litigation, 98, **274**
Mediator, 184
sodium valproate concerns and litigation, 103, 105–6
funding and costs, 265
after-the-event insurance, 12
before-the-event insurance, 12
conditional fee agreements, 12
contingency fee basis, 11
cost-shifting, 12
England and Wales, 12
insurance policies, 12
legal aid, 12
United States, 11
hormonal pregnancy tests, 91
hormone replacement therapy:
multi-county litigation, 136
multi-district litigation, 136
human growth hormone, 197
human insulin, 188–89
isotretinoin:
UK, 118
USA, 116–17
legal aid, 122–23, 162
Lipobay, 207
Manoplax, 203
Mediator, 184
mefloquine:
civilian claims, 215
military claims, 215–16
Micturin, 236
MMR vaccine, 148–49
multi-county litigation (MCL), 13
Accutane, 116–17
hormone replacement therapy, 136
urogynaecological mesh, 263

multi-district litigation (MDL), 13
  Accutane, 116–17
  anti-obesity drugs, 179
  cerivastatin, 207
  hormone replacement therapy, 136
  Norplant, 130
  pramipexole, 169
  silicone breast implants, 219
  urogynaecological mesh, 259–63
nomifensine, 156
Norplant:
  UK, 131
  USA, 130–31
obesity treatments:
  EU, 180
  France, 180
  USA, 179
Opren
  England and Wales, 171–72
  USA, 171
outcomes, **274–77**
pancreatic enzymes, 192
poly implant protheses (PIP) hydrogel breast implants, 225–27
poly implant protheses (PIP) IMGHC silicone breast implants, 232
  consumer credit claims, 232
  France, 233–34
  Germany, 233–34
  insurer claims, 233
  product liability claims, 232
pramipexole:
  Canada, 169
  England and Wales, 168
  EU, 168
  USA, 169
product withdrawal, 272–74
selective serotonin re-uptake inhibitors:
  group litigation orders, 162
  legal aid, 163
  revived action, 163–64
  third-party funding, 163
  UK (Seroxat), 162–63
  USA (Paxil), 161–62
sodium valproate:
  bellwether process, 106–7
  England and Wales, 105
  France, 105–6
  settlement efforts, 107
  USA, 106–7
thalidomide:
  England and Wales, 85–87
  Germany, 85
third-generation oral contraceptives, 128
trilucent breast implants, 222–23
United States of America, 11
  multi-county litigation, 13
  multi-district litigation, 13
urogynaecological mesh, 259, 264
  multi-county litigation, 263
  multi-district litigation, 259–63
  UK, 263
vigabatrin, 165
Vioxx, 175–76

Macgregor Committee, *see* **Joint Standing Committee on the Classification of Proprietary Preparations**
magnesium valproate, *see* **sodium valproate**
Manoplax, 7, 203
  description, 201
  litigation, 203
  marketing and regulatory history, 201–3
  safety concerns, 201
manufacturer and user facility devices experience database (MAUDE) (USA):
  alerts, 81
  healthcare provider letters, 81
  product recall, 81
  reclassification, 81
  section 522 studies, 80–81
marketing authorisation applications:
  EU, 34
    categories of medicinal products, 37
    distribution authorisations, 37
    information required, 34–36
    manufacture authorisations, 36
    packaging, 38
    patient information, 38
    qualified persons, 36
    refusal of applications, 36
    summary of product characteristics, 37
  USA:
    Abbreviated New Drug applications, 59
    forms, 61
    Investigational New Drug applications, 58–59
    New Drug applications, 59
    over-the-counter drugs, 59
    required information, 62
    types of submission, 61
marketing authorisation holders:
  inclusion on packaging, 38
  qualified person responsible for pharmacovigilance, 41
  reporting obligations, 41–42
MAUDE, *see* **manufacturer and user facility devices experience database**
measles, *see* **MMR vaccine**
Mediator, 6, 184
  description, 181

litigation, 184
marketing and regulatory history, 181
EU, 181–84
safety concerns, 181
Medical Devices Agency (MDA) (UK), 33
breast implants, 222, 224
Medical Devices Directive (MDD) (EU), 43
clinical investigations, 45–46
conformity assessment procedures, 47
essential requirements, 44–45
reporting requirements, 47–48
Medicines Act 1968 (UK), 19, 84, 87
Licensing Authority duties, 33
licensing of new medicines, 24–25
Medicines Commission, 90
regulation of devices, 120–21
Medicines and Healthcare Products Regulatory Authority (MHRA) (UK), 33, 44
breast implants, 229–31
clinical investigations, 45–46
HRT, 134–35
isotretinoin, 115
mefloquine, 214
Prozac, 157
sodium valproate, 103–4
SSRIs, 159
urogynaecological mesh, 257
vigabatrin, 164–65
Vioxx, 175
Medicines Control Agency (MCA) (UK), 33
MedWatch (USA), 65, 71, 79, 80
mefloquine, 8, 216
description, 212
litigation:
civilian claims, 215
military claims, 215–16
marketing and regulatory history:
UK, 213–14, 215
USA, 212–13, 214–15
safety concerns, 212
Merital, *see* **nomifensine**
Micturine, 9
description, 235
litigation, 236
marketing and regulatory history, 235–36
safety concerns, 235
Mirapexin, *see* **pramipexole**
MMR vaccine, 4, 149
description, 145
measles, 145
mumps, 145
rubella, 145
individual vaccines compared, 145–46
litigation, 148–49
marketing and regulatory history, 147
composition of the vaccine, 147–48
safety concerns, 147
UK trends, *146*
Monitoring System for Illness Following Immunization (MSIFI) (USA), 141
multi-county litigation (MCL) (USA), 13
Accutane, 116–17
hormone replacement therapy, 136
urogynaecological mesh, 263
multi-district litigation (MDL) (USA), 13
Accutane, 116–17
Anti-obesity drugs, 179
cerivastatin, 207
hormone replacement therapy, 136
Norplant, 130
pramipexole, 169
silicone breast implants, 219
urogynaecological mesh, 259–63
multi-party cases:
discontinued, 15
failed, 16
succeeded, 16
see also class actions; group litigation orders
mumps, *see* **MMR vaccine**
mutual recognition regulation, 31–32
establishment, **27,** 31
isotretinoin, 114
Lipobay, 205
patient reporting, 41

National Childhood Encephalopathy Study (NCES) (UK), 140, 143
National Health Service (NHS) (UK):
cost management, 22
pharmaceutical regulation, impact on, 21–22
unbranded v proprietary pharmaceuticals, 22
National Institutes of Health (NIH) (USA), 104
negligence, 10–11
benzodiazepine litigation, 152
contaminated blood products, 195–96
DTP litigation, 143–44
human growth hormone, 197
thalidomide litigation, 85
1968 settlement, 86
Netherlands:
breast implants, 229
class action settlement procedures, 14
compulsive gambling, 167
DES, 14, 93, **94**
alternative causation, 98, 274
litigation, 98, 99
Halcion, 151
joint and several liability, 274
mefloquine, 214

neuromodulators, *see* **benzodiazepines; nomifensine; selective serotonin reuptake inhibitors; vigabatrin; pramipexole**
New Drug Applications (NDA) (USA), *57*, 59, 61
FDA post-market safety evaluations, 71
New Legislative Framework (NLF) (EU):
Active Implantable Medical Devices Directive, 43
designation of national competent authorities, 43–44
essential requirements:
conformity assessment procedures, 44
performance, 44
safety of products, 44
In Vitro Diagnostics Directive, 43
market surveillance, 47
Medical Devices Directive, 43
clinical investigations, 45–46
essential requirements, 44–45
regulation of medical devices, 43–44
no fault regimes, 10–11
nomifensine, 4, 156
description, 154
litigation, 156
marketing and regulatory history:
UK, 155–56
USA, 154–55
safety concerns, 154
non-steroidal anti-inflammatories, *see* **Opren; Vioxx**
Nordic States:
alternative dispute resolution, 14
risk pooling, 278
Norplant, 4, 131
description, 129
litigation:
UK, 131
USA, 130–31
marketing and regulatory history:
UK, 129–30
USA, 129
safety concerns, 129
Northern Ireland:
legal system, 1

obesity treatments, 180
description, 177
dexfenfluramine, **6**
fenfluramine, **6**
litigation:
EU, 180
France, 180
USA, 179
marketing and regulatory history, 178
Canada, 179
EU, 178–79
USA, 179
safety concerns, 177–78
Office national d'indemnisation des accidents medicaux (ONIAM) (F), 106
Opren, 5, 172
description, 170
ligitation:
England and Wales, 171–72
USA, 171
marketing and regulatory history, 170
safety concerns, 170
oral contraceptives, *see* **third-generation oral contraceptives**
over-the-counter (OTC) drugs:
definition, 59
marketing authorisations, 59
OTC drug monographs, 59

packaging:
information requirements, 38
packaging inserts:
FDA requirements, 61
incorrect information, 36
regulation, **28**
see also labelling
pancreatic enzymes, 6, 192
description, 190
litigation, 192
marketing and regulatory history, 190–91
UK, 191
USA, 191–92
safety concerns, 190
pancreatic function:
diabetes:
Mediator, *see* Mediator
human insulin, *see* human insulin
patient information, 38
EU marketing authorisation applications, 34
USA, 54, 55–56
pelvic inflammatory disease (PID), 119–21
pelvic organ prolapse (POP), 81, 237–38
see also urogynaecological mesh
pelvic prolapse treatments, *see* **urogynaecological mesh**
pertussis, *see* **DTP vaccine**
pharmacovigilance:
EU, 40
centralised system, 41
decentralised system, 41
European Medicines Agency, 40

qualified person responsible for pharmacovigilance, 41
reporting requirements, 41–42
UK:
yellow-card system, 24, 40, 85
USA:
alerts, 72
FAERS, 71
healthcare provider letters, 72
mandatory reporting, 65–70
post-market safety evaluations, 71–72
recall, 73
voluntary reporting, 71
see also reporting requirements
Pharmacovigilance Risk Assessment Committee (PRAC) (EU), *31*, 42
combined oral contraception, 127–28
poly implant protheses (PIP) hydrogel breast implants, 8, 227
description, 224
litigation, 225–27
marketing and regulatory history, 225
safety concerns, 224–25
poly implant protheses (PIP) IMGHC silicone breast implants, 9, 234
composition, **228**
description, 228
litigation, 232
consumer credit claims, 232
France, 233–34
Germany, 233–34
insurer claims, 233
product liability claims, 232
marketing and regulatory history:
adverse events, 231
EU, 230
recapitulation studies, 230–31
safety concerns:
cancer concerns, 229–30
incident reports, **231**
manufacturing process, 228–29
Ponderax, *see* **obesity treatments**
practolol, *see* **Eraldin**
pramipexole, 5, 169
description, 166
litigation:
Canada, 169
England and Wales, 168
EU, 168
USA, 169
marketing and regulatory history:
Canada, 168
EU, 167
USA, 167–68
safety concerns, 166–67
pre-market approval (PMA) (USA):
Class III devices, 73–74, 77–78
humanitarian device exemption, 78
new devices, 77
post-amendment devices, 77
pre-amendment devices, 77
reclassification of devices, 77–78
transitional devices, 77
pre-market notification procedures (USA), 74
abbreviated 510(k) notification, 76
special 510(k) notification, 76
Quality System regulation, 76
third party 510(k) review procedure, 77
traditional 510(k) notification:
purpose, 75
substantial equivalence, 75–76
Primodos, *see* **hormonal pregnancy tests**
private regulation, *see* **litigation**
product development controls:
EU, 34
USA, 60
product development protocol (PDP), 77–78
Product Liability Directive 1985 (EU), 10
product recalls:
medical devices, 81
medicinal products, 73
product withdrawal:
litigation and, 272–74
public regulation:
advantages of, 280–81

reasonableness, 10
recall, *see* **product recalls**
reclassification of medical devices, 75–76, 81
redress:
apologies, 279
care packages, 279
collective redress:
thalidomide tragedy, 86–87
see also class actions; group litigation orders
non-financial redress, 279
see also compensation
Redux, *see* **obesity treatments**
regulation systems (medical devices):
EU:
Active Implantable Medical Devices Directive, 43
conformity assessment, 46, 47
essential requirements, 44–46
harmonised standards, 46
In Vitro Diagnostics Directive, 43
Medical Devices Directive, 43
national competent authorities, 43–44
New Legislative Framework, 42–43

origins, 42
reporting requirements, 47–50
USA:
abbreviated 510(k) notification, 76
approved medical devices, 74
classification system, 73–74
cleared medical devices, 74
MAUDE, 80–81
post-marketing requirements, 78–80
pre-market approval procedures, 77–78
pre-market notification procedures, 74–77
reporting requirements, 79–80
special 510(k) notification, 76
third party 510(k) review procedure, 77
traditional 510(k) notification, 75–76
voluntary reporting, 80

regulation systems (medicinal products), 17–18
development controls in the EU, 33
advanced therapy medicinal products, 39
clinical trials, 34
human tissues and cells, 38–39
marketing authorisation applications, 34–39
pharmacovigilance, 40–42
product development, 34
development controls in the USA, 60
accelerated approval, 62–63
biosimilar applications, 64
breakthrough therapy, 62–63
cellular, tissue and gene therapies, 65
clinical trials, 60–61
expanded use to experimental biologics, 64
fast track, 62–63
marketing authorisation applications, 61–62
pharmacovigilance, 65–73
priority review, 62–63
product development, 60
risk evaluation and mitigation strategies, 62
therapeutic biologics applications, 63–64
EU:
background, 25–26
Brexit, impact of, 26
centralised regulation, 32–33
Committee for Proprietary Medicinal Products of the EU, 28
decentralised regulation, 31–32
development controls, 33–42
European Agency for the Evaluation of Medical Products, 28
European Medicines Agency, 28–29, 30–33, *31*, *32*
increased harmonisation, 28
legislation, **27–28**, **28–29**, **30**
mutual recognition, regulation, 31–32
origins, 26–28
Review 2001, 29–30
European Free Trade Area, 26
marketing authorisations within the EU:
centralised regulation, 32–33
decentralised regulation, 31–32
national regulatory architecture (UK), 33
UK:
legislative provisions, **20–21**
national regulatory architecture, 33
NHS, 21–22
origins, 18–21
statutory regulation, 24–25
thalidomide tragedy, 22–23
voluntary self-regulation, 23–24
USA:
accelerated approval mechanisms, 55
contaminated medicines, 52
current regulation, 56–58
Food and Drug Administration, *see* Food and Drug Administration
formalisation, 53
HIV/AIDS crises, impact of, 55
improved record-keeping, 52
Kefauver reforms, 54
marketing authorisations, 58–59
minimum standards, 52
origins, 51–52
patient information, 54, 55–56
pre-clinical trials, 54–55
prescription-only medicine, 53–54
regulation through deterrence, 13
risk management, 56

reporting requirements:
death, 48, **49**, 67–70, **79**, **80**
EU:
medical devices, 48–50
medicinal products, 41–42
Investigational New Drug adverse drug events, **65**
medical devices:
device user facilities, 79, **79–80**
EU, 48–50
European Commission guidance, 48
importers, 79, **79–80**
manufacturers, 79, **79–80**
manufacturers' reporting requirements, 48–50, **49**
Medical Devices Directive, 48
post-marketing surveillance, 47
UK guidance, 48
UK, 48
USA, 79–81
vigilance requirements, 47
medicinal products:
EU pharmacovigilance, 41–42
human cells, tissues and tissue-based products, 70

investigational new drug reporting, 65–67, **65**
marketing authorisation holders, 41–42
periodic safety update reports, 42
post-marketing reporting of biological products, 69–70, **69**
post-marketing reporting of drug, 68, **68**
prescription drug without approved new drug application, 67–68, **67**
USA, 65–70
serious incidents, **49**
serious public health threat, **49**
under-reporting, risks of, 267–69
unanticipated serious deterioration in state of health, **49**
USA, *268*
medical devices, 79–81
medicinal products, 65–70

risk evaluation and mitigation strategies (REMS) (USA), 62
Roaccutane, *see* **isotretonoin**
rofecoxib, *see* **Vioxx**
rubella, *see* **MMR vaccine**

Sabril, *see* **vigibatrin**
SANCO Directive (EU), 38–39
Scotland:
benzodiazepines, 151–52
contaminated blood products, 195–96
DTP vaccine, 16, 143–44, **275**
legal system, 1
multi-party cases:
Vioxx, 15
Scottish Law Commission:
strict liability, 10
Scottish Law Commission:
strict product liability, 10
selective serotonin re-uptake inhibitors (SSRIs), 5, 163
description, 157
litigation:
group litigation orders, 162
legal aid, 163
revived action, 163–64
third-party funding, 163
UK (Seroxat), 162–63
USA (Paxil), 161–62
marketing and regulatory history:
EU, 160
Japan, 161
UK, 159
USA, 159–60
safety concerns:
suicide, self-harm and aggressive behaviour, 157–59
withdrawal symptoms, 159

self-harm:
SSRIs, 157–59
serious adverse events:
MedWatch, 71, 80
nomifensine, 155
post-market safety evaluations, 71
reporting requirements, 39, 71
Investigational New Drugs, 66
urogynaecological mesh, 245, 257
serious incidents, 48–49
reporting requirements, **49**
serious public health threat:
reporting requirements, **49**
serious suspected adverse reaction:
reporting requirements:
Investigational New Drugs, 66
settlement schemes, 16
breast implants, 219
Dow Corning Settlement Trust, 219, 271
thalidomide:
1968 settlement, 86
1973 settlement, 86
Thalidomide Trust (UK), 85, 86–87
Trilucent Care Scheme (UK), 222–23
Valproate compensation (France) 106
settlements:
class action settlement procedure, 14, 98, 99
clioquinol, 210–11
contaminated blood products, 195
Copper 7 Intrauterine Device, 124
DES, 98–99
Dow Corning breast implants, 217, 219
hormone replacement therapy, 136
litigation outcomes, 274–77
mefloquine, 210–11, 216
Norplant, 130–31
obesity treatments, 179
Opren, 171–72
pramipexole, 169
thalidomide, 85–87
urogynaecological mesh, 259–63
Vioxx, 175, 176
see also litigation
Sifrol, *see* **pramipexole**
sodium valproate, 2
bellwether process, 106–7
compensation fund, 106
description, 100
litigation:
bellwether process, 106–7
England and Wales, 105
France, 105–6
settlement efforts, 107
USA, 106–7

marketing and regulatory history:
Agence nationale de sécurité du medicament et des produits de santé, 103
Europe, 101–4
European Medicines Agency, 102–3
Medicines and Healthcare Products Regulatory Agency, 103, 104
teratogenic nature, 101–2
treatment of epilepsy, 101–2
UK, 101
USA, 104–5
safety concerns, 100–1
somatic cell therapy medicinal products, *see* **advanced therapy medicinal products**
stress urinary incontinence (SUI), 237–39, 245
strict liability, 10
EU, 10
UK, 10, 128
Consumer Protection Act, 148
subacute myelo-optico neuropathy (SMON), 208–11
suicide:
isotretinoin, 110–12, 115–16, 118
mefloquine, 212
SSRIs, 157–61, 163
litigation (Paxil), 161–62
litigation (Seroxat), 162
summary of the product characteristics (SmPC), 37
suspected adverse reaction:
pharmacovigilance, 41–42
reporting requirements:
Investigational New Drugs, 66–67

teratogens, *see* **DES; hormonal pregnancy tests; isotretinoin; sodium valproate; thalidomide**
terodiline, *see* **Micturine**
tetanus, *see* **DTP vaccine**
thalidomide, 2
background to the tragedy, 22–23
description, 82
Germany, 83–84
litigation, 85
liability, 87
litigation:
England and Wales, 85–87
Germany, 85
marketing and regulatory history, 83–85
regulatory response to the tragedy:
Medicines Act and statutory regulation, 24–25
UK, 23–25
USA, 54
voluntary self-regulation, 23–24
safety concerns, 83
UK, 23–25, 83–85
litigation, 85–87
USA, 54, 83
Thalidomide Trust (UK), 85, 86–87
therapeutic biologics applications, 63–64
third-generation oral contraceptives, 3, 128
background, 125
litigation, 128
marketing and regulatory history:
EU, 127–28
Germany, 126
UK, 125, 126, 128
safety concerns:
venous-thromboembolism, 125
tissue-engineered products, *see* **advanced therapy medicinal products**
Trilucent breast implants, 8, 223
description, 221
litigation, 222–23
marketing and regulatory history, 221–22
safety concerns, 221

unanticipated serious deterioration in state of health:
reporting requirements, **49**
under-reporting:
risks of, 267–69
unexpected adverse event:
reporting requirements, 41, 66–69
unexpected suspected adverse reaction:
reporting requirements, 66
United States of America:
arbitration, 13–14
class action procedure, 12–13
damages and costs, 13
development controls for medicinal products, 60
accelerated approval, 62–63
biosimilar applications, 64
breakthrough therapy, 62–63
cellular, tissue and gene therapies, 65
clinical trials, 60–61
expanded use to experimental biologics, 64
fast track, 62–63
marketing authorisation applications, 61–62
pharmacovigilance, 66–73
priority review, 62–63
product development, 60
risk evaluation and mitigation strategies, 62
therapeutic biologics applications, 63–64
legal system, 1
litigation, 11
multi-county litigation, 13
multi-district litigation, 13

regulation systems (medical devices):
  abbreviated 510(k) notification, 76
  approved medical devices, 74
  classification system, 73–74
  cleared medical devices, 74
  MAUDE, 80–81
  post-marketing requirements, 78–80
  pre-market approval procedures, 77–78
  pre-market notification procedures, 74–77
  reporting requirements, 79–80
  special 510(k) notification, 76
  third party 510(k) review procedure, 77
  traditional 510(k) notification, 75–76
  voluntary reporting, 80
regulation systems (medicinal products), 17–18
  accelerated approval mechanisms, 55
  contaminated medicines, 52
  current regulation, 56–58
  Food and Drug Administration, *see* Food and Drug Administration
  formalisation, 53
  HIV/AIDS crises, impact of, 55
  improved record-keeping, 52
  Kefauver reforms, 54
  marketing authorisations, 58–59
  minimum standards, 52
  origins, 51–52
  patient information, 54, 55–56
  pre-clinical trials, 54–55
  prescription-only medicine, 53–54
  regulation through deterrence, 13
  risk management, 56
regulation through deterrence, 13
reporting requirements:
  human cells, tissues and tissue-based products, 70
  investigational new drug reporting, 65–67, **65**
  post-marketing reporting of biological products, 69–70, **69**
  post-marketing reporting of drug, 68, **68**
  prescription drug without approved new drug application, 67–68, **67**
strict liability, 10
see also individual case studies
urinary incontinence treatments, *see* **Micturin; urogynaecological mesh**
urogynaecological mesh, 9
  description, 237–38
  litigation, 259, 264
    multi-county litigation, 263
    multi-district litigation, 259–63
    UK, 263
  marketing and regulatory history:
    510K approvals, **240–44**
    EU, 256–59
    section 522 studies, **245–55**
    USA, 239–56
  safety concerns, 238–39

Vaccine Act 1813 (USA), 51–52
vaccines, *see* **DTP vaccine; MMR vaccine**
valproate semisodium, *see* **sodium valproate**
valproic acid, *see* **sodium valproate**
valpromide, *see* **sodium valproate**
venous-thromboembolism (VTE), 125–28, 134
vigabatrin associated visual field loss (VAVFL), 164–65
vigabatrin, 5
  description, 164
  litigation, 165
  marketing and regulatory history:
    EU, 164
    UK, 164–65
  safety concerns, 164
Vioxx, 5, 176
  description, 173
  litigation, 175–76
  marketing and regulatory history, 174–75
  safety concerns, 173–74
voluntary compensation schemes, *see* **compensation schemes**
voluntary reporting, 71, 80
voluntary self-regulation (UK), 23–25

Walter Reed Army Institute of Research (WRAIR):
  anti-malarial treatments, 212–13, 214
whooping cough:
  USA reported incidents, *139*
  see also DTP vaccine
withdrawal symptoms:
  benzodiazepines, 150–51
  nomifensine, 154–55
  SSRIs, 159
  Seroxat, 162–63
World Health Organization (WHO):
  anti-malarials, 213
  collaboration with European Medicines Agency, 40
  DTP vaccines, 138, 142
World War I:
  impact on regulation, 19–21

yellow-card reporting system (UK), 24, 40, 85, 87, 149, 199